THE GREENWOOD ENCYCLOPEDIA OF

ROCK HISTORY

The Greenwood Encyclopedia of Rock History

Volume 1
The Early Years, 1951–1959
Lisa Scrivani-Tidd

Volume 2
Folk, Pop, Mods, and Rockers, 1960–1966
Rhonda Markowitz

Volume 3
The Rise of Album Rock, 1967–1973
Chris Smith

Volume 4
From Arenas to the Underground, 1974–1980
Chris Smith with John Borgmeyer, Richard Skanse, and Rob Patterson

Volume 5
The Video Generation, 1981–1990
MaryAnn Janosik

Volume 6
The Grunge and Post-Grunge Years, 1991–2005
Bob Gulla

THE GREENWOOD ENCYCLOPEDIA OF
ROCK HISTORY

The Grunge and Post-Grunge Years,
1991–2005

BOB GULLA

GREENWOOD PRESS
Westport, Connecticut • London

Library of Congress Cataloging-in-Publication Data

The Greenwood encyclopedia of rock history.
    p.   cm.
  Includes bibliographical references and index.
    ISBN 0–313–32937–0 ((set) : alk. paper)—ISBN 0–313–32938–9 ((vol. 1) : alk. paper)—ISBN
0–313–32960–5 ((vol. 2) : alk. paper)—ISBN 0–313–32966–4 ((vol. 3) : alk. paper)—ISBN
0–313–33611–3 ((vol. 4) : alk. paper)—ISBN 0–313–32943–5 ((vol. 5) : alk. paper)—ISBN
0–313–32981–8 ((vol. 6) : alk. paper)   1. Rock music—History and criticism.
  ML3534.G754   2006
  781.66'09—dc22   2005023475

British Library Cataloguing in Publication Data is available.

This book is included in the *African American Experience* database from Greenwood Electronic
Media. For more information, visit www.africanamericanexperience.com.

Library of Congress Catalog Card Number: 2005023475

ISBN 0–313–32937–0 (set)
       0–313–32938–9 (vol. 1)
       0–313–32960–5 (vol. 2)
       0–313–32966–4 (vol. 3)
       0–313–33611–3 (vol. 4)
       0–313–32943–5 (vol. 5)
       0–313–32981–8 (vol. 6)

First published in 2006

Greenwood Press, 88 Post Road West, Westport, CT 06881
An imprint of Greenwood Publishing Group, Inc.
www.greenwood.com

Printed in the United States of America

The paper used in this book complies with the
Permanent Paper Standard issued by the National
Information Standards Organization (Z39.48–1984).

10 9 8 7 6 5 4 3 2 1

CONTENTS

 **SET FOREWORD**

Rock 'n' roll, man, it changed my life. It was like the Voice of America, the real America, coming to your home.

—Bruce Springsteen[1]

The term *rock 'n' roll* has a mysterious origin. Many have credited legendary disc jockey Alan Freed for coining the term. Some claim that it was actually a blues euphemism for sexual intercourse, while others even see the term rock as having gospel origin, with worshippers "rocking" with the Lord. In 1947, DeLuxe Records released "Good Rocking Tonight," a blues-inspired romp by Roy Brown, which touched off a number of R&B artists in the late-1940s providing their own take on "rocking." But many music historians point to the 1951 Chess single "Rocket 88" as the first rock record. Produced by Sam Phillips and performed by Jackie Brenston and Ike Turner's Kings of Rhythm (though released under the name Jackie Brenston & His Delta Cats), the record established the archetype of early rock and roll: "practically indecipherable lyrics about cars, booze, and women; [a] booting tenor sax, and a churning, beat-heavy rhythmic bottom."[2]

Although its true origins are debatable, what is certain is that rock 'n' roll grew into a musical form that, in many ways, defined American culture in the second half of the twentieth century. Today, however, "rock 'n' roll" is used with less and less frequency in reference to the musical genre. The phrase seems to linger as a quaint cliché co-opted by mass media—something that a *Top Gun* pilot once said in voicing high-speed, mid-air glee. Watching MTV these days, one would be hard-pressed to find a reference to "rock 'n' roll," but the term *rock* survives, though often modified by prefixes used to denote the growing hybridization of the genre: There is alternative rock, blues rock, chick rock, classic rock, folk rock, funk rock, garage rock, glam rock, grunge rock, hard rock, psychedelic rock, punk rock, roots rock, and countless other sub-genres of rock music. It seems that musicians found more and more ways to rock but, for some reason, stopped rolling—or to paraphrase Led Zeppelin's "Stairway to Heaven," the music world opted to rock, but not to roll.

Call it what you will, rock music has never existed within a vacuum; it has always reflected aspects of our society, whether it be the statement of youth culture or rebellion against adult society; an expression of love found, lost, or never had; the portrayal of gritty street life or the affirmation of traditional American values; the heady pondering of space-age metaphysics or the giddy nonsense of a one-hit wonder, rock music has been an enduring voice of the people for over five decades. *The Greenwood Encyclopedia of Rock History* records not only the countless manifestations of rock music in our society, but also the many ways in which rock music has shaped, and been shaped by, American culture.

Testifying to the enduring popularity of rock music are the many publications devoted to covering rock music. These range from countless single-volume record guides providing critics' subjective ratings to the multi-volume sets that lump all forms of popular music together, discussing the jazz-rock duo Steely Dan in the same breath as Stravinsky, or indie-rock group Pavement with Pavarotti. To be sure, such references have their value, but we felt that there was no authoritative work that gives rock music history the thorough, detailed examination that it merits. For this reason, our six-volume encyclopedia focuses closely on the rock music genre. While many different forms of rock music are examined, including the *influences* of related genres such as folk, jazz, soul, or hip-hop, we do not try to squeeze in discussions of other genres of music. For example, a volume includes the influences of country music on rock—such as folk rock or "alt.country"—but it does not examine country music itself. Thus, *rock music* is not treated here as synonymous with *popular music*, as our parents (or our parents' parents) might have done, equating whatever forms of music were on the charts, whatever the "young kids" were listening to, as basically all the same, with only a few differences, an outsiders' view of rock, one that viewed the genre fearfully and from a distance. Instead, we present a six-volume set—one that is both "meaty" and methodical—from the perspective of the rock music historians who provide narrative chapters on the many different stories during more than five decades of rock music history.

The Greenwood Encyclopedia of Rock History comprises six information-packed volumes covering the dizzying evolution of this exciting form of music. The volumes are divided by historical era: *Volume 1: The Early Years, 1951–1959*, spans from the year "Rocket 88" (arguably the first rock single) was released to the year of the infamous "Day the Music Died," the fatal airplane crash that took the lives of Buddy Holly, Ritchie Valens, and J. P. Richardson (a.k.a. The Big Bopper). *Volume 2: Folk, Pop, Mods, and Rockers, 1960–1966*, covers the period when the British Invasion irrevocably changed the world, while such American rock scenes as Motown and surf rock held their own. In *Volume 3: The Rise of Album Rock, 1967–1973*, Chris Smith chronicles the growing experimentation during the psychedelic era of rock, from *Sgt. Pepper* to *Dark Side of the Moon* and everything in between. In *Volume 4: From Arenas to the Underground, 1974–1980*, Smith et al., record how rock became big business while also spawning hybrid forms and underground movements. *Volume 5: The Video Generation, 1981–1990* starts with the year of MTV's debut and captures the era when video threatened to kill the radio star. Finally, in *Volume 6: The Grunge and Post-Grunge Years, 1991–2005*, Bob Gulla captures the many innovations of millennial rock music and culture. Within each volume, the narrative chapters are supplemented by a timeline, discography, bibliography, and a glossary of encyclopedia entries for quick reference.

We hope that librarians, researchers, and fans alike will find endless nuggets of information within this reference. And because we are talking about rock, we hope you will find that reading *The Greenwood Encyclopedia of Rock History* will be a whole lot of fun, too.

Rock on.

Rob Kirkpatrick
Greenwood Publishing Group

NOTES

1. Rock and Roll Hall of Fame and Museum home page, http://www.rockhall.com.
2. All Music Guide entry for Jackie Brenston, http://www.allmusic.com.

 **PREFACE**

Writing a book of historical import on a subject that hasn't yet qualified as history is a prickly matter. Where more weathered subjects, in this musical case the Beatles or Carl Perkins or Led Zeppelin, have closed up shop permanently—allowing for more accurate analysis and a bird's-eye perspective—the subject of music in the 1990s and beyond doesn't yet have that luxury. Many groups of the period are still together, and those that aren't haven't really spent a sufficient amount of time in history's rearview mirror to determine what role they actually played in the whole scheme of things.

And so, without making excuses, I tried to arrive at whatever consensus I could, using whatever sources I could drum up. I consulted printed matter, to the extent that it exists, to corroborate events, dates, and statistics. I'm happy to report that enough documenting, if not actual research, had been accomplished during the time in question so that I could at least ensure the veracity of the details covered in the book.

Then again, there's another source of consternation. Just as historical perspective on the subject hasn't yet arrived, neither have "scholarly" sources on the subjects. Yes, there are Web sites dedicated to rock music in the '90s, more than I'd care to count. But the information they contain doesn't necessarily rate as "scholarship," not by a long shot. It's like consulting a high school newspaper to catch up on world events.

Thanks to the myriad Web sites and blogs that seem to pop up every day, everyone has become an authority on something in the '90s and through the present. In many cases, bona fide online research encyclopedias like *Wikipedia* invite their frequent users to contribute to their subject matter, which adds to the questions about authority and reliability of sources found on the Internet.

I do, however, have the advantage of writing about a subject that I have actually witnessed; had I undertaken the '60s rock music volume in this series, I wouldn't have had the same luxury. Having been on the scene throughout much of the decade and the time since, and having written about it in various publications, I believe I have a reasonable grasp on the subject matter. And I have been able to put the various trends within the time frame in proper perspective.

Which brings me to the book's "site mapping": I have attempted to stand as far back from the decade as possible to squeeze it all into my own fish-eye camera lens. In so doing, I have managed to group the various musical explosions (and I do mean "explosions") into practical subsets. This worked well for most of the decade, largely because the '90s ranks as one of the most fractious and splintered eras in all of rock history. Even more so than the '60s, the musical boomlets of the '90s were separate and distinguishable from everything else going on at the same time. Only two chapters of the fifteen in this volume veer from this tidy categorization. Chapter 4 includes a random survey of the decade's biggest alternative stars, grouped together based on one common element: their success. And due to the incredible ongoing evolution of heavy metal music, Chapter 13 contains a vast cross section of movements and styles, all qualifying as heavy metal. The final chapter is an A-to-Z arrangement focusing on the major albums, artists, movements, and events of our time frame. In a pinch, just head there to find what you're looking for.

You will also find some interesting front and back matter in the book, a timeline of important events in the era, and two lists, one of bestselling albums, the other of influential recordings of the period. The Reference Guide brings together listings of important books, articles, Web sites, festivals, and films of 1991 to the present.

Is this book for you? Well, if you happen to be a fan of today's rock music, or any rock music for that matter, I'd have to say, most humbly, "Yes." An immense amount of collating, synthesizing, factoring, mulling, writing, rewriting, thinking, and rethinking went into the book you now hold. If you don't mind my saying so, it was dreadfully laborious. Of course, that doesn't mean it's dreadfully laborious to read. Great pains were taken to ensure that the text isn't too musty and academic. It's rock and roll we're talking about, after all.

ACKNOWLEDGMENTS

I'd like to apologize to my editors, Rob Kirkpatrick and Anne Thompson, who are likely fed up with my endless pleas for deadline extensions. Their patience is certainly virtuous, and I am indebted to them for it. Finally, I'd like to thank my wife Kathleen for her incredible patience while I dwelled on this project. She's had champagne on ice for months now, awaiting its end, hoping that one day I'd emerge from my office with a smile on my face and two words coming from my lips: "I'm done." Well, I guess I *am* done at this point, done with keeping rock-and-roll hours on a project that didn't offer the fun and excitement of a great rock show. Of course, it has given me a tremendous sense of accomplishment: the knowledge that I was able to record the first legitimate "history" of a time in music that has not yet seen definitive documentation.

# INTRODUCTION

In the winter of 1990, on a slushy January evening, I recall the first time I met Kurt Cobain and Chris (born Krist) Novoselic of Nirvana. Scruffy and run down, the band was not yet over the hump of a lengthy national tour meant to bring attention to their debut album, *Bleach*. At the time, few if any mainstream rock fans had heard of the band, but it didn't bother them much. They were doing what they loved—playing music for a living. They were happy to come away each night with enough money to gas up, make the rent, and grab a cheap meal. Nirvana was, after all, an independent band in the age before commercial alternative rock; their needs were few.

Kurt and Kris were amiable and forthcoming; they welcomed the attention of a genuinely enthusiastic fan, and we spent the night speaking the language of rock 'n' roll at a noisy Italian bistro. At the table, the band went unrecognized, our interview uninterrupted. At the time, they had just recently emerged from the first few sessions for their second album, the follow-up to *Bleach*. Preliminary reports from Kurt himself were diffident. "Right now I think it sucks," he told me, without smiling. "It's not as rock and roll as the last album. We'll probably lose all of our fans. They'll hate us for it."

The comment, of course, is revealing, not only for its irony, but also for what it tells us about Kurt's inner voice. Here he was, on the verge of making the breakthrough rock record of the '90s—*Nevermind*—and he was worried about losing his fans. It's that kind of darkness that would contribute to Kurt's eventual undoing.

Although the band had no inkling *then* of their accomplishment, *Nevermind* became the record that changed everything. It defined the decade and popularized alternative rock. After Nirvana hit the charts in the winter of 1991, "alternative rock" (as defined by journalists and radio program directors) was the term applied to the bands and artists on commercial radio that didn't sound like any other music on the dial. Alternative bands brought unconventional sounds, new attitudes, and new perspectives on music making. They satisfied the hunger listeners harbored for something new following the blasé rock and pop of the '80s. *Nevermind* embodied the excitement and possibilities of rock 'n' roll; its growling punk and corrosive sentiments sandblasted the crusty buildup of popular music and became the new standard. The funny thing is, no one was ready for it. When their label, Geffen, ordered the title, they only earmarked 50,000 CDs for shipping to stores. It would go on to sell over 10 million.

It also served as an invitation to rock fans everywhere. Come one, come all to the underground! Hear the next new thing in alternative rock! *Nevermind* topped the charts, and ruled radio and video. But the party was such a success, it had to find a roomier location. That location? The mainstream. Since early 1992, "alternative rock," a term that started out in the '80s as a secret password, has grown from buzzword to household word.

Following the flowering, an everything-goes attitude took effect in alternative rock. Music of all kinds, no matter how experimental, received a second, serious look—from the purple psychedelia of the Flaming Lips and the big-beat electronic rock of the Chemical Brothers, to the bristling UK Britpop of Oasis to the crass punk of blink-182. The curtain had now lifted on an entire banquet of new music and adventurous fans had an open invitation to eat it up.

Because of that flowering, many movements in the wake of Nirvana's success were touted as Next Big Things. The UK act Prodigy broke electronica open in 1994; Uncle Tupelo hailed the beginnings of the alt.country movement in 1990. Oasis and Blur heralded the Britpop invasion. Korn and Limp Bizkit, followed by a cavalcade of others influenced by the hard rock of Seattle and the rap of their youth, mixed the two, giving birth to nü metal. Other important demi-movements also factored in: ska, industrial rock, and the second wave of punk.

In the end, though, too many entrants vied for attention; listeners were eager to sample, but not ready to buy into anything too quickly. Genres and subgenres came and went so quickly, bands rose and fell so rapidly, that it was difficult to focus, like watching a quick-cut video edit job. Only the fastest, most decisive fans found what they were looking for and stuck by it. All others were passive bystanders, waiting for a ride to slow down before jumping on.

There was also a sharp downside to the "alternative revolution." As the '90s progressed, and the alternative style became more absorbed into the mainstream (and alternative started actually *becoming* the mainstream), it flushed bands out of the underground. These bands were looking for fame, big contracts, and higher visibility. In fact, many underground bands received these things, at least ephemerally, during the initial boom of the early '90s, but, while the alternative nation climate was receptive for a time, it was not receptive to everything.

Many bands that broke away from the comfort of their independent roots weren't welcomed by the mainstream and radio. Many flouted that lack of acceptance and retreated to their cubbies, but as many or more broke down and broke up, never to be heard from again. As a result, the exodus from the underground wounded the independent rock scene seriously.

The alternative revolution also threw rock music into a state of categorical confusion. Just what was alternative rock? Most releases in the '90s would get lumped into the alternative category. Ani DiFranco, Sonic Youth, Collective Soul, and Oasis have virtually nothing in common, other than being modern musicians, but they are all referred to as "alternative." This dilution proved confusing for fans of mainstream rock. Alternative acts meant virtually anyone that was playing (or looking) different from those stars currently in the mainstream; it was a catch-all.

Not that alternative rock was the be-all/end-all of the period. Throughout the '90s, grunge was balanced by the reemergence of a number of so-called "dinosaur acts." These acts, referred to that way because of their longevity, became one of the biggest draws on the concert circuit, if not consistently in album sales.

Aerosmith continued their string of hits that began in the late '80s with the 1993 disc *Get a Grip*. That, and a hits package of their Geffen label material, *Big Ones*, fulfilled their contract with that label. The band, seemingly forever young, signed a multimillion-dollar contract with Sony and made an incredible impact on commercial rock throughout the decade. Now well into their fifties, the band is as active and as high profile as ever. The Eagles, broken up since 1982, reappeared on the scene with a surprising reunion tour and subsequent hit album in 1996, *Hell Freezes Over*. The tour, which was widely acclaimed, was heavily criticized for its high ticket prices. The Rolling Stones stayed relevant throughout the decade as well. They reconvened to record and tour for the *Voodoo Lounge* album, produced by Don Was. They put out an unplugged album in 1995, recorded and supported *Bridges to Babylon* in 1997, made the live album *No Security* in 1999, and *Live Licks* in 2004.

Bob Dylan had his most acclaimed decade since the '60s with albums like *World Gone Wrong*, the Grammy-winning *Time Out of Mind*, and *Love and Theft*.

Finally, in the '90s, Bruce Springsteen left his much-loved E Street Band behind to record as a solo act. On albums like 1995's *The Ghost of Tom Joad* and the more recent *Devils & Dust*, Springsteen opted for a rotating cast of musicians to fill out his sound. His period-defining *The Rising*, however, done after the 9/11 tragedy, was the album that seemed to best encapsulate the sadness and frustration the country was experiencing.

The fact that these superstar acts remained viable throughout a musical era dominated by alternative music is a testament to their authenticity, and the tremendous initial impact and success, which has created ripples through a decades-long career. However, the present volume, *The Grunge and Post-Grunge*

Years, does not focus on these acts largely because much of their activity during this time was either a recycling of past accomplishments or a pale imitation of the same. This is not to diminish the achievement of, say, the Stones, who have had the kind of unparalleled career that will never be rivaled in the modern era. The same can be said of Dylan: That the gravelly voiced songwriter can still hold audiences enrapt with his classics some three decades after writing them proves how powerful the originals truly were. Clearly, though, these artists made their biggest impact early in their careers.

Historically speaking, when all is said and done, the '90s and early twenty-first century will be best known for the explosion of "alternative rock" and the birth of an "alternative nation." Just as Nirvana journeyed from that modest trio in the '80s at that Italian bistro in Boston to become one of the biggest rock bands of our generation, so too rock 'n' roll has continued that journey it began way back in 1955. The only constant? Change.

TIMELINE: 1991–2005

1991

March:	Chicago's Smashing Pumpkins signs a long-term deal with Virgin Records, which would soon prove beneficial to both parties.
April 17:	Nirvana performs a song called "Smells Like Teen Spirit" live at a Seattle club. Later this month they sign a recording contract with Geffen Records imprint DGC for a debut advance of $287,000.
July 18:	Lollapalooza, Perry Farrell's alternative-rock road show, opens at Compton Terrace in Phoenix, Arizona. Jane's Addiction, Siouxsie and the Banshees, the Butthole Surfers, Living Colour, and Henry Rollins perform on the main stage.
August:	Metallica's landmark *Metallica* album is released and debuts at No. 1 in both the United States and the United Kingdom.
	Noel Gallagher, a roadie for Oasis, offers to join the band if they perform his songs and he retains complete control over the band's creative direction. They agree.
September:	Guns N' Roses ships over 4 million copies of their two albums, *Use Your Illusion I* and *II*, the largest opening shipment in pop history.
	Nirvana ships only 50,000 copies of their debut major label set, *Nevermind*. It would eventually rack up more than 10 million in sales and open the door to hundreds of alt-rock acts throughout the decade.

November 24:   Queen's Freddie Mercury, an icon of pop-rock with an operatic vocal range, dies of pneumonia-related complications from AIDS at the age of 45.

December: In Oxford, England, Radiohead forms, first calling themselves On a Friday.

1992

April: The Red Hot Chili Peppers album *Blood Sugar Sex Magik* sells over a million copies and is certified platinum.

June: The H.O.R.D.E. Tour, featuring Blues Traveler, the Spin Doctors, Phish, and Widespread Panic, kicks off this summer and jumpstarts the so-called jam-band movement originally embraced by the Grateful Dead.

1993

July: Beck delivers his first single, "Loser," to a California radio station.

Rage Against the Machine appears at a Lollapalooza date completely nude with the letters PMRC scrawled across their collective chests. They were protesting the efforts of the Parental Music Resource Center and their attempt at labeling objectionable content on recordings.

Kurt Cobain overdoses on heroin in the bathroom of his New York City hotel room. His wife Courtney Love revives him with an illegal drug.

August: Estranged from her band the Sugar Cubes, Icelandic singer-songwriter Bjork begins her solo career with *Debut*.

September: Suede UK wins the prestigious Mercury prize for their self-titled debut.

November: Nirvana records an "unplugged" concert in New York City. The resulting set would top the charts.

1994

February: Alice in Chains' *Jar of Flies* is the first EP (extended play) to ever top the charts.

Green Day's third album, *Dookie*, hits the charts and eventually peaks at No. 2. It would go on to sell twelve million copies worldwide, becoming the best-selling punk album of all time.

March: Sheryl Crow's debut, *Tuesday Night Music Club*, enters the U.S. album chart and begins a vital, decade-long career.

April 5:   Kurt Cobain commits suicide, in a controversial conclusion by the Seattle Police Department. His body is discovered three days later. He was 27.

May: The Eagles reunite to play their first gigs in over fourteen years, and produce the aptly titled *When Hell Freezes Over*. It debuts at No. 1.

June: Aerosmith makes their music available on the Internet, marking a major event in the history of music delivery.

July: Oasis makes their American debut with a performance in New York City.

August: The three-day Woodstock 1994 festival in Saugerties, New York, attempts to stay true to the spirit of the original Woodstock, some twenty-five years later. Candlebox, Aerosmith, Collective Soul, Sheryl Crow, Live, and the Cranberries play, among others. Joe Cocker and Crosby, Stills & Nash, two veterans of the original Woodstock, also play.

October: Shock rockers Marilyn Manson are banned from Utah's Delta Center. Bandleader Brian Warner responds by shredding a copy of *The Book of Mormon* before their scheduled set and tossing it into the audience. He'd be arrested in a month for performing part of his set naked.

November: The Rolling Stones become the first major band to have a segment of a gig broadcast live over the Internet.

1995

January: Courtney Love is hailed by the media as "Queen of the Riot Grrrls," a movement begun at least in part as a female response to the male-dominated grunge scene.

March: Bruce Springsteen's "Streets of Philadelphia" wins three Grammy awards including Song of the Year, as well as an Oscar.

April: The first new single by the Beatles in twenty-five years, "Baby It's You," is released.

May: Jewel, an itinerant, free-thinking poet of a songwriter, debuts with *Pieces of You*. Over the next two years, the record would sell in the millions.

June: Alanis Morissette's domestic debut album, *Jagged Little Pill*, is released in the United States. Then age 21, Morissette will go on to become a mega-platinum superstar based on the success of this album.

The UK electronic rock act Chemical Brothers debut domestically with *Exit Planet Dust*, which is praised as groundbreaking.

July 4: Courtney Love is found guilty of fourth-degree assault on Bikini Kill's Kathleen Hanna during a Lollapalooza gig.

August 9: Jerry Garcia dies of a heart attack, ending the incredible run of improvisational kings the Grateful Dead.

The Dave Matthews Band, in support of their breakthrough album, *Under the Table and Dreaming*, hits their stride, so far selling 3 million copies of their disc.

September 2: The Rock and Roll Hall of Fame opens on the banks of Lake Erie in Cleveland, Ohio. It cost $92 million to build and was designed by I. M. Pei.

October 21: Blind Melon singer Shannon Hoon is found dead of an overdose, ending the band's fast ascent to stardom in mid-arc.

November: Green Day's Billie Joe Armstrong is arrested for mooning the audience at a Milwaukee gig.

1996

March: The Sex Pistols announce a reunion tour twenty years after splitting.

April: Rage Against the Machine performs on *Saturday Night Live* with upside-down flags hanging from their amps, protesting the network (NBC) and its corporate ownership. They're barred from performing a second song and joining the end of the show lineup.

KISS announces a reunion tour of their original members. It's the first time in fifteen years all four have played together and worn their original makeup.

June: The Beastie Boys host the two-day Tibetan Freedom Concerts in San Francisco.

September: Ozzy and Sharon Osbourne's first Ozzfest tour gets underway in Alaska.

1997

May 29: Promising songwriter Jeff Buckley, son of folk icon Tim Buckley, dies in a freak swimming accident in the Mississippi River.

June:	Radiohead's feverishly acclaimed recording, *OK Computer*, brings them from hit-oriented rock act to career artist.
July:	The all-female singer-songwriter ensemble roadshow called Lilith Fair, conceived by Sarah McLachlan, opens before a sell-out crowd at the Gorge in George, Washington.
	Prodigy's smash breakthrough *The Fat of the Land* becomes the first electronica recording to cross over to a rock-pop audience. It debuts in the United States at No. 1.
August:	The classic lineup of Fleetwood Mac returns with *The Dance*, an effort that earns several Grammy nominations.
	Phish, performing before 65,000 fans at the Great Went Festival in Maine, begins to inherit the jam-band mantle of the Grateful Dead.
September:	Elton John's musical tribute to Princess Diana, "Candle in the Wind 1997," sells 32 million copies in a little over a month, making it the best-selling single of all time.

1998

March:	Matchbox 20 takes the pop-rock world by storm, having sold over 3 million copies of their debut, *Yourself or Someone Like You*, since January.
May 14:	Frank Sinatra dies of a heart attack at the age of 82.
September:	Aerosmith has their first No. 1 hit with "I Don't Want to Miss a Thing" from the *Armageddon* soundtrack.
	Korn's breakthrough album, *Follow the Leader*, enters the U.S. charts at No. 2. The band's Family Values Tour with Orgy, Limp Bizkit, and Rammstein essentially legitimizes the term "nü metal."

1999

The merger of two major recording labels, Universal and Polygram, causes upheaval in the recording industry. It is estimated that the new company, Universal Music Group, controls 25 percent of the worldwide music market.

June:	Napster, a file-sharing service started by 18-year-old Shawn Fanning, becomes available on the Internet. In October, major labels abandon plans to join forces with Napster, and instead focus efforts on eliminating it.
	Fred Durst is rewarded for his popularity with a post as Senior Vice President of Interscope, and is given his own Flip imprint

to run. He signed Staind, and later Puddle of Mudd. Kid Rock joins forces on tour with Limp Bizkit, riding his own wave of popularity with his long-awaited breakthrough effort, *Devil Without a Cause*.

July: Woodstock '99 is held at a deserted Air Force base near Rome, New York. It is a disaster, as chaos erupts around Limp Bizkit's set. Bonfires rage out of control, hot weather and high prices escalated tensions. Rape and other criminal activity stood in stark contrast to the original Woodstock's mantra of "peace, love, and understanding."

September: David Bowie's newest album, *hours . . .* becomes the first by a major artist available by Internet download, at $17.98. It is issued in the Liquid Audio format.

November 10:   It is announced that the Eagles have the biggest-selling album of the millennium (in the United States), when *Greatest Hits 1971–1975* reaches the 26-million mark.

2000

February: Carlos Santana makes it into the record books when he collects eight Grammy Awards for his *Supernatural* album and its singles. The achievement caps an incredible return to center stage for the guitarist, and is based largely on the stunning chart run of his hit "Smooth," written with Matchbox 20's Rob Thomas.

April: Metallica states their intention to sue Napster for copyright infringement. It begins a long steady slide for the band, which is in this case perceived as greedy rock stars intent on taking money from the hands of their fans. Still, the lawsuit is legitimate in the eyes of many.

June: Fred Durst, Limp Bizkit frontman, incites a feud with Creed frontman Scott Stapp. Both bands are among the biggest on the rock scene and the conflict creates quite a stir.

               Nine fans are trampled to death during Pearl Jam's set at the Roskilde festival near Copenhagen.

October: Pearl Jam sets a new *Billboard* record when they debut five new albums on the chart in the same week. All are double CDs recorded on their recent tour.

November 7:   Warner Brothers releases the first batch of DVD audio discs with Emerson, Lake, and Palmer's *Brain Salad Surgery* album.

               Music file-sharing is growing in popularity at sites like MP3.com and through the use of Napster software, before lawsuits from the large record companies and the RIAA (Recording Industry Association of America) bring the free services to a halt.

December 2:   The Smashing Pumpkins play their final show at Chicago's Cabaret Metro. The performance lasted nearly five hours.

2001

January: Five years after her death from cancer, a relative unknown named Eva Cassidy finds a place on the charts in England and the United States with her posthumous album *Songbird*.

April 15:   Legendary punk rocker Joey Ramone dies from lymphoma at the age of 50.

June 21:   Blues icon John Lee Hooker dies in his sleep at the age of 83.

July: A federal judge rules that Napster must cease operation.

Coldplay and Staind begin to dominate the pop and rock music scenes.

September/
October: A multinetwork fundraiser, "America: A Tribute to Heroes," takes place in the wake of 9/11, with proceeds donated to victims and victims' families. Bruce Springsteen, Billy Joel, Sheryl Crow, Paul Simon, Neil Young, the Dixie Chicks, and Tom Petty perform, among many others. Another fundraiser, "The Concert for New York City," also features major star performers, including Eric Clapton, David Bowie, and Elton John.

November 29:   George Harrison dies of cancer at the age of 58. "Horse to the Water," the last recording he appears on that is released during his lifetime, is a song he co-wrote with son Dhani.

Apple introduces a new portable music device called the iPod. The size of a deck of cards, it can hold up to 1,000 songs in the MP3 format. Evolutions in its manufacturing would multiply that number substantially, and the product would eventually incite a revolution in portable music technology.

December: *Billboard*'s top album of the year is *1* by the Beatles. It comes thirty-one years after the group's split.

2002

February: Four Concerts for Artists' Rights take place in the Los Angeles area to raise funds for the Recording Artist Coalition (RAC). The Eagles, Sheryl Crow, No Doubt, Weezer, the Offspring, and many others support the cause, which is focused on reversing adverse issues in artists' contracts.

March 5:   "The Osbournes," MTV's new reality series based on the family life of Ozzy Osbourne, becomes the network's highest-rated premiere.

April 19:   Alice in Chains lead singer Layne Staley is found dead of a drug overdose in his apartment at the age of 34.

Norah Jones, who recorded her debut for the Blue Note jazz label, begins to gain momentum. She makes her first U.S. TV appearance on the CNN network and her album, *Come Away with Me*, catches fire at radio. It would go on to become one of the year's biggest sellers and a sweep at next year's Grammys.

Linkin Park's debut album, *Hybrid Theory*, is certified eight times platinum and is officially the year's biggest-selling record. They played 324 dates in the past twelve months.

Former alt.country band Wilco, led by Jeff Tweedy, breaks free of their creative constraints and records *Yankee Hotel Foxtrot*, an album that their label, Warner Brothers, refuses to release because it is deemed uncommercial. Unwilling to change the album to make it more viable, the band bought the finished studio tapes and left the label. It would become their most successful effort to date.

June 5:   Dee Dee Ramone, a founding member of the '70s punk rockers, dies, just fourteen months after Joey Ramone succumbed to cancer.

June 27:   Who bassist John Entwistle dies in his Las Vegas hotel room on the eve of Who's North American reunion tour.

Elvis Presley reclaims the record in the United Kingdom for the most No. 1 singles, with eighteen, when a remix of "A Little Less Conversation" hits the top.

Avril Lavigne's debut, *Let's Go*, is released. The skate-punk pop-star-in-waiting is just 17.

July: John Mayer kicks off his first substantial American tour in support of his platinum debut album, *Room for Squares*.

August: Bruce Springsteen performs "The Rising" to open the MTV Music Awards from his yet-to-be-released album of the same name.

September: Coldplay's anticipated second album, *A Rush of Blood to the Head*, begins to dominate charts the world over.

Courtney Love settles her differences with the Universal Music Group and Nirvana's remaining band members over the treatment of Nirvana's recorded legacy. The settlement paves the way for issuance of unreleased Nirvana material and a box set (2004).

December 22: Clash frontman Joe Strummer dies suddenly of a heart attack at the age of 50. His band was due to reunite next year, when Clash would be inducted into the Rock and Roll Hall of Fame.

2003

Time magazine names Apple's iTunes Music Store the coolest invention of 2003. You can buy songs for $1 and download them from your computer to an MP3 player.

The Recording Industry Association of America (RIAA) launches its long anticipated legal assault on file-swappers by filing 261 civil lawsuits against individuals accused of illegally distributing copyrighted music through peer-to-peer (P2P) networks. Individuals accused of distributing copyrighted files on P2P Networks Kazaa, Grokster, Imesh, Gnutella, and Blubster were targeted in this initial round. Under U.S. law, damages for copyright violations range from $750 to $150,000 per copyrighted work infringed.

World sales of recorded music fall by 7.6 percent in value in 2003, the year-on-year decline slowed by a stronger second half in the U.S. market, combined with resilient sales in the United Kingdom. The fourth consecutive year of falling music sales is attributed to the combined effects of digital and physical piracy and competition from other entertainment products.

The White Stripes and the Strokes both prove that they are worthy of their new mega-star status by releasing successful follow-up recordings. The White Stripes release *Elephant,* while the Strokes issue *Room on Fire.*

April: Yeah Yeah Yeahs, led by iconoclastic singer Karen O, release *Fever to Tell,* their debut, and in the process add more legimitacy to the quirky garage-rock movement underway.

2004

August: Sony Music Entertainment and Bertelsmann Music Group (BMG) finalize a merger. The merger makes Sony BMG the second-largest record label, only slightly behind Universal Music Group. Each controls approximately one quarter of the global market in recorded music. There are now only four major labels: Warner Music Group, Sony BMG, Universal Music Group, and EMI.

2005

July: Live 8 was a series of concerts that took place in 2005 in the world's wealthiest nations—the G8 (Canada, France, Germany, Italy, Japan, United Kingdom, United States)—to raise political consciousness and pressure world leaders to drop the dept of the world's poorest nations, increase and improve aid, and negotiate fairer trade rules. Ten huge shows were held the first week of July, and on July 7, leaders of the G8 responded, pledging to increase aid to Africa. Many of music's biggest acts responded with their time throughout these eight concerts. Here are some of the highlights of what was the biggest series of pop-rock shows in 2005: Coldplay, Elton John, and Paul McCartney played London's Hyde Park. Andrea Bocelli, the Cure, and Sheryl Crow hit Paris. Green Day, Audioslave, and CSN played Berlin. Duran Duran, Faith Hill, and Tim McGraw played the Circus Maximus in Rome. Dave Matthews, Def Leppard, and Linkin Park played the Museum of Art in Philadelphia. Deep Purple, Jet, and Our Lady Peace played Park Place in Barrie, Canada. Bjork and Good Charlotte hit the stage in Tokyo. Lucky Dube and Orchestre Baobab joined together in Johannesburg, South Africa, and the Moscow stage presented the Pet Shop Boys, among others.

THE GRUNGE ERA

Seattle 1988. This city by the sea had little to distinguish itself besides a colorful fish market, an above-average tolerance for rain, and a superhuman penchant for caffeine, which seemed to be increasing by the day. A metropolis with a provincial, small-town attitude, Seattle has always been an isolated place, sheltered by mountains, protected by the sea, and bordered by Canada to the north. In a way, Seattle, known as the "Emerald City" for its lush vegetation, was detached from the rest of America, insulated from so many of the influences that touched musicians in other American cities more directly.

It is for this reason, and perhaps this reason alone, that Seattle and the entire Pacific Northwest, including Portland, Oregon, and Seattle's sister city of Tacoma, have a long history of giving rise to volcanic musical forces. Back in the early '60s, when rock 'n' roll was still in its infancy, Seattle gave birth to the rumbling sounds of garage rock. Seminal bands like the Kingsmen, the Sonics, and the Wailers defied conventional music making by fusing the energy of early rock performers like Elvis Presley and Chuck Berry with the shouting of electric Chicago bluesmen like Buddy Guy and Muddy Waters, artists who were just being discovered at the time by white audiences. The Kingsmen hit it big with "Louie Louie" in 1964, a song that single-handedly defined the loud, distorted, simplistic garage-rock style, while the Sonics, turning the sound of early rock into something downright dangerous, bewitched audiences with visceral screams and raunchy guitar playing way before it had become socially acceptable to do so.

Another Seattle native, Jimi Hendrix, also revolutionized rock 'n' roll. Born in Seattle in 1942, the guitar player bided his time as a hired gun on the soul circuit with acts like Little Richard and the Isley Brothers before making his mark on the rock scene with his own stunning debut, *Are You Experienced*, in 1967. Undoubtedly influenced by the uncompromising music of his Northwest upbringing, Hendrix took that vocabulary, merged it with his rhythm 'n' blues (R&B) experience and, with a little magic, liberated the instrument from the constraints of rock 'n' roll formula with incendiary fretwork.

And so it was that "grunge," a brash, distorted style of loud music not far from the lo-fi sounds of garage rock, arose from this tradition of uncompromising musical values. Young musicians in damp and disconnected Seattle have often given voice to isolated paroxysms of sound, and grunge is no different. The musicians who would later come to play in the bands associated with the first wave of grunge all grew up listening to indigenous garage rock, as well as the sounds of early metal and punk: Black Sabbath, Blue Cheer, the Stooges, and Led Zeppelin. Records like the Stooges' *Raw Power*, Zeppelin's *Houses of the Holy*, and Sabbath's *Volume IV* circulated widely among aspiring musicians in the region's burgs. As the '70s progressed, that spectrum also embraced other recordings: Flipper's *Generic*, the Ramones' *Rocket to Russia*, and Neil Young's *Rust Never Sleeps*. As the '70s turned into the '80s, post-punk bands like the Minutemen, the Meat Puppets, and Hüsker Dü became touchstones, as did two Australian outfits, the Scientists and a maniacal gang led by gloomy baritone Nick Cave called the Birthday Party.

These bands all shared a certain reckless abandonment, a wild-eyed, caution-to-the-wind attitude that combined a passion for music with an unwillingness to conform to traditional music standards. Generally, the musicianship was coarse, sometimes unskilled, the writing haphazard, and the lyrics often afterthoughts, yet the energy and urgency of the music itself gave these works emotional and physical power. That power, and that energy, would show up later on the best works of the grunge years.

The music scene in Seattle, like the epic scenes in mid-'60s San Francisco and early '90s London, was also built on humor and sarcasm. The generation of young people that had come of age during the Reagan years had grown disaffected by the overwhelming affluence, some would say greed, of the time, an indulgence they witnessed yet never participated in. Called "slackers" or "Generation X-ers" because they (seemingly) couldn't be bothered with politics, social causes, careers, or the general state of humanity, these teens and twentysomethings were jaded and media-savvy. They were ready for the real world, but not inspired to become a part of what they saw. They were disillusioned by politics and pop culture. To them, even punk rock, long a bastion of free and liberal thinking, had become boring and predictable. Worse still was that popular music at the time was thought by many to be abysmal—the blippity blip of synthesizer-based pop or the grandstanding randiness of '80s metal, also called "shred" or "hair metal," did little to satisfy the appetites of serious music fans.

By the late '80s, all of these styles had run their course. They had worn music fans down with shallow expression and uninspired writing. Slackers were looking for something exciting to remedy its dissatisfaction. Indeed, they were ready for a change, both culturally and musically. They would soon receive both.

In the mid '80s, change was imminent. The slackers started forming bands. Portland's the Wipers, Seattle's the Melvins, and the U-Men, the Screaming Trees, and Green River—all from the Pacific Northwest; all fed from the trough of punk, '70s metal, and classic rock—began to merge their post-punk aesthetics with a revision of the music of their upbringing. The result was received with skepticism, even humor. Their sounds were radically different, often unlistenable, at least by conventional standards. Still, change, they believed, was essential.

Yet even amid the ranks of these young bands there existed restlessness. Few groups in this early transitional period of rock 'n' roll in the Northwest could maintain stable lineups, perhaps because the musical evolution of these groups was visionary, and thus unsettled. Most made their mark by remaining around long enough to spawn splinter groups; the musicians within their ranks, inspired by change and equipped with innovation, would fan out, creating dozens of bands that would eventually comprise Seattle's new scene.

Around 1985, the city still lurked undetected on the nation's music radar screen. But the musical undercurrent began to pick up its pace. The cataclysm of punk rock had come and gone nationwide and, oddly enough, while the independent rock scenes in cities like Chicago, Los Angeles, and New York were in the process of going musically haywire, Seattle was quiet, biding its time as if it was poised for its own revolution on its own schedule.

Green River, a band inspired by the U-Men and the Wipers—as well as the aforementioned '60s and '70s rock movements—would be the first of many to step forward as one of Seattle's truly explosive bands. Named after the site of the city's worst serial murders, Green River—consisting of Mark Arm, Steve Turner, Stone Gossard, Jeff Ament, Bruce Fairweather, and Alex Vincent—only stayed together for three years and released just a handful of songs. But the band's long-term effects were enormous. They shrugged off the haze that hung over Seattle, and began filling clubs with both people and a sense of purpose. At their best, they made explosive, distorted guitar rock; at their worst, they served up a sludgy, depressing mess. Somewhere in between these extremes lived the very definition of grunge.

Green River also served as the first band signing to the city's resident upstart rock label, Sub Pop. The label, started by Jonathan Poneman and fellow aspiring musician Bruce Pavitt, first began in the early '80s as a fanzine, called *Subterranean Pop USA*. In it, Pavitt provided commentary and off-handed riffing on music, culture, and politics. He was a blogger of his time.

Green River debuted on the label in 1985 with *Come on Down*, a distorted, metallic effort that derived as much from Iron Maiden as it did from messier, guitar-driven post-punk bands like Hüsker Dü. But, like many early Seattle bands, Green River, who would go on to release two more EPs, were better known for their alums than for their recorded output. Snarky singer Mark Arm and guitarist Steve Turner would go on to form enduring grungers Mudhoney, while bassist Jeff Ament and guitarist Stone Gossard would stay together in an ill-fated group called Mother Love Bone, a band which would later segue into the phenomenally successful Pearl Jam. Bruce Fairweather formed the acclaimed but less familiar outfit Love Battery.

At the same time, also in 1985, another fledgling label was corralling a handful of bands. C/Z Records, originated by Chris Hanszek and Tina Casale and later operated by Skin Yard bassist Daniel House, brought together six bands—Skin Yard, Malfunkshun, the U-Men, the Melvins, and Soundgarden—on a single album and called it *Deep Six*. It is widely regarded as the first album to feature what we now know as "grunge."

These early grunge projects altered Seattle's reputation as a second-rate music city almost immediately, giving it a nascent identity that it seized readily. The Sub Pop label almost immediately became the hip house for hot Seattle music. Pavitt and Poneman, two entrepreneurs who already had their finger on the city's pulse, rose up to take advantage of the fast-growing scene, and signed more bands like Soundgarden, Blood Circus, and Swallow. In the wake of Green River's dissolution, they signed Mudhoney, a band that, more than any other, would come to define the grunge ethos, perhaps not commercially, but aesthetically. Their first single and subsequent EP, "Touch Me I'm Sick" and *Superfuzz Bigmuff*, respectively, provide not so much the inspiration but the very templates of grunge as a style, with ear-splitting distortion, yelping vocals, and a live performance that on good nights often verges on chaos. With Soundgarden and Mudhoney as cornerstones, Seattle and its rising music scene were poised to take flight.

Nationally, the rock scene was also in a bit of flux at the same time. Independent rock, also known as "indie rock" (that is, rock independent of the major label corporations), had seen recent success in cities like Los Angeles (Jane's Addiction), Minneapolis (the Replacements, Soul Asylum, Hüsker Dü), Chicago (Naked Raygun, Big Black), and Austin (Butthole Surfers). These successes had created a demand among college radio stations and the underground club circuit for more inspired alternatives to the mainstream music they had been hosting previously. Timing was good for Seattle, Sub Pop, and grunge in general to take advantage of what was an open invitation.

In 1989, Sonic Youth, an edgy, urban avant-garde rock band from New York City that had been big fans of Green River, invited Mudhoney to join them for a British tour, and soon the Seattle crew found themselves the talk of the UK rock press (a cabal, it should be noted, with a penchant for sensationalizing). Ballyhooed as the next big thing, Mudhoney and *Superfuzz Bigmuff* landed on the British indie charts and stayed there for the better part of a year. The band wasted no time in returning for a headlining tour, complete with massive press coverage and riotous shows. Word of Mudhoney's reputation in Europe quickly returned to the United States, and the band had become the new heroes of Seattle's underground rock scene by the time their first full-length album,

Mudhoney, came out in late 1989. College radio, always the milieu of unconstrained record spinning, jumped all over the new Seattle sound, and soon, the heavy vibes from the Northwest spanned across the country and found their way to the corners of the globe.

In the wake of Mudhoney's success, a number of other Sub Pop acts began making big noise on college radio and the indie club circuit, including Soundgarden, Tad (from Boise, Idaho), the Fluid (from Denver, Colorado), and a trio of young, relatively ambitious music fans from Aberdeen, Washington, called Nirvana.

NIRVANA AND THE SEATTLE MUSIC SCENE

When Kurt Cobain and Chris Novoselic formed Nirvana in 1987, they, like other musicians in the grunge movement, had brought with them an upbringing in the classic rock and metal of the '70s. Nirvana was also well-grounded in the roots of the '80s independent movement, around Seattle and elsewhere. They grew up watching the Melvins, a Black Sabbath–inspired metal/noise band that indirectly influenced more area bands than any other with their extreme waves of unpredictable rumbling. Nirvana also dug deeply into the do-it-yourself (DIY) realm of bands in the surrounding area, such as Olympia, and overseas.

Like Chicago and Minneapolis, Olympia, Washington was a breeding ground for the independent music aesthetic. But unlike those scenes, Olympia did not possess the balance presented by the slicker, major-label bands that also hailed from those cities. The city's most prominent band, Beat Happening, formed in 1982, and served as the linchpin of the town's arts scene. With their unpretentious approach to creating rock music, and their politely rebellious attitude toward the same, Beat Happening and the Olympia pop music scene perhaps unwittingly became Ground Zero for DIY music, an ethos that exists to the present day. It also functioned as a catalyst, an affirmation of sorts, for what was happening in Seattle. (Beat Happening bandleader Calvin Johnson even helped to assemble Sub Pop's first few fanzines in the early '80s.) Olympian musicians adopted a stance in direct opposition to the accepted norms at the heart of rock music. They ignored otherwise de rigeur issues of professionalism and stardom and created raw sounds, by turns charming and unschooled, that combined the punk DIY ethic with a sort of playful, rather than angry, attitude. In taking this approach to the extreme, Beat Happening democratically rotated vocal, guitar, and drum duties between members, and disregarded bass altogether. The aesthetic was devastating in its simplicity and a marvel of genuine sincerity. Other pretty pop bands like Heavenly and the Orchids helped to further define that musical aesthetic. In contrast, the Riot Grrrl movement (see Chapter 9), also conceived in Olympia, would provide a sharp and angry counterpoint to that naïve simplicity.

At Sub Pop, Poneman and Pavitt took Olympia's shaggy artistic aesthetic, plugged it into a stack of Marshall amps, and doused it with the nostalgic sound of '70s rock and a hint of rebellion. Up until grunge, there had always been a line drawn between popular and underground music, with the sterile commercial rock of bands like Journey and Boston on one side and punk rockers like X and the Dead Kennedys on the other. Somehow, grunge managed to appeal to both sides. It was loud and hip enough for fans of underground music—the buzzword "alternative" had not yet surfaced—and it was melodic and powerful enough for fans of commercial hard rock. Nirvana, a band at the very fulcrum of those two entities, proffered the perfect blend.

Kurt Cobain and company released their first full-length album, *Bleach*, in 1989 to relatively little fanfare. Marked by its signature guitar assault, melodic flourishes, and stop-start dynamics, the record was made (so touted on its back cover) for $606.17 by producer Jack Endino, a name credited on many an early grunge recording. Also released at that time were important discs like Tad's debut, *God's Balls*, and Soundgarden's *Ultramega OK*. Both were characterized by throttling guitar riffs, lots of distortion (to hide the imperfections) and wah-wah guitar effects, and maniacal singing.

As grunge and the Seattle scene gained momentum, musicians, inspired by the city's Everyman approach to music making, assembled bands, hundreds of them. In the process, they gave little consideration to the rock star posing of their youth, choosing instead to dress down; most wore flannel shirts and jeans—the same clothes they wore to their day jobs. (Many, ironically, worked at the Muzak factory based in Seattle.) Their down-to-earth style closed the gap between audience and performer, essentially knocking the rock star image off its pedestal and placing it on the floor next to the ticket buyer. In the process, rock 'n' roll became infinitely more accessible, more immediate, and music fans responded.

Because of this immediacy, the label's national reach caught on rapidly with a hip, young, white audience already trolling the underground for new sounds. The independent label scene, serving as a bristling undercurrent to the bland corporate sounds of the '80s and '90s, was issuing true alternatives to the musical mainstream, from the maniacal musings of Minneapolis' Cows and Edmund's Flaming Lips to the punk-inflected rock of Smashing Pumpkins and the Pixies. Independent alternatives were flourishing.

"It was the energy," writes British journalist Everett True, who first came to Seattle in 1988 to cover the city's growing rock scene. He is occasionally credited, though wrongly, with inventing the term "grunge."

> It was the insane amount of energy rising up through the boards of that town's clubs, the musicians with their long, greasy hair and unflagging, sick humour, the thrill of loud music. Bodies tumbling on top of bodies, faces smiling and grinning and lapping up the pain, musicians such as Mudhoney's Mark Arm and the mighty Tad Doyle and any number of interchangeable grunge bands all merging into one sweat-soaked, glorious whole. (True 2001)

Pearl Jam, 1996. Courtesy of Photofest.

Now that eyes were on Seattle, a few of the most worthy bands began attracting the attention of big corporations. Soundgarden, Nirvana, Pearl Jam, Alice in Chains, and many others were all signed by major labels even though few had sold many records nationally, and even fewer enjoyed widespread radio airplay. Still, Seattle had become a geyser of talented bands and musical excitement; it did not take long for the majors to move in, scoop up the best bands, and begin capitalizing on their potential.

In 1990, both Soundgarden and Alice in Chains released major-label records. Soundgarden's *Louder Than Love*, the follow-up to their *Ultramega OK* EP on Sub Pop, received a Grammy nomination that year for Best Metal Album. In August, Alice in Chains' *Facelift* also came out, but because they had virtually no hip cache, no affiliation with Sub Pop or any other indie label, the band's grunge connection was minimal. They were a Seattle band, yes, and benefited by its location, but the band was not immediately associated with the underground surge.

Temple of the Dog was another compelling band that did not have a direct indie connection, but still had immense impact on Seattle's reputation. It was

Alice in Chains (left to right) Mike Inez, Layne Staley, Jerry Cantrell, and Sean Kinney. Courtesy of Photofest.

conceived in 1990 as a side project/tribute to the late Andrew Wood, the lead singer of short-lived, proto-grunge/metal band Mother Love Bone as well as the seminal Malfunkshun, and the victim of a heroin overdose in 1990. Temple of the Dog featured Wood's bandmates Jeff Ament (Pearl Jam, bass) and Stone Gossard (Pearl Jam, guitar), along with Chris Cornell (vocals) and Matt Cameron (drums), both of Soundgarden.

Temple of the Dog released their only disc at the end of 1990 on A&M Records, a major label. But the album didn't chart until the summer of 1992, when Pearl Jam, led by then-unknown singer Eddie Vedder and guitarist Mike McCready, formed in the wake of the tribute, had its own smash hit with their debut, *Ten*. Temple of the Dog's single, "Hunger Strike," a moving duet between Pearl Jam's Vedder and Soundgarden's Cornell, reached the Top 10 and pushed the disc to platinum status before the end of 1992.

"The Seattle Sound," now in full swing, bled well outside the protected confines of the Pacific Northwest. Soon enough, the city's grunge movement would never again belong to the city itself. Nirvana would see to that.

Nirvana's Cultural Importance

Kurt Cobain and Kris Novoselic grew up in Aberdeen, Washington, a smelly papermill town 100 miles outside of Seattle. Cobain, a Beatles fan early on, was passed from relative to relative as a child, a downbeat latch-key kid and victim of a divorce. Buzz Osborne, guitarist of the Melvins, also from Aberdeen, introduced Kurt to Kris, and turned them both on to the classic Los Angeles punk rock of bands like Black Flag and Flipper.

Both Cobain and Novoselic had strong feelings of alienation, both social and political, so the rebellious nature of punk rock resonated deeply. They

Nirvana, 1994 (left to right), Kurt Cobain, Krist Novoselic, David "Dave" Grohl. Courtesy of Photofest.

found a like-minded soul in drummer Chad Channing, later replaced by the more powerful Dave Grohl. Early on, they crafted their sound at gigs around the Olympia area, particularly at the liberal clearinghouse for independent music, Evergreen State College. Together, like the musicians of grunge, Nirvana fused their affinity for Led Zeppelin and Black Sabbath with their newfound punk sensibility. *Bleach*, their debut, only hinted at Nirvana's potential.

On September 13, 1991, the band followed up its debut with *Nevermind*, the epic recording that would, quite simply, change the way people would hear popular music in the 1990s. Perhaps no other record in the modern era, and inarguably in the alternative era, would have so great an impact. It virtually defined every other rock subgenre that would follow and obliterated the memory of the music it immediately followed. Why? Timing. *Nevermind*, and specifically the first single of the album, "Smells Like Teen Spirit," hit record stores at a time when audiences were aching for change. Not only were they sick of the music they'd been hearing on their radios for a decade, they were bursting with anticipation for something new. Up until now, even grunge bands like Mudhoney and Soundgarden, two marquee acts that beat Nirvana to record stores, were not quite what wider audiences were looking for. Nirvana hit radio in the fall of 1991 when the stars were aligned perfectly. Their songs, intensely aggressive, were also melodic and hummable. They possessed the adrenaline rush of great punk, but with pop sounds friendly enough to sing along with.

Like a cleansing thunderstorm, *Nevermind* swept through popular music, clearing the air and preparing the music industry for the dawn of a new era. An initial shipment of 50,000 units was dispatched in September 1991, but the record kept selling and climbing the charts. Miraculously, that unassuming trio from the Washington backwoods ultimately bumped Michael Jackson off the top of the charts. It remained there for eight weeks and "Smells Like Teen Spirit" dominated both music television (courtesy of a powerful, Samuel-Bayer-directed video) and radio, to date has sold 10 million records, and has stayed in the Billboard Top 200 for five years. It has since become an anthem of the postmodern era and it now stands among the top rock albums in history.

Nirvana's success not only changed what fans wanted from their rock 'n' roll, it also dictated what they didn't want to hear. The anti-musician stance of Kurt Cobain, primarily, and so many of his grunge colleagues—that is, his relative disdain for slick, overly produced material—made the hair metal bands and commercial pop groups of the '80s look like has-beens. Suddenly, any pretense of glamour seemed dated, superfluous. Grunge and the underground music scene had taken over the mainstream and stripped away everything but the music.

Immediately, Artists & Repertoire (A&R) executives, sensing urgency, descended on Seattle waving big-money contracts, tripping over each other in an attempt to sign the Next Big Thing, bands that would follow Nirvana through the door the band had just blown wide open. In Seattle alone, dozens of groups were the beneficiaries of this eager generosity. First wave acts like the Melvins, the Screaming Trees, Tad, and Mudhoney all signed big-money contracts with major labels.

For a few short years in the early '90s, grunge bands and their kin were the only story in rock music. They dominated radio playlists and major-label rosters. They infiltrated the national and international gigging circuits, and, perhaps most significantly, spawned thousands of imitators, all of which wanted to play unpretentious rock 'n' roll for people just like themselves. Many consider the grunge years to have been the first big youth culture movement since punk in 1977.

Soundgarden, Pearl Jam, Alice in Chains, and Nirvana all became platinum-selling acts, drawing huge, arena-type crowds, and adorning the covers of national magazines like *Rolling Stone* and *Spin*. Videos like Nirvana's "Teen Spirit," Soundgarden's "Black Hole Sun" and Alice in Chains' "Would?" monopolized MTV's playlist. Grunge was now on the lips of even casual music fans, and fast on its way to becoming a household word.

The Melvins, 1994 (left to right), Mark Deutrom, King Buzzo, and Dale Crover. Courtesy of Photofest.

Even the film industry paid tribute to the phenomenon. The Matt Dillon vehicle *Singles* starred many grunge musicians in smaller roles. Richard Linklater's landmark debut, *Slackers*, takes place in Austin, but embraces the same Generation X themes that had been occupying Seattle. Ben Stiller's *Reality Bites* also addresses the grunge/slacker zeitgeist against a backdrop of indie rock.

Of these, Cameron Crowe's *Singles*, from 1992, did the most to move grunge further into the spotlight. Using the Seattle music scene as a main character, the story involves Generation X-ers looking for love amid the city's boisterous club circuit. The city itself proved to be as likable as the quirky characters and its sleeper success ensured its exposure to millions.

Like the movie studios, fashion designers also embraced the grunge aesthetic. Some, like Marc Jacobs, Anna Sui, and Christian Francis Roth created exotic, high-fashion lines out of grunge's standard issue flannel shirts, threadbare cardigans, and ripped jeans. Like any fad or trend worth its hipness, grunge had become a commodity.

The Degeneration of Grunge

As this phenomenon seeped into multiple facets of society, the musicians who initially gave birth to it became suspicious and disillusioned. Expectedly, the scene soon degenerated from the inside. Suspicious of outsiders by nature, the city's musicians and scene-sters retreated, refusing to participate in a trend the likes of which they had risen up against. Kurt Cobain, for one, whose own rise and subsequent fall paralleled the triumphant-to-tragic arc of grunge, became wary of his success as soon as he experienced it and expressed it often in interviews. "I've had days where I've considered this a job," he said in an interview with *Melody Maker* back in 1992, "and I never thought that would happen. It makes me question the point of it all. I'm only gonna bitch about it for another year and then, if I can't handle it after that, we're going to make some drastic changes" (True 1992). Says UK journalist True, who befriended Kurt on his rise, "Grunge started to die the moment it became exposed to the outside world, as all scenes do. As soon as the hangers-on and major label A&R men in town started to outnumber the creative people, the artists, musicians and fanzine editors. Kurt Cobain's suicide was the final straw for most" (True 2001).

In the liner notes to the soundtrack of the film *Hype!* (1996), scene queen and frontwoman of Seattle's Dickless Megan Jasper talks about the effect the explosion had on musicians:

> Imagine sleepless Seattle, circa '92—A&R cannibals gobbling up tons of Seattle bands, journalists attempting to shed a light on Seattle's dark side, and the fashion industry telling us that our $3.50 wack slacks now cost 150 buckaroos in fine department stores. Those of us going for the ride were trying to decide whether to be jaded, bummed, stylish, psyched to make a buck, or just too proud to even say the wretched "G" word.

The more prominent and successful Nirvana had become, the less comfortable Kurt Cobain had become. Not in a million years could he, a hard-luck kid in the backwoods of Washington state, have anticipated the fame he would receive. Inadvertently, he became a pop icon, a spokesperson for a generation. But the limelight nauseated him, made him feel awkward in his own skin. As a comfort, perhaps, he sought solace in a relationship. He married controversial artist Courtney Love, frontperson of the band Hole, in February 1992. In August of that year, Love gave birth to the couple's only child, Frances Bean.

Cobain's love and devotion to his family brought real happiness and hope into his life for the first time, but the constant media attention was a distraction to that placidity, and it gave way to troubling bouts of depression. He did not welcome fame. He detested the idea that people wanted to know what he thought about issues, musical or political. Although he never shied away from a debate, his opinions were personal to him, not meant for international consumption, which they eventually became. An intensely private person, Cobain's words were oftentimes scrutinized and criticized. The attention rattled him.

Still, Nirvana soldiered on. They fulfilled record company wishes by touring heavily worldwide. They subsequently released *Incesticide*, a rarities and b-sides collection, in December 1992. *In Utero*, an uncompromising return to the abrasive sound of their punk roots, came out two years after *Nevermind*, in September 1993. For the project, they enlisted rabble-rousing producer Steve Albini (Big Black, Rapeman), and while the abrasive set didn't have the same commercial success as *Nevermind*, it remained true to Nirvana's artistic raison d'être. After becoming a glossy punk phenomenon in the wake of *Nevermind*, though, the band's only aim was to remain true to its own vision.

Many critics, like the *All Music Guide*'s Stephen Thomas Erlewine, deemed *In Utero* a foreshadowing of Cobain's suicide.

Even though the band tempered some of Albini's extreme tactics in a remix, the record remains a deliberately alienating experience, front-loaded with many of its strongest songs, then descending into a series of brief, dissonant squalls before concluding with "All Apologies," which only gets sadder with each passing year. Throughout it all, Cobain's songwriting is typically haunting, and its best moments rank among his finest work, but the over-amped dynamicism of the recording seems like a way to camouflage his dispirited-ness . . . *In Utero* remains a shattering listen, whether it's viewed as Cobain's farewell letter or self-styled audience alienation. Few other records are as willfully difficult as this. (Erlewine 1997)

Increasingly demonized by drug use, plagued by chronic stomach problems and depression, and completely ill-accustomed to attention, the embattled Kurt Cobain took his own life on April 8, 1994. He was 27.

The mourning was intense and widespread. The city of Seattle was devastated. Not since John Lennon died back in 1980 did the passing of a rock star receive such attention. Vigils were held nationwide, the most famous of which involved Love, Kurt's outspoken widow, reading Kurt's own suicide note to a crowd of hundreds. On the other hand, cynics claimed that Cobain deliberately turned his life into a sort of rock 'n' roll martyrdom. By taking his own life, he secured a reputation as the Jim Morrison of the '90s. There were also murmurings of a conspiracy—that Cobain's death, despite the official coroner's report, was a murder made to look like a suicide. The main talking points on that topic alleged that there were no fingerprints on the gun he used to shoot himself, or the pen with which he wrote his note. It is also alleged that Cobain had so much heroin in his system it would have been physically impossible for him to pull the trigger of a gun. The drugs would have rendered him comatose, insinuating that he may have been dead even before the gun shot.

A film titled *Kurt & Courtney*, Nick Broomfield's 1998 documentary that Love tried valiantly to table, explored these

 KURT COBAIN'S SUICIDE NOTE

To Boddah

Speaking from the tongue of an experienced simpleton who obviously would rather be an emasculated, infantile complain-ee. This note should be pretty easy to understand.

All the warnings from the punk rock 101 courses over the years, since my first introduction to the, shall we say, ethics involved with independence and the embracement of your community has proven to be very true. I haven't felt the excitement of listening to as well as creating music along with reading and writing for too many years now. I feel guilty beyond words about these things.

For example when we're back stage and the lights go out and the manic roar of the crowds begins, it doesn't affect me the way in which it did for Freddie Mercury, who seemed to love, relish in the love and adoration from the crowd which is something I totally admire and envy. The fact is, I can't fool you, any one of you. It simply isn't fair to you or me. The worst crime I can think of would be to rip people off by faking it and pretending as if I'm having 100% fun. Sometimes I feel as if I should have a punch-in time clock before I walk out on stage. I've tried everything within my power to appreciate it (and I do, God, believe me I do, but it's not enough). I appreciate the fact that I and we have affected and entertained a lot of people. It must be one of those narcissists who only

KURT COBAIN'S SUICIDE NOTE
(continued)

appreciate things when they're gone. I'm too sensitive. I need to be slightly numb in order to regain the enthusiasms I once had as a child.

On our last 3 tours, I've had a much better appreciation for all the people I've known personally, and as fans of our music, but I still can't get over the frustration, the guilt and empathy I have for everyone. There's good in all of us and I think I simply love people too much, so much that it makes me feel too fucking sad. The sad little, sensitive, unappreciative, Pisces, Jesus man. Why don't you just enjoy it? I don't know!

I have a goddess of a wife who sweats ambition and empathy and a daughter who reminds me too much of what I used to be, full of love and joy, kissing every person she meets because everyone is good and will do her no harm. And that terrifies me to the point to where I can barely function. I can't stand the thought of Frances becoming the miserable, self-destructive, death rocker that I've become.

I have it good, very good, and I'm grateful, but since the age of seven, I've become hateful towards all humans in general. Only because it seems so easy for people to get along that have empathy. Only because I love and feel sorry for people too much I guess.

Thank you all from the pit of my burning, nauseous stomach for your letters and concern during the past years. I'm too much of an erratic, moody baby! I don't have the passion anymore, and so remember, it's better to burn out than to fade away.

Peace, love, empathy.
Kurt Cobain

Frances and Courtney, I'll be at your alter [*sic*].
Please keep going Courtney, for Frances.
For her life, which will be so much happier without me.

I LOVE YOU, I LOVE YOU!

conspiracies through interviews with inner-circle witnesses. Ostensibly a look at various aspects of the A-list couple's relationship, including its shared drug habits, the film served to draw even more attention to an already inflammatory subject. Legal complications blocked this film from a December 1997 BBC airing and a showing at the 1998 Sundance Film Festival.

Cobain's death put an emphatic end to the grunge movement in Seattle. The country and indeed the world had co-opted the music, but its city of origin wanted no further part in it. The commercialization and slick packaging unwittingly and ironically engendered by grunge was rapid and, to many of those involved in its creation, demoralizing. Radio and music television had scrapped their pop playlists completely and replaced them with playlists consisting mainly of something now known as "alternative rock."

Not that alternative rock did not exist before. In fact, it had been around since the early '80s, used as a term to describe bands that existed outside the mainstream. It was a catch-all term for rock bands, most of which owed their debt to punk in the wake of that genre's 1976 revolution. There was virtually no commercial pretense to the original wave of "alternative bands," which ranged from post-punk and gothic styles to New Wave and hardcore. As alternative rock became more popular in the mid-'80s, it spread widely to other college radio stations, leading to the name "college rock." R.E.M. and U2 rate most famously as the quintessential "college" bands.

But now, alternative rock embraced grunge as one of its styles as well. This meant that grunge, once the mode of expression favored by the slacker proletariat, now the new commercial rock, brought the term "alternative" into the mainstream. Mainstream rock has not been the same.

POST-GRUNGE

With original grunge bands, that is, first-wave grunge bands beating a hasty retreat, record labels were left with second-rate imitators, bands like Bush (London), Live (Pennsylvania), Green Apple Quick Step (Seattle), Loudmouth (Chicago), and Candlebox (Seattle) who took their cues from grunge, but possessed little of the dynamism and edginess of the originals. The radical fringe—again, like the Melvins—were still doing their thing as they had all along, while the mainstream became saturated with unoriginal alternative bands styled after grunge.

The mass market—radio and retail outlets—didn't bother to distinguish the imitators from the original. They had a hunger to feed; the demand for the heavy, slightly angry guitars of grunge still existed and the new bands satisfied it, even though they were twice removed from the original movement. This was seen by critics as crass and exploitative, especially in light of Kurt Cobain's death. Bands created and inspired by the sounds of grunge were vilified for taking advantage of a trend whose hero had so freshly taken his own life. The visceral reaction against these bands reinforced what many already knew, that grunge had become an American rock cliché, and was, despite its continuing commercial viability, headed into a downward spiral.

Optimists insist that grunge served as a launching pad. It dismissed the tired and indulgent music of the past, erased the ennui of music fans in the process, and gave them something to get excited about. The phoenix-like rise of alternative rock as a result of grunge's breakthrough altered the landscape of music indefinitely. It destroyed the staid, normally unchanging formats of radio by proving that underground music could indeed succeed in the mainstream. Commercial rock music—rigidly defined by radio program directors since disco back in the late '70s—no longer existed. Because Nirvana and its kin had proven what few thought possible, the entire musical playing field was now open to all comers. In the wake of grunge, any genre or subgenre of music was a commercial possibility. Many young bands continued to wear flannel shirts and Chuck Taylor hi-tops, but just as many were inspired to succeed on their own terms, another lesson learned in grunge's wake.

Young musicians realized that they no longer had the stringent code of popular music to abide by. They could now make their own rules, play their own music, express their own opinions, without succumbing to the record industry. At last, the mega-corporations had to answer to the young and creative types, as they had back in the '60s with the hippie movement. The next big thing, experts predicted, could be anything.

Music fans also learned to take nothing for granted. For a brief window, popular music had become open-minded, willing to look at and listen to just about anything. Of course, that window closed almost as quickly as it had opened. But it still allowed plenty of refreshing new sounds to seep in, and inquisitive ears to hear what was going on "outside." One of the results of this enlightenment saw the production of popular music increase tenfold between the years

1988 and 1998 (Christgau 2000), ending with 35,000 record releases annually. Much of this increase in production can be attributed to Nirvana's success, along with the advent of the digital era and the explosion of the compact disc medium.

In the introduction to his book *The Nineties*, London-based journalist John Robb sees the decade this way:

> The Nineties was a time when the barriers came down. It was a time when you could cross-pollinate and grab any scene you wanted . . . Pop culture continued to be fractured but you could smash and grab across all the different scenes. The age barrier disappeared, different generations pilfered each other's styles and sounds. New music rubbed shoulders with old styles . . .
>
> It has given musicians greater freedom to create, escaping the dark days of scene-orientated rock. After all, pop is meant to be some sort of adventure. You have to follow your nose and fuck all the rules off, otherwise what's the point? (Robb 1999, 4)

2

ALTERNATIVE COUNTRY

The story of country rock, or rockin' country, has always been about outsiders looking in. From the earliest days of country merging with rock in the '50s right up to the present with performers like Steve Earle, Emmylou Harris, and Ryan Adams, what has come to be known as "alternative country" (or alt.country), in the '90s has been a long history of pop music's great haven for outlaws and outsiders, artists who simply didn't care to abide by the country music industry's stringent rules.

Of course, in rock 'n' roll, rules were made to be broken. In the '60s, artists like Gram Parsons and the Byrds went against the grain of rock 'n' roll by fusing the big beat of psychedelic rock with the twang of country. Parsons, who died in a motorcycle accident in 1970 and has since become the crown prince of alternative country, had a huge influence even then on bands like the Rolling Stones. Keith Richards, who partied extensively with Parsons, infused songs like "Sweet Virginia" on their classic *Exile on Main Street* with a country flavor, at least in part due to his relationship with Parsons. Some say Richards returned the favor by allowing Parsons to record the definitive version of "Wild Horses" with his band the Flying Burrito Brothers, even before the Stones themselves recorded it.

The Byrds, thanks in part to Parsons, subverted the psychedelic revolution—which they participated in—and recorded the country-rock cornerstone *Sweetheart of the Rodeo*. The contributions of Parsons, as well as gifted songwriters David Crosby, Roger McGuinn, and Gene Clark, enabled the band to become the lynchpin of alternative country.

After hijacking the Byrds' *Sweetheart* sessions, turning them into a barn dance of sorts, Parsons left the band in 1967 to form the Burritos. It was here

Gram Parsons with friends, Keith Richards and Anita Pallenberg, at the Joshua Tree National Forest. Courtesy of the Library of Congress.

that Parsons, along with bandmate/roommate Chris Hillman (also a former Byrd), made his biggest impact. Only a few albums came of that period. *The Gilded Palace of Sin* and *Burrito Deluxe* were the band's first two albums—the only two with Parsons in the lineup. But they were enough to allow the original lineup to carve a very definite place in alternative country history. Another critical group during this early confluence of folk, country, and rock was Buffalo Springfield with Neil Young, Stephen Stills, Bruce Palmer, and Richie Furay. Although they were only together for two years beginning in 1967, only the Byrds, and arguably, the Flying Burrito Brothers had as much impact on the sound of country rock.

A few years later, the Nitty Gritty Dirt Band was looking to merge country with folk and rock. Formed in 1965 as a jug band, they journeyed to Nashville from their native Santa Monica in 1972 to make a record of traditional country numbers in a jug/folk-rock style. What resulted remains a landmark in country rock: *Will the Circle Be Unbroken* is on the short list of masterpieces in alternative country.

In the '70s, the so-called "space cowboy" movement got underway in Texas with Jerry Jeff Walker, Doug Sahm, Guy Clark, and Townes Van Zandt, all country-styled songwriters who refused to do business the conventional way.

Fond of drugs (hence the moniker), these talented artists found ways to establish themselves without caving in to industry expectations.

Another school of rebels, the so-called "outlaws," came together in Nashville. These were by and large country artists who also remained outside the country system. Johnny Cash, Waylon Jennings, Willie Nelson, Kris Kristofferson, and David Allan Coe among others, were considered mavericks, musical bullies who drank heartily and took no prisoners.

In California, a bunch of midwestern ex-patriots, including Don Henley, Glen Frey, Bernie Leadon, and Randy Meisner began exploring the possibilities of merging folk with rock and country. Leadon played with Parsons in the Burritos, after forming country rockers Poco. Frey and Henley played in Linda Ronstadt's band, the Stone Ponys. Leadon and Meisner also played with Ronstadt, though briefly. It was long enough, however, to bring them together as the Eagles.

"Alt.country has added an aggressive attitude and an anti-establishment spirit from these forms to the nostalgic reverence associated with country," writes John Molinaro, a music journalist who published his thesis, "Urbane Cowboys: Alt.Country in the '90s" in 1998. "It also includes artists who have worked within country or roots-rock but who have been branded as outlaws or pariahs for ideological, political, or social decisions (i.e., public and unrepentant drug abuse, refusal to conform to current trends in Nashville, etc.)" (Molinaro).

Throughout the '80s, Southern California proved to be an able incubator of twang-rock hybrids. Punk bands like the Gun Club (whose frontman, singer Jeffrey Lee Pierce, is described as the missing link between the Eagles and Nirvana), X (made a full-on country record as the Knitters), Social Distortion (covered Johnny Cash's "Ring of Fire"), and Rank & File (once played on the country television program *Austin City Limits*) all injected a country taste into otherwise turbulent sounds. The Blasters welded a raging blues and rockabilly sound onto their rock and punk, and its singer, Dave Alvin, has since gone on to become a principal player in the world of alternative country. Others, like Jason and the Scorchers, the Silos, the Bodeans, and Lone Justice found fertile ground in the gray areas between pop, rock, and country. Paisley Underground bands (the Dream Syndicate, Green on Red, and the Long Ryders) merged heady psychedelia with an undercurrent of Burrito Brothers' aesthetics.

As the '80s progressed, a handful of artists—Dwight Yoakam, Jim Lauderdale, Kelly Willis, and Shelby Lynne—attempted to move mainstream country music forward, by keeping it from straying too far beyond its traditional boundaries. All have since become successful Americana artists, which basically means they're not making the kind of music that mainstream country music radio is anxious to play.

Los Lobos, a Hispanic-American band borne in East Los Angeles, proved shortly after forming in the mid-'80s that they were one of the most original bands in the country. Albums like *By the Light of the Moon* (1987) and *Kiko* (1992) fall on the Tex-Mex side of alternative country and roots rock, but they still managed to captivate an alternative audience with their gorgeous blend of Latino and American grooves.

These major amalgams of country and rock provide a rough lineage and foundation, a sort of family tree root system of the alternative country music explosion of the '90s. Oddly enough, though the bands mentioned above had a tremendous impact on the future sound of rock music, they existed as random occurrences, separate bursts of genius that had very little thread other than the fact that they were all efforts at fusing disparate genres: country music and rock 'n' roll.

WHAT EXACTLY IS ALTERNATIVE COUNTRY?

Billboard columnist Chet Flippo wrote in 1996, "If you're not played on mainstream country radio, then you're alt.country," which is as good and as wide open a definition as you will hear. It also means that when it comes to alternative country, anything goes. The genre is currently referred to by a variety of nicknames, also characteristic of its no-borders approach: alt.country (named after the momentum it developed on the Internet), No Depression (after a Carter Family tune), Insurgent Country, Cowpunk, Y'Alternative, or Country Grunge, among others.

> Historically, the blending of country and rock music is as old as Elvis Presley's recording of Bill Monroe's "Blue Moon of Kentucky" back in 1954. Johnny Cash and Bob Dylan helped tear down the walls between the two genres with their famous collaborations in the 1960s. Gram Parsons took the Byrds all the way to the Grand Ole Opry; Waylon Jennings covered Rolling Stones songs and got a standing ovation opening for the Grateful Dead in the 1970s; and Neil Young got hippies singing "Are You Ready for the Country" while Merle Haggard's "Okie from Muskogee" was still fresh in most Americans' minds. (All Music Guide)

Alternative country music has, over the years, come to embrace many kinds of music, from twangy Bakersfield swing to folky, Bluebird Café outcasts who had made an effort in Nashville but never clicked; from greasy rockabilly and roots rock acts to blustery punks offering mere hints of a dusty West. The array now, which also includes a genre called Americana—a not-so-subversive version of alternative country—is quite vast. For example, the magazine designed to cover the genre, appropriately named *No Depression*, features a Top 40 retail chart. Artists as diverse as folk singer John Prine, country swingers Asleep at the Wheel, London art-rocker Beth Gomez, pop country divas the Dixie Chicks, and bluegrass virtuoso Bela Fleck comprise the list in a single month.

The Dixie Chicks, 2001 (left to right), Emily Robison, Natalie Maines, and Martie Seidel (Maguire). Courtesy of Photofest.

The category is fluid, says Molinaro.

> Alt.country draws from a number of rock and country influences creating a hybrid sound that is neither country or rock. To understand it fully, its influences, liminal artists from a wide spectrum of popular styles need to be examined: country artists like Johnny Cash or Willie Nelson who border on rock and/or folk; rock stars like R.E.M. and Bruce Springsteen that border on country-folk; punk bands like the Replacements or X who border on roots-rock . . . Alt.country, while drawing from all these liminal styles, defies categorization. Both the artists and audience recognize that this is something different.

Finally, Peter Blackstock and Grant Alden, the editorial tandem of *No Depression*, a publication started in 1995 to cover this multifaceted genre, put it this way in their liner notes to *No Depression: What It Sounds Like (Vol. 1)*, a various-artist collection released in 2004:

> If, in fact, alternative-country music actually exists—and this remains a curious riddle open to furious debate—what does it sound like? . . . Indeed the definition is elusive precisely because, as with all true art, this music

pays no mind to strictures or bounds. And yet somehow, somewhere, there is a commonality, a harmonizing chord struck between the cracks of the styles and the genres that blend together amid the artists portrayed in our pages.

Therein lies the challenge of composing a definitive overview on alternative country for historical purposes. One thread that holds this genre loosely together is the artists' relative disdain for the highly polished, actively handled image-making and marketing that characterizes other branches of country and pop music. These artists generally have steadfast control of their careers and make their own decisions regarding them. Even the Dixie Chicks, a hugely successful, multiple-platinum-selling act on a major multinational corporation label, Sony, handle all of their own business affairs, having the final say on everything that has anything to do with the band.

Stylistically, the Nashville thread of country music has always taken its cue from traditional types of acoustic music from the '20s, '30s, and '40s, including Jimmie Rodgers, Hank Williams, and the Carter Family. But Nashville's country music updates itself continually, adjusting its sound to the themes of modern life. Certain country music styles—in particular bluegrass, hillbilly, folk, and other acoustic roots music—remain traditional and implicitly connected to the past, reflecting life as it was in more agrarian times. Not so with mainstream country, which is written, for better or worse, to reflect today's life experience. This is one reason mainstream country music experiences vicissitudes of commercial success. It adheres closely to the emotional ups and downs of our national, social, political, and economic climate.

Alternative country is set in direct opposition to that. It eschews ideas of modern-day existence in favor of a more traditional view of American rural life, a sort of Depression-era, "Grapes of Wrath" perspective more akin to Woody Guthrie than Garth Brooks, closer in spirit to the primal mountain music of Tennessee than to the highly polished twang of Nashville's urban cowboys. Alternative country maintains a direct connection with the past, a sort of black-and-white photograph of a rural America characterized by honesty, endurance, and humility, and a time when the simple life along the Appalachian Trail ruled.

But it is the punk strand, the "alternative" hemisphere of alternative country that has determined its audience. Punk has always appealed to a disaffected young and white demographic which stares the prospect of mass "downward mobility" in the face. This is in stark contrast to their relatively affluent upbringing throughout the '80s, otherwise known as the Reagan years.

1980–1988

During the Reagan years, 1980–1988, the social landscape shifted radically. Prosperity reigned. Baby boomers, benefiting from the stock market and real estate spikes, again had money at their disposal. Reagan turned back two decades of federal welfare, EPA legislation against big business, and attempted to enact something he called "the trickle-down theory." This stated that his big business tax cuts would ultimately trickle down to the middle and lower classes: businesses would hire more, pay better, and this money would reach the less fortunate, who would then, in turn, invest their own small windfalls.

Unfortunately, greed subsumed the money classes and the trickle never reached the bottom strata. There were investment scandals, a market crash, hostile takeovers, and the like. Companies looking to stretch already healthy profits opened businesses or sent work overseas. In the process, 10 percent of the richest Americans became richer while the poor remained so.

In musical terms, this wealth disparity and injustice gave rise to rebellion the same way it did during the original wave of punk in the mid-'70s. Then, as here, disillusioned music fans were drawn to hardcore and punk, modes of extreme expression adopted by those angry and frustrated kids left behind. But instead of the punks being drawn to alternative country following the Reagan years, the slackers (also known as Generation X), suffering from the same frustrations, took to the genre instead. Slackers have always had a famously passive reputation, however, choosing to sit idly as an opportunity-less life passes them by. This is in contrast to punks, who have historically taken a much more active political approach to their plight. Fans of alternative country have never bothered with this heightened level of activism. Rather, in characteristic fashion, they enjoy an equally active involvement with their music and their bands, without all the protestation.

So how do punk and country coexist in a single genre? Irony. Alternative country undermines the reverence of its traditional past by welding it to a very progressive future—its punk and post-punk heritage. Punk, on the other hand, with its extreme leanings and its pretense to rip down convention, might seem to be at odds with the deep monochromatics of the Carter Family and Hank Williams. But the relationship allows punks to enhance their indie rock with a credible and authentic voice, the respected voices of time-honored artists steeped in tradition, while reaching a new audience with that voice.

Similarly, old-time country and folk music was about honesty and directness. Like punk, these styles were built on candor, erected on a foundation of independence and autonomy, and populated by artists who were rarely professionally trained, yet inspired in their own right. In this way, alt.country and punk rock have always had a great deal in common.

Few fans of today's country music have an opportunity to hear the gritty voices of the genre's forbears because commercial country radio specializes in the sanitary purview of mainstream Nashville. Cowpunks have co-opted the hardscrabble voices of the tradition's great, homespun voices and have made it their own to share.

ESSENTIAL ALT.COUNTRY PERFORMERS

Uncle Tupelo

Although the genre has been long in the making, alternative country is, by and large, a product of the late '80s and early '90s. Many experts in the field agree that one band was responsible for jumpstarting it: Uncle Tupelo.

Jeff Tweedy and Jay Farrar were high school buddies who grew up in small-town Illinois, in a farm-belt burg called Belleville. Inspired by bands like Clash and the Ramones on the punk side and Bob Dylan and the Byrds on the folk/rock side, they formed a band called the Primatives [sic] in the mid-'80s. Early on they would rent local civic halls and play cover songs for up to 500 of their fellow students, making a name for themselves with a gritty, speeded-up blend of punk, rock, and country music. "The records we were listening to early on from the '60s (the garage stuff)," said drummer Mike Heidorn in the liner notes to the band's classic 1990 disc *No Depression*, "morphed into the other side of the '60s: the Byrds, the Flying Burrito Brothers, the Band, Neil Young. Jeff always had Dylan tapes around and Jay always had a Johnny Cash song on hand. But now it seemed we wanted to branch away from just doing '60s covers."

In late 1987, the band began to ramp up its songwriting. Tweedy and Farrar scribbled lyrics down on random scraps of paper; they rehearsed nightly in a cramped rehearsal space in downtown Belleville, searching for an aesthetic to call their own. Little did they know that the pieces for such an aesthetic were already in place. They just had to start making some records.

Uncle Tupelo began putting their music on tape at friends' home studios beginning in 1987 and 1988, all the while making a name for themselves on the area's live circuit, developing a following specifically in St. Louis, the closest metropolitan area.

Their demo tape, *Not Forever Just for Now*, landed in the hands of many independent label representatives—including Sub Pop and Caroline—but only one imprint responded. Giant Records, later called Rockville, took a particular interest in the Uncle Tupelo sound and signed them with a verbal agreement. The boys would go on to win the Best Unsigned Band contest at 1989's CMJ Music Festival in New York City and, with the blessing of Rockville, traveled to Boston's Fort Apache Studio to begin recording their debut album.

No Depression, named after their cover of a late '30s tune by the Carter Family, "No Depression in Heaven," hit the stores in the summer of 1990. It was reviewed positively by the press and received well by indie music fans. But few at the time anticipated the larger impact the album would later have. In fact, Uncle Tupelo's impact has essentially been defined not by the effect it had musically—recording for recording—but by the stampede of imitators it precipitated during and after its brief lifetime as a band.

No Depression was followed by another landmark album, *Still Feel Gone*. Released in September 1991, the album was a transitional one for the band, exhibiting a deeper and more varied approach to both country and rock. The alliance between both sides of the band's creativity didn't mesh quite as well as it did on their less complicated debut. Still, it served to push Tweedy, Farrar, and Einhorn slightly forward in their quest for the perfect compromise between rock and twang.

March 16–20, 1992, the band's third album, named for the week in which it was made, sees the pendulum swinging back toward the band's acoustic roots. Produced by R.E.M.'s Peter Buck, it's a mix of originals and covers, yin and yang, sadness and joy, all made with acoustic instruments on a demo-tape budget. "Halfway through the week," Buck says in the album's liner notes, "I thought, Gee, this is like working on a classic Rolling Stones album. This is going to be a great record and it's going to be around for a long time."

As Buck predicted, the album ended up breaking open Uncle Tupelo's legend. Like their first two records, it was an explosion in sound, an authentic exploration of style, and a brash statement of intent. "Part of it was our contrarian spirit," said Tweedy in a 1997 interview with *Rolling Stone*, "as if doing something so arcane, we were actually inventing something" (*Rolling Stone*, March 1997).

Indeed, it became known as alt.country. It was also when the myths surrounding Uncle Tupelo began circulating. Some surmised that they were coal miners, that they spent their time on a back porch in the rural Midwest strumming these songs while sipping on moonshine from the still out back. The myth held that they were never meant to be discovered. The publicity machine often surrounding popular bands hadn't begun rolling for Tupelo and new fans, believing they had discovered something truly unique, spread whatever word they had heard about the bucolic band. Much of that dissemination took place on the Internet. Thus one of the genre's nicknames: alt.country.

While many felt Tupelo wrote original tunes, which they did often, they also had discovered a mother lode of esoteric folk songs from the '30s and '40s themselves. "We learned the songs at the library," said Tweedy, "bought 'em on record. I'd stumble on things from working in a record store, and buy anything that looked like a Folkways album and Jay would go to the local libraries and check out anything in the folk section" (*Mojo*, May 2002).

The truth is, Farrar's dad, an accordionist, did move to Belleville from the Ozark Mountains, and he did, in fact, teach his four sons the songs and sounds of his upbringing. Tweedy's own father worked the railroad as a diesel mechanic for decades, so he was brought up in the kind of hardworking, blue-collar family that taught their children the songs and culture of the working class.

Still, the legend of these two remarkable songwriters grew exponentially with the release of *March 16–20, 1992*. In sharp contrast to the band's first two discs, the songs on this album resonated with the low-budget folk and acoustic music they cherished as kids. Covers of traditional songs like the Louvin Brothers' "Atomic Power" and the traditional "Satan, Your Kingdom Must Come Down" coexisted with simpatico originals like Tweedy's "Black Eye" and Farrar's "Shaky Ground." Oddly enough, *March 16–20, 1992* found Tweedy and Farrar, lifelong soul brothers, growing apart slightly. Their relationship, says drummer Heidorn, "always had an edge," but their love for this kind of music, this unique creation of theirs, had until now kept them firmly together.

It was Uncle Tupelo's first and only major-label album, *Anodyne*, released in 1993, that is now referred to as their magnum opus. Having taken on drummer Ken Coomer—Mike Heidorn left to spend more time with his family—and part-time instrumentalists Max Johnston and John Stirratt, the band laid down *Anodyne* totally live at Cedar Creek Recording in Austin with engineer Brian Paulson.

Although the rift between Tweedy and Farrar had widened during the recording of the album, they managed to stay together harmoniously enough to get through the sessions. Those on the scene could actually attest to the fact that the duo had never been more attuned to each other. Songs like "Acuff-Rose," "The Long Cut," and the title cut "Anodyne" have since become alt.country classics and the album as a whole is a true country-rock milestone in much the same way the Byrds' *Sweetheart of the Rodeo* was back in 1968.

A subsequent tour in support of the album, a long and grueling jaunt dictated by Warner Brothers, their label, resulted in Farrar and Tweedy splitting acrimoniously. On May 1, 1994 (the story has it), after a triumphant set, Jay Farrar walked off the stage in their shared hometown of St. Louis following the last date of the band's tour and never returned. At the very peak of their popularity and with a bright future ahead, the band could no longer tolerate the routine and called it quits. Legend also has it that the two longtime friends haven't spoken a word to each other since.

Uncle Tupelo Epilogue

Since their split, both Jay Farrar and Jeff Tweedy have remained quite busy. Farrar assembled a band called Son Volt. Tweedy's band became known as Wilco. Tweedy recruited his band from the original Uncle Tupelo lineup, while Farrar rang up founding Tupelo drummer Mike Heidorn and a few old friends, including the Boquist brothers, Dave and Jim, for Son Volt.

Farrar's band has turned out to be the more traditional of the two offshoots. Son Volt's recordings, namely *Trace* and *Straightaways*, are respectful tributes to the music of his upbringing: folk, acoustic blues, and roots. After 1998's *Wide Swing Tremolo*, Farrar set out on a solo career, denying the breakup of Son Volt. His first solo album, *Sebastopol*, was issued in 2001. Critics of the band were troubled by Farrar's backwards progress, which belied the groundbreaking nature

Wilco, 2001 (left to right), Glenn Kotche, Mike Jorgensen, Jeff Tweedy, and John Stirratt. Courtesy of Corbis.

of his former band, Uncle Tupelo. Rather than finding a fertile creative niche to explore, Farrar retreated, choosing to fall back on the music of his youth.

Wilco, conversely, has attempted to escape their alternative country branding altogether. On albums like *Summer Teeth* and *Yankee Hotel Foxtrot*, Tweedy has become something of a Brian Wilson (Beach Boys) songwriter, crafting elaborate, moody pieces rife with the sounds of pop and rock, and light on the twang. His work has managed to hold on to its jangly charm, only now it's adorned with somewhat gaudier musical accoutrements. The artistic bifurcation of these two talents and former friends only serves to buttress the reasons for their actual falling out, a split now attributed to "creative differences."

Both bands were unable to retain their former label, Warner Brothers. Son Volt made three records before exiting, while Wilco did the same beginning with A.M. in 1995, *Being There* in 1996, and *Summer Teeth* in 1999, each disc more acclaimed than the last. Their falling out with the Warner Brothers label was articulated on the acclaimed documentary *I Am Trying to Break Your Heart*. In it, the label is depicted as desiring a more commercially viable work in place of the album Wilco delivered, the aforementioned *Yankee Hotel Foxtrot*. Unwilling to comply, the band was unceremoniously released. In the wake of the split, however, the album became one of 2002's most acclaimed recordings.

MERMAID AVENUE

Woody Guthrie was the archetypal political folksinger, a troubadour activist with the wit and vision of a poet and the heart of a lion. Some call him the most important American folk music artist of the first half of the twentieth century. Certainly, he is one of the spiritual fathers of Americana and alternative country, a classic outsider. By the time he gained recognition in the 1940s, Guthrie had written hundreds of songs, many of which remain folk standards to this day. When the Dust Bowl singer was interviewed by musicologist Alan Lomax for the Library of Congress in March 1940, Guthrie sang some of his most popular tunes, including "So Long, It's Been Good to Know You," "Dust Bowl Blues," "I Ain't Got No Home," and many other songs, all of which were recorded for posterity. Guthrie later went on to write songs like "Pastures of Plenty," "The Grand Coulee Dam," and his masterpiece, "This Land Is Your Land." He died in 1967.

During the spring of 1995, Woody's daughter Nora Guthrie wanted to pay tribute to her dad on the thirtieth anniversary of his passing. To help her commemorate the date, she contacted like-minded British urban folk troubadour Billy Bragg about completing some of her father's unfinished songs. Specifically, there were sets of lyrics Woody had completed before his death, but the music had yet to be written. In fact, Guthrie left behind over 1,000 sets of lyrics written between 1939 and 1967, all of which had no music other than his own vague notations.

Bragg set about choosing a number of songs, and he recruited Wilco's Jeff Tweedy (working with bandmate Jay Bennett) for assistance. Nora Guthrie impressed upon the two that they should write in the spirit of Guthrie, as if collaborating with him. Both Bragg and Tweedy completed more songs than could fit on an album and they chose fifteen to fit on the first installment of *Mermaid Avenue*, issued in 1998. Each tune is faithful to Guthrie's rowdy élan but also reverent. The project was successful, and true enough to the cause to earn itself a Grammy nomination. Not only that, it yielded a sequel, *Mermaid Avenue, Vol. 2*, which featured more selections from the band's collaborations with Bragg on Woody Guthrie's unfinished songs.

Lucinda Williams

Alongside Uncle Tupelo, another artist was able to enjoy the same kind of respect and admiration from an ever-blossoming group of fans, without having to conform to any sort of industry standard of mainstream country music. Lucinda Williams was born in 1953 in Louisiana, the daughter of a poet/professor, and she came of age in ambitiously intellectual surroundings. A gifted writer with a hunger for early blues and folk, Lucinda grew up listening to Dylan, Leadbelly, Woody Guthrie, and Joan Baez, before delving into the blues of Robert Johnson and Howlin' Wolf.

In 1978 she recorded the first of two traditional acoustic blues albums for the Smithsonian Folkways label, debuting with the self-titled *Ramblin' on My*

GOLDEN SMOG

In the late '80s, Minneapolis was a raging indie rock town, led by bands like the Replacements, Hüsker Dü, and Soul Asylum. The sounds were loud, the clubs were packed, and the records of these Minneapolis bands were selling beyond all reasonable expectations. At the height of their popularity, members from several local bands, including Soul Asylum, the Jayhawks, the Replacements, Wilco, Honeydogs, and Run Westy Run, came together secretly as an all-star country rock band called Golden Smog.

Their design was to be a sort of Klaatu-meets-Spinal-Tap situation in which the true identities and pedigree of the band members were not to be revealed. Their record company, Rykodisc, went so far as to fabricate a history of the band, complete with pseudonyms, so Golden Smog would be treated not as a super-group side-project, but as a new, original act unto itself. The band's Web site features an extensive ersatz history of the band—describing it as "nine young men from Norway"—broken up into long-winded chapters, tracing its recorded roots all the way back into the '60s.

Actually, the band's first disc, an EP of cover tunes called *On Golden Smog*, was issued in 1992. It was very well received despite (or perhaps because of) the fact that it was shrouded with a sort of wry secrecy. Of course, it didn't take long (only a handful of live shows) to determine who was in the band. In fact, it was a rotating cast of characters from around the Minneapolis scene, all of them eager to break temporarily from their main gigs, to play something fresh, something alt.country to recharge the batteries.

In 1995, the band released *Down By the Old Mainstream*, their first full-length album, and followed that up three years later with *Weird Tales*. In the interim, the Golden Smog cabal, trying to keep an air of history about the band, put out a special promo-only box set, *35 Years of Golden Smog*, which actually included one real disc, *Down By the Old Mainstream*, and two empty jewel boxes, titled *Swingin' Smog People: The Swingin' Sounds of The Golden Smog* and *America's Newest Shitmakers: The Newest Sounds of The Golden Smog*.

Mind. The second, *Happy Woman Blues*, followed in 1980. But a series of professional and personal setbacks prevented her from recording another album until a full eight years later. Professionally, she struggled to maintain independence in the face of intense record company directives, unfavorable contracts, and executives who pressured her artistically. Personally, alcohol also proved to be a major stumbling block. But in 1988, she pulled her act together to record *Lucinda Williams*, a beautifully realized effort sparked by songs like "The Night's Too Long" and "Passionate Kisses," the latter of which won Williams a Grammy for Best Country Song after Mary Chapin Carpenter recorded a version of her own. Her sound bridged the gap between country, folk, and rock, with Lucinda's voice—tender and soulful but with a blues grit—and literate wordplay, serving as her focal point. Like Uncle Tupelo, she absolutely

Lucinda Williams performing on the television show *Crossroads*, 2002. Courtesy of Photofest.

adored the old-time music of America's rural past and it fully informed her sound.

Seized again by record company red tape as well as personal problems, Lucinda wouldn't put another record out for four years, unable to capitalize on the momentum she established with her 1988 title. In 1992, she finally released *Sweet Old World*, a highly anticipated album (at least critically) that proved her fan base to be a loyal one. But her record company, Chameleon, went out of business soon after and she lost the support of the one label with which she didn't have philosophical differences. It would be another six years before she'd record again, this time signing on with Rick Rubin's American Recordings. Unfortunately still, American went through corporate changes just as Lucinda was readying the release of her album, *Car Wheels on a Gravel Road*, stalling its release. By now, Williams' recording misadventures were becoming the stuff of legend. A story in the *New York Times* magazine on September 14, 1997 was titled, "Lucinda Williams Is In Pain"; it detailed her struggles with labels; her frustration with remaining in artistic control; and her falling out with producers, friends, and bandmates (Frey 1997).

Yet despite it all, Williams triumphed with the new album and nearly won success outside of the alternative country coterie. By now she had become the biggest and most respected act in the genre, and was rewarded with a second Grammy, this time for Best Contemporary Folk Recording in 1998. After only three short years, Lucinda recorded *Essence*, an introspective collection highlighted by the song "Get Right with God," a song that won her a third Grammy, this time for Best Female Rock Vocal. The fact that Lucinda Williams has upto now won Grammys in three different categories—rock, folk, and country—is characteristic of a great alternative country artist, one that will go down in history as a star of the genre.

THE FLOURISHING

Uncle Tupelo and Lucinda Williams sparked a stampede of like-minded artists. The underground rock scenes across the country, in Seattle, Boston, Minneapolis, Chicago, and Austin, among other cities, were teeming with talented bands, many of which had created a thirst for new and original music. Uncle Tupelo brought them just that.

Other bands at the time were making similar inroads. In Boston, a band called the Blood Oranges, led by fiddler Jimmy Ryan, were early purveyors of alt.country before it had become hip to pursue the sound. At the time, there were few rock and pop bands with a country vibe, so their sound was less a part of a trend and more a novelty. Still, their debut disc in 1990, *Corn River*, a mix of folk, bluegrass, and hard blues-rock, serves as a critical entry in the genre's canon. In Minneapolis, the rise of the Jayhawks, led by Gary Louris and Marc Olsen, almost paralleled that of Uncle Tupelo. Their 1991 album *Hollywood Town Hall* is another significant cornerstone in the alt.country pyramid. Across the border in Toronto, the Cowboy Junkies had begun asserting themselves in an understated way, in the late '80s. They had a vaguely western feel, courtesy of Michael Timmins' expressive guitar playing and sister Margot's hushed singing style. The Cowboy Junkies made their biggest impact with a cover of the Velvet Underground's "Sweet Jane," and that song's commercial impact prevented them from being fully embraced by the alternative crowd, which preferred its music less "discovered."

In Louisville, Freakwater, a duo starring former punk rockers Janet Bean and Catherine Irwin, reinvented themselves with a backwoods acoustic sound

Cowboy Junkies, 1991. Courtesy of Photofest.

reminiscent of Appalachian folk. They debuted on record in 1991, but broke through with their 1993 disc, *Feels Like the Third Time*. Their old-time folk sound, reminiscent of the Carter Family, opened the door to other old-timey aspirants, including Lambchop, Iris DeMent, Palace, Sparklehorse, and Gillian Welch, all of whom have at one time or another been hailed as pioneers on the acoustic byway of alternative country. Palace's Will Oldham and Sparklehorse's Mark Linkous have become, with their mysterious personalities and abstract folk sounds, underground cult heroes.

In Chicago, a very different roots rock sound was brewing. Nan Warshaw, a music fan tired of both the existing country and punk scenes, endeavored to put together a roster of acts that were more relevant to fans of modern music. They coined it "insurgent country," and issued their first compilation, *For a Life of Sin*, back in 1994. Since then, Bloodshot has been one of alternative country's most dedicated and revered labels, putting out recordings by Nashville escapee Robbie Fulks, Paul Burch, Neko Case, and the Sadies.

Two Bloodshot acts, the legendary Waco Brothers and Alejandro Escovedo, deserve special mention. The Waco Brothers were formed from the remnants of a Chicago band called the Mekons, a sloppy, lovable punk band that's been making music on its own terms since its formation in 1977. That band's leader, artist/songwriter/renaissance man Jon Langford, fronts the Waco Brothers. Sally Timms, also from the Mekons tribe, has recorded for Bloodshot, as has accordionist Rico Bell, who fronts his own bluesy country-rock outfit, Rico Bell and the Snakehandlers. Together, Mekons alums have helped shape a large part of the Bloodshot imprint's ethos, not to mention the ethos of alternative country at large.

With a lineage in bands like the Nuns, Rank & File, the True Believers, Alejandro Escovedo ploughed a furrow straight through punk, cowpunk, roots rock, and the blues without skipping a beat. The Austin, Texas–based artist is a favorite among alternative country aficionados. His music, intensely personal and often sparsely arranged, is vividly rendered without much commercial consideration. Albums like *With These Hands* and *Gravity* serve as the creative foundation of his solo oeuvre. So powerful is his artistry, Escovedo was named "Artist of the Decade" in 1998 by the editors of *No Depression* magazine, beating out a number of worthy contenders. Today he records as a solo artist for Bloodshot.

The Dead Reckoning label found a place to exist behind enemy lines—in Nashville, that is, the clearinghouse for mainstream country music in America. Dead Reckoning, founded by Kevin Welch, Tammy Rogers, Kieran Kane, Harry Stinson, and Mike Henderson, serves as a repository for these A-list talents, all of whom continue to spend time writing and performing with mainstream acts. The Dead Reckoning label allows these acts to make the kind of roots, blues, and traditional country material they felt was sorely lacking in mainstream country music.

Two of alternative country's more renowned artists—Dale Watson and the Derailers—have also spent a career in two of country's more traditional offshoots. Dale Watson, a heavy honky-tonker, comes from a place populated by truck drivers and greasy spoons, playing music in beer-soaked barn dances and hot-rod hoedowns. He's defiantly anti-Nashville and not afraid to say so in his songs, choosing to search for his audiences along the country music fringes. The same goes for the Derailers, nudie suit-wearing, Telecaster-wielding contemporary purveyors of Bakersfield country. Although their sound is classic western-style music, with intricate guitar work and smooth harmonies, the Derailers' sound has been called too country for country radio, which just about says it all.

Rockin' Renegades

Another Minneapolis band, the Replacements, formed in the wake of punk in the early '80s, influenced a great number of alt.country bands and cowpunks alike with their ragged sound and penchant for sloppy, hard-partying live shows. Bands like the Old 97s, the Honeydogs, Slobberbone, the Bottle Rockets, and the Drive By Truckers all take their cue from the Replacements by adopting their no-holds-barred approach to twangy rock 'n' roll.

Dale Watson, 1996. Courtesy of Photofest.

The Bottle Rockets, from Festus, Missouri, kickstarted by former Uncle Tupelo roadie Brian Henneman, veer between hard rock, honky-tonk, and rootsy ballads. Slobberbone, perhaps the quintessential barroom rockers of the '90s, features singer Brent Best leaving his heart on the stage everywhere they travel. His band developed a sizable following based solely on their passionate performances. The Honeydogs follow the same formula as their metro-mates, the Replacements, with a boozy brand of twangy rock, though they encountered label troubles that hindered their progress. Still notable though, is their fiery self-titled debut of 1995.

The Oxford, Mississippi–based Blue Mountain was founded in 1993 by the husband and wife team of vocalist/guitarist Cary Hudson and bassist Laurie Stirratt after their previous band, the punk-inspired Hilltops (which also included Stirratt's twin brother John, who later enlisted in Wilco), dissolved. Like Tupelo before them, Stirratt and Hudson brought a punk aesthetic to their foot-stomping, country-flavored roots music on discs like *Dog Days* (1995) and the inspired *Homegrown* (1997). Unique to Blue Mountain was the fact that despite their flannel shirt and tattered jeans approach, they had signed a deal with Roadrunner Records, at the time one of heavy metal's most prominent labels.

Whiskeytown

In 1994, a punk band from Raleigh, North Carolina, came together with a feisty singer-songwriter named Ryan Adams in control. It didn't take long for their shows—fast, confrontational, and exhilarating—to become legendary, due mainly to Adams' propensity for bar fights and hard liquor. Their 1996 debut, *Faithless Street*, showed a writer and a band strongly indebted to both Gram Parsons and Johnny Rotten, an outfit that could swing without hesitation between hardcore punk and honky-tonk ballads. In a very brief period, Whiskeytown built one of the biggest cult followings of any alternative country band—and had a promising future as well—until Adams jumped ship after only three discs, choosing to go it alone as a solo artist. The fact that he had trouble maintaining a stable lineup had something to do with Adams' solo venture. But since establishing himself as such, he has retained, even enhanced his reputation as one of the style's brightest voices. Yet, while his material is sounding more diverse, and his projects become more and more ambitious, Adams sounds on record as if he is disavowing his country/punk roots to become a pop star. He can still cut deep with a cowboy-style ballad, or hit the honky-tonk pretty heavily, but it's pop star status he's after right now.

Rhett Miller of Dallas's Old 97s had the same idea. He formed the Old 97s in 1994. The quartet recorded a couple of indie rock albums, including one for the Bloodshot label, before signing to a major for the release of 1997's *Too Far to Care*. The record was generously received and the band became stars on the alternative country scene. In the meantime, Miller, like Adams only without the crazed temperament, took temporary leave to record a solo album, *The Instigator*, in 2002. Miller also records with another band, the Rancheros, an outfit originally formed to test out songs for the Old 97s, but which soon took on a life of its own.

Other bands on the brink of fame in the genre include the Pernice Brothers, Beachwood Sparks, the Postal Service, Gingersol, Thad Cockrell, and Moviola. Hundreds of other worthy units aspire to the throne, leaving avid listeners with the hope that, unlike many trends that emerged fully formed in the '90s and then went on to flame out and disappear, alternative country is one that is likely to stick around for a lot longer.

3

THE REBIRTH OF PUNK

When they first came together in 1988, the Rodeo, California, trio by the name of Green Day was just another snotty young punk band. At the time, underground punks were a dime a dozen and to the many punk rockers on the scene during the original wave of punk (1976–1980), the Green Day version of punk was little more than déjà vu.

But Green Day, fronted by singer and guitarist Billie Joe Armstrong, wasn't concerned with appealing to older punk fans. There was a younger, and fast-growing audience hungry for speedy, aggressive tuneage with singalong choruses and hummable melodies. To them, the sound of Green Day's angry but melodic bursts of noise hit precisely the right three chords. Their mega-reception at the dawn of the '90s, first in the underground and then with major-label support, sent ripples resonating through the music industry. Ultimately, Green Day would become one of the top three or four most influential bands of the '90s.

Punk rock came about originally at the hands of seminal acts like the Ramones, the first punk band in New York City, and the Sex Pistols, the first punk band to emerge from London. While there's an argument to be made that the seeds of punk were sown up to ten years earlier with bands like the MC5, the Stooges, and the Velvet Underground, it wasn't until these bands became true forces that punk rock became a musical and cultural phenomenon. Until the '90s, punk rock had more or less remained a constant on the pop scene, occasionally bubbling up from the underground, but never in a big way. The music's appeal remained with college and club-goers, where the punk culture found unified reception. In New York City, where bands like Television, the Patti Smith Group, Blondie, and the Ramones all came together on the city's Lower East

Green Day performing on *Last Call with Carson Daly*, 2005. Courtesy of Photofest.

Side, the scene was especially strong. In the city of Los Angeles an equally active punk scene sprang up shortly after the birth of punk to appease its large, youthful, and artistic population. Bands like X, the Dils, the Germs, and the Avengers assaulted audiences with aggressive, primitive noise.

Isolated pockets of the punk rock movement popped up around the United States in the decade-plus following its birth. But the fact is, it never really took hold in a commercial way, never grabbed the attention of the music industry. Rockers didn't enjoy punk's uncompromising sound—neither did radio or major labels for that matter. Punk's message, at least the intentions of true punk, which was strongly anti-establishment, remained defiant and nonconformist, refusing to temper its political, social, or cultural beliefs in hopes of wider acceptance. Punk and punk bands wanted justice, they wanted equality, they wanted to be left alone. So the music industry granted that wish. That is, until Green Day and a wave of neo-punk bands arrived.

While punk remained the bedrock of underground and alternative rock throughout the '80s, it wasn't until the early '90s, when the corporate music industry, empowered by the success of Nirvana and encouraged by the possibilities of alternative music in general, co-opted a few punk rock bands. These bands possessed different motivation than the original punks. In 1977, the original punks, decked out in safety pins and Mohawks, were inspired by anti-socialism and rebellion. Twenty years later, that rebellion softened into a mild form of disillusion. The punks, having just lived through eight "prosperous" years under the Reagan administration in the '80s, saw that the trickle-down effect of Reaganomics didn't exactly trickle down quite as far as they found themselves. But rather than seethe and act out, these new punks, many of which were members of the slack Generation X, merely pouted.

THE REVIVAL

Green Day and the Offspring were the primary movers of this punk revival, both of whom brought the brash sound of punk to commercial radio. Green Day independently released its first EP, *1,000 Hours*, in 1989. Soon after, the group—Armstrong, Tres Cool, and Mike Dirnt—had signed with an independent label, Lookout, and their first disc, *1,039/Smoothed Out Slappy Hour*, was released later that same year. Throughout the early '90s, Green Day cultivated an enthusiastic cult following, a process that received a critical boost with the release of their second album, 1992's *Kerplunk*. The underground success of *Kerplunk* led to big-time interest from corporate imprints and the band eventually opted to sign with Reprise.

Dookie, Green Day's major-label debut, was released in the spring of 1994, and thanks to support from radio and music television, the initial single, "Longview," became a massive hit, as did the second single, "Basket Case," which spent five weeks on the top of the American modern rock charts. At the end of the summer of '94, Green Day stole the show at Woodstock, again boosting sales. The album's fourth single, "When I Come Around," benefited, enjoying a seven-week stay at Number One on the modern rock charts in early 1995. *Dookie* eventually sold over 10 million copies worldwide and turned Green Day into modern-day punk superstars. *Dookie* also won the 1994 Grammy for Best Alternative Music Performance. A punk rock band had achieved the unthinkable: it became a household word. The genre would never be perceived in the same way again.

Green Day didn't exactly sustain their success. *Insomniac*, their follow-up, only sold 2 million, but the impact was still present. Green Day had done for punk rock what Nirvana did for alternative rock: it pricked the ears of the music industry, opened the doors to all kinds of like-minded bands, and created an appetite for a type of music where none previously existed. Their music wasn't innovative; it merely updated the sound of the late '70s to a new generation. In so doing, a flood of American hardcore punk, post-punk, and punk metal, came gushing forth.

The Offspring, another northern California group, was the first and biggest of the bands to follow up on Green Day's foray. Originally signed to Epitaph Records, an important imprint for punk's new school, the Offpsring, together since 1985, released their breakthrough album *Smash* in 1994. It was the third album of their career and it sold millions, bolstered by the strong radio play of singles like "Come Out and Play" and "Self Esteem." Like Green Day's

The Offspring, 2004 (left to right), Atom Willard, Greg K, Dexter Holland, and Kevin "Noodles" Wasserman. Courtesy of Corbis.

"Longview," these songs crossed over from punk and alternative audiences into a larger, mainstream rock context. The band, fronted by Dexter Holland and flanked by guitarist Kevin "Noodles" Wasserman, bassist Greg Kriesel, and drummer Ron Welty, soared to stardom. They had played small clubs for nearly a decade. Now arenas beckoned.

At first, the Offspring rejected the prospect of signing a contract with a major label. They were slightly older, and truer, to the original punk rock ethos of the '70s. They were also content to stay with Epitaph, a label that had been faithful to them and to many independent punk bands. But in 1996, they succumbed to tremendous pressure and potential financial windfall, and made the switch to Columbia Records, a Sony imprint. The move to a more corporate setting ran counter to their DIY philosophy and independent beliefs. The underground punk community, which still existed at this point, felt betrayed, as did Epitaph and the corps of musicians that had rallied behind them to represent the independent music spirit. The controversy threatened the Offspring's future success and the future of indie punk. But then, punk rock was changing. Thanks to the success of Green Day and Nirvana, punk rock was now viable for a commercial audience. And if the Offspring sacrificed a fraction of their hardcore punk audience by signing to a corporate label, surely they could make up for it with the new punk fans that radio and the merging of punk into the mainstream would create.

Columbia released the band's follow-up to *Smash*, titled *Ixnay on the Hombre*, in 1996. Sales started slowly and remained that way, but the band retained enough of an audience to remain important to the genre. While the group did lose a percentage of their original loyal fans, they managed to compensate for it with *Americana*, the disc that followed in 1998, which featured the hit "Pretty Fly (For a White Guy)." In mid-2000, the Offspring again stirred the pot, truer to their punk roots, with a decision to offer their latest album, *Conspiracy of One*, free of charge on the Internet prior to the initial release date. Their parent company didn't agree with the move and threatened legal action, forcing the band to abandon that specific plan. Individual singles, however, were made available for download at no charge. *Splinter*, their sixth album, was released in 2004.

The success of Green Day and the Offspring helped to solidify cult followings for scores of other punk-related bands, many of which were based in California around the Bay Area scene. Berkeley's Rancid almost squeezed in the same door that Green Day and the Offspring had jarred open. For a moment in 1994, when their Clash-inspired sophomore effort, *Let's Go*, bestowed on them huge underground success, it appeared that they had succeeded in following

Rancid, 1998. Courtesy of Photofest.

those footsteps. But it was only temporary: the band's bold lyrics and radical politics proved to be too extreme for mainstream audiences.

Formed in 1991 and led by Tim Armstrong and Matt Freeman, Rancid came from the ashes of ska icons Operation Ivy, so they were no strangers to enthusiastic followings. But it was the album they released in 1995, . . . *And Out Come the Wolves*, that had the music industry drooling. Rancid's fusion of that same reggae-inspired ska sound with a dash of punk rock and a daring look generated excitement about the band. Would they become the next Clash? The title of the album, a reference to the major-label buzz surrounding the band and other punk bands, gives a good indication of their perspective on the corporate music industry.

Ultimately, that record went platinum, and Rancid, alongside Green Day, briefly became the face of punk. Unlike the Offspring, however, the band decided to turn down all major-label offers, choosing to stay on Epitaph. Publicly, they felt no major corporation could give them the same kind of creative freedom that Epitaph could, and they were most likely correct. Rancid continued to work their records at the grassroots level; albums like *Rancid* (2000) and *Indestructible* (2003) helped to maintain the band's healthy fan base, even while stardom and financial success on a large scale eluded them.

Tim Armstrong, one of the band's founding members, started up his own Hellcat label in the mid-'90s. Since then, the company, affiliated with the Epitaph imprint, has been very active, recording and releasing Rancid's own recent discs, as well as stylish, old-school punk and punk offshoot albums by the Dropkick Murphys, ska-punkers the Slackers, the Distillers (who eventually signed with Warner Brothers), and others.

BAD RELIGION

Even punk stalwarts Bad Religion, formed in 1980 in Los Angeles and inspired by the original wave of punk, attempted to capitalize on the commercial acceptance of punk rock in the '90s. They released their very first major-label effort, *Recipe for Hate*, in 1993 on Atlantic. While that may not sound peculiar, the fact that one of the band's original members, Brett Gurewitz, owned the Epitaph label and was spending considerable time retaining successful punk bands on his own imprint, certainly was. In fact, Gurewitz left the band after his label issued the Offspring's *Smash* to nurture business, which was booming in light of

NOFX, still another Berkeley punk rock band formed in the aftermath of the original punk movement, has been slogging away since 1983. They've no doubt succeeded in nurturing a solid audience and their records, beginning with their 1989 debut *S&M Airlines*, released on Epitaph, and culminating, thus far, with 2003's *War on Errorism*.

Unlike higher-profile bands before them, NOFX, starring "Fat" Mike Burkett on vocals, Eric Melvin on drums, and Aaron "El Hefe" Abeyta on guitar, insisted on staying closer to their fans, at ground level. They were thrust occasionally, and reluctantly, into the limelight. To counter what they felt was unwarranted attention, they acted out defiantly, naming their albums crassly (*White Trash; Two Heebs, and a Bean; The*

P.R.M.C. *Can Suck on This*; and *Pump Up the Valuum*), and writing their signature gross-out tunes. At one point, NOFX lured radio programmers in with a song called "Play This Song on the Radio," a melodic punk song with a big hook that began promisingly before descending into a stream of unsavory language. It was this kind of sophomoric behavior that struck an important chord with even younger punk bands to follow, like blink-182 and Sum 41.

Pennywise came together in 1989. They attended the same high school in Hermosa Beach, California, and shared an enthusiasm for surfing and snowboarding. The band's blend of hardcore, skate-punk, and funk caught the ear of Epitaph president Brett Gurewitz, and they have sailed ever since, cultivated their audience—largely fans of sports like surfing, skateboarding, and snowboarding—by remaining true to their indie roots. The band has released all of their records on Epitaph, despite selling in fairly large numbers. The band experienced a setback in 1996 when Jason Thirsk, their original bass player, on leave to recover from an addiction, committed suicide after binge drinking. Despite the shock, Pennywise marched on. Their 1997 disc, *Full Circle*, released in the wake of Thirsk's death, was among their most dynamic, full of pathos and frustration. Their latest disc, *From the Ashes*, continues in the strong Pennywise tradition.

Formed in 1991 from the remnants of

 BAD RELIGION *(continued)*

the punk explosion. Ironically, the Offspring left Epitaph following *Smash* to vie for a bigger piece of the pie, and so did his own band. The truth is, Epitaph did not have the machinery or the financial means in place to send its patented punk music overseas to international audiences, and even to the corners of the United States.

Miraculously, Bad Religion, despite selling its tunes through a corporate pipeline, managed to maintain the fandom they worked so hard throughout the '80s to build. They did this by focusing, and indeed reemphasizing, their strengths: hard-hitting, meaningful lyrics, and intelligent song structures that rocked with brains. Singer Greg Graffin, a biochemist by trade, voiced frustration with unprecedented eloquence, at least in the punk genre, and the band established itself early on as an important spoke in the idiom's wheel. They continued to release albums on Atlantic throughout the '90s, peaking with *Recipe for Hate* and 1994's *Stranger Than Fiction*. But sales slipped steadily throughout their tenure with the label and in 2000 the band was dropped. Without wasting time, they headed quickly back to Epitaph, where former founding guitarist Gurewitz was awaiting them, still running the label. He rejoined the band (having been out of it for six years) for the impressive *The Process of Belief* in 2002. They have since released *The Empire Strikes First*, their most emphatically political release in a decade.

popular indie bands like All, Clawhammer, and the Chemical People, Down By Law quickly captured the imagination of the underground with hard, fast, and creative punk rock structures. Their 1994 album, *Punkrockacademyfightsong*, on Epitaph, proved the band could go toe-to-toe with the best punk bands in the business. They soon split from Epitaph and began a journey that saw them searching restlessly for a new home. Their 2003 album, *Windwardtidesandwaywardsails*, is on the Union Local label.

Bad Religion, 2002. Courtesy of the Library of Congress.

BIG-TIME

Once the major labels got a whiff of the possibilities of punk, they began to seek out bands with punk sensibilities. Because many original punk and even some punk revivalists often refused to cooperate with industry reps, companies sought means to assemble and hire the kinds of punk acts that they could actually work with, and that could appeal to what was fast becoming one of commercial rock's most viable new genres. At the same time, these contrived acts still had to at least appear to possess the same kind of "snotty" punk attitude adopted by the style's more authentic groups.

This meant that many of the majors' newest charges had compromised punk values. Not a bad thing, of course, but a dilution of the genre's mainstay principals nonetheless. The sound of big-time punk also changed in the hands of the majors. What was once a blur of three chords and a shouted chorus became slower, precisely recorded tunes with overtly melodic hooks, closer to rock than to punk. The rhythms eased up a bit, emphasizing power and sonic impact over any sort of strident message.

Beyond Green Day and the Offspring, Weezer became the first pop-punk band to make a popular impression. In 1994, with Harvard student and singer-songwriter Rivers Cuomo at the helm, the band released their self-titled debut,

Weezer. The record tempered punk into something more listenable and less confrontational. Weezer's music was saturated with a quirky sense of humor and an endearing awkwardness—emphasized by Cuomo's nebbish looks—that turned songs like "Undone (The Sweater Song)," "Buddy Holly," and "Say It Ain't So" into big modern rock hits during 1994 and 1995. It helped immeasurably that all their singles were boosted by clever videos. In fact, Weezer became the first "punk" band to fully utilize the medium. One of their stunning videos came with the song "Buddy Holly." Created by noted videographer Spike Jonze, a man who would go on to produce dozens of major videos throughout the '90s, this was an innovative film splicing the group into old footage from the '70s sitcom *Happy Days*. The single, also a novelty, quickly became a hit, boosting the album to multiplatinum sales as well. By the time the album's final single, "Say It Ain't So," was released in the summer of 1995, the group had gone on hiatus, with Cuomo returning to Harvard.

Weezer reconvened in 1996 to make *Pinkerton*, a more cohesive and fully envisioned album than their debut, but somewhat less successful. Cuomo refused to duplicate the success that had pushed his debut over the top. He laid off the attention-getting videos, so the band seemed to disappear quietly by the time the *Pinkerton* album cycle played out. Rubbing salt in the wound, *Rolling Stone* named *Pinkerton* the Worst Album of 1996. The band took some time off to reassess their goals. Rumors circulated that they were breaking up. Not so. Buoyed by the changes in music and the fact that *Pinkerton* seemed to be rediscovered even as the band's profile diminished, they reassembled to make *The Green Album*, so-called because its cover was green and self-titled again, which came out in 2001. Its lead single, "Hash Pipe," went a long way in recovering the band's initial fan base. Weezer released *Maladroit* in 2004.

Originally, blink-182 made a name for themselves mining the same vein as Pennywise and other Cali punk bands, selling themselves to surfing, snowboarding, and skateboard crowds. Hailing from San Diego, the band, consisting of Mark Hoppus, Tom Delonge, and Travis Barker, debuted in 1993 and has been on an up escalator ever since. A slot on the Warped Tour, a popular traveling road show for punk and its outgrowths, alongside Pennywise and NOFX, helped the humorous band build credibility. In the summer of 1999, they released their first album for a major label, the MCA project, *Enema of the State*. It was a hands-down commercial triumph, selling over 4 million copies. Like Weezer, blink-182 developed a stylish video image to accompany their prurient sense of humor, with skillfully directed videos for songs like the cheesy, '70s-inspired "First Date" and the faux elegant "Miss You." *The Mark, Tom, and Travis Show* exhibited that funny-guy image on a full-length scale. Delonge and Hoppus joke around onstage about various crass topics, and engage in the kind of horseplay and harmless immaturity that separates the band from many of their super-serious counterparts. Critics often deride the band for what they perceive as over-the-top juvenilia and silly jokes. But the band, with a natural penchant for this, obviously revels in crass humor and has developed a following of appreciative jokesters because of it. A more sober album, *Take Off Your Pants and Jacket*, emerged in 2001. A still more expansive, and less self-centered worldview, musically and lyrically, grace the self-titled *blink-182*, their album from 2004.

Ontario's Sum 41 embraced a similar brand of toilet-bowl humor with their version of pop-punk. Island Records snapped up the band in 1999 as its own answer to blink-182, and the band responded with a couple of quick hit singles, "Fat Lip" and "In Too Deep." Led by the cartoonish guitarist Dereck Whibley and bandmates Dave Baksh, Cone McCaslin, and Steve Jocz, the band excited audiences with whirlwind punk/metal performances and the kind of immature humor originally perpetrated by blink-182. *All Killer No Filler* (2001), produced by Green Day/blink-182 producer Jerry Finn, and *Does This Look Infected?* (2003) are graced by punchy deliveries, crisp performances, and just the right amount of craziness. *Chuck*, a disc released in late 2004, and named after the man who saved their lives at a video shoot in the war-torn Congo of Africa, finds the band branching into ballads, pop songs, and—at the other end of the spectrum—thrash metal.

Punk isn't exactly an apt description of the much criticized Good Charlotte, the post-teen cabal of upstart ska-punkers. Many say they were merely in the right place at the right time—and barely familiar with their instruments—when they signed with the Sony label in the late '90s. High school buddies, they formed after being inspired by a Beastie Boys gig in 1995. They fused their

Good Charlotte, 2002. Courtesy of Photofest.

admiration for metal, ska, punk, and hip-hop and came up with what could accurately be described as derivative. Still, Good Charlotte, led by twin brothers Joel and Benji Madden, were sincere and indefatigable in their pursuit of an audience. Their debut, a self-titled effort released in 2000, found the band searching for a sound, throwing together standard fare punk and ska-punk. It also hinted at the band's quasi-Christian leanings both in their lyrics and in the liner notes, sending mixed messages between the occasionally harsh stories within their songs and their commitment to religion.

Their first big break came when the Maddens—often decked out like stereotypical punks from the '70s—secured a gig as hosts of MTV's late-night program *All Things Rock*. The visibility gave the band an immense push, and by the fall of 2002, Good Charlotte released *The Young & the Hopeless*. Their hits "Lifestyles of the Rich and Famous" and "Anthem" vaulted the band into the ranks of the mainstream teenyboppers, especially with fans of the MTV teenybopper program *Total Request Live (TRL)*, a compromise seen as running counter to the ambitions of all folks who called themselves "punk." Regardless, Good Charlotte is now viewed as the band that allowed punk rock to trickle down to fans of teen-beat music, a lucrative move seen as a blasphemous crossover to some and a boon to the corporate purveyors of the genre.

In 2003 and beyond, Good Charlotte toured relentlessly, sharing dates with another mainstream punk band, New Found Glory. Florida's New Found Glory, perhaps less contrived and a bit more experienced than Good Charlotte, formed in 1997 and quickly built a reputation for their optimistic approach to the idiom and their energetic live shows. Their combination of chunky metal and pop-punk found its best manifestation in the 2002 release *Sticks and Stones*. Subsequent efforts to graduate to the elite class of the genre, including the recent, ambitious sonics of 2004's *Catalyst*, fell just short.

There were many other important punk rock bands in the '90s. Columbus, Ohio's New Bomb Turks consists of four English majors from Ohio State University, made a name for themselves by interlacing the hard, fast rules of punk with a bold, noisy approach. Face to Face, SoCal (Southern California) punks since 1991, have had a long and satisfying career recording and performing, with high points including their 1996 major-label album *Face to Face* and their 2001 covers disc *Standards & Practices*. They disbanded in 2003 after thirteen years and six albums together.

The Vandals, who released *Hollywood Potato Chips* in 2004, have been a mainstay on the punk scene for more than two decades. The real impact they've achieved, however, has been helping to set the tone of sophomoric humor many Southern California pop-punkers adopted as their own, including blink-182 and Green Day.

New Jersey–born pop-punkers Bouncing Souls spent lots of time touring and paying dues before getting picked up first by BYO Records and then by Epitaph. Their earnest brand of sing-along punk caught on eventually with albums like *How I Spent My Summer Vacation* (2001) and *Anchors Aweigh* (2003).

No Use for a Name assembled in 1987 in Sunnydale, California, but didn't gain momentum until signing with the popular punk label Fat Wreck in 1993 for their *Daily Grind* disc. They've released albums steadily since, despite losing their guitarist Chris Shiflett to alt-rock stuperstars the Foo Fighters.

Chicago's the Alkaline Trio first came together through a love of punk and as occasional drinking partners. They made a name for themselves initially in the Midwest, where punk wasn't as prevalent as it was on the coasts, and their brand of highly combustible, emotionally sophisticated punk and hard rock drew lots of attention. Their debut, *Goddamnit*, emerged in 1997, and their most recent release, *Good Mourning*, came out in 2004.

Punk bands continue to emerge every month in popular music. Thanks to showcases like the Van's Warped Tour, an annual summer tour of punk and indie rock bands, the genre remains as vibrant and important as ever. Young bands of all types are proving that punk is much more malleable as well, as they blend different styles—pop, rock, metal, thrash, reggae, goth, and electronica—together in creating an overarching genre as energized and essential now as any in popular music.

GIRLS NIGHT OUT

Another important entry in the punk rock category, and a band that seems poised to run with the idiom in the twenty-first century, is the Donnas. Described by many as "the Ramones meets the Runaways" (referring to an all-girl band led by Joan Jett in the '70s and '80s), the Donnas won a cult following and considerable media attention in the late '90s after scoring a record deal right out of high school.

Inspired by bands like L7 and the Riot Grrrls as well as a cluster of classic rock-type bands like AC/DC and the Stones, the Donnas worked hard at refining their art. With help from songwriter Darin Raffaelli, they released their debut album, *The Donnas*, in 1997. It was so unexpectedly successful that the band found themselves taking a week off during their senior year in high school to tour Japan. In the meantime, the band had encountered some problems with Raffaelli; some accused him of exerting excess control on the girls. It was during this controversy that the Donnas severed ties with him. Postponing college came next, as the band collectively decided to sign with Lookout! Records, the original home of fellow Bay Area punks Green Day. Their label debut, *American Teenage Rock and Roll Machine*, was released in early 1998. The Donnas quickly became underground punk favorites. Their third album, *Get Skintight*, appeared in 1999 and marked the first time the band composed their material with no outside assistance. *The Donnas Turn 21* saw the band move even further from punk in favor of a more classic metal sound, ala Aerosmith and KISS. But the shift didn't deter Atlantic Records, a major label, from signing the band to a long-term contract. In 2002, the Donnas released their most popular effort to date and their first on Atlantic, titled *Spend the Night*. MTV and its teen show *Total Request Live* latched onto the band, and the record proceeded to sell in the millions, turning the girls into a not-quite-overnight sensation.

PUNK STYLES

Just as metal and electronica splintered into dozens of fragmented categories after breaking through, courtesy of the alternative rock explosion, so too did punk. Many of these offshoots, inspired by the hardcore, grunge, and metal styles that came before them, developed niche audiences of their own. Many remain underground, while some, like Third Wave ska and Emo, have set foot on more commercially successful terrain.

Hardcore

Impossibly fast and heavy, hardcore punk has always served as the most extreme variation of punk rock. Characterized by simple guitar riffs played at warp speed and shouted vocals, hardcore was largely a DIY genre populated by bands with an intense interest in politics, looking to get social and political issues off their collective chests. Like pop-punk, hardcore musicians didn't need the skill—their songs were elementary, in many cases, and easy to play. The hardcore scene germinated in Los Angeles and New York City, but has since spread to all reaches of the nation. Important early bands include the Dead Kennedys, the Exploited, Black Flag, D.R.I., Bad Brains, Circle Jerks, and Fear. Much hardcore in the '90s morphed into metal, as production techniques and a taste for louder guitars came to pass following the breakthrough of Nirvana. Important recent bands: Sick of It All, Murphy's Law, Hatebreed, Refused.

The Third Wave Ska

The Third Wave ska revival rose up in the late '80s, when certain members of the American punk underground began returning to the sounds of British ska bands like Madness, the Specials, and the Beat. These bands injected that sound with a dose of hardcore punk and even more frenetic rhythms. During the early '80s, this Third Wave, two waves removed from the original ska movement from Jamaica, where it gave birth to reggae, continued to grow. Bands cropped up all over the country, but many of the most popular were based in California. Eventually, Third Wave revivalists broke into the American mainstream; the first band to benefit was Rancid, quickly followed by No Doubt, who experienced incredible chart and financial success, Goldfinger, Dancehall Crashers, and the Mighty Mighty Bosstones, a leading figure on the scene in the early '90s that all followed. Tragedy struck one of the most popular acts,

Sublime, when their lead singer and driving force Brad Nowell, died of an overdose.

Third Wave ska reached its peak in 1996, becoming one of the most popular forms of alternative music in America. From there, though, it took a turn, as a heavier guitar sound began to take over. Soon, but for a few stalwart bands like Goldfinger and Reel Big Fish, both of which changed their sound entirely to remain viable, the movement died out completely.

Emo

Originally an arty outgrowth of hardcore punk, Emo became an important force in underground rock by the late '90s, appealing to modern-day punks and indie-rockers alike. Some Emo leans toward the progressive side, full of complex guitar work, unorthodox song structures, arty noise, and extreme dynamic shifts; some Emo is much closer to punk-pop, though it's a bit more intricate. Emo lyrics are deeply personal, usually either free-associative poetry or intimate confessionals. Although it's far less macho, Emo is a direct descendant of hardcore punk and its preoccupations with authenticity and anti-commercialism. It grew out of the conviction that commercially oriented music is artificial and calculated, and that the music inadequately expresses genuine emotion. Rites of Spring, Hüsker Dü, Fugazi, and to a lesser extent, Weezer, are seen as the genre's original forbears.

Other important bands: Promise Ring, the Get-Up Kids, Jimmy Eat World, Glassjaw, the Used, Finch, Jets to Brazil, Pedro the Lion, Joan of Arc, and Mineral.

Riot Grrrl

Weary of what they perceived as a sexist punk scene and alienated by the lack of women getting involved in uncompromising music, the Riot Grrrl scene carved out new territory for female artists, beginning around 1992. It was a grassroots feminist movement started in the punk scene and personified by leading bands like Bikini Kill and Bratmobile, also Queercore bands. Riot Grrrls fused politics and activism with punk rock, addressing gender-related issues like rape, domestic abuse, male domination in society, and female empowerment. Hole, led by Courtney Love, Babes in Toyland, and L7 existed before the term, certainly, but fit the spirit of the style.

Other important groups: Sleater-Kinney, Huggy Bear, the Butchies, 7 Year Bitch.

Queercore

Queercore is punk rock or a similar-sounding music played wholly or in part by homosexual musicians. Many feel that the Queercore movement solidified when it became an early offshoot of the underground feminist-inspired Riot Grls in the early '90s, but a few bands had existed before then like Pansy Division and Fifth Column.

Other important bands are: Team Dresch, God Is My Co-Pilot, Tribe 8, Double Zero, Cheesecake, Bikini Kill, Sister George, Bratmobile.

Straight-Edge

Straight-edge refers to a philosophy whose most basic tenet promotes a clean, drug-free lifestyle. It came about as an offshoot of the punk rock/hardcore scenes of the early 1980s. It is widely believed that the term was coined by Ian Mackaye of the seminal hardcore band Minor Threat (later Fugazi) in "Straight Edge," a song of the same name. Mackaye eschewed the nihilistic tendencies of punk rock, promoting a simplistic philosophy of "don't drink, don't smoke, and don't [have sex]."

Other important bands: Youth of Today, Earth Crisis, Snapcase, Mouthpiece, Strife.

Skatepunk

It's not exactly obvious what makes skatepunk differ from its standard punk and pop-punk counterparts. Originally derived from hardcore punk, and so named because of its popularity among skateboarders, there are a small handful of stylistic trademarks. Skatepunk tends to be high energy, with fast tempos and thrashy guitars. It also tends to have a smart-alec sense of humor, mainly because it serves as a soundtrack for skateboarding. And it is also staunchly anti-corporate, its fans preferring its bands signed to indie labels based on nothing more than principle. Many credit skatepunk with giving birth to the Third Wave ska revival because of its energetic approach. The first true skatepunk band was Suicidal Tendencies, whose members Mike Patton and Robert Trujillo went on to many other reputable projects. Pennywise, Samiam, Down By Law, Unwritten Law, MxPx are some of the latest, successful skatepunk bands.

Rockabilly/Psychobilly

Like ska's Third Wave, rockabilly came around a few times itself, the first time of course, in the '50s, then again in the '80s at the hands of the Stray Cats, and most recently in the '90s. The '90s rockabilly bands, occasionally referred to as Psychobilly because of their whacked-out musical antics, earned regular audiences by touring nonstop. The best examples of the genre include the Reverend Horton Heat along with the long-running Southern Culture on the Skids, the Amazing Crowns, Deadbolt, and Necromantix.

PUNK LABELS

Many labels emerged throughout the '90s, staking a claim on a particular style or school of punk. Epitaph, of course, has been mentioned frequently, and has always been one of the most revered and successful in the business of releasing punk rock. But there are several other labels, smaller concerns that have made a considerable impact on the sound of punk in the '90s.

Drive Thru

Drive Thru Records, co-owned by the brother-sister team of Richard and Stefanie Reines, has been one of the most successful of the punk labels, specializing in pop-punk and Emo with bands like New Found Glory, FenixTX, Something Corporate, Starting Line, and Finch. They arranged a deal with MCA/Universal, a distribution and promotion agreement that has allowed the company the ability to sign the bands it wants and market each with major-label muscle.

Lookout!

Lawrence Livermore and David Hayes both planned on starting record labels in 1987. Livermore already had some experience, having released an album the previous year by his own group, the Lookouts. Hayes had been responsible for a series of cassette compilations of Bay Area punk. They both had an idea to document the scene of up-and-coming punk bands centered around the Gilman Street Project, the all-ages cooperative punk venue founded by *Maximum Rock 'n' Roll*'s Tim Yohannon, which had opened on New Year's Eve 1986. The groups who populated the stage of the small club in West Berkeley, California, were unlike much of the hardcore music dominating the punk scene of the time; this was something new. Instead of starting two labels, Livermore and Hayes combined their efforts and consolidated their releases under the label name that Livermore had haphazardly chosen for the back cover of his band's LP. And Lookout! was born. Since then, they've released early albums by breakthrough bands like Green Day and the Donnas, as well as high-profile punkers like the Pansy Division, Screeching Weasel, the Mr. T Experience, and Ted Leo and the Pharmacists.

Tooth & Nail

Tooth & Nail Records is a Seattle-based independent company with close to 200 releases to its credit, as well as numerous outgrowth labels like Solid State. Tooth & Nail is best known as the launching pad for such massively popular bands as MxPx, Further Seems Forever, the Juliana Theory, and P.O.D. Much controversy revolves around the label's roster and its religious leanings. While many bands on the Tooth & Nail roster may contain members who are Christian,

Tooth & Nail itself has never claimed to be a strictly "Christian" label. As religion has always been an intensely divisive issue within the punk rock sector, many of these groups have been ignored by fans.

Vagrant

Vagrant Records' label sampler, *Another Year on the Streets*, gives a pretty good indication of its strengths, with Emo and pop-punk acts like the Get Up Kids, Face to Face, Saves the Day, as well as harder-to-categorize outfits like Rocket from the Crypt and Alkaline Trio. Founded in 1991 by Richard Egan, the label got a huge boost from the super-success of Emo singer-songwriter Chris Carabba and his band Dashboard Confessional.

Victory

An inveterate presence on the punk scene, Chicago's Victory label takes credit for over 200 releases since its formation in 1994, and has asserted itself as one of the driving forces in independent punk and hardcore music over the past decade. Past bands on the label comprise a Who's Who of hardcore: Bad Brains, Shelter, Boy Sets Fire, Earth Crisis, Grade, Hatebreed, and Refused. Today, Victory has softened its stance—aligned itself (controversially) with a major label in Island Records, and met with further success with bands like Snapcase and the commercially successful bands Thursday and Taking Back Sunday.

Crypt

Tim Warren launched Crypt Records, now based in Germany, in the early '80s to reissue some of his favorite punk and garage tunes from the '60s and '70s. That task in time began to embrace raunchy active groups in the late '80s and throughout the '90s. Best known today for bands like the Oblivians, Nine Pound Hammer, and New Bomb Turks, the company's garage punk labor of love, the *Teenage Shutdown* series, is also noteworthy.

Jade Tree

Founded by straight-edgers Darren Hayes and Tim Owen in 1990, Jade Tree has been a thinking person's punk label since its inception. They've signed earnest, provocative, hard-to-pigeonhole bands like Joan of Arc, Jets to Brazil, Promise Ring, and Pedro the Lion.

BYO

The BYO label came into its own back in the early '80s, when brothers Shawn, Mark, and Adam Stern, in a popular punk band called Youth Brigade, formed the Better Youth Organization to help give punk rock a good name. At the time, the genre had been slagged by the press as nothing more than a spectacle with little musical merit. Since then the band has championed punk rock consistently, including records by the Bouncing Souls, Rancid, and other icons on the circuit, past and present. Run by Shawn Stern for over two decades now, the label is a story of dedication and perseverance.

Fat Wreck Chords

Founded by "Fat" Mike Burkett, Fat Wreck Chords has been releasing premier punk revival albums since the late '80s. Its philosophy is more politically strident and overtly humorous than many of its counterparts, as evidenced by its issuing bands like Anti-Flag, Sick of It All, Good Riddance, Against Me, and NOFX, whose latest album is called *The War on Errorism*.

Burning Heart

Örebro, Sweden's Burning Heart Records, has launched some of the most noteworthy bands of the '90s, including European acts like Millencolin, the (International) Noise Conspiracy, the Hives, and Refused. The label has a close affiliation with Epitaph Records and shares distribution of a number of releases each year. The label is now home to the reunited Norwegian group Turbonegro and serves as the European home for several popular North American acts like the Weakerthans and Give Up the Ghost.

Nitro

Founded by the Offspring's Dexter Holland, Nitro Records has been the home to popular outfits like AFI, the Vandals, and Guttermouth.

MOJO

The California-based label specialized most successfully in Third Wave ska or ska-punk bands like Goldfinger and Reel Big Fish, as well as swing revivalists Cherry Poppin' Daddies.

Side One Dummy

Roommates and relatively successful musicians Joe Sib and Bill Armstrong started this punk label in 1995 with their life savings and a taste for punk rock. Their inaugural release, a Swinging Utters collection, was the first of many reputable discs by the likes of the Mighty Mighty Bosstones, Avoid One Thing, and Suicide Machines.

Revelation

Starting with a Warzone 7" in 1987, California label Revelation Records, started up by Jordan Cooper, has been home to some of the most influential and trendsetting hardcore and post-hardcore bands of the past fifteen years, including Quicksand, Texas Is the Reason, Sick of It All, Gorilla Biscuits, the Movielife, and Sensefield.

MAJOR ALTERNATIVE ROCKERS

Original alternative music of the '80s and its accompanying DIY ethic it espoused morphed into the grunge music of Seattle, thanks to bands like the Butthole Surfers, the Melvins, Jane's Addiction, and the Pixies, whose own guitar rock provided an early blueprint for grunge. Grunge became the early '90s movement—in the hands of bands like Nirvana, Pearl Jam, Soundgarden, and Mudhoney—that inadvertently allowed mainstream rock to hijack the idea of "alternative rock" into the mainstream. Previously, "alternative" meant nothing more than its literal definition; it was an umbrella term for a diverse collection of underground rock bands who chose to play the kind of music considered to be an alternative to mainstream music. But Nirvana and Pearl Jam, and their seething, aggressive rock, crossed over to the mainstream with its astonishing commercial success, and suddenly "alternative" had become something very specific. It had narrowed down to a sound defined by these bands.

Over time, the newly defined "alternative rock," or "alt-rock," came to embrace many other genres, most often hyphenated offshoots of the core guitar-centric style originally inspired by grunge music. Following the breakthroughs of early Seattle bands, and the reception of it by commercial radio and music television, champions of alternative rock began to emerge. These acts succeeded on multiple levels. Many melded styles of music into a single, cohesive style. Many appealed to commercial audiences with enough accessibility to attract fans of all tastes. Many emerged from the alternative revolution with a visionary sound, wholly unique and strikingly different from that of their contemporaries. Because of this, many of the acts mentioned here didn't fit neatly into one of the trend chapters covered in this book. And perhaps because they avoided trends, or jumpstarted one single-handedly, they were able to transcend the fashionable tendencies of alternative rock throughout the '90s and enjoy longer, more fruitful careers.

THE VISIONARIES

The Beastie Boys

One of the acts not particularly influenced by the impact of Nirvana is New York City trio the Beastie Boys. Born in the early '80s, the Beasties—Adam Yauch, Mike Diamond, and Adam Horovitz—started out as hardcore punk rockers, but ended up making it big as the first noteworthy group of white rappers.

Inspired by the fury of punk and the street smarts of hip-hop, the trio originally seemed like a band of comic rappers, frat-boys intent on having fun during their ten minutes of fame. Their first big hit, "Fight for Your Right (To Party)," from their 1986 album *Licensed to Ill*, embodied that goofball persona. But their album titled *Paul's Boutique*, released in the summer of 1989, altered that image decisively. The dense and sophisticated disc depicted the band as not only hard-rocking punkers who dabbled as hip-hoppers and samplers—that is, excerpting the work of other artists to use in their own music—but a mind-bending mix of all three. In fact, *Paul's Boutique* foreshadowed a radical sort of genre blending that occurred after the original alt-rock revolution in the early '90s.

The Beastie Boys (left to right) Mike D (Mike Diamond), Ad-Rock (Adam Horovitz), and MCA (Adam Yauch). Courtesy of Photofest.

Early in their career, the band had sampled freely. *Paul's Boutique* is a case in point, a testimony to sampling as an art form. But as the legal ramifications of sampling became apparent, the Beasties backed off the usage of other artists' work. Still, they had earned a reputation as visionaries. They subsequently opened up their own record label, Grand Royal; shed the frat-boy image, and began taking their recording careers more seriously. Their next album, *Check Your Head*, bowed in 1992, and made an immediate impression. Easier to grasp than *Paul's Boutique*, the disc resonated with the band's signature eclecticism and the witty, lyrical interplay of its three members.

Ill Communication followed in 1994, the same year the band co-headlined the Lollapalooza tour with Smashing Pumpkins. The record, an extension of *Check Your Head*, took the top slot on the *Billboard* album chart the first week of release. It cemented the band's status as superstars and allowed them the luxury of tackling side projects, stumping for political and social causes (Adam Yauch put on the high-profile Tibetan Freedom Concert in 1999), and focusing on their own label.

Grand Royal impacted the business as it issued a number of creatively successful discs of various genres, including bands like the pop act Bis and the extreme electronics of Alec Empire. The most successful band to emerge on the label was Luscious Jackson, a jazzy pop collage of a band—all women—that reflected the Beasties' own colorful palette of music. Kate Schellenbach, the band's drummer, was also the Beasties' original drummer, back when that band played hardcore in the early '80s.

A couple of EPs followed over the years, including a soul jazz collection, *The in Sound from Way Out*, and a hardcore EP. But the band didn't finish their next full-length disc, *Hello Nasty*, until 1998. Another six years passed before the trio released their latest album, *To the Five Boroughs*, an old-school homage to vintage rap, and a scaled-back exercise of three men who have, since the early '90s, graduated from b-boy rabble-rousers to respected, alternative elder statesmen.

Jane's Addiction

In many ways, the decade of the '90s and beyond has been defined by the many major alternative acts that sprouted up during the period. Nirvana, of course, was the first truly huge alternative act and its affiliation was with grunge. But in some ways, the opposite was true: "alternative" was defined by the music made by many original bands.

Jane's Addiction, for example, took the fury of punk, the glamour of '80s metal, and elements of folk in creating their particular blend of noise. They debuted in the mid-'80s—many say paving the way for Nirvana's explosion—but didn't make any real impact until 1988 with their Warner Brothers set, *Nothing's Shocking*, one of the first commercial "alternative" albums released by a major label. Led by Perry Farrell and guitarist Dave Navarro, Jane's Addiction was nothing if not audacious in approach, in image, in performance.

Jane's Addiction, early 1990s. Courtesy of Photofest.

There was plenty of hype surrounding the Los Angeles band, and it didn't take long for their star to shine. The record spent almost nine months on the charts.

Their follow-up album, *Ritual de lo Habitual*, released in 1990, found the band breaking through commercially, selling in large amounts, even before the alternative explosion. Motivated by his success and a surfeit of creative ideas, bandleader Perry Farrell spearheaded the Lollapalooza Festival, which began in 1991. The tour, originally designed as a string of farewell shows for his band, ended up being so successful that it would continue through the summers of most of the '90s and beyond.

In 1992, Farrell and Jane's drummer Stephen Perkins formed a sequel to Jane's Addiction, which had indeed folded, called Porno for Pyros. Even more experimental than Jane's, the group met with lukewarm reception. In 1993, guitarist Navarro joined the Red Hot Chili Peppers.

Farrell continued trumpeting Lollapalooza after Jane's Addiction ceased, holding on to Porno for Pyros until 1997. Later that year, Farrell announced he'd be reforming Jane's, a bright prospect, considering that many thought the band had broken up with some potential still unmet. *Kettle Whistle*, which compiled classic live performances and demos alongside a few newly recorded tracks, followed their reuniting. The album didn't fare well, but the reunion tour certainly did, proving Jane's Addiction was more a live phenomenon than a studio project.

In 2001, Farrell, ever restless, released his first solo work, *Songs Yet to Be Sung*. Navarro bowed with his own solo debut, *Trust No One*, the same year. Both were moderately successful, but not successful enough, apparently, to prevent them from announcing still another Jane's Addiction reunion. The band released *Strays* in 2003, eleven years after announcing their first breakup.

Smashing Pumpkins

Unlike Nirvana or Jane's Addiction, both of whom were rather destructive, Smashing Pumpkins established a blueprint for the career success of an alternative rock band. The Pumpkins, a quartet hailing from Chicago, did eventually succumb to a flurry of destructive occurrences, but not until the band had

Smashing Pumpkins. Courtesy of Photofest.

become one of the most commercially successful and durable outfits of the '90s. Billy Corgan, son of a jazz guitarist, supplied the motivation behind the Pumpkins, a band that also included guitarist James Iha, bassist D'arcy Wretzky, and drummer Jimmy Chamberlin. Inspired by progressive rock as well as punk and indie sounds, the Pumpkins began writing together, led by Corgan's angst-laced lyrics and his powerhouse guitar playing. Their first gig, incidentally, was opening in Chicago for none other than Jane's Addiction.

Smashing Pumpkins sold out of their first two singles, "I Am One" and "Tristessa," and the buzz grew loud enough to start a "bidding war," or competition between labels intent on signing them. In 1991, the band signed with Virgin Records, but instead of releasing the Pumpkins' debut, it licensed the record to an independent label, Caroline. This way, the band had the backing of a major label but was still perceived in the marketplace as "independent." The strategy worked. *Gish* was a towering work of rock 'n' roll, with progressive, metallic flourishes and punk rock undertones. Opening slots with hot bands like Pearl Jam and the Red Hot Chili Peppers followed, exposing the young group to a critically important demographic. *Gish*, however, took its toll on the band. The pressure sent Corgan into a depression, drummer Chamberlin became addicted to drugs and alcohol, and Iha and Wretzky, romantically tied, went through a nasty breakup.

Corgan plunged into his work. He wrote and played and immersed himself in the craft of songwriting. In fact, he became so absorbed, he decided to write and play all the instruments but the drums on the band's highly anticipated follow-up, *Siamese Dream*. Released in 1993, *Siamese Dream* debuted in the Top 10 and established the group as true rock stars. It has since become one of the '90s' most noteworthy rock albums.

The Pumpkins maintained a fairly high level of exposure throughout the '90s, touring extensively, a highlight of which was headlining 1994's Lollapalooza, and releasing acclaimed, but high-minded albums like *Mellon Collie and the Infinite Sadness*. Released in 1995, the band's epic encompassed everything they liked to think they were: loud, passionate, skilled, poetic, immense, and indulgent. The two-record, 28-song set spawned a trio of singles and sold 4 million copies. It pushed the band into larger venues and made them mega-stars. But tragedy struck when their touring keyboardist Jonathan Melvoin died of an overdose while with the drummer, Chamberlin. Subsequently, the band fired Chamberlin and went on hiatus to regroup. During that time, Iha and Wretzky dabbled in other projects, including starting their own record label. Corgan set to work on the band's next album.

Adore came out in 1998 and marked a significant change in the band's sound. There appeared to be substantially more tenderness on the album, and Corgan experimented with keyboards and synthesizers. This was a result of the impact and influence electronic music was having on popular music at the time.

Chamberlin returned to the group and D'Arcy exited prior to the early 2000 release of *Machina: The Machines of God*. Several months later, Corgan made clear his intentions to dissolve the band before the year was out. With former Hole bassist Melissa Auf Der Maur, the Pumpkins embarked on their farewell tour in 2000. Virgin chose not to release the band's final album, officially titled *Machina II: The Friends of Enemies of Modern Music*, so the band issued it on the Internet free. On December 2 of that year, the group played a mammoth final show at their hometown venue, Chicago's Metro (the place they had played their first show back in 1988), before officially disbanding. Corgan would take time off before setting out on a solo career.

Beck

One of the more courageous performers of the '90s went by the name of Beck—Beck Hansen, actually. He was the son of a Bibbe Hansen, a groupie in Andy Warhol's Factory clique of bohemian hipsters, and a classical conductor. The Los Angeles–born parvenu asserted himself as an artist in the early '90s with a loopy pastiche of styles, on his way to becoming one of the decade's most unique artists. From the beginning of his career, Hansen drew on a kaleidoscope of influences, synthesizing and implementing everything from Delta blues to hip-hop, acoustic folk to lounge, pop to jazz. His creative fearlessness and his utter lack of regard for the conventions of traditional pop and rock music—particularly on albums like *Mellow Gold* and *Odelay*—led him down some intriguing paths. The drum machine/slide guitar/silly rap of his breakthrough single "Loser" opened the door, and once through, Beck toyed with every idiom he could grasp.

Beck's major-label debut, *Mellow Gold*, came out in 1994, and as part of his agreement with the Geffen label, he was allowed to continue his lo-fi side projects. These

 GONE TOO SOON

Many rock and rollers saw their stars extinguish prematurely in the '90s and beyond, including Andrew Wood (Mother Love Bone), Kurt Cobain (Nirvana), Shannon Hoon (Blind Melon), Mia Zapata (the Gits), Layne Staley (Alice in Chains), and Mark Sandman (Morphine). But two in particular had their brightest moments still ahead of them.

Sublime

Sublime began in the Long Beach area of California with the intention of being a laid-back but serious group of punk revivalists, a style that was, as mentioned in another chapter, intensely popular in the state. But as a trio, Sublime—Bud Gaugh, Eric Wilson, and leader Brad Nowell—was a little different. They embraced both the yin and yang of music and life, tempering their feverish punk with smooth reggae/dub vibes, and alternating their mosh pit frenzies with ocean surfing. In their first seven years, the band released just two recordings, both low-budget efforts, but ones that earned them a loyal local and regional following.

With their self-titled third disc, they finally made a national impact. *Sublime* the record, and Sublime the band, were on the brink of breaking through to stardom, with major-label support and a growing, fanatical base of appreciators. But just two months before the album's release, after the disc was already done and being prepared for release, singer/songwriter Nowell, the motor and the heart of the band, died of a drug overdose.

Ironically, several tribute bands popped up in the wake of Sublime, at first serving as sincere homages to their fallen stars. But a few of them still remain, playing the music of Sublime as if they were Sublime themselves, and they've been successful in carrying on in lieu of the original.

GONE TOO SOON (continued)

Jeff Buckley

In 1994, Jeff Buckley, son of cult hero/folk icon Tim Buckley, released *Grace*, one of the most acclaimed album projects of the '90s. Buckley was an intoxicating personality, supremely talented, often profound, and completely grounded. His art, veering from the tactile compassion of Van Morrison to the high-art hard rock of Led Zeppelin, had at its core Buckley's ability to sing with the voice and soul of an angel.

Grace ended up making many Ten Best lists in 1994. In 1995, his tune "Last Goodbye" began to take Buckley from underground rock hero to pop star, with frequent radio play. But the singer-songwriter wasn't preoccupied with the prospect of stardom and he began, leisurely, to write a follow-up: *My Sweetheart the Drunk*. Buckley finally got down to work recording in Memphis during the late spring of 1997. On the night of May 29, he and a friend traveled to the local Mud Island Harbor, where Buckley decided to take a swim in the swift currents of the Mississippi River. He waded into the water fully clothed and disappeared a few minutes later. They found his body a week later. He was 30 years old.

Buckley has enjoyed more fame posthumously than he did while alive, almost as if he never left, that he was still around to continue on. Magazines, especially those in the United Kingdom, exalt his work to this day, and his reputation continues to grow in the States as well. An expanded edition of *Grace* appeared in 2004, complete with outtakes and archival video.

projects have defined him as much as his major recordings. *Stereopathic Soul Manure*, for example, featured lo-fi noise rock, while *One Foot in the Grave* dished out acoustic blues and folk.

A year after showcasing for the first time on a national level in the 1995 edition of Lollapalooza, Beck released his second album, *Odelay*. Unanimously praised, it would become one of the most acclaimed works of the decade, receiving a Best Alternative Performance at the Grammys in 1996. The funky *Midnite Vultures*, the artist's official follow-up to *Odelay*, came after a few more side projects, and was somewhat less enthusiastically received. In 2000, Beck earned another Grammy for Best Alternative Music Performance for his album *Mutations*. *Sea Change*, the second album produced by Radiohead producer Nigel Godrich, followed in 2002, and a subsequent tour found Beck backed by members of the Flaming Lips.

The Flaming Lips

Along with '80s originals like the Pixies and the Butthole Surfers, the Flaming Lips helped clear a path for bands of the alternative revolution of the '90s. Although never selling large amounts of records, the Lips, formed in 1983 in Oklahoma by Wayne Coyne, found ways to win large audiences. Their art, characterized by its quirkiness (reflecting the unique personality of its members), was too idiosyncratic for mainstream tastes, but accessible enough for adventurous rock fans.

The Lips made their recording debut in 1985 and released several albums in the second half of the '80s, all of which were continuations of the psychedelic and rock explorations originally begun in the '60s. They were also heartily accepted by an audience of indie rock fans who appreciated their whimsical approach and their true "alternative" perspective on rock. In 1990, the band issued one of their finest discs, *In a Priest Driven Ambulance*, a loosely thematic album addressing religion and conflict. By the time it came out, "alternative" had become something of a hot topic, and the Lips managed to parlay that into a major label recording contract with Warner Brothers. Their first album for the label, *Hit to Death in the Future Head* emerged in 1992, followed by 1993's *Transmissions from the Satellite Heart*, both of which found the band toning down their acid-tinged rock with melodic pop elements. A single, "She Don't Use Jelly," found radio reception, and the Lips started inching up the charts.

But their rising commercial stature seemed to increase their quirkiness. They came up with bizarre songs like "Guy Who Got a Headache and Accidentally Saves the World" and "Psychiatric Explorations of the Fetus with Needles," and album titles like *Clouds Taste Metallic*. Onstage, they were frequently seen in odd, plush animal outfits, with vertiginous light shows and deafening orchestral backing tracks. But their music, always unorthodox and unpredictable, managed to maintain just enough mainstream pop elements to keep them in the running for prestigious soundtrack slots and other more mainstream alternative opportunities. In 1999, the band released the highly acclaimed *The Soft Bulletin*, and in 2002 they came up with the characteristically titled *Yoshimi Battles the Pink Robots*.

Radiohead

One of the leading lights of the English rock revival of the mid-'90s, Oxford's Radiohead premiered in 1993 with *Pablo Honey*. Fronted by songwriter Thom Yorke and a daunting three-guitar attack, the recording yielded the band's breakthrough single, "Creep." That song, with its intensely self-deprecating lyrics, became an unexpected hit worldwide, and established the young lads from Oxford as a band to watch. Their closely scrutinized follow-up, *The Bends*, proved Radiohead was no one-hit wonder. The disc portrayed a

Radiohead, 1993. Courtesy of Photofest.

group unafraid to delve beneath the surface of ordinary rock into issues of alienation, paranoia, and politics, enhanced by elements of forward-thinking rock. Yorke, the visionary in the band, served as thoughtful leader, and his lyrics were empathic, revealing.

But it wasn't until the band's 1997 album that Radiohead showed what they were truly capable of. *OK Computer* was a work of remarkable depth and passion. Laced with electronics and ambient flourishes, the recording went way beyond the typical guitar band project into more cerebral territory, skillfully straddling the gray area between the rock of today and the rock of the future. *Spin* magazine, which voted the disc number two in its year-end music poll, said, "It's not the gadgetry that makes this album fly, it's the embattled musicianship, the tightly wound arrangements, the whacked-out but tangible humanity."

Radiohead continued to travel down abstract avenues with their next recordings: *Kid A*, which debuted at number one on the charts in October 2000, *Amnesiac* (2001), and *Hail to the Thief* (2003). All three of these late-period albums demonstrated a desire to move away from their early guitar-band roots into more musically and emotionally complex areas. With their track record thus far, Radiohead has earned a spot on that critically acclaimed and much sought-after "career artist" list. That status, in which artists aren't relied on to sell in copious amounts to be considered successful, keeps the band immune to the finicky vicissitudes of radio, radio programmers, and consumer trends.

Bjork, 2001. Courtesy of Photofest.

Bjork

Trained in classical piano as a child, Bjork, the Reykjavík, Iceland–born artist, began singing at an early age, making her homeland debut at age 11. But Bjork, born Björk Guðmundsdóttir, had bigger things in mind when she joined the arty rock band the Sugar Cubes as lead singer. Also based in Iceland, the Sugar Cubes earned international recognition, thanks in large part to the idiosyncratic, otherworldly vocals of their elfin-like singer. Her Sugar Cubes success led to larger things for Bjork. In 1990, after the demise of the band, she recorded her first solo record of any consequence, *Gling-Glo*, a collection of jazz standards and originals. But jazz was just another facet of Bjork's artistry and, as she did with classical, she stowed it away and moved further into futuristic pop, dance, and club culture.

Her pop debut, aptly coined *Debut*, found Bjork inspired by the club and house music of her new home in London. Now aligned with dance music maestro Nellee Hooper (Tricky, Massive Attack) of the United Kingdom, Bjork began to build an audience, first in Great Britain, where she was voted Best Newcomer in the *NME* (*New Musical Express*) year-end poll, and then in the United States, where her record eventually sold enough to go gold.

Post came next, in 1995, and was met with the same enthusiasm she enjoyed with her debut. Accolades followed, and Bjork began to come into her own as a truly creative, if eccentric, artist. To flex her creative muscle, Bjork released a remix album of the *Post* tunes, called *Telegram*, in 1997, and followed that with *Homogenic*, her most experimental studio effort to date. In the spring of 2000, she indulged a different aspect of her creativity, as the lead in Lars von Trier's Palme d'Or–winning film, *Dancer in the Dark*. For her work in the downbeat drama/musical, Bjork was named Best Actress by jurors at the Cannes Film Festival. *Selmasongs*, her score for the film, reunited Bjork with her *Homogenic* collaborator Mark Bell, arriving in the fall of 2000. The full-length follow-up, *Vespertine* was released one year later, in 2001.

Despite her inability to break into the mainstream, Bjork continues to inspire and excite her niche fan base with impressive displays of boldness and creativity.

POST-NIRVANA GRUNGE

Stone Temple Pilots

The story of Los Angeles' Stone Temple Pilots is one of glory and humiliation, success and disaster. Formed in 1992 by brothers Dean and Robert DeLeo, Eric Kretz, and singer Scott Weiland, STP combined the bluster of alternative rock with the swagger and rock-star presence of the arena rock bands of the '70s. Starting out, STP was vilified by critics for what seemed, on the surface, a remarkably derivative version of what had come immediately before: grunge, hair metal, and classic rock. But despite the qualms, their debut album, *Core*, was immensely successful, selling over 3 million copies upon its release in 1992.

Competent musicians and proven performers, STP had obvious chemistry. That dynamic kicked in on *Core*'s follow-up, the much-improved *Purple*, which debuted at No. 1 on the *Billboard* album chart when it was issued in the spring of 1994. Fueled by successful singles like "Interstate Love Song" and "Vasoline," the album was a quantum leap over *Core*, and a conscious effort to distance themselves from their post-grunge copycat image.

Unfortunately, it didn't take long for things to fall apart. (In fact, this roller-coaster ride of experiencing great highs and miserable lows would become a trend with the band.) Following *Purple*, they took some time off, a luxury that led to lead singer Weiland's arrest and subsequent rehab for drugs. Upon his release in 1996, the band eked out *Tiny Music . . . Songs from the Vatican Gift Shop*, before Weiland relapsed and needed further treatment. Their lack of presence on the touring circuit hurt sales and the band's morale began to flag. Still battling addiction, Weiland focused long enough to make his solo debut, *12 Bar Blues*, while the three remaining band members proceeded to form a side project called "Talk Show," releasing an album of the same name.

To the surprise of many, STP reunited long enough to record *No. 4*, before Weiland was once again sent to rehab. No touring presence following that studio effort damaged the band's chances of selling in big numbers—despite its quality, radio-friendly content. A sober Weiland rejoined the band in 2001 to make *Shangri-La Dee Da*, one of the band's most compelling works. But Weiland couldn't stay sober long enough to cut it, and the band ultimately decided to call it quits in 2003, after years of trying to stay together and fulfilling tremendous potential. As a coda to their career, the band compiled *Thank You*, a greatest hits collection. After dissolving, Weiland went on to join Velvet Revolver, with former members of Guns N' Roses, while the DeLeo brothers and Kretz worked at producing records.

The Foo Fighters

Following the death of Nirvana's Kurt Cobain in 1994, bassist Chris Novoselic and drummer Dave Grohl contemplated working together on Grohl's own material before going their separate ways. The politically active Novoselic stayed busy musically with Sweet 75, a duo featuring singer Yva Las Vegas. Grohl, after playing with several luminaries as a freelance drummer, decided to put his own band together. At the same time, he dusted off some of the material he was working on while plugging away with Nirvana. Branded as the Foo Fighters, Grohl abandoned the drums, and opted to front the band, singing, writing, and playing guitar. The Foos' self-titled debut of 1995 reflected Grohl's work with Nirvana: hard, fast, punk-derived tunes with lots of melody. Each subsequent album—1997's *The Colour and the Shape*, and 1999's *There Is Nothing Left to Lose*—increased the band's audience until they were one of the biggest alt-rock draws of the late '90s. In 2005, Grohl and company released *In Your Honor*, a double CD led by the single "Best of You."

A private personality with a quirky sense of humor, Grohl didn't encounter conflict post-Nirvana until 2001, when Courtney Love sued him, Novoselic, and the Universal label over control of Nirvana's master recordings. The lawsuit turned messy, dragging on for over two years, before it was resolved with a single-disc retrospective of Nirvana material in 2003.

Bush

This London quartet began their career backwards in several respects. First, though hailing from London, they met with their initial success in America.

Turned down by nearly every label in their homeland, Bush focused its efforts on the States, a move that actually made sense, considering they played the kind of guitar rock fervently embraced by domestic audiences. Britain, on the other hand, was in the throes of Britpop, a fairly narrow category in which Bush, guitar heavy and grunge derived, clearly did not fit. But then, when they did sign to an American label, Trauma/Interscope, following the breakthrough of grunge in 1994, they were seen as followers, copycats, or worse, opportunists. Kurt Cobain had just died, and their sound, uncannily like that of Nirvana, specifically in frontman Gavin Rossdale's Cobain-esque voice, emerged at precisely the wrong time.

Sixteen Stone, the band's debut, came out in 1994 to unanimously bad reviews, largely because of the aforementioned bad timing and the record's lack of originality. But radio picked up on it because it served up neatly the perfect blend of trademark grunge elements: abrasive guitars, visceral singing, and fierce dynamics. Singer-songwriter Rossdale had a debonair look to match his striking vocals and Bush began to attract a remarkably young audience. This was another aspect of the band that exasperated critics. In an attempt to counter the immense criticism, Bush made a grab for artistic integrity by hiring producer Steve Albini. Albini was the man behind such uncompromising acts as the Pixies and the Big Black, and he possessed the street credibility Bush desperately wanted. *Razorblade Suitcase*, a vociferous, spontaneously recorded album, came out at the end of 1996 and it impressed enough people to help the band stay relevant.

In contrast to their hit-strewn, mega-platinum debut, *Razorblade Suitcase* sold only 2 million copies and yielded only one hit single, "Swallowed." *Deconstructed*, a collection of electronic remixes, appeared in late 1997, and in the fall of 1999 Bush returned with *The Science of Things*. That album found the Bush sound swinging gently back to that of their debut—injected with electronic flourishes.

In late 2001, they went back to basics entirely with the guitar-driven effort *Golden State*. Although it didn't climb the charts, the band's fans still showed support, helping Bush sell out shows countrywide. Founding guitarist Nigel Pulsford announced his departure in 2002, leaving Rossdale with drummer Robin Goodridge and bassist Dave Parsons along with new guitar recruit Chris Traynor. Significantly, Rossdale married No Doubt's charismatic frontperson Gwen Stefani, and the band took a backseat to his personal life in the early part of the new millennium.

Marilyn Manson

Dismissed by critics and denounced by fundamentalist groups for his antireligious/blasphemous comments and stage shows, Marilyn Manson, nee Brian Warner, was one of the most controversial figures of the '90s. Against great odds, and passionate enemies, the band's thundering blend of hard rock, punk,

Marilyn Manson at the 1997 MTV Video Music Awards. Courtesy of Photofest.

and '80s metal climbed the charts, slotting Manson behind Alice Cooper and KISS as the latest in a long line of shock rockers.

Born in Canton, Ohio, the social outcast relocated to Florida as a teen and started his first band in the Tampa area. He met guitarist and fellow outsider Scott Mitchell; the two adopted unusual stage names: the first name came from a pop-culture starlet, and the surname from a notorious mass murderer. For example, Mitchell rechristened himself Daisy Berkowitz and Warner adopted the name Marilyn Manson. With the addition of bassist Gidget Gein and keyboardist Madonna Wayne-Gacy, the group, originally called Marilyn Manson and the Spooky Kids, began gigging and putting music out on their own label. Their gothic stage show, notable for Manson's elaborate makeup and homemade special effects, attracted enough regional attention to qualify as one of the biggest rock bands in south Florida.

It was at this time that Trent Reznor, impresario of the popular industrial rock band Nine Inch Nails, came calling. Reznor offered the band a contract and an opening slot on his band's 1994 tour. *Portrait of an American Family*, the band's debut, came out in the summer of 1994.

The Manson live show, a circus of horror with a high-decibel soundtrack, quickly developed an infamous reputation. The Church of Satan's founder Anton Lavey bestowed upon Manson the title of "Reverend," a mantle he donned with the ultimate irony. Despite the outcry, or perhaps because of it, Manson's popularity, mainly with disaffected suburban teens, grew exponentially throughout the decade. Radio responded as well, spinning his remake of the Eurythmics' "Sweet Dreams (Are Made of This)" off the band's second record, *Smells Like Children*.

Their third disc, *Antichrist Superstar*, was the band's most anticipated, as was the accompanying tour, which climaxed with Manson's staged crucifixion, an outrageous tableau of grotesque characterizations and bizarre nihilism meant to titillate and incite. The album debuted at No. 2 on the *Billboard* chart. Manson's popularity soared and, in the process, he succeeded in separating himself from Reznor, a man many credited for his success.

On *Mechanical Animals*, the band's 1998 disc, Manson put his industrial metal behind him in favor of straightforward glam rock. Led by the notorious single "The Dope Show," the disc featured the band taking on a David Bowie–like persona, named Omega, in a concept album meant to redefine his well-established Marilyn Manson character. Musically, the experiment succeeded, but the fans that relied on Manson for his cartoon characterizations and outrageous behavior were disappointed.

The high-powered *Holy Wood*, out in November 2000, continued in that punk-inspired rock 'n' roll vein. In 2003, Manson released his most accessible disc to date, *The Golden Age of Grotesque*. Ostensibly set in Weimar Republic–era Berlin, the set is an over-the-top theatrical odyssey that puts Manson at the front and center of his own cabaret. It's a nihilistic cabaret, patterned after Manson's own life with dark and angry melodrama.

The true impact of Manson's career has perhaps already come and gone, his shock value now but a distant echo from the late '90s, his musical peak. But appearances at Ozzfest in 2004 and other high-profile moments have served to keep him in the public eye, as has a greatest hits collection, *Lest We Forget* (2004).

COMMERCIAL POP CROSSOVERS

A handful of bands were crossover successes, meaning they went from alternative rock success to attracting mainstream pop audiences. Bands like Toad the Wet Sprocket, Sugar Ray, Hootie and the Blowfish, Goo Goo Dolls, Train, Vertical Horizon, Shawn Mullin, 3 Doors Down, John Mayer, and Five for Fighting, among many others, all managed to appeal to mainstream audiences with hefty doses of melody leavening their acoustic rock sounds. Smash Mouth, a San Jose quartet formed in 1994, hit the big time with their rock/surf sound best heard on infectious tracks like the Zombies rip-off "Walkin' on the Sun" and the ubiquitious "All Star," which gained new life in Dreamworks' animated hit film *Shrek*.

No Doubt

No Doubt also made huge waves during the '90s, shuttling between rock and pop audiences. Stalwarts on the Los Angeles scene, together since 1987, the band got its start as ska revivalists with a punky flair. Despite the explosion of a harder rock sound in grunge, the band, led by striking platinum-blonde lead singer Gwen Stefani, stayed the course. In 1994, after grunge dust began to settle, No Doubt released *Tragic Kingdom*, and toured endlessly to support it.

Music television eventually picked up on the group's colorful visual image, inserting songs like "Spiderwebs" and "Just a Girl" into increasingly heavy rotation. By 1996, the band hit the Top 10 on the *Billboard* album chart. Shortly thereafter, another single, the ballad "Don't Speak," gave the record, and the band, an even greater chart boost. In the process, Stefani became a sort of role model for young girls. Her image, clean and professional, talented and thoughtful, appealed to a wide cross section of fans, from young kids to their parents, from Top 40 music fans to punk rock Riot Grrrls. Her high-profile relationship and subsequent marriage to Bush frontman Gavin Rossdale kept her in the gossip columns and on magazine covers.

In 2000, No Doubt finally released a sequel to *Tragic Kingdom* called *The Return of Saturn*, an album that included singles "Ex-Girlfriend" and "Simple Kind of Life." Their fifth album, *Rock Steady*, appeared in 2002.

Other Top 40 Radio Stars

As the decade wore on, Top 40 radio began to opt for a more aggressive, harder rock sound. At the turn of the century, guitar-based rock groups like Nickelback, Creed, P.O.D., and Linkin Park hit the pop charts, tempering Top 40's dance orientation and closing the gap between mainstream pop and melodic hard rock. Edgy bands like Aussie garage rockers Jet, Maroon 5, and Hoobastank had all made deep impressions on a general American pop audience.

5

THE JAM BAND/ NEO-HIPPIE/IMPROV MUSIC SCENE

The lively, diverse, musical and cultural phenomenon known as the jam band scene stems directly from the long-standing legacy of the Grateful Dead, whose own improvisational skills have been well documented. The Dead, helmed by Jerry Garcia, were known for their unique and eclectic songwriting style— which fused elements of psychedelia, rock, folk, bluegrass, blues, country, and jazz—and for its extended jams, many of which were offshoots of the band's fondness for hallucinogens.

These various influences were distilled into a unique new music—a synthesis of all American folk music forms to date. It paid homage to previous forms, and also reflected a sense of adventure and a continuous quest for the "musical unknown." More often than not, that involved exploration and a search for a deeper musical place, a newness—these jams and their metaphysical destinations were hallmarks of the Dead's live performances.

When guitarist Garcia passed away in 1995, the band essentially called it quits. They continued on in various permutations, one of which was simply called the Dead; the other, a band cheekily referred to as the Other Ones. But Garcia's leadership had been critical to their unity; he was the heart and pulse behind those creative explorations, and it was not possible to continue the Grateful Dead as they had been since the mid-'60s. Following Garcia's death, a jam ethos, or hippie rock scene, characterized by the Dead's tie-dye splash of colors and penchant for hallucinogens, formed in his wake. Initially, the scene began merely as a search for the Dead's progenitor, an heir to the improvisatory throne. And while no single band seized the opening with any authority, many cropped up to fill the void vacated by the band's ample creative girth. When this movement first bubbled up in the early '90s, most of the bands aspiring to the throne were pegged as Grateful Dead or even Allman Brothers copyists. Indeed, the so-called bands of the young jam scene were synthesists, sponging elements of all kinds of popular music, from classic rock and folk to bluegrass, jazz, and world music.

The initial wave of bands actually referred to as "jam bands"—the Spin Doctors, Blues Traveler, Big Head Todd and the Monsters, and Widespread Panic—assumed a pop-rock stance. That is, they played a loose type of melodic rock music that easily incorporated lengthy improvisational passages. But as more and more bands formed in the Dead's stead, the stylistic subgenres multiplied and the scene's diversity grew richer.

From the mid-'80s to the mid-'90s, peaking with the stunning success of the Dave Matthews Band, the jam scene enjoyed a long, slow build. Many bands within this new scene cropped up in colleges across the country: Phish at the University of Vermont, the Disco Biscuits at the University of Pennsylvania, .moe at the University of Buffalo, and so on. This perhaps reflects the more intellectual and studied approach to the music of the jam scene. While the commercial rock of the '90s ended up being the product of the studio and studio producers, played by serviceable musicians, the music of the jam scene came in large part from cerebral, gifted, and musically educated performers.

Over time, the jam scene gradually split into two separate but equal schools: one thread involved the traditional jam bands still focused primarily on improvisational techniques, and the other a newer breed of musicians looking to merge aspects of improvisation with more tangible rock song structures. Inspired by the success of the working class Matthews (see Chapter 6), the new school of jam rockers concentrated more on the structures of their songs, rather than leaving them open-ended, ala the Dead, the Allmans, or even George Clinton's outrageous funk outfit, Parliament Funkadelic. Acoustic pop bands were reluctant to walk the shaky plank of improvisation—where musical dexterity is essential. Bands like the Spin Doctors, G. Love & Special Sauce, the Samples, Vertical Horizon, and Agents of Good Roots paid more attention to lyrics and hooks, latching on to pop melodicism in an attempt to stay in the hunt for commercial success, while still retaining their appeal to jam-hungry fans.

Ultimately, this bifurcation would lead to the same place, with the jam scene morphing into one big kitchen sink of bands. Literal jam bands like Phish, .moe, and Deep Banana Blackout were lumped in with figurative ones: pop bands, bluegrass fusion, acid jazz, funk groove, and southern rockers like Medeski, Martin and Wood, Ben Harper, Galactic. Today, the lines between these bands are blurred, largely due to huge festivals like the recent H.O.R.D.E. and today's Bonnaroo, which books them all together, regardless of style and individual approach to the jam idiom.

SELLING RECORDS VERSUS SELLING TICKETS

While the audience for this type of material is large and active, few artists within the scene sell many records. This could be because few ever attain widespread media exposure through radio or music television. The only ways these acts gain visibility are by word of mouth, touring, and Internet mailing lists. Their albums, often on independent labels, become secondary priority to touring, which makes them money and in turn helps them sell their recordings.

The Grateful Dead, too, sold surprisingly few records. Its biggest seller, *American Beauty* (1970), sold a little over 2 million. Instead, the Dead became one of rock's most successful acts by literally giving its music away. Rather than buy the band's official recordings in the stores, Dead Heads, the nickname for the band's fans, enjoyed their countless concerts—on tape and distributed free of charge among fans, or tape trading, with the band's blessing. The Dead always remained one of the largest grossing acts on the touring circuit, and had no problem sustaining itself on the road without requisite substantial record sales.

Where the Dead's fans employed cassettes and the mail service to swap music, Jam band fans now employ updated technology to do their trading, like CD burners and the Internet. Still, the result is the same: bands sacrifice record sales in favor of selling more concert tickets. Indeed, because they don't stress about record sales, few of today's jammers choose to sign with major record labels. But jam bands still boast hordes of dedicated fans and considerable profits as a result.

Additionally, set lists, always a topic of compelling interest among true fans of this style, would be published and debated. The jam within a song was more interesting to hardcore fans than the jam itself—a three-minute song would extend to ten or even twenty minutes. Many even allow tapers to come to shows early to set up equipment and plug in through the venue's official audio board. The prevailing wisdom of this is that interest in the band's official recorded music will increase with the ownership of these bootleg recordings.

Not all groups feel this way. The Dave Matthews Band issued a handful of quickly produced live recordings to offset the damage done by mass-producing bootleggers the band felt were taking a bite out of their bottom line. In the same way, Pearl Jam, not by any stretch a "jam" act, released low-budget live recordings from every date on their 2000 concert tour, even

The Dave Matthews Band performing in 2002. Courtesy of Photofest.

two from the venues they played on consecutive days, in order to head bootleggers off at the pass. .moe, one of the scene's fastest-rising acts, released a series of albums under the name *Instant Live* in 2003. Another popular band in this school, String Cheese Incident, released a series of live albums from their 2002 tour on their own Sci Fidelity label, nearly sixty in all.

MAKING MONEY, JAM-BAND STYLE

Twenty years ago, the Vermont-based Phish, the genre's biggest success story, toured nonstop across the northeastern bar circuit. Along the way, they encouraged new fans to make recordings of their gigs and swap them freely. Since then, the band's popularity has grown exponentially and their shows have become real events. So while tape trading has certainly taken a bite out of

Phish, 1996 (front to back), Trey Anastasio, Jon Fishman, Mike Gordon, and Page McConnell. Courtesy of Photofest.

the band's record sales—they typically sell about 200,000 units—they had become, before breaking up in the summer of 2004, one of the highest-grossing acts on the touring circuit. Scalpers commanded $600 a ticket for the band's high-profile shows, like their Madison Square Garden date on New Year's Eve in 2003. Because they made their infrequent live shows true events, 60,000 Phishheads often came to see them play.

For many mainstream acts, a successful tour means tying live shows together with the release of a recording. Not so for jam bands. Because they rely less on recording, they can tour without supporting an album and sacrifice little in the way of audience. Jam bands fly under the pop culture radar and, by necessity, shun expensive tastes and costly entourages. Widespread Panic, which started seventeen years ago and is now tailed by thousands of devoted "Spreadheads," keeps expenses down by traveling light. This allowed the Athens, Georgia–based band to net $3 million on $10 million of gross touring revenues in 2002, a high percentage in comparison to many touring acts.

The bands keep costs down for their fans as well. Jam bands charge half of what mainstream acts charge and often sell tickets directly to customers rather than forcing them to pay ticket outlet fees. Some acts, such as the String Cheese Incident, even book travel for fans. The end result is a colorful and flourishing scene of students (avid jam band fans), corporate executives (or "suits"), and legions of neo-hippies, all of whom think nothing of driving hundreds of miles to concerts.

THE DEAD CONTINUE

Following the passing of Jerry Garcia in 1995, the remaining members of the Dead formally decided to disband and pursue various solo projects. Bob Weir formed Ratdog, Phil Lesh called his project Phil Lesh and Friends, and drummer Mickey Hart increased his involvement in various solo works, including music for the 1996 Olympics. These factions reunited occasionally for a major festival, one they called Further Fest. Further was an annual gathering of bands that began in 1996, designed to share and remember the spirit of the Dead as well as their penchant for improvisation. Weir, Bill Kreutzman, Lesh, and Hart reunited in 2002 as the Other Ones and embarked on a fall tour throughout the eastern half of the United States.

Because the Dead were considered a sacred institution by their fans, many of these side projects took a while to catch. Starting up, these bands based their music on the sound of the Dead but attempted to move in slightly different directions. The Grateful Dead amassed an extraordinarily loyal following in its thirty-year career, so following it up proved to be difficult. The Other Ones with Lesh and Weir attempted to avoid that conflict by hiring keyboardist Bruce Hornsby and realigning their sound accordingly. Hornsby handled most of the vocals associated with Jerry Garcia.

Weir's Ratdog, formed in 1995, included bass player Rob Wasserman, who had accompanied Weir on his solo performances for some time; guitarist and harmonica player Matt Kelly, who had been a member of Kingfish with Weir as early as 1974; and drummer Jay Lane. Just after the band launched their first tour in August 1995, Garcia died, and Ratdog suddenly became his primary performing unit. They released their first album, *Evening Moods*, as Bob Weir and Ratdog, in 2000. A year later, the band released *Live at Roseland*, recorded at the Roseland Theater in Portland, Oregon.

On February 14, 2003, reflecting the reality that was—and the still-gaping hole left behind by the much-loved Grateful Dead—Weir, Lesh, Hart, and Kreutzman reunited and renamed themselves "the Dead," keeping the word "Grateful," out of respect for Garcia, in retirement.

JAM'S NEW HEIRS: PHISH

Of all the bands on the cerebral jam scene, Phish towered above the rest. Together, guitarist Trey Anastasio, bassist Mike Gordon, keyboardist Page McConnell, and drummer Jon Fishman possessed eclectic musical influences, uncanny technical abilities, and a dash of goofball humor. Stylistically, they weren't really like the Dead, but they shared one distinct similarity: they, too, sold more tickets than records.

Phish formed in 1983 when Anastasio, Fishman, and original guitarist Jeff Holdsworth were attending the University of Vermont. After meeting and jamming in their dorm room, they posted gig flyers across the campus to recruit a bassist. Mike Gordon answered the ad. In the fall of 1984, the band hired percussionist Marc Daubert and, later, a part-time vocalist/lyricist who called himself the "Dude of Life." His role was patterned after the Grateful Dead's own lyricist Robert Hunter. Soon after, the group was playing concerts on nearby campuses. Musician Page McConnell, who organized one of the band festival gigs, became a fan of the band and later joined on keyboards. Shortly after McConnell joined Phish, Holdsworth left. This lineup would remain for the duration of the band, a full twenty years.

Phish debuted in 1988 on a cassette-only release called *Junta*, and then followed quickly with *Lawn Boy* in 1989. When their indie label went bust in 1991, they jumped over to Elektra Records, a major, which released *A Picture of Nectar* in February 1992, and reissued their independent discs. *Rift*, the band's fourth album and the first recorded with a producer, appeared in February 1993. During their 1993 tour in support of the album, Phish set blocks of tickets aside exclusively for tapers. The gesture did not go unnoticed, and fans began to understand the quirky nature of these Vermonters.

Several other albums followed, including the popular *Hoist* in 1995, all of which sold steadily, but not spectacularly. Critics often cited the band's unevenness in the studio as part of the problem. Despite sluggish sales, the quartet proved to be a mega-draw on the road. Like the Dead before them, the band attracted the kinds of fans, nicknamed "Phishheads," who would attend more than a single show, even follow them on tour. This fanaticism turned their shows into rituals for serious fans, and events for the more casual enthusiast.

Because they knew many of their fans followed them from date to date, venue to venue, Phish focused intensely on their set list, changing it from night to night in an attempt to excite, amuse, and inspire the many fans who traveled with them. They worked up different covers to surprise their audiences, and made it a point to engage in deep, groove-inspired left-field jams. The band's legendary annual Halloween concerts featured the band reproducing entire classic albums, like the Who's *Quadrophenia* and the Beatles' White album.

But in 2000, worn out from all the touring, eager to indulge in solo projects, and frustrated by the lack of time spent with their young and growing families, the band announced a temporary breakup, a hiatus. It lasted less than two years. Bowing to pressure from fans and their record company, they reunited in 2002. Their rededication involved a massive series of live concert discs, twenty in all, issued in the spring of 2002. After releasing the studio effort *Undermind* and touring further, however, the band was haunted by the same frustrations that prompted them to call it quits in the first place. In June 2004, Phish broke up for good.

Their dissolution left a significant gap in the jam scene. At the time of their breakup they had begun to approach the importance of the Dead, and the jam scene flourished while the band was at the helm. Since the early '90s and the dawn of Phish, the entire jam culture has grown into a musically important, commercially viable, and artistically successful community. It remains to be seen who will step in, as Phish did, to fill this place of prominence on the jam landscape.

 PHISH SIDE PROJECTS

For a span toward the end of the '90s, the ever-ambitious cast of Phish ventured outside their band cocoon and into different sonic directions with noteworthy results. Guitarist Trey Anastasio released a series of demos before hooking up with Primus bassist Les Claypool and former Police drummer Stewart Copeland for a rather unconventional Oysterhead project. A stir-crazy and fecund artist, Anastasio also worked in improv jazz in Surrender to the Air, with the Vermont Youth Orchestra, an instrumental project called Seis de Mayo, and others. Keyboardist Page McConnell dedicated time to recording with Vida Blue and contributed keyboards to music/comedy duo Tenacious D's first record. Drummer Jon Fishman worked with his side project Pork Tornado and the touring jazz combo Jazz Mandolin Project. Bassist Mike Gordon became engrossed in film, doing work in and on several films. He also rejoined his former band Col. Bruce Hampton. Both Gordon and McConnell worked on Warren Haynes' Gov't Mule album *The Deep End, Vol. 1*. As a band, Phish was given a flattering vote of confidence when invited to appear on Matt Groening's animated series *The Simpsons*.

OTHER FLAMEKEEPERS

In 1989, Warren Haynes nailed down one of the best gigs in the world of guitar players: he was hired to play in the Allman Brothers Band, as the second replacement to the inimitable Duane Allman. Haynes had the chops to fill Duane's shoes, but not the experience. That would soon change over time, as he made the position his own. Bassist Allen Woody enjoyed the same compliment, being invited to join ABB on bass. As they reaped the instrumental fruits of the jam-happy southern rockers, Woody and Haynes started planning a side project. With the seed planted by the Allmans' legendary music, the two, joined by drummer Matt Abts, started Gov't Mule in 1993.

The Allmans' influence is apparent in Gov't Mule. Their knack for jamming and loose song structures, particularly live, turned quickly into the band's predominant hallmark. But they tempered that looseness with a harder rock flavor, a psychedelic blues edge that the Allmans never explored. Gov't Mule debuted on Capricorn Records in 1995 and within a few years had released a handful of live and studio albums, including the limited edition four-disc set *With a Little Help from My Friends*.

The band was dealt a setback in the summer of 2000 when founding bassist Woody was found dead in a New York City hotel room. The cause of death was listed as a heart attack. Reluctantly, Haynes and Abt marched on, this time with a special project dedicated to Woody. That project, *The Deep End*, was a two-installment deal that enlisted notable bassists to play on each of the band's new songs, essentially filling Woody's shoes. Included on the list of contributors were luminaries like Flea of the Red Hot Chili Peppers, Bootsy Collins of Funkadelic, and Phish bassist Mike Gordon.

In 2003, the band released a live album of the subsequent *Deep End* tour, called *The Deepest End*, which emphasized the band's comfort touring and continued to demonstrate the sheer power and accomplishment of Gov't Mule as an instrumental act.

Another accomplished instrumental group is Widespread Panic, a southern-style rock/jam band based in Athens, Georgia. A cornerstone of today's jam scene with roots that go all the way back to the early '80s, the band has built an enormous following, mainly in the South, based on a working-class image, skilled players, and tireless touring.

Widespread's appearance on early installments of the H.O.R.D.E. tour ("Horizons of Rock Developing Everywhere," see Chapter 7) helped them and many other regional bands gain exposure to audiences outside their home base. Widespread Panic released their energetic debut LP *Space Wrangler* in 1988 on the Landslide label. After several years of relentless touring, they signed to major label Capricorn, an early home of southern rockers like the Allman Brothers, Sea Level, and Wet Willie. Capricorn issued the group's self-titled sophomore outing in 1991.

Blues Traveler, 1994. Courtesy of Photofest.

The viability of H.O.R.D.E. and the success of a handful of its bands prompted the rising emergence of many other like-minded outfits. The Ominous Seapods, Rusted Root, God Street Wine, the Samples, the Aquarium Rescue Unit, and Allgood were some of the first bands to impress within the jam scene in the late '80s and early '90s. Blues Traveler (whose own singer, John Popper, helped found H.O.R.D.E.) and the Spin Doctors were commercially successful acts at that time, which perhaps excluded them from being taken too seriously by jam aficionados. The Dave Matthews Band also falls within that category. The success of these groups, while indeed excluding them from frontline acceptance within the jam community, opened the door for scores of instrumentally ambitious bands with the same goals.

Big Head Todd and the Monsters, another act on the H.O.R.D.E. bandwagon, formed in Colorado in the late '80s and debuted on record in 1989. Their 1993 disc, *Sister Sweetly*, went gold. A second Colorado band, the aforementioned String Cheese Incident, formed at about that time, 1993, but didn't debut on record—recording sporadically is a hallmark of jammers—until

The Spin Doctors, 1991 (left to right), Chris Barron, Aaron Comess, Eric Schenkman, and Mark White. Courtesy of Photofest.

1997. They steadily built a reputation based on nonstop touring and grassroots marketing. Their self-described "sacreligious mix of bluegrass, calypso, salsa, Afro-pop, funk, rock and jazz" was a smash on the club circuit. Today, SCI owns their own label (Sci Fidelity) and averages over 150 shows a year.

Buffalo, New York's .moe is another touring monster. The band came together in 1991, with a passion for experimentation and a flair for the unexpected. They earned a slot on the 1997 Further Tour, a H.O.R.D.E.-styled roadshow originated by a few remaining members of the Grateful Dead, and since then have become a major presence on the jam scene. *Wormwood* (2003) and a well-received live album, *Warts and All*, helped to enhance their already positive reputation.

In genuine, eclectic jam band fashion, the Disco Biscuits conjure a radical fusion of elements, cobbling together seemingly incongruous styles. Their mixture of rock, techno, jazz, soul, blues, dance, and classical—reminiscent, in fearlessness, of a voracious eccentric like Frank Zappa—quickly vaulted them to the upper reaches of the jam/groove scene. Guitarist/lead vocalist Jon Gutwillig has declared that the goal of the group is to create the wildest music of all time and the band's execution of that mission, dubbed "Trance Fusion," is convincing.

Galactic and Deep Banana Blackout derive their grooves from the Funkadelic-inspired faction of the jam scene. DBB, affiliated with Allman Brother percussionist Butch Trucks' Flying Frog label, exhibits a vast spectrum of influences, from Latin to calypso, funk to jazz. Galactic, from New Orleans, takes that city's hard R&B sound and laces it with pop and jazz to get the joint jumping. On the jazzier side, Medeski, Martin and Wood emerged from New York City's downtown scene in the early '90s. They made a name for themselves by fusing funk and jazz grooves and making large, improvisational leaps. Their touring ethic, the same as those dedicated to the rock side of the jam scene, gave them a boost, and some adventurous affiliations, including one with longtime jam kingpin Colonel Bruce Hampton, earned them a positive reputation among jam-friendly audiences.

Tenor sax player Karl Denson built a reputation in rock music by hooking up with Lenny Kravitz in the late '80s. When that stint expired, Denson plunged into his first love by forming a danceable acid-jazz band called the Greyboy Allstars. The act, based in San Diego, went over well for three years, before the restless Denson assembled another band, Karl Denson's Tiny Universe. Influenced by funk gurus like Maceo Parker and James Brown, the band has unexpectedly crossed over successfully between jazz and jam band audiences, with a flair for zesty, unpredictable performances.

An even more unlikely jam hero of the '90s is former trad-bop-fusion guitarist John Scofield. He made a name for himself accompanying jazz greats like Miles Davis, Chet Baker, and Charles Mingus. But these days, he is entertaining a far younger audience with his funky fusion of jazz and jam. Few guitarists are more capable of changing colors than John Scofield and he demonstrates it fully on albums like *A Go Go* (1997) and *Bump* (2000).

Another veteran has become an icon of sorts for the jam nation. Bluegrass/banjo legend Bela Fleck and his band the Flecktones have become the standard to which many roots-oriented jam bands aspire. Several bands don't jam per se, but have become major attractions for jam audiences. Ben Harper and his band the Innocent Criminals bring an organic, hippie vibe to their shows that have become almost spiritual. Philly's G. Love & Special Sauce adds a laid-back, funky flair to their evocative, acoustic hip-hop and blues. Their heavy touring and reputation established early on at H.O.R.D.E. earned the band a young and enthusiastic audience, though recording has been sporadic.

Acoustic pop band Vertical Horizon is a jam band in the Dave Matthews mode, meaning they appeal to the commercial side of the scene, emphasizing pop-rock flair over improvisation. Solo performer Keller Williams, signed by the String Cheese Incident's own label, has crafted a reputation based on virtuosity, eccentricity, and humor. His guitar instrumentation is dazzling, and his songwriting is by turns poignant and expressive. Onstage, he is a one-man show, unafraid to challenge audiences with his voice, his personality, and an array of guitars.

Touring and more touring has served as the modus operandi for the Pat McGee Band, a Richmond, Virginia–based sextet formed in 1996, and it has remained thus ever since. Playing over 250 shows a year, the band has developed an audience with positive energy and a good-time attitude. Their latest album, *Save Me*, was released in 2004 on the Warner Brothers label.

WHAT EXACTLY IS IMPROVISATION?

While the Grateful Dead are generally accepted to be the founders of the jam band scene, the concept of improvisation, which plays such a large role within their music (mainly live) is, of course, not of their invention. Early jazz musicians pioneered the spontaneous form of expression as far back as the beginning of the twentieth century.

The hundreds of bands that comprise the jam scene, like the Dead, feature improvisation as an integral cog of their songs. But what is it, exactly, and why are so many bands (and fans) drawn to it? Plainly stated, improvisation in music is the act of deciding what to play on a spontaneous basis. Each decision a musician makes during an improvised tune is based partly on his past experience as a musician, partly on the experience of the musicians with which he shares the stage, and partly on the parameters of the song itself. By and large, there are two kinds of improvisation. Most jam band improvisations are based around existing chord progressions of composed songs. That is, they are variations on notes already written following tempos already determined. This technique occurs as a logical progression from a solo taking place within a song—on guitar, bass, keyboard, or any other instrument on stage. This type of improvisation generally occurs within pop or rock jams.

Then there are the jams that are more free form, jams that completely improvise the notes, tempo, and structure of the music. Like most rock jams, they jump off existing arrangements, but they journey farther from a song's core and often end up sounding nothing like the original songs. This generally happens in jazz, but certain jazz-rock-type bands like Phish possess the sort of adventurous spirit that often results in this second type of improvisation.

Many of the best rock improvisers like the Dead and the Allman Brothers possess deep experiences in musical conversation, which is why their onstage language activity runs with such fluency. Generally speaking, veteran improvisers have more interesting things to say, which is why experienced players like the Dead's Jerry Garcia and Bob Weir were so respected in this regard. Of course, many jazz players are actually educated in the art of improvisation and are expected to exercise their skills whenever they play within some areas of the genre. This is in contrast to traditional rockers, who rarely use those skills and are more accustomed to rote playback of material.

6

COMMERCIAL ROCK

Following the alternative rock boom of the early '90s, a number of important offshoots surfaced, nearly all of which are addressed elsewhere in this book. One of the most commercially popular tributaries was commercial pop-rock, a style similar to the sound of rock prior to the alternative boom, only trimmed with a slightly more '90s aesthetic.

Many of the most popular bands of this ilk took their cues from the Everyman image of the grunge movement. Like the grunge and early alternative bands that arose in rebuttal to the souped-up glam of the late '80s, these pop bands were modest and low-key. They avoided the rock-star poses and provocative fashions of Top 40 rock, opting instead to present their music with more candor than contrivance. Their music and expressive performances, they felt, spoke for themselves. In essence, this type of commercial pop-rock became alternative music for a more mature audience, hence its official moniker: adult alternative pop/rock.

The genre took off immediately. In contrast to grunge, which was heavy and often uncompromising, adult alternative pop/rock softened the edges, tempered the frustration, and clarified the melodies. The change in tone and the easing of decibels was refreshing and adult alternative became the vox populi of an aging generation.

Commercial radio ate it up as well. Early on, bands like Blind Melon, Blues Traveler, and the Spin Doctors blended the laid-back sounds of classic and Grateful Dead–oriented rock with '90s edginess, combining the best of the old and new styles for mature listeners. The Spin Doctors and Blues Traveler in particular also had the benefit of being able to play their instruments well, so while their rock was lightweight in comparison to other alternative styles, it did have musical credibility. In some cases, groups like the Samples, the Dave Matthews Band, and Big Head Todd and the Monsters added flecks of jazz, also attractive to older audiences.

Detractors called the music disposable, expendable. Indeed, at its worst, adult alternative pop/rock felt insubstantial and uninspired. Anxious to make music that was pretty and likable, some adult alternative artists wound up inoffensive to the point of blandness; others self-consciously tried to sound "deep," resulting in forced melancholia and heaps of overwrought, amateurish poetry. But at its best, the style sounded great on the radio and it gained significant exposure for artists who were ambitious, intellectual, and/or idiosyncratic, yet still accessible enough to meet the requirements of mainstream radio programmers who wanted to spin more sophisticated music that wasn't loud or overly disturbing.

What binds this overarching genre together is quite simply a sense of maturity. Essentially, it's the mainstream, pop-rock of the '90s, a type of music that appeals to a more mellow adult sensibility; people who still appreciate rock, but don't have the patience for the noise of their youth. Rather, the stresses of adult life—kids, bills, work, and civic responsibilities—have shoved music into the background. A new CD purchase is no longer the single reason to take a drive in the car. Music now serves as a stress-buster, a soundtrack of positive energy, easygoing tunes to help many meet difficult daily challenges.

BEGINNINGS OF ADULT ALTERNATIVE ROCK
IN THE 1990s

Adult alternative pop/rock is more a sensibility than a particular sound. Its artists specialize in a spectrum of styles: intelligent guitar-pop (Barenaked Ladies), pop jangle (Gin Blossoms), acoustic folk rock (Vertical Horizon), confessional poetry (Indigo Girls), roots rock (Sheryl Crow), or moody electronica (Portishead), among others. In fact, as with many of the relatively new genres that sprouted in the '90s and beyond, the genre itself wasn't defined until critics and pundits in the industry could take a step back and survey the new crop of bands. In so doing, you can better understand groupings and trends. One of the bands that helped jumpstart a commercial alternative grouping was a bunch of small-town Pennsylvanians called Live. Starring Ed Kowalcyk and supported by guitarist Chad Taylor, drummer Chad Gracey and bassist Patrick Dahlheimer, Live debuted in 1991 with *Mental Jewelry*, an album that introduced the band's passionate performance style and conviction for the art form. These elements would soon become their signature. Together since high school, the band capitalized on their deep, long-standing relationship by adjusting quickly to stardom. Radio, playing songs like "Pain Lies on the Riverside," welcomed the band with open arms.

Their luck continued with the heavily anticipated *Throwing Copper*. That album, released in 1994, launched the band into the mainstream with fervent tunes like "Selling the Drama," "Lightning Crashes," and "I Alone." The recording turned the band into superstars and one of the key players in the post-Nirvana world of alternative music.

Over the next several years, a sporadic release schedule and shifted priorities derailed the band's momentum. They still attracted a sizable fan base for their albums in the late '90s, but never recaptured their original glory. In 2003, they released *Birds of Prey*.

Like Live, Blind Melon began the '90s with great promise, spinning out a hit early with the infectious "No Rain." Singer Shannon Hoon, a boyhood friend of another Indiana native, Axl Rose, perfectly embodied the young naïve talent, one part hippie, one part good friend, one part pop star. His band, a back-to-basics bunch of midwesterners transplanted to Los Angeles, complemented him perfectly. Blind Melon was nominated for two Grammys in 1994, Best New Artist and Best Rock Performance. Hoon sang with Rose and his band Guns N' Roses. The group played a memorable Woodstock show that year and opened for the Rolling Stones on several dates. Things, as they say, were looking up.

But amid the rise to fame, drugs took hold of Hoon. In 1995, after a stint in rehab, the band's promising career was cut tragically short when Hoon, with a dangerous addiction to heroine, overdosed and died on October 21. The void left by a band with such promise was quickly filled from all sides.

Hootie and the Blowfish, an acoustic pop-rock quartet formed by University of South Carolina students back in 1989, released their blockbuster break-through, *Cracked Rear View*, in 1994. The disc, bolstered by several hit singles

Hootie and the Blowfish accept the award for Best New Artist in a Video during the 1995 *MTV Video Music Awards*. © AP/Wide World Photo.

including the anthemic "Hold My Hand" and "Let Her Cry," went on to dominate the mid-'90s sound, selling 13 million copies.

San Francisco's Counting Crows also released their breakthrough, *August and Everything After*, in 1994. Grafting singer-songwriter Adam Duritz's skewed romanticism onto the band's '70s pop-rock, the band's sound appealed to new and classic rock fans alike. The record, led by the up-tempo, Van Morrison–esque rocker "Mr. Jones" and Duritz's free-spirited image, quickly captured the adult alternative imagination and *August* ended up selling in multiplatinum numbers. Given the success of stylistically related bands like the rootsy Spin Doctors (*Pocketfull of Kryptonite*, 1991), Blues Traveler (*Four*, 1994), and former punk rockers the Goo Goo Dolls (*Superstar Car Wash*, 1993), the roots pop revival had momentarily become the sound of American mainstream rock.

As part of that new sound, the Wallflowers held a special connection to one of the offshoot's original inspirations. The band's leader, singer-songwriter/guitarist Jakob Dylan, is the son of legend Bob Dylan. And though the Wallflowers shared more similarities in sound with roots rockers like Tom Petty and the Band, his folk-rock intentions aren't ever far in the distance. The band released its self-titled debut in 1992, but enjoyed its breakthrough album, *Bringing Down the Horse*, four years later, when the single "One Headlight" hit the Top 40 and won two Grammys. Since then the characteristically quiet Dylan and company have toured and sold records successfully in support of subsequent albums, *Breach* (2000) and *Red Letter Days* (2002).

Compared to the rootsy sound of the Wallflowers, bands like Matchbox 20, Collective Soul, and Third Eye Blind were downright grungy. All of these bands crawled underneath the pop music radar with relatively inoffensive guitar-based rock that took its cue from the lighter side of bands like Pearl Jam and Soundgarden. All of them were able to succeed in spite of withering criticism (once critics discovered them), leveled at the bands for being derivative and bland. Each had frontmen who were indistinguishable and sounds that were interchangeable. Still, their best melodies sounded great on the radio and each of these bands had immensely gifted central songwriters.

Collective Soul, the veteran of the bunch, having assembled in 1992 outside of Atlanta, is led by writer/guitarist Ed Roland. The son of a strict preacher, Roland attended the Berklee School of Music in Boston, despite his father's reluctance to expose his kids to popular music. Roland dropped out of Berklee due to lack of funds, but he continued to write and demo material. The demo of one of Roland's best songs, "Shine," found its way into the hands of several radio stations and generated a significant amount of interest, including some from Atlantic Records. Roland hastily assembled a group and inked a contract with the label. "Shine" became a massive hit, and the band's subsequent records, including *Hints, Allegations and Things Left Unsaid*, produced by Matt Serletic, and *Disciplined Breakdown* went on to sell in platinum numbers.

Matchbox 20 is fronted by Rob Thomas, a high school dropout and army brat. He assembled the band during his meanderings in the Orlando, Florida, area and commenced producing a collection of demos with Collective Soul producer Matt Serletic. The demos attracted the attention of Lava Records, then a subsidiary of Atlantic, and the band recorded and released *Yourself or Someone Like You* in late 1996.

Several hit singles, including "Push" and "3am," followed, propelling the band into the limelight. Although critics derided the disc for its blandness and studio sheen, Matchbox 20 was named "Best New Band" in 1997's *Rolling Stone* Reader's Poll. In 1999, leader Thomas was invited to collaborate with guitarist Carlos Santana on a record the guitarist intended to revitalize his career. The first single on the disc, "Smooth," was that collaboration, and it exploded, powering the disc to sell millions.

Rob Thomas of Matchbox 20 performs at the *30th Annual American Music Awards*, 2003. Courtesy of Photofest.

It also rekindled attention for Matchbox 20's work, which was ebbing slightly at the time. In 2005, Rob Thomas issued his first solo album, *Something to Be*, and it debuted in April at the top of the charts.

CORPORATE ROCK

The concept of corporate rock began in the '70s, the same decade that spawned another concept, that of the rock superstar. The story goes like this:

Excess became the norm for bands like Led Zeppelin and the Rolling Stones, KISS, and Aerosmith. They were not only earning huge amounts of cash, courtesy of successful tours and generous contracts with their record labels; they were incredibly decadent in more ways than one. Stage and studio effects grew more elaborate and costly. The sheer scale of rock album sales gave musicians—and their ever-growing entourage of managers, lawyers, and accountants—the upper hand in negotiations with record companies. During this time, successful rock bands became, quite literally, corporations, employing dozens and earning money in several ways—onstage, on recordings, and through merchandise. For most of the decade, until punk and the DIY ethic brought corporate rock down to earth, it seemed that the greater the artistic self-indulgence the bigger the financial return.

In the early '90s, corporate rock rose up once again, though with a slightly altered definition. Beginning in 1990, many popular alternative bands bit on the big-money contracts waved at them by the major labels. Many even became the subject of bidding wars. As a result of their substantial investment in these big-money contracts, many underground and marginally commercial bands became willing corporate partners with the labels.

In the beginning, much of the music coming from the majors was courageous and challenging. The labels, thankful to have adventurous bands on their rosters—Nirvana, Helmet, the Pixies, and the Melvins come to mind—were issuing intelligent and compelling rock music. The majors were also co-opting independent labels in an attempt to capitalize on the expertise these smaller labels had in the independent music marketplace. Atlantic Records, for example, developed a relationship with the creatively successful New York imprint Matador in 1993, to shore up that label's alternative roster. In 1995, the credible Sub Pop label, hungry for cash, sold 49 percent of its company to the Warner Music Group for $20 million. These moves and several others blurred the line between major and indie, mainstream and alternative.

Yet over the next few years, faced with diminishing returns on these signings and contractual agreements, corporations were forced to exert more pressure on their bands. The bands that cooperated were rewarded with support. This led directly to a change of perspective and the second wave of corporate rock. Bands that abided closely to their parent labels were seen as subservient to their companies, a real role reversal given the history of band–label relationships. Many bands began to rely on their handlers to help them with image, style, music, and promotional opportunities. Critics derided these bands as being mere puppets of their record companies. On the other hand, many bands that played by these rules and succeeded made frequent trips to the bank.

Before signing their major-label deal, Seattle's Sub Pop had t-shirts and bumper stickers printed with the slogan "Corporate rock sucks." Clearly, independent labels and bands were at odds with their counterparts on the corporate side. That battle was waged for just a few years, with the independent side losing ground at an alarming rate. Soon, the punky grunge sound of original alternative and indie rock would fall out of favor, only to be replaced by a more palatable, more melodic, easier listening blend of heavy guitars and rock. This happened for a variety of reasons. At the time, boy bands and girl bands began to dominate Top 40 radio. That sound, characterized by simplistic and love-obsessed teen acts like the Backstreet Boys and Britney Spears, helped to tame the feisty rock beasts of punk and grunge. So melodically accessible rock bands like Creed, Nickelback, and Three Doors Down rose up to fill a new void: rock bands that sounded comfortable alongside the teen acts on Top 40 radio. Throughout the latter part of the '90s and into the '00s, pop radio made these bands mega-stars. For that reason, they were overwhelmingly successful. They were also roundly criticized.

Creed

Creed formed in Tallahassee in the mid-'90s. The original lineup of Scott Stapp and Mark Tremonti, influenced by the hair metal of the '80s and grunge of the early '90s, combined those two sounds—creating an anthemic amalgam, with slightly Christian overtones, that hit all the right notes. While their grunge contemporaries were attempting to regain their roots after selling out to the mainstream, Creed did so unabashedly, writing songs tailor-made for radio.

The ploy paid off. Creed became one of the top-selling bands of the late '90s. Their debut, *My Own Prison*, was originally released in 1997 on the band's own label, Blue Collar, before getting picked up by another fledgling label, Wind-Up. Wind-Up polished the record, added a slightly heavier sound, and worked the record on the radio side. The labor paid off. Creed moved 5 million units of its debut, and tallied no less than four chart-topping singles.

The band's follow-up, *Human Clay*, also did spectacular numbers. Upon its release in 1999, while *My Own Prison* was still converting listeners into fans, it bowed at No. 1 on the *Billboard* album chart. The record eventually sold over 10 million copies, yielded a pop hit with "Arms Wide Open," and earned the band a Grammy for Best Rock Song.

For its next album, the band worked through the better part of 2001. *Weathered* appeared amid some controversy. Their

 THE CORPORATIZATION OF RADIO

The fact that radio was becoming more corporate as well made the lives of these corporate rock bands somewhat easier. A U.S. federal law passed in 1996 lifted restrictions on radio ownership, increasing the number of stations a corporation can own in a single market. Under the old rules, companies could only control two radio stations per market and no more than forty nationwide. But under the new Telecommunications Act, companies could own up to eight stations in one market and an unlimited number across the country. Over half of all radio stations in the country have changed hands since the Federal Communications Commission (FCC) last relaxed ownership rules in 1996. Texas-based Clear Channel Communications is now the largest radio company in the United States with more than 1,200 stations and about 100 million listeners. That's roughly one-third of the U.S. population.

Because of these laws, commercial radio—and, most importantly, the music it plays—is increasingly coming under the control of corporations. In some cases, those corporations have financial interest in record companies. Cynics say that this allows radio to have a say, even dictate, what goes on the air. This also creates a situation involving dubious bedfellows, with radio and the recording industry developing a relationship that is, without a doubt, too close for comfort.

bassist, Brian Marshall, was fired from the band. Stapp engaged in a lively feud with Limp Bizkit frontman Fred Durst, which made headlines. Stapp even began to distance himself from his bandmates, for which he was publicly criticized. Still, *Weathered* debuted in November 2001 at the top slot on the chart and remained there for eight straight weeks. Hit singles followed, as did a tour. But the tour was interrupted by a violent car accident involving Stapp, which shelved the band's promotional plans for the album.

But the gap widened between Stapp and Tremonti. Some called Stapp egotistical and difficult to work with, including his bandmates. Ultimately, that

Creed (left to right) Scott Phillips, Scott Stapp, Brian Marshall, and Mark Tremonti. Courtesy of Photofest.

strained relationship led to the band's demise. They broke up officially in June 2004, after months of inactivity.

Tremonti formed the band Alter Bridge and released his debut, *One Day Remains*, in the fall of 2004. Stapp is at work on a solo album.

3 Doors Down

3 Doors Down, from a small town outside Biloxi, Mississippi, created a buzz on local radio with their tune "Kryptonite." That buzz was heard all the way in New York City, when, in 1999, they played a showcase gig at a small club. That gig helped secure the band a major-label recording contract with the Republic label, a subsidiary of Universal. *A Better Life*, the band's debut, came out in 2000, and, powered by "Kryptonite," proceeded to achieve multiplatinum status. The band lingered on the charts for a few years, touring relentlessly, before recording a follow-up. *Away from the Sun* emerged in late 2002, and entered the charts in the Top 10.

Nickelback

Vancouver-based post-grunge rockers Nickelback initially gained visibility in their homeland with the single "Leader of Men," released to radio at the end of 1998. The song, and the album it was on, *The State*, originally released independently, received generous attention and earned the band a major-label contract.

Like many corporate rock bands, Nickelback, fronted by singer-guitarist-songwriter Chad Kroeger, toured ceaselessly, often playing over 200 shows a year. They joined forces with other similar bands, including popular acts like Creed and 3 Doors Down, and played to sizable audiences.

Nickelback's popularity grew exponentially with the release of *Silver Side Up* in 2001. Kroeger confirmed the possibility that he was an adept melodist in the rock realm with another smash hit, "How You Remind Me." The single ascended pop charts around the world and made Nickelback into superstars. The single hit No. 1 in both the United States and Canada, making the band the first act since the Guess Who to accomplish the feat.

Kroeger made the most of his newfound fame, writing and collaborating with pop and country stars. He co-wrote "Hero" with Saliva frontman Josey Scott, for the *Spiderman* feature film soundtrack. Saliva, a southern rock band on the corporate tip, also toured rigorously and has had several rock hits.

Other Popular Rock Bands

A hefty handful of other popular rock bands also fall into this corporate rock category. Some lineups, like those of Matchbox 20 and Linkin Park, discussed elsewhere in this book, were actually assembled by producers, and had their short- and long-term plans laid out for them well in advance. Third Eye Blind, Fuel, and the Verve Pipe also had some luck establishing audiences and good album sales figures in the late '90s. Incubus, the Killers, Maroon 5, and Hoobastank (produced by Nickelback's Kroeger) all have made a substantial impact on rock beyond that time period on into the present, with hit singles, a constant touring presence, and steady promotional opportunities—all things consistent with the corporate rock concept.

THE WOMEN TAKE CENTER STAGE

Alanis Morissette

Alanis Morissette's career began at the ripe age of 10, when she became a regular on a TV program, *You Can't Do That on Television*, in her native Canada. With the money she received on the show, she entered the studio to make her first single, which was released when she was still 10.

At 14, she signed a publishing deal with MCA Canada, increasing the stakes of her musical career. Her debut, *Alanis*, did well, selling 100,000 copies in

Alanis Morissette performs on *The Early Show*, 2002. Courtesy of Photofest.

Canada. She followed that recording up with another, *Now Is the Time*, which also did well in Canada. But success in America eluded Morissette, so she relocated to Los Angeles. While there, she hooked up with successful songwriter Glen Ballard, whose experience writing with Michael Jackson made him an in-demand talent.

Morissette and Ballard began writing together when Alanis was just 20. At the time, the alternative revolution was in full swing, and even though both Morissette and Ballard had straight-up pop backgrounds, they decided to go for an edgier sound. The material would become the duo's first full-length project together, *Jagged Little Pill*, recorded for Madonna's Maverick label.

On the strength of the disc's first single, "You Oughta Know," the album became one of the '90s best-selling albums. Released in 1995, the record continued to sell three years later, ultimately moving an incredible 16 million copies. Follow-up singles like "Ironic" and "Hand in My Pocket" helped keep Morissette on the charts consistently during that time. In 1996, she won a slew of Grammys, including Album of the Year and Song of the Year. Her much-anticipated follow-up, *Supposed Former Infatuation Junkie*, was released in the autumn of 1998. While no one expected it to do as well as its predecessor, it still sold 3 million copies. *Unplugged*, which appeared a year later, sold 1 million copies. Morissette, by this time fatigued from several years of relentless public exposure and touring, took some time off to recharge.

In 2002, eager to break free of her guru-like association with Ballard, she decided to terminate her songwriting relationship with him amicably. Her subsequent recording, *Under Rug Swept*, while critically lauded, didn't meet with the same reception by radio and failed to sell in substantial numbers. Her idiosyncratic way of being super-descriptive lyrically—her songwriting signature—reached an apex on the album, and her creative flow seems to be taking on a life of its own. In 2005, Morissette released an acoustic version of *Jagged Little Pill*, again with Ballard.

Sheryl Crow

One of the few women to take advantage of the commercial popularity of the roots rock sound, Sheryl Crow debuted in 1993 with *Tuesday Night Music*

Club, a record that yielded the hit "All I Wanna Do." The disc concept was based on a Los Angeles songwriters group she belonged to that met on Tuesday nights, and it had a loose, ramshackle feel.

Born in 1962, Crow began her professional career singing backup for Michael Jackson, and was even rumored (falsely) to have been his lover. But when she tried to secure a record deal of her own, she met with resistance. Labels familiar with her work tried to convince her to become a dance diva. But Crow, a rocker at heart, wanted to apply her writing and singing skills to a more classic

Sheryl Crow performs on *Soundstage*, 2004. Courtesy of Photofest.

rock context. The difficulty of the task and the apparent futility sent her into a six-month depression. After resurfacing, she resumed her role as a backup vocalist on sessions with an array of top acts: Rod Stewart, Stevie Wonder, Sting, and Don Henley, to name a few. She also refined her writing skills, and placed her songs with artists like Eric Clapton, Wynonna Judd, and Celine Dion. Based on her work, producer Hugh Padgham signed Crow to the A&M label. But Padgham misread Crow's intentions and channeled her into making an album full of downbeat ballads. That recording experience, frustrating for Crow, resulted in the label shelving the project, which in turn sent Crow into another bout of depression.

But in 1993, the inspiration supplied by the Tuesday Night Music Club rescued Crow, and her subsequent recording of the same name was released in August of that year. Since then, she has been one of the decades most reliable performers. A string of hit singles and Grammys beginning in late 1994 set in motion a wave of successful career moves. That success was not without its fallout, however. Members of Crow's Tuesday Night Music Club felt betrayed by her success, charging that she gave little credit to the members of the group for her success and adding that Crow had little to do with the music that originated in the club.

Adding insult to injury, her friends in the group spoke critically of Crow after her highly publicized appearance on *The Late Show with David Letterman* in 1994. On the show, Crow told the host that her hit "Leaving Las Vegas" was autobiographical. In fact, the song was mostly written by Club member (and Crow friend) David Baerwald and was based on the book by Baerwald's good friend John O'Brien (which had also inspired the film of the same name). Having been burned by the industry already, some of the members of the Tuesday Night Music Club took Crow's comment as a refusal to give proper credit for their contributions. Baerwald felt betrayed, and, when O'Brien committed suicide not long after Crow's Letterman appearance, the clouds accumulated over Crow's already precarious reputation.

Touring was the answer. Crow toured nonstop for two years following the release of her debut, and, with the help of radio, which glommed onto Crow's mix of lite and roots rock, she soon left her problems behind. When she set about writing and recording her new album at the beginning of 1996, she assumed the added pressure of having to prove she could write without her Tuesday Night Music Club. Written in collaboration with her guitarist Jeff Trott, the sequel to her debut, *Sheryl Crow*, proved just that. The singles "If It Makes You Happy," "Everyday Is a Winding Road," and "A Change Would Do You Good" were all radio smashes, and "Home" also became a minor hit. *Sheryl Crow* went triple platinum, and Crow brought home Grammys for Best Rock Album and another for Best Female Rock Vocal (for "If It Makes You Happy").

More success ensued, with a couple of warmly received albums (*The Globe Sessions* in 1999 and *C'mon, C'mon* in 2002). In 1999, she gave a free concert in New York City's Central Park, with the help of several invited guests: Eric Clapton, Keith Richards, Chrissie Hynde, the Dixie Chicks, and Sarah McLachlan. This luminous guest list provides some indication of Crow's superstar stature in the new millennium. A new album, *Wildflower*, hit stores in the fall of 2005.

Tori Amos

Beyond Crow, a handful of other women made huge names for themselves in this world of adult-oriented pop. Tori Amos, for example, combined the music of the '70s with eccentric personality, unusual fashion sense, and an affinity for alternative music, to become one of the '90s most-loved pianists. A musician who began her career in the church choir and continued it through the prestigious Peabody Conservatory, Amos served to bring the piano back to the rock music idiom. Since then, artists like Ben Folds, Vanessa Carlton, Charlotte Martin, Regina Spektor, and many others have come back to the keyboard as a hip, songwriting tool and effective performing instrument.

Amos initially made noise with her 1992 album *Little Earthquakes*, due in part to strident, often socially aware lyrics and unconventional song arrangements. She continued to attract audiences with 1994's extraordinary *Under the Pink*, a disc that yielded such Amos standards as "God" and "Cornflake Girl." Since then, she has consistently produced quality material, on ambitious albums like *From the Choirgirl Hotel* (1998) and the stirring *Scarlet's Walk* (2002). She is a thoughtful, introspective woman with a uniquely personal perspective on herself and her art.

Sarah McLachlan

Canadian Sarah McLachlan's rise parallels Amos'. Sarah released her debut a bit earlier, in 1989, but didn't issue her attention-getting *Solace* album until

1991. McLachlan's appeal draws striking similarities to Amos'. They both compose and perform on piano and both are captivating singers with ethereal qualities to their voices.

Born in Halifax, Nova Scotia, McLachlan trained in classical piano, voice, and guitar as a teen. She began writing songs with a New Wave band called October Game before signing on with Canadian label Nettwerk Records as a solo artist in the late '80s. Her debut, *Touch*, introduced McLachlan as a sensitive songwriter with a magical voice and the album eventually achieved gold status in Canada. *Solace*, a more mature set and a great leap in songwriting, came next and helped to earn the artist a much larger audience. The personal *Fumbling Towards Ecstasy*, issued in 1994, eventually went platinum. But it was her central role in the development of Lilith Fair (see Chapter 7), and a much-lauded fourth effort, *Surfacing*, that pushed McLachlan into superstar territory. *Afterglow*, her first studio album in six years, has only enhanced her revered status as a pop music icon.

Sinead O'Connor

Two rock acts from Ireland, the Cranberries from Limerick, and Sinead O'Connor of Dublin, became powerful voices on the '90s pop music scene, not only in the United States, but internationally. O'Connor debuted in 1987 with the phenomenally successful *The Lion and the Cobra* and its hit "Mandinka." An outspoken punk rocker and petty thief as a teen, she worked through her hardship as a youth and made a name for herself by singing with potency and passion and speaking powerfully (and controversially) in interviews about social causes and injustices.

But O'Connor remained a cult figure until her follow-up disc in 1990, the sublime *I Do Not Want What I Haven't Got*. Elevated by the album's first single, a cover of Prince's "Nothing Compares 2 U," the record became O'Connor's breakthrough and a supreme validation of her early success. But controversy followed her everywhere. She pulled out of the Grammys in 1991, despite being nominated in four categories. She refused to appear on *Saturday Night Live* when she discovered a misogynist comedian, Andrew Dice Clay, was also slated to appear. But she got the biggest reaction of all in 1992, when, following an appearance on the same *SNL* program, she ripped up a photograph of the pope, protesting his leadership in the Catholic Church. The fallout was enormous and O'Connor became a virtual pariah in pop music.

Time and distance, along with a six-year hiatus, has enabled O'Connor to regain at least a portion of her audience and find her way delicately back into the public eye. Since the debacle, she has kept a lower profile, focusing on bringing up her children and recording acclaimed but little-heard recordings. Her 2002 studio album, *Sean-Nos Nua*, features O'Connor singing a collection of her favorite traditional Irish tunes. Her reputation remains intact at this time, as a performer who irrevocably changed the image of women in rock music.

The Cranberries

Another Irish act, the Cranberries started the '90s off with a bang as well. At the outset of the decade they were pictured on the cover of English music weekly *New Musical Express* on nothing more than the strength of a six-song demo. In fact, the four teens from Limerick were quite nearly overwhelmed by all the premature attention. Still, it didn't take long for the band to justify the hoopla. That demo incited a bidding war among major labels, resulting in the band signing with Island Records.

Their first two albums, *Everybody Else Is Doing It So Why Can't We?* (1993) and its follow-up, *No Need to Argue* (1994), were successful from the outset, selling over 6 million records combined. The teens from Limerick were headed quickly and unwittingly toward superstar status.

The Cranberries, 1999 (left to right), Feargal Lawler, Dolores O'Riordan, Mike Hogan, and Noel Hogan. Courtesy of Photofest.

The strength of the Cranberries lay in Dolores O'Riordan's emotional vocals; her voice is infused by a sense of strength and optimism amid what at the time was a sea of dark grunge bands. The diminutive singer, from country stock and a church-singing background, embodied the kind of trustworthy brightness—with a range from a whisper to a scream—the band needed to move forward. In the words of the *New York Times'* David Thigpen:

> Fans seem mesmerized by the contrast between her waifish look, her powerful voice, and the direct, no-nonsense style she affects on stage—jeans, boots and simple, short, blond hair. In the same way people were taken by Sinead O'Connor's fierce power a few years ago, O'Riordan seems to have grabbed the public's fancy—and the torch from O'Connor—and run with it. (Thigpen 1994)

The Cranberries as a unit—also featuring Mike Hogan on bass, his brother Noel on guitar, and Fergal Lawler on drums—tapped into an audience both at home in Ireland and in the United States that desperately needed hope and possibility in its future. Their refreshing sound—coined "alterna-lite" and described as "quiet storm music for the alternative generation" by *Entertainment Weekly*—bridged the gap between the alternative rock of the late '80s/early '90s like the Smiths, and the melodic, commercial pop of acts like Tori Amos and Toad the Wet Sprocket.

High points followed. In August 1994, the band performed at Woodstock, shortly after they captivated millions with a live performance on *Saturday Night Live*, and to top it off, O'Riordan herself graced the cover of *Rolling Stone*. O'Riordan took some time off to raise a family with her husband, tour manager Don Burton, and then connected once again with albums like 1999's *Bury the Hatchet* and 2001's *Wake Up and Smell the Coffee*.

Aimee Mann

Aimee Mann, formerly of the '80s New Wave band 'Til Tuesday, overcame severe record-company complications as a solo artist in the '90s to become one of the decade's most critically acclaimed singer-songwriters. Her solo debut, *Whatever*, came out in 1993, and its follow-up *I'm with Stupid* hit shelves two years later, but a tangle of corporate red tape—and her own bitter disillusionment—stunted her career. A breakthrough came with her score of the popular Hollywood film *Magnolia*, which was then followed by the predictably acclaimed *Bachelor #2* in 2000. Since that difficult period, Mann has become something of a poster child for all of the talented artists victimized by the faceless corporate structure of the record industry and its bottom-line emphasis, where would-be stars take a backseat to other, more immediate promotional priorities. *Lost in Space* followed in 2002.

EVA CASSIDY

The story of Eva Cassidy is as heartrending as any in the '90s. A singer in the Washington, DC, area, Cassidy had a wonderful instrument in her voice, and a gift for song interpretation that crossed all boundaries of style. Initially, she refrained from recording, in part because record labels were confused as to how to market her—Cassidy adamantly refused to be pigeonholed as a singer—and because she enjoyed the art of performance. In January 1996, she played two gigs at the DC club Blues Alley, which were recorded and released as *Live at Blues Alley*. Despite her dissatisfaction with the performance, the album received great reviews. Sadly, it would be the only album to appear during Cassidy's lifetime.

A melanoma she had removed in 1993 spread to her lungs and bones. Cassidy started chemotherapy in spring of 1996, but it was too late. A benefit show in her honor was staged in September, and Cassidy found the strength to give her last performance there, singing "What a Wonderful World." She died on November 2, 1996. *Eva by Heart*, the album she was working on at the time of her death, was released in 1997.

Virtually all of Cassidy's commercial success has come posthumously. Blix Street Records picked up her material and compiled it in 1998 in an album called *Songbird*. The BBC Radio network in the United Kingdom began playing Eva's version of "Over the Rainbow," and the reception was enormous. Video of Cassidy singing the song surfaced on a British television show, "Top of the Pops." The exposure was monumental in keeping Cassidy's legacy alive. *Songbird* climbed to the top of the British album chart and sold millions worldwide. Since then, two other collections of her material have been released, one sanctioned by her family, *Time After Time*, and one not, *No Boundaries*. In August 2002, a compilation of live recordings, *Imagine*, was also released.

Cassidy's success, years after her death, and something she desperately craved, only on her own terms, proves just how random, serendipitous, even cruel, the music industry can truly be.

Natalie Merchant, Meredith Brooks, Fiona Apple, Alana Davis, and Heather Nova

Natalie Merchant also fronted a band in the '80s, the popular roots pop band 10,000 Maniacs. When Merchant left that band to go solo, she managed to take most of her former band's audience with her, enabling her to enjoy a fulfilling solo career. After several albums and seventeen years on Elektra, a major label—including her well-recognized debut, *Tigerlily* in 1995 and *Motherland* in 2001—Merchant formed her own record company, Myth America, and now disseminates products through the Internet and limited retail channels. Considered a risky career move, so far she has turned her new operation into a worthwhile venture.

Meredith Brooks, Fiona Apple, Alana Davis, and Heather Nova all experienced some degree of success thanks to the doors opened by Crow, Amos, and McLachlan. Meredith Brooks hit it big with her womanpower anthem "Bitch" in 1997. Apple earned a contract with a vulnerable approach to confessional songwriting that many seemed to relate to, and others considered uncomfortable. Her 1996 debut *Tidal* garnered much attention, while her follow-up, the ostentatiously titled *When the Pawn Hits the Conflicts He Thinks Like a King What He Knows Throws the Blows When He Goes to the Fight and He'll Win the Whole Thing 'Fore He Enters the Ring There's No Body to Batter When Your Mind Is Your Might So When You Go Solo, You Hold Your Own Hand and Remember That Depth Is the Greatest of Heights and if You Know Where You Stand, Then You Know Where to Land and if You Fall It Won't Matter, 'Cuz You'll Know That You're Right*, began what would become a barrage of criticism and ridicule, from which the singer has never truly recovered. She was preparing a sequel to her album, eight years in the making, for release in late 2005.

WORLD-BEAT AND JAM BAND INFLUENCES

The Dave Matthews Band

The South African born singer/songwriter named Dave Matthews set a precedent in the early '90s with his unassuming but riveting mix of world-beat stylings (ala Sting and Paul Simon) and the jam band ethos of the Grateful Dead. Matthews, a former bartender, became a constant road warrior, a fixture on the college circuit, and word of mouth spread so quickly that the band became underground heroes even before they self-released their first CD, *Remember Two Things*, in 1993. His grassroots approach to building a fan base was a throwback to the '60s and '70s, when marketing meant going door-to-door recruiting fans, and promotion meant selling CDs after the show.

Matthews and the band ultimately signed with RCA based on their extraordinary self-made success, and the label, after properly reissuing his debut, released *Under the Table and Dreaming* in 1994. The album proved that the band's early success was no fluke, spawning the hit single "What Would You Say" and going on to multiplatinum sales heights. The single also won a Grammy for Best Rock Group Vocal Performance.

Through it all, Dave Matthews has honed his reputation as rock's Regular Joe, an accessible guy with an all-too-human personality; a man who insists that, despite his immense popularity and superstar status and despite the fact that his band was pegged to tour with the Rolling Stones, he is just like everybody else. In an interview with *Guitar* magazine in 1996, Matthews described his biggest source of anxiety.

> "My fear of being seen as a star at least in part ensures that I won't behave that way," says Matthews. "I see it to different degrees in people that I know. Overall, I've managed to keep it away from us as a band. But I'm obsessed, in the same way I'm obsessed with music, with the idea that I'm gonna end up maggot food like everyone else, so any delusions of grandeur are more pathetic than they are realistic." (Gulla 1998)

It is this humility that enables Matthews and his band to reach across genre lines to fans of rock, pop, jazz, jam, folk, and fusion. While his fans idolize him, they can also relate to him, a strange combination for a music celebrity, most of whom are placed on pedestals.

In 1996, the Dave Matthews Band issued *Crash*, an album that debuted at No. 2 on the charts on its way to ringing up multiplatinum sales. Two years later, they released another studio album, *Before These Crowded Streets*, an attempt by the band to capture the improvisatory nature of the group's live set. As a result, it was the band's least commercial effort. Still, it became their first No. 1 album, notching the top slot on *Billboard*'s hit list.

That same year, Matthews released one of his pet projects, an all-acoustic outing with friend and guitarist Tim Reynolds called *Live at Luther College*. In

2001, he reassembled the band for 2001's *Everyday* and the odds and sods collection *Busted Stuff*. He also issued a few official live recordings in an effort to head off bootlegged recordings.

 BOOTLEG RECORDINGS

The Dave Matthews Band's rabid fan base created a market for bootleg recordings (that is, those recordings made illegally, with no authorization from the artist), which Matthews and his management attempted to squelch with assistance from the federal government. Matthews also tried to beat the bootleggers at their own game with the release of 1997's *Live At Red Rocks 8.15.95*, the first in a series of official live albums released on the band's own Bama Rags imprint designed to address the bootleg proliferation problems the band frequently experiences. It went platinum unexpectedly, debuting at number three on the charts and selling a million copies within its first five months.

In his fights against bootleggers, Matthews also targeted stores that were selling semi-legal copies of his live performances. His combative efforts resulted in an unprecedented crackdown of bootlegged material in early 1997—with nearly all of the major foreign bootlegging companies placed under arrest by the United States. This action essentially curbed the entire underground industry.

Like many acts in the Jam Band scene, all of which take their cue from the Grateful Dead, the Dave Matthews Band allows audiotaping at almost every live performance. Bands like the Dead and Phish have enjoyed a proliferation of something called Tape Trading, band-sanctioned activity involving one taper trading a tape of his show to another taper who has a tape of a show he may be missing. Because bands like Phish, the Dead, and Matthews change their set lists and performances nightly, these tapes become eminently collectible. A statement on the band's Web site reads: "We feel that each show is unique and want to offer our fans the opportunity to recreate the live experience through the audio reproduction of our shows."

But that liberty has also been the source of headaches for Matthews and the band. "The proliferation of commercial resale of recordings of our concerts has become a concern to us," the Web site states. "Commercial bootlegs are not only excessively priced and of inferior quality, but primarily, they are an illegal use that threaten the taping privileges of everyone. Due to the efforts of a few unscrupulous tapers the privilege of recording live performances has been jeopardized. Once again we turn to you to assist us with putting a stop to this use of our music" (www.davematthewsband.com).

The once prosperous bootleg industry has since suffered at the hands of Dave Matthews and his band's legal maneuvering. What was once a multimillion dollar industry has now been strangled and left for dead.

JAZZ PLUS

With Dave Matthews smoothing their jam-pop over with some jazz and R&B undertones—courtesy of a fusion-esque violin sound and a saxophone—there arose a school of young bands that also tried their hand at plugging funk, jazz, and R&B into the mix. God Street Wine, the Samples, Big Head Todd, and Blessid Union of Souls all combine the melodicism of alt-pop with the musicianship of the jam bands and the rhythmic tendencies of R&B. This school of rock has frequently been associated with the so-called "jam bands." But these bands, while instrumentally dexterous, keep their tunes honed to a sharp pop edge.

Of this thread of acts, many have developed sizable and loyal audiences, and are able to sustain themselves as touring entities. But few have broken through to the mainstream and remain regional phenomena. Phish, for example, a band referred to in greater detail in Chapter 5, is the best example of a cult band whose success falls just short of commercial. Kindred spirits like God Street Wine and the Samples, also referred to in Chapter 5, dabbled with major labels. It was believed that with the right song a band like this could release a single, hit it big on the radio, while still maintaining their iconic status among jam band fans. This hypothesis, though, has not been successfully proven.

CONTEMPORARY CHRISTIAN MUSIC (CCM)

As a legitimate genre of pop-rock, Contemporary Christian Music (aka Christian Rock or CCM) originated in the mid-'70s as a counterpoint to the perceived hedonistic rock of the period. As a form of religious expression, the focus of CCM remained largely on the music's Christian message. Although there are many Christian music acts in the mainstream music industry, the term CCM today usually refers specifically to artists within the genre that are played excusively on Christian radio.

During its initial decade, the genre existed in a universe parallel to pop's own big world, never crossing over into the popular mainstream, but often including mainstream artists with a spiritual bent, like U2 (occasionally), Bruce Cockburn, and T-Bone Burnett. Then along came an artist named Amy Grant. Already huge with Christian music fans at the time, Grant crossed over to the mainstream in 1985 with the song "Find a Way." A short time later, the pop metal band Stryper (which stands for "Salvation Through Redemption Yielding Peace Encouragement and Righteousness") enjoyed widespread success in the late '80s with albums like *To Hell with the Devil* (1986) and *In God We Trust* (1988). In the '90s, Christian rock music has flared out into a number of narrow subgenres. Today edgy styles like metal, alternative, electronica, and rap, among others, exist in CCM with audiences unto themselves. This splintering is a mirror image of the pop music of today, with audiences and bands becoming ever more specialized and categorized.

Also in the '90s, a handful of record labels like Frontline, Exit, and Refuge popped up to accommodate the flourishing alternative Christian scene. At the outset these artists were ignored by the mainstream CCM industry, with only a few exceptions. Where CCM is often viewed as a tool for ministry—with the music itself taking a backseat to the message—alternative Christian music put music first, with the message remaining buried, or shrouded in metaphor. Bands like dc Talk, Jars of Clay, Sixpence None the Richer, P.O.D., Newsboys, and Audio Adrenaline, made a real impact on mainstream alternative and pop music charts as Christian artists. And they did it so discreetly that fans of many of the bands exposed to their music on mainstream radio barely realized they were hearing the teachings of Christianity.

Jars of Clay specifically set the stage for the breakthrough of many other successful Christian alternative bands, like dc Talk and Sixpence. They did this in part by laying off the preachy or judgmental images of CCM and writing solid rock music. Their breakthrough album, *Jars of Clay*, addressed secular as well as spiritual topics and did so with tact. They toured with some secular bands when the album took off and their single, "Flood" became a radio hit. For a brief span they became one of the mid-'90s' biggest young bands.

There was a bit of a backlash, however, that affected the band from both sides of their audience, a peril for many Christian crossover bands. Christian fans resented their being co-opted by a secular audience, and touring with secular bands—and all the excesses that rock 'n' roll road tripping represents—while radio programmers and CD buyers, initially smitten with the band, felt hoodwinked when they realized there were Christian messages hidden in many of their songs. Presently, many bands of the ilk have settled on straddling both spheres. Jars of Clay, for example, have proven themselves worthy of mainstream radio and sales figures, and remain respected by their core Christian audience.

In the 2000s, sales of all Christian music have continued to soar, with its biggest artists like Amy Grant and Michael W. Smith regularly placing high on the mainstream *Billboard* charts, thanks to their ever-growing audience and a genre that has infused a healthy dose of spirituality into an ordinarily heathen context.

ADULT ALTERNATIVE FOR THE FUTURE

While the style has ebbed considerably since it first emerged in the mid-'90s, adult alternative continues to produce appealing acts. The most notable of those, Norah Jones, has seemingly appeared out of nowhere to become a household word. A key to the sweet-voiced singer's success has been her incredible attraction to an older audience without alienating younger fans. Growing up, Jones, the daughter of legendary sitarist Ravi Shankar, didn't really explore music seriously until she attended Dallas' Booker T. Washington High School for the Performing and Visual Arts. There, she won the *Down Beat* Student Music Awards for Best Jazz Vocalist and Best Original Composition in 1996, and earned a second Best Jazz Vocalist award in 1997. Jones also worked toward earning a degree in jazz piano at the University of North Texas for two years before moving to New York City for the summer. She never made it back to Texas; the lure of the folk coffeehouses and jazz clubs proved too strong and she began composing her own songs.

Her appeal crosses over and back into many genres and to many audiences—largely due to the startlingly simple mélange of styles she presents: blues, folk, pop, jazz, country, roots, and jazzy pop standards. Her debut album *Come Away with Me* was a runaway success in 2002, dominating radio, selling 18 million copies worldwide, and earning eight Grammy awards. In 2004, Jones released *Feels Like Home*, and while her debut was certainly a hard act to follow, and modern audiences have proven fickle, Jones' new album has extended her appeal.

Train, Five for Fighting, and John Mayer, three artists signed to the immensely successful, Sony-affiliated Aware label, all gained attention and success as late entries to the adult alternative genre. Mayer, himself linked romantically to Norah Jones at one time, went from a slashing, Stevie Ray Vaughan–type guitar hero to pop icon in two albums: his debut *Inside Wants Out*, his major-label debut *Room for Squares*, released in 2001, and his 2003 set, *Heavier Things*. Mayer tunes like "Her Body Is a Wonderland," sexily sung with adept guitar work and candid lyrics, struck a chord with radio, traversing several musical demographics, from rock and blues to pop and alternative.

John Ondrasik's Five for Fighting and Train have both enjoyed ongoing success. Ondrasik, essentially a one-man band and a talented singer-songwriter, hit it big following the tragic events of 9/11 when he performed his song "Superman (It's Not Easy)" at a concert for New York City. The subsequent album, *America Town*, went platinum. San Francisco's Train, formed in the early '90s, had time to hone their sound before debuting on Aware with their self-titled debut in 1998. Their breakthrough, *Drops of Jupiter*, followed in 2001, and *My Private Nation* came out in 2003.

7

FESTIVALS

Festivals, as with many other trends and movements in the '90s and beyond, were a continuation, or at least an extension of a precedent, something that came before. The concept of the music festival originated back in the '60s, when pop was still in its adolescence. Events like the Newport Jazz and Folk Festivals began very early on, in the late '50s and early '60s, respectively. The Newport Folk Festival, which still exists today, featured its first amplified act, Bob Dylan, in 1965. The Monterey Pop Festival back in 1967—sporting acts like the Who, Hendrix, and the Rolling Stones—became the first large-scale pop festival, while Woodstock, the mother of all musical gatherings, was not long to follow in the summer of 1969. With its massive attendance (400,000) and political significance, Woodstock, also known as "Three Days of Peace, Love and Understanding," is considered a landmark historical event, eclipsing its musical impact with its far-reaching sociocultural repercussions.

The decade of the '90s had its own versions of Woodstock, quite literally. The first reprisal of the festival took place in August 1994 in Saugerties, New York, and featured thirty bands, including Santana, a veteran of the original Woodstock in 1969; Irish pop stars the Cranberries, Berkeley punks Green Day, and industrial heroes Nine Inch Nails. Temperate behavior ruled, with the exception of a little mud-slinging—a result of rainy weather and soggy conditions.

In July 1999, thirty years after the original Woodstock, festival organizers decided to try it all again. Unfortunately, the third time proved not to be the proverbial charm. The weekend, plagued by steaming hot weather and poor coordination, turned out to be a violent, malevolent reincarnation of what in its

Mud-covered "moshers" (dancers who slam into one another) cavort in front of the stage at the Woodstock '94 festival in Saugerties, New York. © AP/Wide World Photo.

prior incarnations had been a peaceful event. Woodstock III organizers John Scher and Michael Lang had good intentions. "The goal is to create a space where people feel safe, secure, unguarded, open," promoter Lang explained to Dave Samuels of *Harper's* magazine before the event took place. "Somehow in this circumstance people seem able to do that. And to do that you need to feel vulnerable. And the result of feeling that vulnerability is that you come out of the experience feeling less alone" (Samuels 1999).

In fact, just the opposite happened. The extreme heat, high vending prices for food and water, and generally unsanitary conditions created something approaching anarchy among the 200,000-plus in attendance. Inflammatory sets by firestarters like Limp Bizkit, Metallica, and Rage Against the Machine proved to be the permission slip to violence and trouble many riled up concertgoers had been waiting for. They started fires, turned over cars, and engaged in brawls. Incredibly, women were raped. Disorder prevailed. In the words of *Harper's* Samuels, "What happened isn't really that hard to describe. With nothing larger to hold them together, the crowd endured the heat, and the sewage, and the trash, and the drugs until all that was left was the feeling of standing in a tired, dirty crowd of people at the end of the day and knowing that you are alone."

Lollapalooza

In the summer of 1991, Perry Farrell, the frontman of the controversial and successful alternative rock band Jane's Addiction, conceived of a traveling festival, a road show dedicated to alternatives in all musical genres, bands that you wouldn't normally assemble in one place on the same stage. Initially, Farrell envisioned Lollapalooza to be a farewell tour for his band, along with a few special guests. But it blossomed into a genuinely alternative festival where a single audience could enjoy electronica, punk, rock, rap, and metal all in the same day.

Farrell's vision proved prophetic. Lollapalooza turned into Generation X's own Woodstock, and it embraced youth culture from left field, with little corporate intervention. The festival ran successfully in consecutive years through 1997, each time offering entirely different lineups. Unlike previous music festivals, which were ordinarily onetime events held in a single venue, Lollapalooza

The crowd attends A Perfect Circle's performance at Lollapalooza 2003 in California. © Tim Mosenfelder/Getty Images.

was a touring show that brought music to the fans, delivering bi-coastal underground culture to cities that normally had no access to it. Because of this, many more people witnessed the spectacle of Lollapalooza than had been to any previous music festival. It was an important vehicle for disseminating the alternative music of the period and it helped to define not only the music, but the alternative counterculture of the '90s.

Another integral concept behind Lollapalooza was the inclusion of nonmusical features. Performers like the Jim Rose Circus, a modern-day freak show, or the chanting Shaolin Monks defied the limitations of traditional rock shows. There was a tent for display of art pieces, virtual reality games, piercing booths, poetry readings, and political/environmental activism. After 1991, the festival incorporated a second stage (and, in 1996, a third stage) for up-and-coming bands or local acts. It began a sort of cause-and-effect for alternative music. As underground bands broke through to the mainstream, they drew listeners to Lollapalooza, who would then see the next generation of underground bands on the second stage. Many of the bands that played second stage at Lollapalooza later enjoyed more widespread commercial success. Was it because of their exposure at Lollapalooza, or because the timing was right for those particular acts? It is indeed hard to say, but Farrell and his organization proved prescient in selecting acts to play their festival's stages.

When grunge music broke through to the mainstream in 1992 and 1993, the timing couldn't have been better for Lollapalooza. Festival organizers used Seattle bands like Alice in Chains and Soundgarden as the marquee acts to draw popular audiences. The aggressive music helped to make exclusively punk rock club activities like moshing (or "slam-dancing") and crowd-surfing more mainstream pursuits.

The year 1994 was another turning point for Lollapalooza, and a year of tragedy for rock music. Nirvana, the Seattle band appointed to headline that summer's show, canceled when their leader Kurt Cobain committed suicide. Cobain's widow Courtney Love made surprise guest appearances at several shows, speaking to the crowds about the loss.

At the time, Farrell was also beginning to lose his conviction in the tour. A rise in accidents at the shows demoralized him, as did the growing violence. Poor organization helped break down the sense of community that made the festival special. When Farrell pulled out (to create another festival, the ill-fated ENIT) the festival lost its way further. Ideas and musical genres that had been edgy and risque at the beginning of the 1990s had now become fully absorbed into the mainstream or even outdated. Alternative music was beginning to lose its way as well. By 1997, the Lollapalooza concept faltered, and in 1998, the effort to find a headliner turned up no willing and able participant. The tour called it quits.

A few years later, in 2003, Farrell wanted to announce the reunion of his band Jane's Addiction, and he scheduled a new tour, a Lollapalooza, in fact, to announce it. And while he had some problems rekindling the fire that had once stoked young rock fans to attend back in the early '90s—some dates had to be canceled for lack of interest—it did reasonably well in many markets. It grossed almost $14 million from twenty-five shows.

In 2004, the ninth installment of Lollapalooza, however, met with a very different fate. The show, which booked Morrissey, the Flaming Lips, the String Cheese Incident, Modest Mouse, and Polyphonic Spree to play the main stage, had to cancel its entire tour due to abysmal advance ticket sales. Pundits point to the fact that the economy was still ailing and ticket sales for all of the summer's major concerts were extremely soft. Concertgoers had little disposable income to attend shows, and many opted to spend their money on the metal tour, Ozzfest. In addition, alternative music was in the process of redefining itself and hadn't really settled on any particular style or image. It still hasn't. Tour organizers and concert promoters, faced with several million dollars worth of losses and an uphill climb to jumpstart ticket sales, made the decision to pull the tour.

LOLLAPALOOZA'S ARTISTS

Here's a listing of artists that appeared on the stages of Perry Farrell's alternative rock road show from the years 1991 to 2003.

Lollapalooza 1

Began July 18, 1991

Jane's Addiction, Siouxsie and the Banshees, Living Color, Nine Inch Nails, Fishbone, Violent Femmes, Ice-T/Body Count, Butthole Surfers, Rollins Band. No side stage.

Lollapalooza 2

Began July 18, 1992

MAIN: The Red Hot Chili Peppers, Ministry, Ice Cube, Soundgarden, the Jesus and Mary Chain, Pearl Jam, Lush, Temple of the Dog.

SIDE STAGE ARTISTS: Jim Rose Circus, the Cows, Sharkbait, Archie Bell.

Lollapalooza 3

Began June 19, 1993

MAIN: Primus, Alice in Chains, Dinosaur Jr., Fishbone, Arrested Development, Front 242, Babes in Toyland, Tool, Rage Against the Machine.

SIDE STAGE ARTISTS: The Runties, Sebadoh, Cell, Unrest, Tool, Mercury Rev, Mosquito, Free Kitten, Royal Trux, Tsunami, Mutabaruka, A Lighter Shade of Brown, the Coctails.

Lollapalooza 4

Began July 7, 1994

MAIN: Smashing Pumpkins, the Beastie Boys, George Clinton and the P-Funk All Stars, the Breeders, A Tribe Called Quest, Nick Cave and the Bad Seeds, L7, Boredoms, Green Day.

SIDE STAGE ARTISTS: The Flaming Lips, the Verve, the Boo Radleys, the Frogs, Guided by Voices, Lambchop, Girls Against Boys, Rollerskate Skinny, Palace Songs, Stereolab, FU-Schnickens, the Pharcyde, Shudder to Think, Luscious Jackson, King Kong, Charlie Hunter Trio, Shonen Knife, Blast Off Country Style, Souls of Mischief, Smashing Pumpkins, Green Day, Cypress Hill, Black Crowes, L7.

Lollapalooza 5

Began July 4, 1995

MAIN: Sonic Youth, Hole, Cypress Hill, Pavement, Sinead O'Connor, Elastica, Moby, Superchunk, Beck, Jesus Lizard, the Mighty Mighty Bosstones.

LOLLAPALOOZA'S ARTISTS *(continued)*

SIDE STAGE ARTISTS: Coolio, Doo Rag, Possum Dixon, Poster Children, Yo La Tengo, Brainiac, the Coctails, the Geraldine Fibbers, Moby, the Dambuilders, Laika, the Pharcyde, Tuscadero, Superchunk, Built to Spill, Helium, Redman, St. Johnny, Dirty Three, Mike Watt, Versus, Hum, Blonde Redhead, the Roots, Blowhole, the Zeros, Pork Queen, Thomas Jefferson Slave Apartments, Sabalon Glitz, Psychotica, Patti Smith Group, the Mighty Mighty Bosstones, Beck, Pavement, Gary Young, Overpass, Jesus Lizard.

Lollapalooza 6

Began June 27, 1996

MAIN: Metallica, Soundgarden, Cocteau Twins, Waylon Jennings, Rage Against the Machine, Cheap Trick, Violent Femmes, Wu Tang Clan, Steve Earle, Devo, Ramones, Rancid, ShaoLin Monks/Kung Fu of China, Screaming Trees, Psychotica.

SIDE STAGE ARTISTS: Beth Hart Band, Girls Against Boys, Ben Folds Five, Ruby, Cornershop, You Am I, Soul Coughing, Sponge, the Melvins, Satchel, Jonny Polonsky, Fireside, Chune, Moonshake, Lutefisk, Capsize 7, ShaoLin Monks, the Cows, Long Fin Killie, Thirty Ought Six, Varnaline, Crumb.

Lollapalooza 7

Began June 25, 1997

MAIN: Orbital, Devo, Prodigy, the Orb, Tool, Snoop Dogg, Tricky, Korn, James, Julian and Damian Marley and the Uprising Band, Eels, Failure.

SIDE STAGE ARTISTS: Eels, Summercamp, Artificial Joy Club, Jeremy Toback, Radish, Old 97's, Inch, Porno for Pyros, Failure, the Pugs, Lost Boyz, Agnes Gooch, Demolition Dollrods, Skeleton Key, Molly McGuire, Orbit.

Lollapalooza 8

Began July 3, 2003

MAIN: Jane's Addiction, Queens of the Stoneage, the Donnas, A Perfect Circle, Incubus, Audioslave.

SIDE STAGE ARTISTS: The Distillers, Rooney, Jurassic 5.

LILITH FAIR

In the mid-'90s, women had at last begun making appearances on the rock and pop charts. Up until that point, rock bands and men had dominated radio and retail with hair metal and grunge movements putting loud, masculine music front and center. But the winds began to shift after the death of Kurt

Cobain in 1994. Music quieted, perhaps in deference to Cobain's death,
and women's voices came to be heard.
At the forefront of that movement
arose names like Tori Amos, Liz Phair,
Sheryl Crow, Alanis Morissette,
Fiona Apple, and Aimee Mann. Suddenly, and perhaps for the first time
ever, women were driving the music
industry. Macho rock music had taken
a backseat, if only momentarily, and
women in music were poised to take
over the controls.

One interesting aspect of this
transfer of power was that it gave
women the spotlight and the opportunity to break down stereotypes. Until
this time, women were either angry
Riot Grrrls, sappy girl groups, or
overly sensitive singer-songwriters

Sarah McLachlan, right, joins Heather Nova for the last song of
Nova's set during Lilith '98 at Jones Beach, New York, Wednesday,
July 15, 1998. © AP/Wide World Photo.

that appealed to niche audiences. The crop of talent that surfaced in the mid-
'90s were essentially all, and none, of the above. Artists like Jewel and Alanis
and Sheryl were pop, rock, and folksingers who blurred the traditional lines between men and women. Sheryl Crow's 1993 effort, *Tuesday Night Music Club*,
started things off, selling steadily for almost two years. Alanis Morissette's 1995
album, *Jagged Little Pill*, an outspoken, confessional, alternative rock album,
took the music world by storm in the summer of that year, ultimately winning
four Grammys and selling millions and millions of albums worldwide. Jewel's
debut, *Pieces of You*, was originally released in 1994, but didn't catch fire until
almost two years later, eventually selling 10 million copies internationally.
Women were indeed winning the musical battle of the sexes.

The incredible success of these women paved the way for still another success story: Lilith Fair. The brainchild of Sarah McLachlan, Lilith Fair was conceived as a vibrant meeting place for fans of women in music, an outlet that
gave a host of emerging female singer-songwriters room to showcase their talents. Women were being embraced as never before by radio stations, record
labels, and the broader pop industry and Lilith Fair gave them a significant
platform.

In 1996, the Fair began with a small handful of dates to test the receptivity
of such a novel idea. When it succeeded, the tour expanded to a full complement of summer dates in 1997 and following suit the next two years. Founder
Sarah McLachlan was the toast of fans and media alike for assembling artist
bills which deemphasized ego and posturing, inserting instead a bevy of tragically overlooked talent. In spite of the festival's success, it still was met with

criticism. Ardent feminists didn't think McLachlan's Fair was feminist enough while some in the mainstream media thought it was too exclusive. For McLachlan, though, who found herself unwittingly at the center of the controversy, Lilith wasn't about excluding men or making a statement; it was about giving a multitude of talented female musicians an opportunity to play their music for thousands of fans. The tour was also set up to raise significant funds for a variety of women's charities.

When McLachlan decided not to book the festival following the summer of 1999—to focus on raising her first child—the current of popular music had already begun to move away from the women-in-rock concept. Hip-hop, teen-beat, and nü-metal—all genres with firm viewpoints and dominant personalities—began to eclipse feminism and feminine perspective in rock music. Soft voices with soft messages were drowned out by harder sounds, louder beats, and sexual glossiness. Four years after Lilith and the like were touted as one of the biggest happenings in the music business in the '90s, the phenomenon that prompted many to proclaim one or several of the years around the mid-'90s "The Year of the Woman," almost completely disappeared.

Without a stage from which to sing, Lilith artists, who enjoyed their fifteen minutes of fame, foundered. With Sarah McLachlan's seal of approval now a nonfactor and the cries of Girl Power Now! only echoes in the distance, many of the artists who benefited drifted away from the scene. A few—like folk-poet Jewel and indie queen Liz Phair—redefined themselves in more sexually charged, pop-minded directions. Others, however, have had great trouble reviving their careers.

H.O.R.D.E.

The Horizons of Rock Developing Everywhere tour, or H.O.R.D.E. Festival, began in 1992 as a showcase for bands that excelled playing live but who also wanted to avoid playing the summertime club circuit. Conceived by Blues Traveler frontman John Popper and colleague David Frey, the festival, which rallied annually during the summer through 1998, also served to assemble like-minded "jam" bands that appealed to an audience big enough to sell out amphitheaters.

Inspired by the previous summer's success of Perry Farrell's Lollapalooza Festival, Popper and Frey called upon their compatriots in Widespread Panic, the Spin Doctors, Aquarium Rescue Unit, and Phish—all "neo-hippie" jam rock bands with a penchant for free-form improvisation. Together, their fan bases and musical styles were similar, as was their attitude and approach to music. What originally separated this festival from many similar events was the bands' approach to playing live. Popper, an improvisational musician at heart, encouraged band members to sit in with other bands, as he often did, to inspire the cross-pollination of sounds and styles. In fact, Popper himself made it a point to sit in with every band on the main stage. Unlike many modern rock shows, where tightly orchestrated performances ruled, H.O.R.D.E. promoted jamming and collaboration, moments in which musical ability could stand out. The vibe itself at these shows was different, almost Dead-like, where fans were encouraged to record shows and tie-dye fashions were the order of the day.

Also, unlike other multi-hour festivals, H.O.R.D.E. never pitted the main stage acts directly against second-stage bands. With careful scheduling, a band finished on the main stage, and just minutes later, tunes cranked up on the second stage. As the second-stage act finished, the next main stage band kicked into gear. The spirit of H.O.R.D.E. relied on this brotherhood and fans never had to make a choice on which act they could miss.

The first year saw the festival, in which the traveling caravan stopped in eight venues, barely breaking even financially. But for everyone involved, the experience proved valuable; all but one band on the bill would continue to play a role in H.O.R.D.E. in future installments. Over the years, the tour grew from these humble beginnings into a forty-date mega-show, a big-dollar revenue generator with top-notch acts. In 1994, the Allman Brothers headlined and up-and-comers the Dave Matthews Band held a supporting slot. In 1995, Atlanta's Black Crowes headlined. That year, the festival was marred by an anti-drug protest in Stanhope, New Jersey. Officials there cited the Crowes and other bands on the tour's presence on a new collection titled *Hempilation*, a CD whose proceeds were funneled to the cause of legalizing marijuana.

The year 1996 proved to be the festival's best year. It emerged from the shadows of the other traveling festivals, including Lollapalooza and Ozzfest, to become a legitimate draw with superstar appeal. Lenny Kravitz, Blues Traveler, and Rusted Root all nailed down the main stage for the entire forty-date, twenty-six-city tour. Neil Young, who made a single, surprise appearance on this tour, would go on to headline H.O.R.D.E. in 1997, along with Leftover Salmon, and pop sensations Toad the Wet Sprocket.

That year, H.O.R.D.E. began to weaken. Widespread Panic, one of the bands that helped establish the tour's aesthetic, was given a second-stage slot rather than one on the main stage, so it pulled out, apparently in protest. In fact, there was an overall undercurrent of dissatisfaction with the bookings this year. Non-jam-type bands like Beck, Primus, and the Mighty Mighty Bosstones were all on the bill in 1997, and none brought with them the kind of instrumental approach most appreciated by the tour's loyalists.

The same happened in 1998, the tour's swan song. Canada's pop-rock stars Barenaked Ladies, the headliner, came as a controversial choice. They didn't fit the mold, certainly, and didn't even have the same popularity among American rock fans as they did at home. At the last show on September 5, 1998, John Popper upheld a long-standing tradition of sitting in with every band, amounting to seven hours of running around playing harmonica. With the last stop in Oregon the curtain fell on H.O.R.D.E. for the last time.

BONNAROO

Taking place on a 530-acre farm sixty miles southeast of Nashville, Bonnaroo, a three-day event named after Dr. John's 1974 album *Desitively Bonnaroo*, has established itself as the heir apparent to H.O.R.D.E. While it is a one-weekend-only event annually, ala Woodstock, it is the mecca, a required pilgrimage, for fans of jam-oriented, hippie-vibe music.

Building upon the experiences of smaller, regional, multistage summer festivals like the Gathering of the Vibes and Berkfest, Bonnaroo for the weekend becomes a small city in itself, offering music on two stages and in two tents, a variety of food vending, an amusement area, ample facilities, and a general store for last-minute needs.

The first year, 2002, the festival was attended by 70,000 fans, and with good reason. Bonnaroo featured H.O.R.D.E. alums Widespread Panic, Primus' Les Claypool, Phish's Trey Anastasio, jam faves .moe, and soulful, college-rock icon Ben Harper. A total of fifty bands played the summer's most successful festival. The next year, festival organizers, encouraged by their success, attempted to add a second Bonnaroo to their annual slate, this time called Bonnaroo NE, meaning Northeast. But venue complications arose at their Long Island destination and plans were scrapped. The Tennessee date, however, went off successfully, with performances by jam bands of all stripes, including James Brown, Sonic Youth, Nickel Creek, and two staples of the genre, the Dead and Neil Young and Crazy Horse.

Bonnaroo 2004 and 2005 continued its ambitious booking policy, embracing the likes of Bob Dylan, the Dead, Dave Matthews, Willie Nelson, and former alt.country favorites, Wilco. The event continues to grow, attracting over 90,000 fans despite the hot summer sun of Tennessee.

Dan Marsala, lead singer of Story of the Year, is held up by fans during a performance, Saturday, June 26, 2004, in Dallas. The band joined several others during the Dallas stop of the 2004 Vans Warped tour. © AP/Wide World Photo.

WARPED TOUR

With two stages and a party pack of upwards of twenty bands, the Vans Warped Tour is the longest-running of the summer festival concepts. As a less pretentious and less pricey alternative to tours like Ozzfest and Lollapalooza, the Warped, which celebrated its tenth year in the summer of 2004, has shown some real staying power. Sponsored by Vans, a skateboarding/casual shoe company, the festival has always leaned toward the kind of music skateboarders would listen to while practicing Ollies on the halfpipe: punk rock and all its permutations. It is, in fact, an annual mosaic, a frontline report, on the state of punk rock music.

The festival combines high-decibel tunes with the pursuit of "X-Game" type sports (aka Extreme Sports)—BMX, skateboarding, rock climbing, and motocross stunts. Similar to Lollapalooza, the Warped Tour also features a village of sorts, with shops and activist tents where concertgoers can learn about non-profit organizations and political causes.

The tour's low ticket prices guarantee a diverse and sizable audience, and its interest in punk rock—long a bastion of the underground underdogs—fosters a warm, communal spirit. Contributing to that spirit, many of the bands who play the festival, some as young as the fans, have a booth or some sort of station set up to sell merchandise, sign autographs, and chat with fans. The ploy works, bringing fans and musicians together more closely, cultivating a deep feeling of identification going in both directions, selling tickets, and, ultimately, selling records as well.

The first Warped Tour took place in 1995. It featured bands like girl rockers L7, edgy urban punks Quicksand, West Coast thrashers Orange 9mm, and ska-punkers Sublime. This variety within the punk idiom would come to characterize the festival's booking policy right up through the present day.

Since its early origins, punk rock has grown from an underground, cult-audience phenomenon to a fully realized commercial musical style. Warped Tour vets like Green Day, the Used, blink-182, have all since gone on to become full-fledged superstars, as punk rock music, commercial radio, and market expectations have grown more aligned than ever. In fact, punk has become one of the recording industry's most reliable subgenres. The Warped Tour has both contributed to and benefited from that reliability. The 2004 version of the Warped Tour was the most successful installment yet, selling over 650,000 tickets, a 30 percent increase over the past year's sales.

OZZFEST

One of the more bizarre success stories in the '90s was the incredible resurgence of Ozzy Osbourne. The former lead singer of influential metal act Black Sabbath resurrected his career first in the '80s, courtesy of the courageous guitar innovations of Randy Rhoads, who died in 1983, then again in the '90s, after reinventing himself through Ozzfest, a heavy metal festival.

Ozzfest originated in the mid-'90s and began officially in 1996. Osbourne, spurned by the organizers of Lollapalooza who labeled him "not cool enough," decided to assemble his own metal concert bill in order to compete. With the help of his manager/wife Sharon, a woman named, incidentally, by *Entertainment Weekly* as one of the most powerful in show business, Ozzfest grew enough to become a force on the summer concert scene. The metal barrage came at the perfect time. Popular music had emerged from grunge and the Lilith Fair sound

THE OSBOURNES

Billed as the first reality sitcom, MTV's *The Osbournes* stars Ozzy's family—wife Sharon, daughter Kelly, son Jack, and one daughter that opted out of the filmed proceedings—in what must be one of the most dysfunctional families in the history of television.

Each episode depicts scenes from the real life of a typical middle-aged heavy-metal multimillionaire. It's clear that years of drinking, drug use, and other repercussions of rock stardom have taken a serious toll on Ozzy. His speech is slurred despite being sober, his movements shaky due to nerve damage, and his body remarkably weak. Combine that with a shopaholic wife (who actually keeps the family together), his rebellious teen offspring—Jack has a fondness for bayonettes and other military paraphernalia, Kelly is a sassy, tattooed, pink-haired, marginally talented pop star—and a menagerie of untrained dogs in an expensive home, and you've got all the elements in place to create utter domestic chaos. The show, miles away from the lives of normal Americans, is laced with profanity to the nth degree, one of the sources of the show's humor.

Still, the show won its first Emmy in 2001 for "Best Reality Series," also called the "Outstanding Non-Fiction Program." In 2002, the show was renewed by the music network for a second and third season at a steep price tag of $20 million. Many say the Osbourne family's net worth is now more than double that. *The Osbournes* has served to catapult Ozzy back into superstardom for the third time. Tickets are moving each summer to his immensely successful summer metal fest and his back catalog, both in Black Sabbath and as a solo artist, are now selling again as well.

with a vengeance. Bands like Limp Bizkit, Korn, Rage Against the Machine, and Deftones were overthrowing the gentler rock acts already on the radio with an aggressive noise of their own, and Ozzfest was there to take advantage.

That first year, fueled by a lineup that included metal stalwarts Slayer, Danzig, Biohazard, Fear Factory, and Sepultura, along with a headlining performance by Ozzy himself, the tour got off to a fast start, despite the fact that Osbourne had to cut many shows on the tour short or cancel them entirely due to illness. Still, the tour was one of the most consistently successful that summer, and by 2001 the Ozzfest caravan had wooed national sponsors, pushing revenues to over $24 million yearly.

In 1997, Ozzfest drove traffic with a Black Sabbath reunion. The first year featured Ozzy singing, with Tony Iommi on guitar, Geezer Butler on bass, and Faith No More's Mike Bordin on drums. Original Sabbath drummer Bill Ward sat out the reunion due to ill health. But in 1999, another lineup that starred Sabbath as headliners, Ward joined the band, making the reunion of Sabbath's original lineup complete.

Of course, given the idiosyncratic and outspoken personalities involved, with Ozzie and wife Sharon particularly, Ozzfest was, and still is, prone to controversy. In 1997, the New Jersey Sport and Exposition Authority announced it would stop ticket sales and cancel Ozzfest at the Meadowlands venue unless rabble-rousing glam-metal icons Marilyn Manson were removed from the bill. Lawsuits were filed on behalf of Marilyn Manson, Ozzy Osbourne, and the promoters. After the NJSEA failed to show cause, a judge ruled the case to be groundless and Manson performed. There were also drug problems. Sharon contracted cancer, Ozzy's ex-bandmates sued him for back royalties, the couple's son Jack entered rehab, bands were tossed off the Ozzfest bill due to unacceptable behavior, and the list goes on. Ironically, it was these types of controversies that kept Ozzie, Sharon, and Ozzfest in the news and the tickets selling. That, and a spectacularly popular television reality show that aired on MTV, called *The Osbournes*.

COACHELLA

Presented by Goldenvoice Concerts, the Coachella Valley Music and Arts Festival in Indio, California, has become an important festival on the rock music circuit. In its fifth year, the 2005 lineup includes more than eighty groups, including Coldplay, Nine Inch Nails, Weezer, Wilco, the Chemical Brothers; the 2004 festival included Radiohead, the Cure, and the reunited Pixies.

8

GARAGE ROCK REVISITED

In the wake of the British invasion of the early '60s, countless American teens were inspired to pick up their guitars. Acts like the Beatles, the Stones, and the Kinks brought a brash rock 'n' roll sound to radios across America, and its effect energized the country's youth. But where the youth of Britain had nurtured their ability to play their instruments before bursting onto the scene, the Americans chose to forego any sort of formal training in favor of picking up an instrument and simply bashing away. After all, why kill the joy with learning when you can start making records with that exuberance immediately? Because of this relative spontaneity, the musicians were considerably cruder, less sophisticated, and lacking in basic songwriting skills of the bands of the time. And so it was that young, aspiring musicians nationwide began picking up guitars and experimenting, and the original wave of garage rock came to be.

Many of the genre's early purveyors were from California and Texas, not only because there were large pockets of progressive populations in the urban centers of those states, but simply because they had climates warm enough, temperatures conducive to spending long hours rehearsing in unheated garages. For a time in the mid- to late '60s, the popular rock formula featured the hallmarks of the movement: fuzzed out guitar, Farfisa organ, and sneering vocals.

The movement rose and fell fairly quickly, even more quickly than some of the fleeting trends of the '90s. Experts attribute the downfall to a variety of factors: college, the military draft, lack of success, the hard rock of bands like Cream and Led Zeppelin, not to mention the advent of drugs leading to psychedelic music. That said, the movement never truly died; rather, it was forced underground. Bands like the MC5 and the Stooges perpetuated the ethic in the early '70s, until punk rock, an offshoot of garage rock, took firm hold in the mid- to late '70s.

In the '80s, the genre rose up again in something of a revival—fueled in part by a resurgence of reissues of the original garage albums. This time the garage sound, not particularly authentic, came with a nod to punk in the music of entertaining and well-meaning bands like the Lyres, Fleshtones, the Chesterfield Kings, the Miracle Workers, and the Fuzztones. During that time, regional labels like Ace of Hearts, Bomp, Norton, Estrus, and Sympathy for the Record Industry began marketing regionally, and managed to develop a cult following for the style.

This time, too, the revival failed to break through to the mainstream, or register much in what was then a healthy underground, or college scene. Perhaps the problem was that where the original '60s bands imitated the bands of the British Invasion like the Stones and the Kinks, the revival bands imitated the '60s originators—right down to the specific instrumentation and production—resulting in an imitation of an imitation, and a significantly less original sound. Even so, well before it had the chance, indie rock and then grunge in the early '90s made certain the garage rock revival of the '80s would forever be a mere footnote in modern pop history.

NEO-GARAGE IN THE '90s

But then something happened in the '90s. After deriving inspiration from the Seattle scene and the Britpop movement in Britain—both highly influential movements for musicians—another wave of garage rock began to take shape. In the early '90s, the dawn of the commercial alternative era, many young music fans were inspired by the accessibility and raw noise that popular acts like the Flaming Lips, the Pixies, Nirvana, and Mudhoney served up. The musically inclined among them ushered in a movement similar to the garage-rock acts of the '60s and '80s: primitive musicians with a plethora of ideas and lots of energy, willing to do whatever it took to turn a dream of a career in music into a reality. Like their figurative "ancestors" in the '60s, many began in garage-type environs.

These musicians, like the best punk and post-punk artists, attempted to strip the existing music down to its basic elements, a framework, and then, piece by piece, reconstruct it in its own primitive image. Some see the new wave of basic garage rock as a reaction to the overcommercialization of popular music, a phenomenon that cropped up in the wake of grunge, courtesy of bands like Matchbox 20, Third Eye Blind, and Hootie and the Blowfish. "Whenever things get a little too slick and professional, the pendulum swings back to a more accessible way of making music," Lenny Kaye says in a 1998 interview with the *Detroit News*. A well-known rock journalist and guitarist for the Patti Smith Group, Kaye compiled the 1972 garage collection *Nuggets*, a set which helped popularize the garage-rock genre posthumously.

Unlike the uniform sound and consistent set of parameters offered by the garage sound of the past, today's new take on garage melds many different rock styles and configurations. Anything that doesn't look or sound too overproduced qualifies, whether it's the intense, two-person dynamic of the White

Stripes and the Black Keys or the classic, post-AC/DC sound of Jet. In this age of so-called garage rock, anything goes.

THE HIVES AND THE SWEDISH INVASION

Back in 1993, a Swedish band called the Hives introduced their version of the standard garage sound. It featured a throttling primitivism, cheeky attitude, and vintage contrivances (including dapper '60s uniforms), recalling '60s bands like the Wailers and the Sonics. The impact that the Hives made in northern Europe was massive, and gave rise to a regional rock 'n' roll revival in that musically progressive area of the world. The Hives' five members go by stage names: Howlin' Pelle Almqvist, Vigilante Carlstroem, Nicolaus Arson, guitar, Chris Dangerous, and Dr. Matt Destruction. Equipped with a faux-haughty attitude, the band dresses nattily in matching black shirts and trousers with white ties and shoes.

Signed to a subsidiary of the Stockholm-based Burning Heart label, the quintet made their full-length recording debut in 1997 with *Barely Legal*. A reputation for entertaining live performances fueled the Hives' growing cache among hipsters, but it wasn't until *Veni Vidi Vicious* in 2001 that the band made their worldwide breakthrough. The album's winning combination of melody, gritty/silly attitude, and primal rock grooves led the band to be hailed as the best of the new garage-rock revival. A follow-up in 2004, *Tyrannosaurus Hives*, solidified that impression.

Other Swedish bands followed suit, either alongside or slightly behind the Hives, including early purveyors the Hellacopters, who signed with grunge

The Hives performing on *The Tonight Show with Jay Leno*, 2003. Courtesy of Photofest.

imprint Sub Pop, the Ramones-inspired Sahara Hotnights, featuring an all-girl frontline, Division of Laura Lee, and the International Noise Conspiracy, led by Dennis Lyxzen, the former frontman for Sweden's notorious punk band Refused. Some called it the "Swedish invasion," which is appropriate, though bands from elsewhere in Scandinavia, like Finland's the Flaming Sideburns (a band the Hives credit as being an inspiration to them), also deserve mention.

All of this success has helped the great northern pacifist countries earn musical comparisons to the world's two leading pop nations: the United States and the United Kingdom. "It is widely reported, both inside and outside our borders," reads the introduction to Sweden's own national Web site, "that little Sweden is the world's third largest music-exporting nation, 'beaten' only by the two superpowers" (Sweden).

Of course, it's doubtful whether the Hives or any one of these new bands will achieve the kind of enduring success experienced by Sweden's own pop legends Abba. But, in their own way, this wave has the potential to affect rock music for years to come, as young and ambitious upstarts attempt to capture the magic of this music in new bands of their own.

STATESIDE

In the States, many bands, coincidentally or not, began popping up concurrently, all vying for the mantle of garage-rock royalty (revisited). In fact, a minor wave of garage bands have buoyed each other with concurrent success and unexpected hit albums. In addition to the Hives, groups like the White Stripes, the Vines, and the Strokes have all made an impact seemingly simultaneously, prompting many to herald a new trend, affectionately referred to as the "The" bands.

The White Stripes

In 1997, Jack and Meg White, a Detroit couple alternately assumed to be husband and ex-wife or brother and sister, came together as a bass-less duet, with Meg (b. Megan Martha White) on drums and Jack (b. John Anthony Gillis) on guitar and vocals. One of a new breed of back-to-basics rock acts to emerge from the city, Jack and Meg were obsessed with turning the music of the Motor City, and rock 'n' roll in general back to its roots. "We have to go back," Jack said, in an online interview. "Digital recording, computers, and all that junk—I think that destroys the creativity of a lot of musicians. It takes the soul out of music" (www.insideoc.com).

Jack, who had previously played guitar in a garage-rock band called the Go and sung for a country band called Goober and the Peas, uses garage rock as a launching point for the Stripes, but delves into folk blues, country, '60s pop, and Broadway show tunes without hesitation. Their striking stage presence, characterized by minimalist red-and-white outfits, reflects in a way their minimalist attitude toward rock music. The band's self-titled debut, which mixed covers (Robert Johnson's "Stop Breaking Down Blues" and Bob Dylan's "One More Cup Of Coffee") with some originals, earned significant praise, and by the time they issued *De Stijl*, their follow-up—named after a Dutch abstract art movement—the media buzz was deafening. Of particular note was the welcome the duo received at the hands of the UK press. The influential music personality John Peel was quoted as comparing their importance to that of Jimi Hendrix and the Sex Pistols.

Peel proved to be correct, at least partially. *White Blood Cells*, their album of 2001, sold over 500,000 copies, bolstered by the single "Fell in Love with a Girl," a song and video that made impact on radio and music television. The band's follow-up, *Elephant*, was made at London's tiny Toe Rag Studios, a recording venue known for using vintage analogue equipment and only eight tracks. The album offered overdue relief from the numbing digital sound of music in the new millennium and was issued to nearly unanimous critical acclaim. It also charted as high as No. 6 on the *Billboard* albums chart and has sold nearly 2 million copies. *Get Behind Me Satan*, released in the summer of 2005, continues the Stripes' impressive run. The White Stripes' presence has not only reenergized the national rock scene, it has also jumpstarted, or at least shone a brighter light on their hometown scene of Detroit.

The White Stripes: Meg White and Jack White, 2003. Courtesy of Photofest.

According to Little Steven Van Zant, the White Stripes bring romance and mystery to an indie underground bereft of those elements. The originator of the nationally syndicated radio show, "Little Steven's Underground Garage," a program that focuses on the garage rock of the past, present, and future, Van Zant has become something of an aficionado in this area.

"First, all art needs an element of mystery to be most effective," he writes on his Web site.

> It needs to be something that cannot be completely explained or understood. And second, people need artists and performers to do the job they are paying them to do. To be in touch with some part of themselves that the average person can't easily access. That access allows the artist and performer to communicate, motivate, inspire, make some sense out of life, or at least help one make it through it. That gift is most effectively communicated by a look and attitude that an audience member may aspire to, or may be satisfied to live vicariously through, but for whatever reason cannot achieve on their own. (Little Steven's Underground Garage)

THE MOTOR CITY SCENE OF THE '90s

Detroit has since the '60s played a major role—much larger than its proportions—in the development of rock 'n' roll. Early on, garage punks like the MC5 and the Stooges helped the metropolis establish its punky foundation, while personalities like Alice Cooper, Ted Nugent, and George Clinton, Commander Cody; and later, the White Stripes, the Gories, the Hentchmen, and so on, have since spent some time atop the city's very eclectic, very rebellious—and very rowdy—rock 'n' roll throne.

The Cass Corridor is a strip of urban turf located between downtown Detroit and Wayne State University. Essentially a slum, this is the dead-end alley where Detroit's garage-rock phenomenon has come to life. Unsurprisingly, most of the city's bands are grimy, no-nonsense garage punks, a product of their tough upbringing and gritty environs.

The White Stripes are the most visible band in the Detroit garage-rock scene, which is a sizable cabal of acquaintances who bonded together largely based on their absolute dedication to great rock music. In fact, Detroit is full of underproduced rock bands all wearing a path on the same bar circuit. (Many of these bands are on the Sympathetic Sounds of Detroit compilation, a collection of Motor City bands Jack White recorded in his living room.) There are the Von Bondies, a sloppy, MC5-ish rave-up quartet and the Detroit Cobras, two of the hottest new acts to emerge. The Come Ons play trad '60s-ish pop. The Dirtbombs bridge the gap between glam, Motown, and sludgy blues-rock. Few of these bands have the kind of cultivation necessary to bring their crazed garage aesthetics and aural damage to the mainstream. Of course, with most garage rock, that's not the point.

The Strokes

Formed in New York City in 1999, the Strokes were, almost immediately, hailed as the next big thing by the city's press corps, a bunch, incidentally, not prone to overstatement. By the end of the next year, the Strokes fulfilled that prophecy in rock circles, and were being hyped as the most important rock band of the new millennium, young as it was.

Julian Casablancas (vocals), Nick Valensi (guitar), and Fabrizio Moretti (drums) first began playing together at a prep-school in Manhattan. Film school student Albert Hammond Jr. (guitar), the son of singer-songwriter Albert Hammond, and Nikolai Fraiture (bass) completed the lineup. All five members enrolled in college, but soon succumbed to the elusive promise of rock stardom.

The quintet debuted onstage in September 1999, and quickly built a reputation on the city's East Side club scene. The band's demo was picked up by the Rough Trade label and released in January 2001 as a three-song EP called *The Modern Age*. A major-label bidding war ensued, with the RCA label earning the right to release the band's major-label bow. That album, *Is This It*, was received enthusiastically by the music press in both the United States and Britain; critics stumbled over themselves to find the proper hyperbole with which to describe them. To refer to them as "critics' darlings" would be an understatement.

An early gig in the UK city of Leeds prompted a UK reviewer for *New Musical Express* (*NME*) to offer: "By the time 'Take It or Leave It' rolls around, it's a shoo-in for rock 'n' roll gig of the year. There is, of course, no encore (five Yanks . . . and they're off). But no one goes home disappointed. Confident, sensitive, thrilling and sexy, the Strokes make being in a great rock 'n' roll band look almost disgustingly easy. Who

The Strokes, 2001. Courtesy of Photofest.

knows how long the magic will last—but for now, no-one can touch them." *The Independent*, a major daily newspaper in London, described the Strokes this way:

> Some bands remain forever hostage to their heritage, unable to leave home either spiritually or musically. Such is the case with the Strokes. There's no evidence here that any of the five musicians, their producer, their manager, or their guru (all given equal billing in the CD booklet) has ever set foot outside the five boroughs of New York City, so rigidly in thrall are they to the city's long-faded musical glories. (www.news.bbc.uk/1/hi/entertainment/reviews/1513745.stm 2001)

The band continued to tour in the United States and the rest of the world, with a defining moment coming in January 2002 when they were musical guests on *Saturday Night Live*. Touring continued throughout the world for all of 2002. The apex came when the band co-headlined shows with the White Stripes in Detroit and New York. After headlining the United Kingdom's Reading Festival the band returned to the United States and toured into November 2002 for their "Wyckyd Sceptre" tour. Then, at last, they stopped, but not before *Spin* magazine put the band on its cover, proclaiming the Strokes as "Band of The Year" for 2002.

In October 2003, the Strokes released their second album, *Room on Fire*, and subsequently landed dates opening for the Rolling Stones. Unlike any garage revival band before them, they broke through on commercial radio with songs like "Last Nite" and "Is That All There Is," from their debut, in the process opening the radio doors, as it were, to bands like the aforementioned White Stripes, who quickly followed them through, as did the Hives and the Vines.

 BILLY CHILDISH: THE ULTIMATE GARAGE ROCKER

Although the facts are a little vague and the evidence even vaguer, it is said that William Charlie Hamper, aka Billy Childish, has, during his twenty-five-year career recorded over 100 LPs with half a dozen or so different outfits. And, if that's not enough, he's brushed over 2,000 paintings, written two novels, and thirty-plus volumes of poetry. He is indeed one of garage rock's true renaissance men.

Born in 1959 in Chatham, England, Childish, a severe dyslexic, was inspired to form his first band during the punk rock explosion of 1977 and has continued to make primitive, garage-rock music ever since under a variety of different banners, including Thee Milkshakes, Thee Mighty Caesars, the Del-Monas, and Thee Headcoats. Since starting out, Childish has been a classic deconstructionist, believing in extreme simplicity—to the point of primitivism—and the idea that music should be made loudly and often. He is the quintessential DIY artist, often knocking out an LP in the time it takes many artists to set up for rehearsal. To wit, Thee Milkshakes were said to have recorded four LPs in a single day, mainly because they were told they released too many records and

The Vines

Of all the bands to squeeze through the new garage movement's briefly opened window, the Vines were perhaps the luckiest and the most unlikely. The Australian trio rose to prominence in 2002 after only a handful of gigs, and an incredible wave of hype generated by a few demo recordings. Led by Craig Nicholls (vocals, guitar), and joined by Patrick Matthews (bass, vocals) and David Olliffe (drums, later replaced by Hamish Rosser), the band was named after an obscure '60s band also from Australia (the Vynes), which featured none other than Nicholls' own father on guitar and vocals.

Inspired by UK bands like Suede, Verve, and Supergrass, the trio set about rehearsing in the mid-'90s, but turned up few gigs. In fact, over their first half-dozen years together, they only played an average of a single gig a year. Instead, they focused their efforts on demoing their first material on Nicholls' four-track. By the end of the decade they released their first musical artifact: "Factory" was released as a limited seven-inch single by UK independent Rex Records in 2001, and received strong coverage in the country's weekly music press. Over the next few months the band's subsequent demos generate considerable interest and the Vines began to play higher-profile gigs. After signing with Capitol for a worldwide deal, they released their debut, *Highly Evolved*, in July 2001. Produced by Rob Schnapf at Sunset Sound Studios in Los Angeles, the disc is an intoxicating blend of heavy psychedelia, Badfinger power pop, primitive riffing, and occasional Nirvana-influenced hard rock.

In March 2002, the Vines went to the United Kingdom for the first time, an introductory tour of four venues, and, as so often happens, they were anointed as the "It" band. Like the Strokes and the White Stripes before them, the Vines found themselves in the middle of a media frenzy nothing had prepared them for. *NME* gushed that their first of four sold-out shows, the first one in Brighton, simply had to be "one of the most sensational" debut gigs ever, while other outlets were equally effusive. Nicholls, a mercurial, unpredictable, and unpolished performer, made the most of this reception by going nearly insane onstage. The Vines returned to Los Angeles to record their first music video and start a small U.S./Canada tour. They played their first music festival at the 2002 Coachella

BILLY CHILDISH: THE ULTIMATE GARAGE ROCKER *(continued)*

were committing commercial suicide in the process. So they acquiesced to prove their detractors wrong.

Childish's many bands have been championed by a succession of more established artists, including Kurt Cobain, Blur's Graham Coxon, and Jack White of the White Stripes, who recently appeared on the British television program *Top of the Pops* with Billy's name scrawled on his forearm after the BBC (British Broadcasting Company) refused to let Billy paint on stage with them during a Stripes performance.

Without exception, Childish and his many bands have remained inconsequential in commercial terms, and even unfamiliar to many hipster indie rock fans. But somehow he has endured in the only way a maverick can: by staying undyingly dedicated to making the music in which he believes. "Billy Childish isn't going anywhere," says Guy Debored of trakMARX.com. "Like a reliable family run garage or a trusty old armchair, he'll remain until the roof caves in or the stuffing falls to the floor. Only then will future generations fully appreciate his true worth."

Valley Music and Arts Festival in California, an event that became their first defining moment in America. Their debut album, *Highly Evolved*, released in July, charts at No. 11 in the United States and number five back home in Australia. *Rolling Stone* Australia writes that the album "meets all the criteria for great debuts," while *NME* says it's a "shiver-down-the-spine" debut. Among the many promotional ventures undertaken by the band was an appearance on *The Late Show with David Letterman* on August 19, 2002. The band tore through their single "Get Free," climaxing with Nicholls throwing himself into the drum kit, a neo-garage-rock moment if ever there was one. A 2004 effort, *Winning Days*, found the band settling down a bit.

CRITICAL, NOT COMMERCIAL SUCCESSES

The biggest difference between this wave of ragged-glory music and the grunge movement of the early '90s—the previous time bands returned to rock 'n' roll basics—was that the garage-rock crew has never been able to find a way to cash in commercially. Their successes are measured almost entirely artistically. Virtually every popular band in this new wave of garage rock burst onto the scene as buzz bands, meaning they debuted with a unique sound pleasing to early listeners and critics alike.

In the United Kingdom, the press has a tendency to overstate its enthusiasm for bands. Whenever a band bows with a unique or courageous sound, no matter where they are from, magazines trumpet them as the Next Big Thing, ballyhooing their creative triumph as nonpareil. This treatment can launch an unsuspecting young band directly into the limelight and onto the charts. Over the years, the list of American bands subjected to this kind of adulation is long and colorful; Throwing Muses, the Pixies, Dinosaur Jr., Mudhoney, Nirvana, the White Stripes, and the Strokes are a few of the most prominent Americans that first earned acclaim overseas, then cashed that notoriety in for audiences stateside.

When the bright light of the media is cast on a young band, the unprepared may find the attention intimidating. In many cases, an act may not be ready to go under the microscope. If the UK press hails a band as the Next Big Thing, and that group becomes the "It" band, expectations rise quickly, and often, unnecessarily. The band feels pressure to produce material worthy of all the attention. While their original material, the songs that earned them attention in the first place, was in most cases created in relative obscurity, the subsequent material is created under a microscope, or at least very different circumstances. The stress of a project in that situation can be daunting.

Still, the bands of the new garage movement have been almost unanimously hailed as artistically triumphant. Commercially, however, because the genre has been marginalized—even since its inception in the '60s—garage rock has been virtually ignored by mainstream rock audiences. Only the Strokes and the White Stripes have sold the kinds of records approaching the equivalent of the national and international press they've received. The Strokes' debut, *Is This It*, was certified gold, with over 500,000 copies sold. As mentioned, the White Stripes, the only other viable commercial act in the movement thus far, sold over 500,000 copies of their commercial breakthrough, *White Blood Cells*, and 2 million copies of their sophomore effort, *Elephant*, which climbed as high as number six on the *Billboard* albums chart.

WRAP IT UP

Other bands were poised to take advantage of the door opened by the new garage acts, but certainly not to the extent of the biggest groups, at least not to date. And with such a fickle musical climate, there is no guarantee the following bands would even make another record. Despite that, a few acts, some even signed to major labels, appear to have what it takes to weather changes in commercial musical tastes. The highest-profile act on the verge of breaking through is New York City's Yeah Yeah Yeahs. Hinging on the manic vocal histrionics of frontperson Karen O, the trio made a name for themselves based on their unusual chemistry. They consist only of two instrumentalists—guitarist Nicolas Zinner and drummer Brian Chase—supporting O's vocals, making for a lean presentation that allows each element to stand out. Their latest album, *Fever to Tell*, released on the major label Interscope, was typically acclaimed, but failed to make commercial impact. Still, the band's unusual sound has helped them amass a dedicated following.

The Raveonettes is another act on the brink of a commercial breakthrough. A Danish act currently living in New York and London, the band formed in the late '90s around the core of guitarist/singer Sune Rose Wagner and bass player Sharin Foo. Their melodic, heavily distorted songs center on the pair's ethereal vocal harmonies and hyperactive lead guitar. The Raveonettes also abided by a rather unorthodox set of rules when it came to writing music. First, they insisted the album be written entirely in b-flat minor, with only three chords, and each song had to be less than three minutes long. *Whip It On*, written on a four-track and drum machine, fused classic garage rumblings with frenzied electronic bits. Extensive touring followed and a full-length album, *Chain Gang of Love*, recorded for Sony Music's Columbia label, suddenly vaulted the band onto the new rock map.

Other bands bubbling close to the surface of widespread recognition, Hot Hot Heat (British Columbia), the Walkmen (New York City), the Catheters (Seattle), the Mooney Suzuki (New York City), the Caesars (Sweden), the Datsuns (New Zealand), and D4 (New Zealand), hail from around the globe. Many retrace the templates of their garage-rock forbears faithfully; others veer in odd stylistic directions. But the truth is, these bands, all presenting fresh, primal takes on new music, are announcing they are indeed ready to be heard.

DEDICATED LABELS

A handful of labels have helped to keep the bloom on garage rock's rose over the years. A trio in particular—Estrus, Norton, and Get Hip—has almost single-handedly breathed life into it at a time when audiences were dwindling. Beginning in the late '80s, Estrus Records capitalized on a distinct Northwest garage sound—one undoubtedly patterned after the original Northwest garage-rock sound of the '60s (the Wailers, the Sonics, the Kingsmen) rose to prominence on the coattails of faithful bands and a dedicated following. Standard-bearing acts the Monomen, the Makers, and the Mummies were among the three most brazen and accomplished examples of '90s garage revivalists, each one fired up by punk rock, but deeply obsessed with the driving R&B sound of the '60s.

In Pittsburgh, the same regionalism occurred, this time at the hands of a label called Get Hip, an imprint whose flagship band the Cynics, featuring label proprietor Gregg Kostelich, led the way. Get Hip also released seminal garage recordings by bands like the Miracle Workers, Electric Frankenstein, and the Billy Childish outfit Thee Headcoats.

In New York City, Norton Records has since its inception specialized in garage rock both old and new, with revival bands like the A-Bones, the Hentchmen, Swingin' Neckbreakers, and surfer/hotrodders Untamed Youth existing side by side with original garage acts like the Sonics and the Wailers.

9

RIOT GRRRLS

WOMEN GAIN PERMANENT ENTRY TO ROCK 'N' ROLL

The late '80s and early '90s was a time of limbo for women. The Reagan presidency's preoccupation with family values lulled middle- and upper-middle-class women into a sense of security and comfort. One of the results of this was a partial abandonment of the feminist values that had become so important to the sex throughout the '70s and early '80s.

But that all began to right itself as the '80s progressed. High-profile accusations of sexual harassment in cases like Justice Clarence Thomas and Anita Hill, and a few with ranking executives in the music industry, brought the issue into widespread focus. The debate polarized the public and galvanized women, especially younger, more progressive women largely centered in urban areas, to take issue with what seemed to be a recession of rights and societal standing.

The battle over abortion rights also gained renewed attention as the legislation of *Roe v. Wade* came under fire during the conservative Reagan and Bush Sr. presidencies. Gillian Gaar, in her book *She's a Rebel: The History of Women in Rock & Roll* (second edition), writes: "Though the battle over abortion rights caused women to recognize the underlying fragility of the gains the feminist movement had made, media focus on other 'women's issues' further illuminated the struggles women continue to face in society" (Gaar 2002, i).

This struggle and the plight of women in the music industry in general, where they seemed to not be considered seriously for positions of power and responsibility, came rushing to the forefront of the media and into the female consciousness. Suddenly, it appeared that the dominant culture, the male culture, was beginning to exert its influence over the industry again, after women had begun to make inroads throughout the late '80s and early '90s.

While all this was going on, there were still some positive things happening for women in the music industry. After the alternative revolution of the early '90s, the record biz's door was open to any and all comers, the more extreme, the more unconventional the better. At this time, the notion of women rockers suddenly became fashionable. Quickly, groups surfaced to take advantage of the opportunities.

THE ROCKER GIRLS

From the '60s through the early '80s, women in bands were all but invisible in commercial music. Of course, there were a few exceptions, like Fanny, the Runaways, the Go Gos, the Slits, the Shags, Calamity Jane, Girlschool, and the Bangles.

Occasionally, someone like Maureen "Mo" Tucker, the drummer for New York's Velvet Underground, would affirm a place in early rock history. But examples of this were far too infrequent to consider these all-girl bands or female instrumentalists little more than daring novelty acts.

Thanks to the egalitarian ethic followed by punk and punk rockers in the late '70s, however, the presence of women in noncommercial musical venture began to change things for the better. Women began to get respect from musicians and clubs and labels in the industry and earn more solid footing in the trade. During that time, beginning in the '70s and into the early '80s, women like Kim Gordon of edgy New York noise rockers Sonic Youth and Tina Weymouth of arty groovers the Talking Heads, both handling bass duties for their respective bands, were among the more prominent artists. Some, like Joan Jett, formerly of the '70s all-girl hard rockers the Runaways, established herself as a frontperson of her own band, while others formed all-girl or mostly girl bands of their own. For some of these bands, having arrived in this form, in the music industry that seemed to hold them down for decades, was simply enough. Their breakthrough assimilation as viable rock bands validated their existence and defined their success. For others, however, existence and viability was not enough. For those bands, members used their voices as means of creating positive social change. In essence, they wanted to change the status quo—a condition that for so long was unanimously inequitable to women—and not go along with it.

The first bands to break through in the '90s with women in their ranks were a result of the more open-minded modus operandi of the alternative music movement. While grunge became the buzzword in many progressive music circles, bands of the grunge era and beyond also began to include women, or, in some cases, all women. Throwing Muses, starring Kristin Hersh and Tanya Donelly, and London's My Bloody Valentine became two of the first of these multigender bands, even prior to the advent of the alternative revolution. The Pixies, too, featured bassist/songwriter Kim Deal.

When the '90s broke wide open musically, women truly began to assert themselves, both musically and figuratively. Bands like L7, Babes in Toyland, 7 Year Bitch, and Hole all became major players on the alternative scene, extracting momentum from convergent directions: from the chaotic rush of alternative bands making impact on rock music during that time and from the novel concept of women making music as loud or louder than the boys.

Babes in Toyland

Babes in Toyland came together in the late '80s in Minneapolis, home of a bustling and innovative music scene. Drummer Lori Barbero and guitarist singer Kat Bjelland found common ground in their adventurous spirit and soon hooked up with bassist Michelle Leon. Together, the band became one of the most influential of all the alternative rock bands of the period, making impressions on the musicians that would soon make up the Riot Grrrl movement.

Babes in Toyland, 1992. Courtesy of Photofest.

They released their first full-length album, *Spanking Machine*, in 1990 on the Twin/Tone label in their home city. With its relentless noise and unorthodox approach—Bjelland sang like a demon, while her rhythm section pieced together lurched with primal force—it was clearly a call to arms. But the most inspiring thing of all was that finally there was a girl band that engendered no comparison to the boys. Unlike Joan Jett, Pat Benatar, and the ladies of the '80s, who made overtures to gain the audiences of male performers, Babes in Toyland left that pretense behind, finding audiences with men and women alike. Not only that, but they rarely played the feminist card. Rather, Babes were expert in using the innate potency of rock 'n' roll as a statement of empowerment. Despite their uncompromising attack, Babes caught the attention of a major label, Reprise. They released *Fontanelle* in August of 1992, with new bassist Maureen Herman. The record impressed critics with its unique, coruscating sound on songs like "Bruise Violet," a tune targeting former Babes member Courtney Love. The record failed to make a dent on the national charts, mainly because of the lack of support given the band by the music video world.

Stung by the snub, Babes contented themselves with touring. But they wouldn't release another album until 1995. Called *Nemesisters*, the album fared even less well and the band, save for a few side projects, tapered off, having left many aspiring girl rockers in their wake.

L7

Another hard-rock outfit that seized the imagination of a national rock audience was L7. Much like Babes in Toyland, they started out strong, with an audacious hard-rock bravura on albums like 1991's minor classic, *Smell the Magic*, which featured the song "Shove," a girl-rock anthem of the early alternative era.

L7, slang for square (the shape of the two figures), formed in Los Angeles in the mid-'80s with Jennifer Finch on bass, Suzi Gardner and Donita Sparks on guitar, and Dee Plakas on drums. Their approach was fast, noisy, and angry, with the band's lyrics depicting women attracted to bad behavior and dangerous men: the perfect combination to horrify parents.

After the indie success of *Smell the Magic*, released on the Sub Pop label (Nirvana, Soundgarden) in 1991, L7 signed to the Slash imprint and released *Bricks Are Heavy* the very next year. Produced by Butch Vig, the man responsible for Nirvana's breakthrough *Nevermind*, the record was infused with cynicism, humor, and metallic guitar chords. The public reacted positively to the album, and radio picked up on "Pretend We're Dead," the disc's robotic first single. But the L7 commercial train soon sputtered; not to say they weren't active. They toured frequently, released *Hungry for Stink* in 1994, and played the Lollapalooza main stage that same year. They also busied themselves with social causes and benefits, earning them credibility with the Riot Grrrl set. But the band began to splinter during the recording of *The Beauty Process: Triple*

L7 performs at the Voters for Choice Concert supporting pro-choice abortion rights. On stage from left are: Suzi Gardner, Donita Sparks, and Jennifer Finch. Drummer Dee Plakas is crouching near her drum kit in back. © Matthew Mendelsohn/Corbis.

Platinum, their 1997 disc, when Finch left the fold. They were dropped from their label and, after making one last album in 1999, broke up for good.

Throwing Muses, Breeders, Tanya and Kristin

Following the Pixies' lengthy hiatus in 1992, bassist Kim Deal joined together with her sister Kelly, guitarist Tanya Donelly (formerly of Throwing Muses), and drummer Jim MacPherson to form the Breeders, a playful band that proved immediately appealing and accessible to a pop audience. After an EP, *Safari*, in 1992, Donelly left, however, to pursue her own star-making vehicle Belly. The Breeders, now with Josephine Wiggs of A Perfect Disaster, released their chart-friendly *Last Splash*, in 1993. Buoyed by the single "Cannonball," the album reached the *Billboard* Top 40, cresting at No. 33.

Complications arose however, and stalled the band's upward progress, with Kelley Deal checking into rehab. It proved to be the band's death knell. They wouldn't reform again in any permutation until 1999, when they released a single, "Collage," on the *Mod Squad* soundtrack.

With Belly, her new band, Donelly found a comfortable creative outlet. Until that point, she had co-starred and co-written with cousin Kristin Hersh (Muses) and shared the spotlight with three other women in the Breeders. As frontperson and songwriter this time, she took advantage, demonstrating her

Throwing Muses, 1997 (left to right), David Narcizo, Kristin Hersh, and Bernard Georges (Tanya Donelly not shown). Courtesy of the Library of Congress.

potential on the band's two recordings, *Star* (1993) and *King* (1995). *Star* drew immediate attention on both sides of the Atlantic. (Throwing Muses had been popular in Europe, thanks to a recording contract with 4AD, a London label.) Donelly was seen as an angelic chanteuse with vulnerable, but empathic style and amiable demeanor. She possessed none of the outward malice, choosing instead to demonstrate deep and troubled obsessions with death through her songs. Belly imploded after *King*, following a lengthy but difficult tour to support the record in 1995. Donelly went on to record as a solo artist. *Lovesongs for Underdogs* (1997), *Beautysleep* (2002), and *Whiskey Tango Ghosts* (2004) all followed.

Donelly's fellow Muse Kristin Hersh went on to record prolifically after her acclaim with her original band. Hersh carried on the Throwing Muses' name after Donelly left the band, amid some creative conflict, in 1992 to join the Breeders. That year Hersh reformed the Muses with drummer David Narcizo and released the band's fourth album, *Red Heaven*. After that, Hersh released a solo album and toured extensively, leaving fans to wonder about the status of the Muses. In 1995, however, Hersh and the rest of the Muses released *University*, followed by *Limbo* in 1996. But the party soon ended with Hersh announcing the band's dissolution in 1997. A collection of rare early material, *In a Doghouse*, followed in 1998. During three weekends in 2002, Hersh's Muses got together to record another album *Throwing Muses*; released the same day in 2003 as Hersh's own *The Grotto*. Former Muse Donelly provided background vocals on some of the songs.

Other women made substantial impact on the rock world. Bands like Dickless lasted only briefly, but their searing tune "Saddle Tramp" is one of the more memorable of the grunge era. Fastbacks, featuring Kim Warnick, Lulu Gargiulo and supporting songwriter Kurt Bloch, were for a time one of the premier punk-pop bands in the Northwest. Albums like *Very Very Powerful Motor* (1991) and *The Question Is No* (1993) earned the band a solid spot in the edifice of '90s rock.

Another band with a dominant creative female force was the Muffs. Kim Shattuck and Melanie Vammen, formerly of the garage-metal girls band called the Pandoras in the '80s, turned heads immediately in the more alternative-friendly climate of the '90s. They signed with Warner Brothers and released their debut album, *The Muffs*, in 1993. After two years of touring, Vammen left the band, leaving them a trio for their follow-up recording, *Blonder and Blonder. Happy Birthday to Me* followed in 1997, trailed two years later by *Alert Today, Alive Tomorrow*; and a rarities collection, *Hamburger*, which appeared in early 2000.

Scrawl began playing their shows in the mid-'90s in and around their native Ohio. Led by Marcy Mays, the trio predated the Riot Grrrl movement by a few years with their fierce sound and gritty sentiment. But distribution problems and label complications prevented Scrawl from earning any widespread popularity. They recorded their first major label album, *Travel On, Rider*, well past the apex of alternative rock and ended up making very little noise with it, despite its talent, integrity, and good intentions.

Courtney Love and Hole

One of the more outrageous and polarizing personalities—male or female—of the '90s and beyond was Courtney Love. Born Love Michelle Harrison in San Francisco in 1965, and raised in Oregon, Love was shut-

Courtney Love performs on *The Tonight Show*, 2004. Courtesy of Photofest.

tled between Oregon and New Zealand in a number of progressive domiciles. Her mother, for one, believed in leading a gender-free life, which meant her daughter was denied conventional dress and toys. Not surprisingly, this issue would become pivotal in her music.

Eventually, Love moved to Los Angeles and began securing bit parts in movies, including appearing as Nancy Spungen's best friend in the lauded flick *Sid and Nancy*, the tragic story of Sid Vicious and his girlfriend. When her Hollywood career stalled out, Love moved to Minneapolis and formed an early version of Babes in Toyland, called Sugar Baby Doll, with friend Kat Bjelland. Contrary to her upbringing, both she and Bjelland would take to wearing little girl dresses on stage as an image staple.

Personalities conflicted however—another recurring theme in Love's career—and Love left the band before recording with them. After moving to Alaska (where she worked as a stripper) and then bouncing around the globe—Japan, England, Taiwan—Love returned to Los Angeles in 1989 to form another band, this one called, provocatively, Hole.

Supported by guitarist Eric Erlandson, bassist Jill Emery, and drummer Caroline Rue, Hole and Love developed a following as a seething band eager to tackle personal issues like sexual abuse, rape, prostitution, and various topics intimate to women. Their first album, *Pretty on the Inside*, made a tremendous impact on the independent rock scene. Primitively played and brutally affecting, *Pretty on the Inside* laid bare Love's mission to sing and write passionately about normally taboo subjects. The record, difficult at times and cacophonous throughout its course, established a template for mean-spirited, though well-meaning rock 'n' roll, a template that would carry through the music of the Riot Grrrls in the Pacific Northwest. It also solidified her status as an outsider in the insider's world of the music business.

Soon after releasing her band's debut, however, Courtney Love's career took a permanent turn. After meeting and striking up a relationship with Nirvana frontman and songwriter Kurt Cobain, the two married in 1992. She became pregnant with his child, and this altered state, seemingly counter to both's desire to remain unconventional, momentarily stalled the progress of her band, if not his. Together, they became a "power couple," perhaps inadvertently, a concept both felt was contrary to their own rebellious and cynical beliefs. Still, Hollywood beckoned. In an interview with the publication *Vanity Fair*, Love's world got a little more complicated. She admitted in the story that she had done heroin while pregnant. After hearing the news, her baby girl, Frances Bean Cobain, was taken from the couple by social workers until the situation, and her drug dependency, was sorted out.

Hole recorded their sequel to *Pretty on the Inside*, called *Live Through This*, in the fall of 1993, and slated its release for the following spring. They had made changes to the lineup, which now included bassist Kristen Pfaff and drummer Patty Schemel. But the album's release was disrupted by the suicide of Love's husband Cobain, who took his life in April 1994. The tragedy was magnified when Pfaff overdosed just two months later. Now, rather than being referred to as a "gold digger" and a "pretender," Love was viewed as a victim, a victim whose album title took on a strangely ironic dimension.

Following her husband's death, Love and her band made little forward progress. The band toured in the summer of that year, but the album stalled out on the charts, and the band decided to go on hiatus. There would be no new music from Hole for four years, during which time Love would transform herself from bereaved punk rock widow to cosmetically enhanced, red-carpet-walking starlet; the details of this transformation have little to do with the overriding concept of this book. Suffice it to say, she spent much time reviving her movie career and fending off a variety of lawsuits.

In 1998, Love pulled herself together long enough to record and release *Celebrity Skin*, Hole's third recording. The mood of the record was brighter, less strident, and radio received it with relative warmth. But in 2000, Love's label, Universal Records, sued its artist for breach of contract. The belligerent one countersued, and, in the process, inadvertently became a spokesperson for artists in the music industry. Love has contended that contractual obligations and financial remuneration were inequitable on behalf of artists.

Another legal wrangle arose when she was accused of manipulating the music catalog of Nirvana, against the best wishes of the band's other two members, Dave Grohl and Chris Novoselic. While the band members wanted to release more Nirvana material, saying it would have been what the departed Cobain truly wanted, Love, with Cobain's trump vote, resisted, citing that Geffen Records, the label Nirvana signed with in the late 1980s, wasn't the same after it was acquired by Vivendi Universal in late 1999. (Eventually, Love and Universal Music Group settled their lawsuit and the company was able to release more product: a Nirvana greatest-hits LP and a box set, *With the Lights Out*.)

In return for granting UMG permission to issue the Nirvana material, Love was liberated from her recording contract with Geffen. She will also gain ownership of all of her previously recorded material, and has waived any re-recording restrictions from some previously released Hole songs. The release of a long-form video with UMG remains an option.

The preponderance of legal activity, combined with her glossy Hollywood makeover and attendant activities, distracted the artist from her primary role as a musician. As a result, Hole dissolved. She released her first album as a solo artist, the cynically titled *America's Sweetheart*, in 2004. The long-awaited disc, put off many times due to Love's troubling drug use and violent behavior, came out amid a barrage of bad press and negative publicity. But it was widely regarded as an album of impressive scope and affecting melodies. Unfortunately, Love has grown ever more distant to the part of her personality that makes music, and her audience has diminished because of it.

THE RIOT GRRRLS

After punk broke, rock music and its definition expanded exponentially. This explosion in music was a breakthrough for women in the evolution of rock 'n' roll. For the first time, they were integrated in rock, punk, noise, and hard-rock genres with little of the marvel and fascination that normally accompanied their presence on the scene. These higher-profile acts paved the way for an underground movement, one that was much more active and vocal than women like Babes in Toyland and L7, who, because of their elevated status in the marketplace and their financed relationships with record companies, were compelled to stay guarded. After all, there was considerable money at stake.

Some bands, however, were not interested at all in the potential financial gain of the music industry. In the progressive Northwest, a hotbed of alternative music, women had already gained a foothold in the music scenes of cities like Portland, Seattle, and Olympia. It was not uncommon beginning in the late '80s to see women in many of the local bands. Communities of artists popped up all over the Northwest, some based in downtown areas, others in small towns, still others at colleges. One particular school that yielded a surprising number of enterprising underground musicians was Evergreen State College in Olympia. As a vibrant community of artists and musicians the college jumpstarted the region's underground music scene with ambitious alumnae like Sub Pop label co-founder Bruce Pavitt and Beat Happening drummer Heather Lewis.

Beat Happening, a band formed in 1983 with Lewis, singer Calvin Johnson, and guitarist Bret Lunsford, would become the first band from this region to attract international attention. Johnson, founder of the upstart K Records, began releasing cassette-only music by underappreciated bands. In 1984, K released Beat Happening's first recording, a five-song cassette. The next year, the band released its first full-length album.

It was not long before the band's simplistic but endearing sound gained widespread attention in the college underground. The success turned Heather Lewis into something of a role model for the region's aspiring teenage musicians. Soon, the Olympia scene began yielding bands in great numbers; outsiders heard about the region's progressive view of music and artist-friendly attitude and began migrating. A scene was born.

One early band formed at Evergreen was Bikini Kill, led by undergrads Kathleen Hanna and Tobi Vail. Both were feminists, musically inclined, and strong-willed, and both published local fanzines to voice their own feminist thinking; they met and decided to continue their mission together. They linked with guitarist Billie Karren and bassist Kathi Wilcox, another Evergreen student, to form the band. A singer-songwriter named Lois Maffeo was also a key proponent of the Evergreen State College scene. A native of Phoenix, Arizona, Maffeo journeyed to Olympia in the early '80s. Her first significant contribution to the city's music culture involved her radio show, "Your Dream Girl," on local station

KAOS. She would eventually go on to perform in her own lo-fi sound and uphold a steadfast membership to the feminist underground in the region.

Another band that cropped up at about the same time was Bratmobile, pioneered by Allison Wolfe and Molly Neuman. Fueled by feminist thinking that had come from Wolfe's outspoken and unorthodox upbringing, Bratmobile added various "special guests" to help them instrumentally. They eventually invited Erin Smith, a guitarist inspired by Beat Happening's Heather Lewis, into the Bratmobile fold. The band's passionate singalongs went over quickly and, like Bikini Kill, they became influential among the region's musically ambitious.

Kathleen Hanna, the vocalist with the band Bikini Kill, performs live on stage. © S.I.N./Corbis.

In the summer of 1991, Bratmobile's Neuman and Wolfe, along with Hanna and Vail of Bikini Kill, pooled their efforts on a fanzine called *Riot Grrrl*. The magazine addressed music issues, but also became a forum for ideas and consciousness raising. Their reach and influence grew. Bikini Kill eventually moved to Washington, DC, to refine their tunes and make records, and Bratmobile did the same while staying in the Northwest, the climate was clearly changing in favor of women in rock.

> Riot Grrrl . . . defied stereotypes of women (and female musicians) as meek, overly sensitive, and lovelorn; and it found a powerful expressive tool in noise. [It] was a blend of personal catharsis and political activism, though most of the attention it drew was due to the latter. Many (but not all) Riot Grrrl lyrics addressed gender-related issues—rape, domestic abuse, sexuality (including lesbianism), male dominance of the social hierarchy, female empowerment—from a radical, militant point of view. The similarly confrontational music favored raging, willfully amateurish blasts of noise, with only a rudimentary sense of melody or instrumental technique. To most Riot Grrrl bands, the simple act of picking up a guitar and bashing out a screeching racket was not only fun, but an act of liberation. To outsiders, the musical merits of Riot Grrrl could be highly variable, but to fans, what the movement represented was arguably even more important than the music. (All Music Guide)

Bikini Kill best embraced this definition. Led by Hanna, a former stripper, the group laced their incendiary live performances with aggressive political stances that challenged the accepted hierarchy of the underground music community. Slam dancers, normally male, were forced to mosh at the fringes of the stage so that women could remain at the front of the crowd. Female audience members were often invited to step up to the microphone to openly discuss issues of sexual abuse and misconduct.

In light of the success and influence of these early bands, dozens of other similar-minded bands popped up. Seattle's 7 Year Bitch, a vociferous hard-rock band starring Selene Vigil and Stefanie Sargent, ascended quickly, eventually going on to record for a major label in 1996. Huggy Bear, from England, made it clear that the growing Riot Grrrl scene was not restricted to the United States, while groups like Team Dresch, Tribe 8, the Butchies, and God Is My Co-Pilot—coined Queercore—brought sexuality of varying degrees to the forefront of their music, presentation, and lyrical content.

During the period from 1990 to 1993, as the movement blossomed, two bands, Heavens to Betsy and Excuse 17, formed and made inroads. Those band have since become known for their role as early vehicles of another more popular band, Sleater-Kinney.

Corin Tucker and Carrie Brownstein met in 1992 in Olympia. Both were overwhelmingly influenced by their precursors in the Riot Grrrl movement and both were interested in moving their musical vehicles to the next level. It would take them a few years to debut on record, which they did with their self-titled release in 1995. Tucker and Carrie Brownstein, both guitarists, didn't bother with a bassist but they hired a drummer, Aussie Lora McFarlane in 1994, then Janet Weiss in 1997. Together, they adhered strictly to the indie ethic of the movement, releasing their albums on the Kill Rock Stars label.

The press from the outset was overwhelmingly behind the band. They combined the passion and fury of Kathleen Hanna's Bikini Kill with more tunefulness and melody. It would take a few years more for the band to become underground rock royalty, which they did with records like *Dig Me Out* (1996), *The Hot Rock* (1999), and *One Beat* (2002). All of those records were highly touted, particularly *Dig Me Out*, which placed the band in the Top 10 of the highly influential "Pazz & Jop" poll of the *Village Voice*. Sleater-Kinney would often see themselves on critic's Top 10 lists.

THE CORPORATE OGRE

All of this activity in the underground was happening not only due to the efforts of communities like the one in Olympia, but because alternative music was fast becoming the reigning buzzword. Smelling profits, the major labels came to invade Seattle and picked off many of the region's successful grunge and heavy rock bands. They eventually made their way to Olympia to pay a visit to the Riot Grrrls and the various style reps in that region. Unfortunately for the labels, they were met with substantial resistance. Indeed, they made one assumption too many. Record labels believed that the Olympia scene had arisen as an offshoot of the grunge alternative scene. While that may be true in theory, it also rose up in opposition to it; the male-dominated ethos that had surrounded rock 'n' roll for as long as its history had also embraced, most likely accidentally, the grunge scene in Seattle as well. Women in the underground music scene had had enough, and saw an opportunity to change all that.

So, when the so-called "corporate ogre" came calling, the bands and labels associated with the scene didn't want what it was offering, namely money, and lots of it. The K label fought off lucrative distribution offers and bands like Bikini Kill and Bratmobile rejected recording contracts. It was more important for these entities to remain independent and in decision-making capacities than it was to be solvent.

Beating back these offers reinforced the mission of the Riot Grrrls and the entire scene began including subgenres like Queercore, love-rock, and twee pop. In doing so, they ensured themselves an anti-corporate posture, and that they would remain musically uncompromised. (Tellingly, the label that released the highest percentage of Riot Grrrl records was named "Kill Rock Stars.")

With the Riot Grrrl philosophy now open to the public, a barrage of press followed. The hype ran in national outlets like *USA Today* and *Newsweek*. Callow stories surfaced by journalists unfamiliar with the base mission and general ethic of the people within the movement. Before they had truly assembled a coherent agenda or political code, they were thrust into the national limelight. As the "trend" stories emerged, many incomplete, the scene became misinterpreted, misunderstood, maligned. Participating bands like Bikini Kill and Huggy Bear felt burned, pigeonholed, and frustrated. Prominent personalities were constantly forced to answer challenges from the press and other skeptics, all of whom were curious about their political and musical approach. Additionally, as these bands grew popular nationally, expectations increased. Now bands were role models, not just for aspiring musicians in the Northwest, but for women worldwide. Shouldering the burden became overwhelming.

This new climate, aloud with skeptics and other hullabaloo, was a far cry from the safe haven of Olympia. Pressure and expectations disrupted the blissful isolation and focus of the major groups. Bikini Kill, Bratmobile, Huggy Bear, and those truest to the cause began feeling the strain.

Bikini Kill released their first full-length album in 1993, *Pussywhipped*. In the following years, the band toured, but stayed away from the studio, with the exception of a few singles. Another incident in that same year also galvanized the Riot Grrrls and, as the murders at the Monterey Pop Festival jarred the hippie movement awake in 1969, so too did this event bring the sting of reality to the Riot Grrrls and their feminist idealism.

A Seattle band on the brink of success, called the Gits, led by singer Mia Zapata, were preparing to record their second album when Zapata was raped and murdered while on her way home from a Seattle club. The incident stunned the scene and was a call to action for women and other artists who had begun to set their sites on the Northwest. It called to mind the fact that no amount of anger and passion—two qualities the Riot Grrrls possessed—could protect them from the evil that lurked in men. While they were making strides to become equals with men, especially on the rock 'n' roll front, and they shared ideas of equality in sexuality and politics as a result of this, they were still in real danger physically.

Zapata's death shone a tragic light on this. Equality, at least in terms of safety—was still well out of reach. As a result, Zapata's death emboldened women to take action. Friends and associates formed Home Alive, an organization created to educate and fund self-defense. The group released *The Art of Self-Defense*, a disc that featured the recordings of Zapata, Joan Jett, Pearl Jam, Nirvana, and many others. The organization also held benefit concerts, using profits to conduct and fund self-defense classes and seminars.

The cause united the movement and illuminated the need for action. The Riot Grrrl mission, now co-opted by the public, spread significantly and garnered support from all different types of artists. This was both positive and negative. While it provided strength and support of all kinds to a worthy cause and did indeed raise consciousness, it also served to diffuse, even defuse the passion once held so dearly by the movement's first wave. Once the concept's original raison d'être loses its focus, it's natural for its founders to abandon it, or at least loosen its grip on it, in order to set their sites on a new cause.

After the death of Kurt Cobain, both Seattle's male-dominated grunge and the Riot Grrrl movement lost steam. Bikini Kill released their *Reject All American* in 1996, the same year Sleater-Kinney issued their brilliant *Dig Me Out*. By that time the jittery rock scene had begun to focus its sites elsewhere. Both records were received well, but the '90s had grown almost peripatetic in its eagerness to embrace the next big thing and the Riot Grrrls were no longer in focus. Kathleen Hanna, Bikini Kill's motivating force and one of the scene's main grrrls, went on to form Le Tigre, laying off the musical violence in favor of a punk-derived electronic and sample-based sound.

The Riot Grrrls indeed served a noble purpose and it would be impossible to gauge the impact they had on thousands of young women who, motivated by their example, would eventually go on to form bands of their own. Rock 'n' roll was no longer the elite boys club, but an egalitarian enterprise where women had (almost) as much credibility as men. It only took the better part of forty years.

POST-GRRRLS, QUEERCORE, AND ALT-FOLK

After the Riot Grrrl scene had more or less run its course, it left a few acts, like Le Tigre and Sleater-Kinney, to wear the mantle, if by default. These acts enjoyed the freedom of expression of the Riot Grrrls but without the expectations and the branding. Seemingly, bands of the Riot Grrrl diaspora split into two separate movements, basically all leading down the same road. Bands like the Gossip, Tracy and the Plastics, Deerhoof, and Erase Errata have all developed sizable, national indie rock fan bases, essentially serving the same purpose as the bands of the Riot Grrrl movement without all the trendy baggage.

Queercore

Queercore, previously mentioned, is a subgenre of punk with an emphasized sense of sexuality originally spawned out of the politically explosive environment of the Reagan years. It gained momentum by latching onto the Riot Grrrls before becoming its own entity after that movement dissolved. Queercore honestly addresses sexual desire, societal prejudice, and the price of being true to one's own self.

The genre gained visibility originally in the pages of Tom Jennings and Deke Nihilson's *Homocore*, and in Donna Dresch's seminal *Chainsaw*. Throughout the '90s, Queercore was most visibly exemplified by the defiant music, political rage, and acidic social commentary of the Butchies Team Dresch, Pansy Division, God Is My Co-Pilot and Tribe 8 on labels like Mr. Lady, Candy Ass, Chainsaw, Kill Rock Stars, Agitprop! and Heartcore. Sporadic festivals have arisen in the name of Queercore, but it has remained a predominantly urban and niche phenomenon.

Alt-Folk

Unexpectedly, Queercore also intersected with an alternative folk movement that grew to embrace more commercial acts. Spearheaded by the phenomenally successful duet the Indigo Girls—Amy Ray and Emily Saliers—the Alt-Folk movement sang delicate and poetic songs from a lesbian viewpoint, and audiences flocked. As the genre became more viable, each year more performers arose to fill the need. Today, the legwork done by artists like the Indigo Girls and Michelle Shocked has paid off for performers like Melissa Ferrick and Catie Curtis.

THE BOLDNESS, THE FRANKNESS

The brutal truths of the Riot Grrrls and various other bands of the early alt-rock movement created a newfound sort of candor among women writing songs. Honesty became a mission. Women began writing music with stark intentions, expressing themselves with a heretofore unseen honesty and expression. Artists maintaining this approach were no longer obligated to drape their songs in metaphors and coy language. At last, women songwriters were now able to express themselves the same way as men did. It was simply another equity long in coming.

The boldness began in the late '80s and early '90s with a plethora of bands, including groups associated with early grunge like L7 and Babes in Toyland, as well as some of the original Riot Grrrls—Bikini Kill and Bratmobile. But others independent of those movements picked up on that candor as well.

ANI DIFRANCO

Ani Difranco, a native of Buffalo, New York, was one of the primary entrants in this quest for honesty in women's music. "Yes, I could think of another word," she said in an interview for *Solo: Women Singer-Songwriters*, "but wouldn't replacing the original thought with something less genuine be a teeny step on the road to writing for some other reason than honesty or personal fulfillment?" (Woodworth 1998)

During the '90s and beyond, Ani Difranco has become the poster child for independent recording artists. More than once in her slow-building career, which began when she was just nine years old and has been rising ever since, Difranco turned down potentially lucrative recording contracts to remain independent and in control of her own artistic career. Today, after a dozen and a half self-released albums, Difranco remains in control of her life, her label Righteous Babe, and her publishing rights along with a small staff. Her exalted status as a successful business woman is unparalleled, especially at a time when artists are so often hostages of their record companies. To be a woman and do these things autonomously is a rarity, even an anomaly.

From coffeehouse gigs, Ani began touring on the acoustic, college, and rock club circuits. With her ability to play guitar and write with convincing authority and in a style all her own—part punk, part folk, part alternative—she began shattering stereotypes and winning unsuspecting fans. Ani started playing Beatles' songs in local bars at age nine but didn't start writing her own material until age fifteen when she moved out of her mother's apartment. By the time she was eighteen she had played every bar in her hometown enough to know that she needed to move. New York was her next destination.

To finance her first album, Ani looted her bank account and borrowed the rest from friends. She rejected offers from indie and major labels alike, and instead started her own record company. She has since sold over 100,000 tapes and CDs on her own. She not only writes and publishes her own songs, but also produces her own recordings, creates the artwork, and releases them. She employs fifteen or so like-minded people in management and staff positions, supports local printers and manufacturers in her hometown, and utilizes a network of independent distributors in the United States, Canada, and Europe. She tours constantly on both sides of the Atlantic.

Still, she does not like to be considered a businessperson, something for which she is constantly given credit. In an open letter to *Ms. Magazine* in 1997, Ani wrote of the irony she's encountered while bucking against the recording industry:

> I sell approximately 2.5% of the albums that a Joan-Jewel-anis-Morrisette sells and get about .05% of the airplay royalties, so obviously if it all comes down to dollars and cents, I've led a wholly unremarkable life. Yet I choose relative statistical mediocrity over fame and fortune because I have a bigger purpose in mind. Imagine how strange it must be for a girl who has spent 10 years fighting as hard as she could against the lure of the corporate carrot and the almighty forces of capital, only to be eventually recognized by the power structure as a business pioneer . . .

ANI DIFRANCO *(continued)*

We have the ability and the opportunity to recognize women not just for the financial successes of their work but for the work itself. We have the facility to judge each other by entirely different criteria than those imposed upon us by the superstructure of society. We have a view which reaches beyond profit margins into poetry, and a vocabulary to articulate the difference.

CONFESSIONAL WRITERS

Artists like Alanis Morissette and Tori Amos developed reputations as writing honest and socially blunt tunes, aiming their lyrics at particular targets—directly at their attackers in some cases, making confessions in others, or taking the point of view of their victims in still others. Teen rocker Avril Lavigne also capitalized on pointed storytelling to great success, especially with her debut album *Let Go* (2002), and on ubiquitous singles "Complicated" and "Sk8er Boi."

All three of these women have achieved popularity as a result of this frank approach and have earned a fan base that has been able to relate to their narratives. (Both Morissette and Amos are given greater attention in Chapter 6.)

Liz Phair

Some artists who've taken that direct approach, however, cannot lay claim to the same commercial recognition. Liz Phair, Lisa Germano, and P. J. Harvey startled the rock scene in the '90s with remarkable debuts. Liz Phair started making her four-track cassette tapes while at Oberlin College in the early '90s under the name Girlysound. She introduced herself on a larger scale with *Exile in Guyville*, one of the most controversial and well-received records of the early '90s. Ostensibly, *Exile in Guyville* was intended to be a riposte in a way, to the Rolling Stones' 1972 album, *Exile on Main Street*, as filtered through the aesthetic of a lo-fi woman's perspective. Its arrival heralded a different kind of sex-positive orientation for women. Rather than the subservient and licentious attitude of many young female pop singers, Phair took the reins of her sexuality, singing frankly about her feelings towards relationships, sexual or otherwise, with candid lyrics providing the focus, supported by a primitive instrumental backdrop. *Exile in Guyville* was enthusiastically praised upon its 1993 release and it spawned a rash of imitators, particularly American female singer-songwriters, in the following years. Ironically, Phair the performer had trouble onstage, where she suffered from stage fright. This prevented her from touring extensively and when she did, she failed to project a positive impression from the stage.

Her follow-up, *Whip-smart*, found Phair rounding out her music slightly in a pop direction. While it wasn't received as unanimously as her debut, it did spawn a radio hit in "Supernova." Still, the pressure mounted. In a stylistic switch precipitated by her indie label's (Matador) new distribution relationship with Capitol, Phair began making her next record for Capitol. In the four years it took her to record it, she married, gave birth to her first child, and scrapped a recording session with R.E.M. producer Scott Litt. *Whitechocolatespaceegg* came out in mid 1998, and despite her well-documented stage fright, she packed her suitcase and joined the Lilith Fair in 1998 and again in 1999. Five years later, she returned with a self-titled effort, *Liz Phair*. That set featured singer-songwriter Michael Penn and pop songwriting team the Matrix in the production seat alongside Phair.

P. J. Harvey

P. J. Harvey made the same huge first impression as Phair. Released in 1992, *Dry* caught an audience completely unaware. During the early '90s alternative rock explosion, several female singer-songwriters rose to prominence, but few were as distinctive or as widely praised as Harvey. Over the course of her first three albums, also including *Rid of Me* and *To Bring You My Love*, Harvey established herself as one of the most individual and influential songwriters of the '90s, exploring sex, God, and love with bracing honesty, dark humor, and an audacious sense of theatricality.

Not only did her music demand to be heard; Harvey herself, raised on an English sheep farm, became a commanding personality. Although she shied away from much publicity, her visual image and her photographic representations were often stunning, intending to subvert traditional concepts of sexuality with a stark and original sense all her own. One need only look at her album covers to understand that Harvey's existence as an artist is as subversive as any within the punk realm. But it was the pretense of convention that she embraced that enabled her to exploit her sexuality as effectively as she did.

Stories from the City, Stories from the Sea, released in 1999, and inspired by her six-month stay in New York City, won the prestigious UK trophy called the Mercury Prize in 2001, making Harvey the first female winner of that award. After extensive touring in support of the album, Harvey split her time over the next two years working on new material and collaborating with contemporaries. She released *Uh Huh Her* in 2004.

Lisa Germano

Lisa Germano has never quite reached the critical heights and seized the popular appeal of Harvey or Phair, but her confessional, self-deprecating style has helped her sustain a worthwhile career. Germano, a native of Indiana, received her first big break in 1987 when a fellow Indiana native John Mellencamp recruited her to play fiddle in his band. Talented as a multi-instrumentalist, Germano stayed with the popular midwestern rocker for seven years before deciding to leave Mellencamp's band to record her own material.

Germano found her own quirky, poetic voice at the age of 30 with the lo-fi *On the Way Down from the Moon Palace*, issued on her own Major Bill label in 1991. It quietly signaled the arrival of a major talent. *Happiness*, Germano's follow-up, was much more melancholy and acerbic when it appeared two years later on Capitol. Sales of *Happiness* were disappointing though, and Germano, unwilling to endure the hardships of being on a major label, decided to leave, choosing to sign with reputable indie 4AD in 1994. After reissuing an altered version of *Happiness*, Germano created her first striking album, *Geek the Girl*. Confessional and uncertain, the material on the album, some intimately biographical, all very moody and atmospheric, painted a picture of an insecure and complicated personality. Her songs were honest to the point of unnerving. The intimacy proved alluring, and Germano began attracting like-minded fans. *Excerpts from a Love Circus*, another striking autobiographical work, this one a little more produced and polished, came in 1996. *Slide* was issued two years later. By this time, bouts with alcoholism and depression interfered with her work. And it wasn't until 2003, after recovering sufficiently from the pressure of her renown, that she recorded *Lullaby for a Liquid Pig*, a harsh, sometimes humorous look at her battle with the bottle.

INDIE ROCK

Sometime in the late '80s, the music of rock's underground scene changed from "punk" to "college music." This was not merely because its audience consisted of college students, but because the only radio stations that played it were those owned by colleges, where playlists, typically concocted by college students, were not accountable to advertisers interested in reaching a specific demographic. Anybody with a radio was free to listen. Or not.

At first, college music was a more intellectual antidote to punk. The bands were more clever, less violent, and less vehement. In fact, a lot of college music was just po-rock music under a slightly different umbrella, without the gloss generally affixed to radio-ready music. Bands like R.E.M., the Smiths, the Cure, and Camper Van Beethoven were among the harmless bands that helped define college rock. At the time, in the early to mid-'80s, they were the true alternatives to the mainstream.

It didn't take long for many of these college rock bands to become co-opted by mainstream audiences. Music fans, hungry for hardier music than the lite pop and metal of the late '80s, began developing a taste for the more subtle work of college bands. U2, for example, began appealing to college rock audiences in the early '80s before busting out as mega-stars later that decade. But as many of these college rock bands began attracting broader audiences and signing to major labels, fans of college rock, chuffed at losing their heroes, began disavowing them and seeking lesser known bands. Thus, the term "alternative rock."

But, in just a short time, alternative rock also became absorbed by the mainstream early in the '90s when Nirvana and Pearl Jam broke through. That breakthrough launched its own radio format, and helped sell records not by the thousands but millions. So, once again, alternative fans were left with nothing to call their own. First their college rock bands were stolen from under them, then their backup—"alternative rock"—was also snatched away by the mainstream. What was left behind? The major labels had swallowed up almost all of the worthwhile bands in the early to mid-'90s, signing them to rich contracts in an attempt to force feed them to the masses. Little did they know that while these masses had a reasonable appetite—witness the impressive success of Nirvana and a handful of others—they were not ravenous. In fact, rock audiences were not about to bite on anything randomly handed to them.

Sadly, this meant that many promising bands of the early alternative movement, eager to capitalize on the genre's serendipitous success, were disappointed at their reception and subsequently broke up. Had they remained true to their independent roots (rather than allowing themselves to be snagged by the corporate recording industry), nurtured their sound, developed an audience first, the results could possibly have been different.

Indie rock rose to prominence as a result of the feeding frenzy perpetrated by the major labels. At first, indie rock consisted of the bands that were either left behind or strong enough to resist the temptation of a big contract. There weren't many. By its nature, indie rock espoused a return to the original ethos of alternative music: low fidelity, elemental performance, basic production values. In many respects, indie rock is modern music made for fans and critics dedicated to the art of rock: it's adventurous, eclectic, defiantly independent, and restlessly creative, all things that keep intense music aficionados content.

> Indie rock takes its name from both the do-it-yourself attitudes of its bands and the small, lower-budget nature of the labels that release the music. The biggest indie labels might strike distribution deals with major corporate labels, but their decision-making processes remain autonomous. As such, indie rock is free to explore sounds, emotions, and lyrical subjects that don't appeal to large, mainstream audiences—profit isn't as much of a concern as personal taste. It's very much rooted in the sound and sensibility of American underground and alternative rock of the '80s. (All Music Guide)

Indie rock is also an underground phenomenon. Even the best indie rock bands—Sebadoh, Yo La Tengo, and Pavement, among others—have existed largely underground and on independently owned labels. When called upon to appear on the national stage, these bands do so hesitatingly, awkwardly. Although the best indie bands are quite accomplished musicians and songwriters, they are not polished performers or personalities, appearing aboveground as if the light of day hurts their eyes.

Like the alternative genre that sprang up in its wake, indie rock is a vast, all-encompassing category that includes a variety of bands and styles, from emo to twee, from lounge to lo-fi, space rock to noise pop, all largely dependent, if you will, on the tastes of the independent labels that have signed the bands. But for purposes of this chapter, we'll stick with the indie rock bands within our given time frame that have made the most impact, and have helped define the genre in general.

THE ROOTS OF INDIE ROCK

Many of the alternative and college rock bands of the '80s became the premier indie rock and commercial "alternative" bands of the '90s. These bands played integral roles in alternative music because at the time, many of the so-called alternative acts—U2, R.E.M., Elvis Costello—had been declawed, homogenized by commercial interests.

Sonic Youth, for example, perhaps the quintessential indie rock band (even though they'd later cash in on the alternative music craze and sign with a major label), blazed a trail for indie rockers to come with albums like *Sister* (1987) and *Daydream Nation* (1988). The band spent years exploring—at times miraculously.

The Pixies (left to right) Kim Deal, Black Francis, David Lovering, and Joey Santiago. Courtesy of Photofest.

Featuring Thurston Moore, Kim Gordon, and Lee Ranaldo, Sonic Youth served as the most emphatic archetype of indie rock band. The Pixies were also immeasurably important during the advent of indie rock with their surging, anarchic noise. (Nirvana frequently cited the Pixies as one of their most important influences.) The Boston band came together in the mid-'80s and proceeded to dominate the underground rock scene with albums like *Surfer Rosa* (1988) and *Doolittle* (1989). The Pixies reformed in 2004 for a tour and renewed recording activity. The band's lead singer and principal songwriter has remained active throughout the last 15 years.

A few British acts, including the Fall and the Jesus and Mary Chain shone rare but influential beams on the development of American underground rock. The Fall, a subversive, post-punk act formed in the late '70s and led by the misanthropic Mark E. Smith, proved to be as enduring and prolific an indie act in the alternative era as any. In 1993, the band signed to Matador and they made a significant push to attract an American audience with albums like *Middle Class Revolt* (1994) and *The Infotainment Scam* (1993). Smith continues to be a snarling icon of punk-inflected indie rock cynicism.

The Jesus and Mary Chain proved just as influential. With albums like 1985's *Psychocandy* and *Darklands*, the band crafted their Velvet Underground–inspired white guitar noise for commercial pop appetites. They remained together through the '90s, mainly on the strength of their emblematic early work. Their career was marked by frequent long absences followed by short periods of activity, including the recording of the charting *Stoned and Dethroned* in 1994 and the epic "I Hate Rock 'n' Roll" single the next year.

Like the Fall, the Mekons came together in the first wave of punk rock in the late '70s and have managed to remain together in one form or another, sporadically, ever since. Helmed by Jon Langford, Sally Timms, and Tom Greenhalgh, the Chicago-based eccentrics have bravely confronted and tackled numerous styles, from three-chord rock to country to reggae. Although they've sailed largely unnoticed even by underground terms, the band continued to release acclaimed albums in the '90s, like *The Curse of the Mekons* (1991) and the *I (heart) Mekons* (1993). Langford and Timms have also contributed to the rise of Americana with their roots side projects, including Langford's wry outfit the Waco Brothers.

A few other bands made deep impressions on the indie rock movement. Both the Meat Puppets and Hüsker Dü originated in the wake of the heavy, cathartic sounds of the original punks. Minneapolis's Hüsker Dü, fronted by Bob Mould and co-songwriter/drummer Grant Hart, melded waves of guitar noise with unexpected melodic hooks. Their 1984 album *Zen Arcade* was one of the most important underground works of the '80s and had a serious impact on many of the indie-oriented musicians to follow. The band also was one of the first alternative acts to sign with a major label, when they inked a contract with Warner Brothers way back in 1986, long before the record industry would hear from Nirvana.

Mould's subsequent work in Sugar retained an air of importance throughout the '90s, propelled by the legitimate breakthrough of alternative rock to more commercial ground. His albums, especially 1992's *Copper Blue*, resonated with the immediacy and passion of Hüsker Dü but with a more viable commercial side. Hart, on the other hand, didn't fare quite as well with his own band Nova Mob.

The Meat Puppets, a zany Phoenix, Arizona, trio together since the early '80s, managed to eke out some fame in the '90s thanks to Nirvana's Cobain who, being a fan, invited them to play with the band on their highly publicized MTV appearance on the program *Unplugged*. The show found its way onto disc and sold in plenteous numbers. The appearance also led to the band's unlikely signing with the London label in 1991, on which they released *Forbidden Places* (1991) and the appropriately titled *No Joke!* (1995). Prior to signing with a major, the Meat Puppets recorded with SST, a critically important indie label based in Lawndale, California. Hüsker Dü and many other influential bands—Black Flag, Screaming Trees—were signed to that label as was Dinosaur Jr., a band starring Joseph "J." Mascis, a drummer known as "Murph," and bassist Lou Barlow.

Formed in western Massachusetts, Dinosaur Jr. (the Jr. was appended after a San Francisco band by the name of Dinosaur objected) was a famously influential band in the late '80s that went on to record important music for a major label in the '90s. Dinosaur Jr.'s early recordings were high-volume distortion assaults long before Seattle's grunge took shape. Bandleader Mascis became something of an anti-guitar hero for the underground, rivaling the unorthodox artistry of "feel" players like Neil Young. Albums like *Bug* and *You're Living All Over Me* in the '80s were essential building blocks for many indie rock fans, as were the band's major-label albums in the '90s, including 1991's *Green Mind* and *Without a Sound*, made in 1994. Following the dissolution of the band in 1997, Mascis went on to record as a solo act, focusing his efforts equally on acoustic and electric guitar. At the same time, he began forging a new band called the Fog, who returned to electric rock form on *More Light* (2000) and *Feel So Free* (2002).

Yo La Tengo is often considered to be the quintessential critic's band. Their creative fearlessness and lack of commercial pretense made the band—initially the married team of Ira Kaplan and Georgia

J. Mascis of Dinosaur Jr. performing at Lollapalooza, 1993. © Tim Mosenfelder/Getty Images.

Hubley—underground favorites. Their sound, bridging the gap between sensitive folk and squalls of electric noise, was as unpredictable as it was sincere.

Named for the way a Spanish baseball player called for a pop fly ("I've got it!"), the trio from Hoboken began making noise early in their career, which commenced with *Ride the Tiger* in 1986. *New Wave Hot Dogs* followed in 1987, but it was *President Yo La Tengo* in 1989, an album that encapsulated the band's schizophrenic approach to songwriting, that started them on the road to ultimate cult status. In the '90s, Yo La Tengo added full-time bassist James McNew and continued impressing critics and fans of underground music. Recordings like *Fakebook* (1990), *Electr-O-Pura* (1995), and *I Can Hear the Heart Beating As One* (1997) were among the '90s' most celebrated indie rock albums.

PREMIER INDIE ROCKERS OF THE '90s

Taking its cue from these icons, the indie rock scene had a firm foundation upon which to move through the '90s. Beyond the reliable contributions of bands like Sonic Youth and Yo La Tengo, a handful of other performers and groups began creating a new indie rock scene, even in the face of the alternative revolution.

Pavement

Formed in Stockton, California, in 1989 by principal members Stephen Malkmus and Scott Kannberg, Pavement initially originated as a studio entity exclusively. But, encouraged by their material, they recruited a full band, including basist Mark Ibold and percussionist Bob Nastanovich, for their 1992 debut, *Slanted and Enchanted*. The recording, widely acclaimed by critics as one of the best "alternative" albums of that year, and certainly the first high-profile indie rock album in the wake of the alternative explosion, helped Pavement establish themselves, reluctantly, as a high-profile act.

The band's sound, unpredictable and "lo-fi" (meaning, recorded relatively quickly and without expensive production values), was refreshing in light of the heavy, obvious, and predictable riffing of the grunge bands. Early singles like "Summer Babe" and "Trigger Cut" were distinctive and new, heralding a true option to the prevailing hard-rock sounds of alternative. Despite the enthusiastic reviews, though, the record failed to generate much in the way of album sales. This would be a recurring theme with the band, and with indie rock in general; most refused to "play the game." That is, because Pavement and other bands were reluctant to get involved in the publicity and demanding tour schedules that many major labels required of them, they accepted less commercial and financial gain as a trade-off.

Not to say that Pavement didn't work hard. Their initial taste of success elevated the bar, so they needed to maintain that high-standard, at least in terms

Pavement, 2004. Courtesy of Photofest.

of songwriting. In 1994, the band released *Crooked Rain, Crooked Rain*, a more pop-focused effort that yielded the tune "Cut Your Hair," a single picked up briefly by music television. As a result, the band was asked to join the 1994 Lollapalooza Festival as a main stage act, a signal that they had arrived. But their reception at Lollapalooza wasn't exactly warm; in fact, they were annoyed with the whole idea of appealing to a mainstream audience. The next year, they released *Wowee Zowee*, a loose, offbeat rock record, in response to that lack of acceptance. The album's eighteen tracks covered a bewildering variety of styles from grunge to country to art-noise. It was as if they'd rather chase fans away than appeal to them. Still, the record is seen as one of their most accomplished.

Brighten the Corners (1997) was a mellower and more focused record, combining the best elements of the preceding two albums. It was at about this time that the band started to self-destruct, with members concentrating more on side projects or on raising a family. But the breakup was delayed until 1999, with the release of their final album *Terror Twilight*. The eleven songs, all written by Malkmus, brought Pavement's witty and oblique style into the context of folk rock, and the album is their gentlest and most emotionally direct.

Sebadoh

Sebadoh was born out of frustration: Dinosaur Jr. bassist Lou Barlow was frustrated by his lack of songwriting contributions, by the ear-splitting decibels plied by his band, and by the lack of chemistry he had with Dinosaur Jr. frontman J. Mascis. In response to that frustration, Barlow began writing and recording his own material on the side. But when Mascis confirmed the mutual malice by ousting Barlow from the band, Barlow's own dabbling turned serious. His side projects, indulgent and primitive, suddenly became full-time. One band was called Sebadoh, and it would go on to make as much of an impact in the '90s as his former band had made in the '80s.

Formed with songwriter Erik Gaffney and a casual collection of semidevoted musicians, Sebadoh developed into a backing band for both Barlow

Sebadoh, 1998 (left to right), Jason Lowenstein, Bob Fay, and Lou Barlow. Courtesy of the Library of Congress.

and Gaffney, as each submitted home-recorded tapes for release and toured behind the albums. They eventually recruited drummer/songwriter Jason Lowenstein, and the trio became popular indie rockers, admired for their unnatural productivity and their strangely schizophrenic sound. Often, Sebadoh flip-flopped between Barlow's acoustic songwriter tunes and Gaffney's unorthodox noise adventures. Sebadoh's diversity and unpredictability became their calling card, and by 1992 they had amassed a loyal following. They had two acclaimed recordings out by this time, *Gimme Indie Rock* (1990) and *III*, released in 1991. *Smash Your Head on the Punk Rock* came out in 1992 and *Bubble and Scrape* appeared the next year.

Gaffney left the band periodically, tired of the lack of acknowledgment he received as a songwriting force in the band, and in turn frustrating his bandmates with his lack of dedication. In 1994 he finally left. With new drummer Bob Fay, Sebadoh produced its most accessible albums, *Bakesale* and *Harmacy*, which helped swell its legion of admirers. But the band remained elusive and somewhat restless creatively. Barlow formed a new band, Folk Implosion, with John Davis, as a lark. But what began on a whim ended up turning into Barlow's biggest success to date, when his soundtrack to the independent film *Kids* spawned the Top 40 single "Natural One" in 1995. Neither of Barlow's bands—Sebadoh or Folk Implosion—could take advantage of the serendipitous success.

A final album, *The Sebadoh*, came out in 1999, and a new Folk Implosion album, *One Part Lullaby*, emerged that same year. In 2003 the band released *The New Folk Implosion*. Despite FI's flirtation with polished production and their fluke success, Barlow and his mates remained steady as cult heroes and became one the touchstones of '90s indie rock.

Guided by Voices

One of the more improbable indie rock success stories of the '90s involved Robert Pollard, an elementary school teacher from Ohio, and his band Guided by Voices (GBV). Pollard first began working under the umbrella of GBV in the early '80s, writing songs with his brother Jim. But it wasn't until 1985, when the band recruited guitarist Tobin Sprout and bassist Dan Toohey,

 ELEPHANT 6

Despite the pillaging many independent labels experienced in the early part of the decade at the hands of major corporations, indie rock held its own throughout the '90s. Because many of the best indie bands were picked up by major labels after the breakthrough of grunge and the advent of alternative music, smaller, independently operated labels were momentarily weakened by the loss of their best bands. But as the decade progressed and many bands discovered that the lure of money at the major labels wasn't everything, indie rock began regaining its strength.

One of the more intriguing musical developments in '90s indie rock was the birth of something called Elephant 6, a musical commune located in Athens, Georgia. A lackadaisical collective of talented musicians, Elephant 6 came about quite casually as a meeting place for musicians interested in the psychedelic sounds of the '60s. These musicians would gather at one ramshackle but colorful home and jam with an array of unusual instruments, toy pianos or otherwise.

ELEPHANT 6 (continued)

The E6 revolution began in Ruston, Louisiana, a small town near Shreveport that was home to the collective's core members: Will Cullen Hart, Bill Doss, Jeff Mangum, and Robert Schneider. Together, they began recording Beatles covers in ninth grade, thanks to a local shop that rented four-track cassette recorders for five dollars a day. They also gorged their musical appetites as young hangers-on at KLPI, the student radio station at nearby Louisiana Tech, absorbing everything from the Art Ensemble of Chicago to Sebadoh. After a few itinerant years spent trading homemade tapes through the mail, Hart, Doss, and Mangum settled in Athens, Georgia.

Their open-door policy in the already fruitful musical environs of Athens resulted in an incredible variety of collaboration. Bands were formed and records were released, many produced at the Elephant 6 compound and released by various independent labels nationally. *Rolling Stone* and *Spin* picked up on the phenomenon in their pages and the indie rock community waited anxiously for the next E6 projects. Premier bands within the Elephant 6 community include Apples in Stereo, Neutral Milk Hotel, Olivia Tremor Control, Beulah, the Music Tapes, Elf Power, the Sunshine Fix, Marbles, the Minders, and Chocolate USA. Epic albums from this eccentric group of musicians—Neutral Milk Hotel's *In the Aeroplane Over the Sea*, Olivia Tremor Control's *Music from the Unrealized Film Script "Dusk at Cubist Castle"*—are ranked high in the pantheon of lo-fi indie rock.

that they became a full-fledged band. During the latter half of the '80s, GBV was largely a recording entity and not much else. They released a clutch of records, but rarely toured. Even then, their recordings were distributed regionally, and their reputation as a band was limited to a few fans and those who worked within their circle.

In 1993, the band signed on with the national indie label Scat Records based in Cleveland and released *Vampire on Titus*. The wider familiarity earned them fans immediately, including many empathetic indie rock musicians who admired Pollard's quirky and prolific songwriting. The attention also helped GBV sign a distribution deal with prominent indie label Matador Records. *Bee Thousand* (1994) was the first album to be released under the new deal and it received a surfeit of critical accolades.

Since that time, Pollard quit his teaching job, an odd occupation for a rock musician, and nurtured GBV into a full-time occupation. True to form, they've continued recording prolifically, even releasing a five-disc collection, *Box*, consisting of their 1980s material. In the fall of 1996, after a lengthy national tour, Pollard and guitarist Sprout both released solo albums, indicating perhaps a break in allegiance to the band.

Indeed, the two had a falling out and Pollard ended up firing not only Sprout but the rest of the band as well. As the last remaining member, Pollard hired the Cleveland-based band Cobra Verde to help him make his next album, *Mag Earwig* in 1996. Switching to the TVT label, Pollard continued his frequent issuance of recordings with *Suitcase: Failed Experiments and Trashed Aircraft*, a four-disc box set featuring 100 unreleased songs recorded in supremely lo-fi over his first twenty-five years as a songwriter. While GBV's second album for TVT, 2001's polished and hard-rocking *Isolation Drills*, received strong reviews, the band hadn't expanded their fan base far beyond their loyal cult, and in 2002 GBV returned to Matador with *Universal Truths and Cycles*, while Pollard also released a number of side projects through his own reactivated Rockathon label. In the spring of 2004, Pollard surprised his fans with the announcement that he would be breaking up Guided by Voices later that year. The band's final album, *Half Smiles of the Decomposed*, was released in the summer of that year, and a farewell tour was scheduled to conclude with a final New Year's Eve show in Chicago.

Superchunk

Often likened to a happier Nirvana, Chapel Hill, North Carolina's Superchunk combined buzzing punk with jaunty melodies on its way to becoming one of the early '90s' most admired indie rockers.

Led by couple Mac McCaughan (guitar, vocals) and Laura Balance (bass), and also including Jim Wilbur (guitar) and Jon Wurster (drums), Superchunk has scored high with their energy and good intentions, even if they have never broken much new ground. Still, the only thing separating the band from wider mainstream success is their disdain for the corporate music industry.

Early on, the band formed its own label, Merge Records, a label that has been releasing material from like-minded indie bands ever since. Superchunk themselves put their first few recordings out—roughly from 1990 to 1993—on

Superchunk, 1991. © S.I.N./Corbis.

the Matador label, before bringing the operation back in house on their own imprint. Recorded highlights include the 1991 release *No Pocky for Kitty* and the compilation *Tossing Seeds: Singles 89–91* (1992).

Superchunk was extremely productive for their first half-dozen or so years, releasing records annually or more through 1995. McCaughan, a busy man with his involvement in the label and his own band, also formed a fairly active side project, Portastatic, an act that differed dramatically from Superchunk with its gentle nature and distant, anti-punk feel.

Palace

The enigmatic country blues franchise that goes by a variety of names—Palace, Palace Brothers, Palace Songs, and Palace Music—is the creation of the mysterious Will Oldham. Like many indie and lo-fi artists, Oldham possesses an eccentricity that keeps him well away from the glare of the spotlight. But that eccentricity also serves as a fascinating focal point for many indie rock fans.

Raised in Louisville, Kentucky, Oldham began his artistic career in film. He starred in the John Sayles picture *Matewan* in 1987 and picked up a few other roles in the years to follow. His Palace Brothers musical work started in the early '90s. His 1993 album *There Is No-One What Will Take Care of You* signaled the onset of an important and unique performance style. It was a collection of obscure, hillbilly dirges sung in an eerie, crackling voice. Oldham, who had no band to speak of, evolved into a more polished artist as his career progressed. *Viva Last Blues* (1995), a Steve Albini–produced recording, and *Arise, Therefore* (1996), a clever collaboration with David Grubbs of the band Gastr Del Sol, were compelling and inspired projects. But because Oldham has prefered to remain in the shadows—he refuses interviews, tours infrequently, and chooses not to list his musical collaborators on his record sleeves—it's difficult to trace his evolution as an artist.

CITY SCENES

Louisville

Louisville may at first seem like an unlikely focal point for the cutting-edge expressionism of indie rock, but the city has indeed yielded a plethora of worthwhile musical talents. Beginning in the mid-'80s with a band of high schoolers who called themselves Squirrel Bait, the Louisville rock scene expanded outward like ripples in a splash. The band spawned an entire family tree of musical activity. Squirrel Bait's Brian McMahan together with Ethan Buckler and Britt Walford formed Slint, a dynamic, highly influential band that was nearly as seminal as its predecessor. It was also equally short-lived, making only two recordings. Slint surprised the indie rock world with the announcement of a tour of the United States, United Kingdom, and Europe in the spring of 2005. The tour featured a reunion of the original lineup and included a headlining date at the prestigious All Tomorrow's Parties indie rock festival, held in Cambers Sands, England. Following the original Slint stint, Buckler and Walford turned some heads in their subsequent band, the entertainingly robotic King Kong, while McMahan created the peculiar For Carnation and spent some time collaborating with Will Odlham's Palace situation.

Squirrel Bait guitarist David Grubbs was the most prolific of the band's albums, though, forming two successful indie rock bands—Bitch Magnet and Bastro. In the early '90s, Grubbs delved into avant-garde rock with Gastr del Sol, a project with multi-instrumentalist and producer extraordinaire Jim O'Rourke. Grubbs also briefly joined O'Rourke in an edgy act called Brise-Glace. When Gastr del Sol disbanded in the mid-'90s, Grubbs issued a clutch of recordings, this time spotlighting his improvisational guitar work, inspired by his work with O'Rourke, himself a highly regarded avant-garde guitarist who made waves working with Derek Bailey and other improvisational icons.

The Chicago/Louisville Connection

When Louisville's David Grubbs moved from Louisville to Chicago he carried a lot of musical impact along with him. Grubbs initially formed a band called Gastr Del Sol in the Windy City with eccentric talents John McEntire, Bundy K. Brown, and Jim O'Rourke. But when Gastr Del Sol broke up in 1997, some say due to the tireless creativity of their principals, the city of Chicago became a veritable clearinghouse for indie rock. McEntire and Brown left to form Tortoise, while McEntire also helmed the quirky jazz-pop outfit Sea and Cake.

Sam Prekop and Eric Claridge, formerly of the seminal Chicago outfit Shrimp Boat, joined McEntire in Sea and Cake, and a great deal of critical commendation, if not commercial success. Another Shrimp Boat veteran, Brad Wood, went on to become a noted producer, working with Chicago artists like Smashing Pumpkins, Veruca Salt and Liz Phair, among many others.

Tortoise has gone on to become a near-legend in their hometown, with their adventurous explorations of jazz, ambient, electronic, rock, and whatever else they stumbled upon. After their first album, *Millions Now Living Will Never Die* on the local indie Thrill Jockey label, the band became icons, and jumpstarted the indie rock subgenre called post-rock.

Tortoise remained important throughout the '90s. O'Rourke and McEntire went on to work on a number of different projects as musicians and as producers. Brown, displeased with the group's accelerated success, left Tortoise before their first full-length recording. Although he maintained ties to the group through his work in various Tortoise spin-offs, Brown, save for his idiosyncratic and daring *Directions in Music* hobby, was without a consistent project for the rest of the decade. Still, the road connecting Louisville and Chicago proved a boon for both cities musically in the late '80s and early '90s, igniting scenes in both metro regions and spawning daring and inspired cliques of musicians who helped keep the indie rock scene aloft throughout the '90s.

Chicago's Alt Mainstream

All of this indie rock activity managed to focus national attention on the city of Chicago and its impressive music scene around the advent of the '90s. The hullabaloo pricked the ears of many major labels in Los Angeles and New York City. That, in turn, sent A&R representatives to investigate the talent. As a result, a few bands were picked up by those labels. Smashing Pumpkins, for example, issued their debut single in 1990 on a local label called Limited Potential. But by the time that and their next single sold out at stores, they were already signed by the Virgin label, where they would go on to become one of the biggest alternative acts of the '90s.

Urge Overkill, a former post-punk, grunge-style band that swapped their power riffs for velvet suits and a more soulful rock approach, didn't fare nearly as well. But they did manage to make some inroads internationally with their pronounced sense of style and distinctive rock. Their ironic detachment, evident early on with their brilliant indie EP *Stull*, prevented them from reaching their goal of "world domination," but they did rope in large audiences with major-label discs like *Saturation* (1993) and *Exit the Dragon* (1995).

Veruca Salt's dalliance with fame ultimately resulted in the same relative indifference. The band, fronted by Louise Post and Nina Gordon, met with some commercial success, in fact, enough to be shunned by most indie rock fans. But on albums like '94's *American Thighs*, originally released on indie imprint Minty Fresh, the band acquitted themselves as capable songwriters. Both women attempted separate solo careers and proved themselves capable of writing and performing with distinction.

Chicago Indie Rock Imprints

One of the reasons the Chicago scene solidified so quickly was the existence of a number of record labels that were set up to take advantage of all the activity. Thrill Jockey, Bloodshot, Southern, Drag City, Touch & Go, Skin Graft, Wax Trax, Atavistic, Minty Fresh, and others all came about to fill the many indie rock niches occupied by bands within the city. Thrill Jockey, Southern, and Drag City signed progressive and experimental rock bands, while Skin Graft welcomed avant-garde and noise acts. Touch & Go, a vestige from the '80s alternative and college scene, thrived by signing indie rockers, while Bloodshot helped to establish alt.country as a viable genre.

MAJOR INDIE ROCK SUB-STYLES

Slowcore/Sadcore

Palace's Will Oldham is at the epicenter of one of indie rock's most unique movements. Often referred to as slowcore or quiet-core, the genre features bands that have deliberately chosen to exist as the antidote to punk and hardcore. With eerily quiet and understated song structures, lingering tones, odd but affecting melodies, slowcore can be a gripping musical experience. Some of the best bands of the genre—Low, Codeine, Rex, Galaxie 500, Palace, and Sparklehorse—possess the ability to manipulate excitement with mild tension, stringing the listener along with enchanting grooves designed to fall softly, a stark contrast to the decibel-abuse of most indie and alternative acts.

Other prominent bands, for example, Lambchop, Mazzy Star, Drugstore, Bedhead and the Radar Brothers, retain elements of slowcore but are not often referred to as principal purveyors of the sound. One more recently acclaimed slowcore act, Sigur Ros, hails from Iceland.

Sadcore, incidentally, takes a similar approach to groove, slowing things down to a thick, turgid tempo. But instead of the abstract lyrical work offered by slowcore writers, sadcore is more deliberately downtrodden, with lyrics that communicate sadness, desperation, paranoia, and tragedy. Prominent performers include American Music Club, whose frontman Mark Eitzel stands as one of the more literate songwriters of the '90s; Willard Grant Conspiracy, whose *Regard the End* (2004) is a genre highlight; and Red House Painters, headed by Mark Kozelek. In the new millennium, Kevin Tihista's Red Terror, a group mixing sadcore with more upbeat rock and pop, proves worthy of carrying the torch.

Post-Rock

The term "post-rock" was coined by critic Simon Reynolds in issue 123 of *The Wire* (May 1994) to describe a sort of music "using rock instrumentation for non-rock purposes, using guitars as facilitators of timbres and textures rather than riffs and powerchords." In other words, it was the most experimental form of rock to take place in the '90s and later.

> Post-rock was something of a reaction against rock, particularly the mainstream's co-opting of alternative rock; much post-rock was united by a sense that rock & roll had lost its capacity for real rebellion, that it would never break away from tired formulas or empty, macho posturing. Thus, post-rock rejected (or subverted) any elements it associated with rock tradition. It was far more concerned with pure sound and texture than melodic hooks or song structure; it was also usually instrumental. (All Music Guide)

Originally used to describe the music of such important bands as Stereolab, Tortoise, Disco Inferno, Seefeel, Bark Psychosis, and Pram, it spread out to be frequently used for all sorts of neo-rock experiments from avant-jazz and Krautrock to dub and electronic projects. Other important bands within the post-rock movement include Ui, Labradford, and Flying Saucer Attack. Two touchstones within the genre include Slint's seminal *Spiderland* album and Talk Talk's *Laughing Stock*, both released in 1991.

At the turn of the new millennium, many critics bemoaned the stasis of post-rock, lamenting the fact that it seemed stalled out as a genre, with the collapse of Tortoise and the relative disintegration of the Chicago post-rock clique. But newer recordings by a handful of bands, such as Dirty Three, Television on the Radio, and Godspeed You Black Emperor have breathed new life into this abstract genre.

Lo-Fi

The term lo-fi originally referred to bands that used primitive recording techniques to make their records. Throughout the '70s and '80s, following the DIY era of punk rock, many bands without the means to record in a professional studio began making their records at home or in spaces crudely approximating studios. But as the '80s progressed, lo-fi also became more than an adjective: it came to encompass all the bands that would regularly record their material on, say, four-track recording devices in their own homes.

Throughout the '80s and on into the '90s, critical lo-fi archetypes Jad Fair and Half Japanese established the blueprint for much of the primitive lo-fi acts to follow. Fair and his brother David took the aesthetic to an extreme, not only recording in lo-fi, but performing with such limited ability and such a rudimentary sense of song craft that many didn't know what to make of them. In doing so, however, they opened the door for aspiring musicians of virtually any talent level, and unwittingly established the template for the much more prominent lo-fi movement of the '90s.

Despite recurrent bouts of clinically delusional behavior, lo-fi artist Daniel Johnston has carved out an influential career as a singer-songwriter. From his first crudely recorded cassette release in 1980 to the more "polished" recordings in the '90s, Johnston climbed the ladder of stardom, becoming the singer-songwriter of choice of the alternative/underground rock scene and championed by members of Sonic Youth and Nirvana, among numerous others.

Prominent indie bands like Sebadoh and Pavement both began as true lo-fi acts, generating their earliest material on their own four-tracks before earning enough money to enter a proper recording studio. Drag City, a successful Chicago label, specialized in the releases of lo-fi groups. Albums by Smog, Silver Jews, and Cynthia Dall all were recorded in lo-fi fashion. Melancholy, poignant, and self-obsessed, these performers' lo-fi output offered unsettling views of oddly insular worlds. All had their own musical themes addressing various alienations and inner turmoils. Many, especially Smog's Bill Callahan, put forth intimate songs chronicling a troubled childhood, failed relationships, and dashed hopes.

Another gifted but troubled four-tracker, David Berman, started his band, the Silver Jews (slang for blonde-haired Jewish people), with future Pavement members Stephen Malkmus and Bob Nastanovich. While the Pavement connection dogged Berman throughout his career, it also helped. Drag City label president Dan Koretzky met Berman at a Pavement show in 1989 and offered to release his music. Since that time, the reluctant live performer has stayed active with and without his Pavement friends, lingering long enough to win a loyal audience.

Another hardworking but hard-luck talent, F. M. Cornog, overcame a battle with alcoholism and mental illness that left him homeless. Today, performing under the name East River Pipe, he spends his time recording at home with his Tascam mini-studio. Credit wife Barbara Powers with his turnaround: in the early '90s, a chance meeting with Powers while he was sleeping in a Hoboken, New Jersey, train station gave him new life. The two married; she bought him equipment and revived his spirit. Soon he signed to the legendary Sarah label in the United Kingdom and the Merge label in the United States. Albums like *Mel* (1996) and *The Gasoline Age* (1999) glow with passionate invention and rate highly among indie albums of the decade.

The early Pacific Northwest scene, jumpstarted by Calvin Johnson of Beat Happening, and prolonged by the Riot Grrrls (see Chapter 9), encouraged their artists to record cheaply. The ploy was effective; the school of rock distanced itself from the more expensive recordings emanating from major labels, and attracted sympathetic throngs of fans to its cause.

In New Zealand, Martin Phillipps of the Chills, David Kilgour of the Clean, and Chris Knox, formerly of the Tall Dwarfs, were by turns brilliant and whimsical on their own four-track recordings. Recording budgets being what they were in late-'80s and early '90s New Zealand—virtually nonexistent—lo-fi recordings were generally the only option.

OTHER GROUPS AND GROUPINGS

Giant Sand/Friends of Dean Martinez/Calexico

Howe Gelb, principal founder and endearing eccentric, moved to Tuscon, Arizona, from his native Virginia in the '70s. He formed Giant Sandworms in the early '80s and began releasing material in 1985. Gelb, antsy and unpredictable, worked with a rotating cast of musicians, rarely establishing a hardworking full-time band. He chose instead to follow his muse, which often led him down strange, abstract musical byways. In the '90s, Giant Sand solidified somewhat with drummer John Convertino. Together, with help coming from various affiliates, Giant Sand began to gel. In 1990 they released *Center of the*

Universe, and in 1993 they issued *Swerve*, both acclaimed and credible indie rock albums with a western flair. Yet despite their progress, the band insisted on branching out. In addition to Giant Sand, Gelb occasionally recorded under the guise of the Band of Blacky Ranchette, an outlet for his pure country leanings. Drummer Convertino moonlighted in the lounge-revival group Friends of Dean Martinez and, along with Giant Sand bassist Joey Burns, also created neo-western indie rock with a Tucson-based band called Calexico.

Mercury Rev

Another band that was more like a long strange trip than a tangible musical entity was Mercury Rev. The band came together loosely in the late '80s in upstate New York, at the hands of a group of musicians—including singer David Baker, guitarist Jonathan Donahue, and a multi-instrumentalist who went by the nickname "Grasshopper" (Sean Mackowiak)—who preferred healthy doses of experimentation with their various collaborations. Donahue broke briefly away from the group to play with the Flaming Lips in the early '90s, effectively stalling his band's progress. But somehow the Rough Trade label in the United Kingdom still managed to get its hands on the band's demo tape, and based on that, signed them to a contract. Their first recording *Yerself Is Steam* in 1991 was wildly received for its brazen originality. Unfortunately, Rough Trade went bankrupt shortly after and momentarily broke the band's back. (In fact, the bankruptcy of Rough Trade sent repercussions throughout the indie rock world.)

The band toured, somewhat successfully, overseas, but continued to meet with tension and conflict. The band members didn't like each other much, and the tension led to erratic behavior both on and off the stage. Still, Sony picked up their record contract and the band stayed together to make a second album. Recorded in a barn in upstate New York, *Boces* came out in 1993 and was hailed nearly as overwhelmingly as their debut. The accomplishment helped the band earn a spot on the 1994 Lollapalooza Festival's second stage. But that gig ended when the band, for a variety of reasons including "excessive noise," was kicked off the tour.

Jonathan Donahue of Mercury Rev performing at Shoreline Amphitheater in California, 1999. © Tim Mosenfelder/ImageDirect/Getty.

After dismissing the difficult Baker, the band made the brighter *See You on the Other Side* in 1995. They changed their name temporarily to Harmony Rockets for the 1995 ambient excursion *Paralyzed Mind of the Archangel Void*, and followed that three years later with the *Deserter Songs* disc, another Mercury Rev release. *All Is Dream* was released on 9/11/2001, and four years later, the band issued *The Secret Migration*.

Luna

After New Zealand native Dean Wareham split rather acrimoniously from his Boston-based breakthrough band Galaxie 500, he moved to New York City and formed Luna, with former Chills bassist Justin Harewood and drummer Stanley Demeski (Feelies). Wareham's work with Luna was something of an extension of his groundbreaking "slowcore" in Galaxie 500. It featured languid guitar lines, his wistful, romantic tenor, and gently propulsive tempos. Luna recorded several noteworthy discs in the '90s, including *Bewitched* (1994), widely considered to be his classic, and their 2002 effort, *Romantica*. Wareham continues to record with Luna, having released *Rendesvouz* in 2004.

Jon Spencer Blues Explosion/Pussy Galore/Royal Trux/ Boss Hog/Honeymoon Killers

When notorious post-punk rockers Pussy Galore broke up in 1990, their unorthodox brand of "scuzz-rock," that is, a style of music characterized by lo-fi recording values and primitive performance splintered in myriad directions. That splintering yielded an indie-based noise rock movement that became more listenable as it strayed further from the musicians' extreme noise roots. Jon Spencer, the frontman for Pussy Galore, formed the Jon Spencer Blues Explosion (JSBE), an act so ironic it almost collapsed under its considerable tongue-in-cheek posing. Still, albums like *Extra Width* (1993) and *Orange* (1994) were exciting post-blues and rhythm and blues and his live show continues to earn converts. In 1996, Spencer teamed up with raw blues icon R. L. Burnside on the acclaimed *A Ass Pocket O' Whiskey*.

Just prior to his forming JSBE, Spencer had branched out of Pussy Galore to form Boss Hog, a side project featuring his then wife and Pussy Galore bandmate Christina Martinez. The duet formed on a lark, coming together spontaneously to fill a last-minute cancellation at New York City's CBGB's club. Their sludgy, lo-fi recordings featured Martinez, rather than Spencer, in the center spotlight. Martinez also performed in a band called Honeymoon Killers, a raw, junk-cinema-inspired New York City outfit that possessed some of the same sense of ironic detachment found in Pussy Galore.

Pussy Galore guitarist Neil Hagerty split to form Royal Trux. At first a duet with partner Jennifer Herrema, Royal Trux was a challenging, often unlistenable project inspired by the copious drugs ingested by the duet. Often, those drugs resulted in fascinating rock-based soundscapes, as on the famously abstruse *Twin Infinitives* and the more accessible *Cats and Dogs*, which is as much inspired by the Rolling Stones as it is by drugs and the band's eccentricity. Occasionally, though, the band was impenetrable and more than an acquired taste.

THE FUTURE OF INDIE ROCK

Indie rock remained strong as the decade of the '90s came to a close. The new school of garage rock buttressed the indie movement toward the end of the decade. Bands like the Strokes, the Hives, the Vines, and the White Stripes, all regarded as up-and-coming stars, initially began as lo-fi indie rockers before breaking through as integral reps of the new wave of garage rock.

A variety of underground-oriented bands are staking their claim to fill the shoes of bygone indie rockers like Pavement and Sebadoh. But with the commercial terrain ever-changing and the stakes for indie bands growing slightly richer, it's difficult to predict whether these bands will remain underground, or whether they'll cash in their credibility chips and vie for a more commercial audience.

As has often been the case, the Matador label, responsible for nurturing the careers of indie stars like Yo La Tengo, Liz Phair, and Pavement, now has promising acts like Cat Power, Sea Change, and Interpol within its ranks.

Hailing from New York City, Interpol derives its influences from the dark, gothic age of mid-'80s New Wave. Glasgow buzz band Fran Ferdinand possesses the same influences and is occasionally referred to as "the Scottish Interpol."

The Walkmen, formed in New York City from a band called Jonathan Fire Eater back in 2000, have gained momentum in the indie rock world with their two recordings, *Everyone Who Pretended to Like Me Is Gone* (2002) and *Bows + Arrows* (2004).

Death Cab for Cutie, a band formed in Washington state in 1997, has increased their cult following with albums like *Transatlanticism* (2003). Modest Mouse, signed to the Epic label, may not be in the indie ranks anymore but they have retained an indie rock aura along with British guitar rock heroes Black Rebel Motorcycle Club, who inked a contract with Virgin Records, and the strangely named And You Will Know Us by the Trail of the Dead. That band, signed to the Geffen imprint, has made inroads with their indie aesthetic and slightly off-kilter approach.

In the early 2000s, a band called At the Drive-In stormed the indie scene from their native Texas with a manic, punk-derived sound. But the band didn't last, and its members split into two separate factions, Sparta and the Mars Volta, both of which show dazzling potential.

Interestingly enough, two bands signed with Sub Pop, the label that unwittingly spawned the new commercial alternative era with its signing of

Nirvana and bands of the grunge era back in the early '90s, have also made significant strides in the indie rock realm. The Shins, from Albuquerque, New Mexico, and Hot Hot Heat, from Victoria, British Columbia, have recorded highly regarded albums, *Oh, Inverted World* and *Make Up the Breakdown*, respectively.

INDUSTRIAL ROCK

Industrial music in the '90s enjoyed widespread commercial success, an ironic occurrence given the music's obscure origins. The first wave of this sound appeared in the '70s in the United Kingdom, with bands like Throbbing Gristle and Cabaret Voltaire, and in Germany with Einsturzende Neubauten. These unorthodox acts fused an early synthesizer sound with the more aggressive racket of punk rock, which was just beginning to take hold, creating an explosive combination of experimental noise. Industrial also employed punk-styled shock tactics, using controversial names, fascistic cover graphics, and explicit lyrical content to create their overall image. For example, the label known as Industrial Records, one of the earliest labels dedicated to this sound, used an image of a gas chamber as its logo.

The term "industrial music" was originally coined by Monte Cazazza as the category of rock purveyed by his Industrial Records label, founded by Throbbing Gristle. The term was meant by its creators to evoke the idea of music created for a new generation of people, and in direct opposition to rock 'n' roll, which could be deemed more "agricultural" and blues-oriented. Industrial grew as an offshoot of electronic music known as "musique concrete," a form of "sound" made by manipulating cut sections of recording tape, and adding very early sound output from analog electronic devices. But the original industrialists had virtually no connection to what we know today as industrial music. Since the late '80s, industrial music takes its place as still another of the myriad offshoots of "alternative." Originally, industrial music, like its punk rock colleagues in the '70s, was challenging noise, purposely difficult to swallow, made by confrontational artists whose intentions had little to do with mainstream taste. In Germany, one of the genre's icons, Einsturzende Neubauten, advanced this approach, performing shows with metal percussion, guitars, and even jackhammers in elaborate stage performances that often wreaked havoc on the venues they played. This utilization of found objects and real-life "tools" helped secure the very meaning of the term "industrial."

In the early 1980s, advances in sampling technology and the popularity of the heavily synthesized pop sound of New Wave helped introduce some of the more accessible industrial musicians to a wider audience. New Wave bands like Depeche Mode and Gary Numan's Tubeway Army adopted the monotonous and robotic experiments of the industrial bands. At the same time, the original industrial groups also began to polish their own sound; Cabaret Voltaire and Throbbing Gristle experimented with dance beats. The "Industrial Revolution," musically speaking, had begun.

In the '80s, the more experimental side of industrial music became almost completely swallowed up by the dance and rock-music cultures. As the genre evolved, pounding beats, allowing for dark-hall danceability, helped transform industrial into an alternative to mainstream dance music. In contrast to pop-based dance music, industrial's trademark sound was acerbic and unsettling, but its rage took a backseat to the relentless repetition of the music, a quality that suited the genre's overarching concept of dehumanization nicely.

Early industrial trendsetters Throbbing Gristle broke up in 1981 and began taking root as one of the genre's extended family trees. One of its members, Genesis P-Orridge, founded a band, Psychic TV, that fused electronically generated music with a dance beat. P-Orridge would go on to become one of industrial's versatile mainstays. In Chicago, Phuture, a band critical to the origination of this industrial dance genre, also known as Acid House, formed in 1985.

THE GROUNDWORK OF INDUSTRIAL ROCK

Front 242 formed in Belgium in 1981 and became one of the more consistently innovative electronic bands throughout the '80s. Originally reminiscent of synth-pop outfits like Depeche Mode, Front 242 began adding a harder and more danceable electronic edge to their music in the mid-'80s. By the end of the decade, the band had become one of the biggest draws on the international industrial music circuit, not to mention one of the first bands on the famed Wax Trax! label to sign over to a major label. By the early '90s, the band stood alongside Skinny Puppy and Ministry as the most popular and commercially viable of the industrial groups.

Ironically, just as the band was helping to attract a wider audience to industrial rock, a flock of bands was beginning to add raging guitars to the mix in an attempt to add metallic power to the genre. When Front 242 resisted rolling with that change, they lost ground, remaining relevant but not particularly important through the rest of the '90s. They issued a challenging disc, *Pulse*, in 2003.

The Vancouver, British Columbia, band Skinny Puppy began attracting some attention with its dark, automated dance grooves. Formed in 1982, they got their start as a duo featuring Kevin Crompton and Kevin Ogilvie. Together, with the able assistance of producer David Ogilvie, the band released important early industrial dance records like *Mind: The Perpetual Intercourse* (1986) and *Cleanse, Fold and Manipulate* (1988).

Another band from the Vancouver region was Frontline Assembly, the best-known of the various electronic music projects undertaken by the productive duo of Bill Leeb (vocals, synthesizers) and Rhys Fulber (synthesizers and samplers). Leeb, in fact, worked under the pseudonym Wilhelm Schroder in Skinny Puppy before forming the industrial/techno-based Front Line Assembly in 1986 with Fulber and synth player Michael Balch. After Balch departed Front Line Assembly in 1990, the duo focused their effort in techno-dance. They released *Caustic Grip*, a techno-dance album, followed by 1992's *Tactical Neural Implant*, a more electro-disco-oriented effort. *Millennium*, released in 1994, showcased their return to guitars, and made some impact on the burgeoning techno-club scene. Fulber left the band in 1997, replaced by Chris Peterson. Leeb and Peterson have been busy ever since, issuing a bountiful array of projects, including the synth-pop of *Epitaph* in 2001 and *Vanished* in 2004.

With Ministry and Skinny Puppy attracting much of the attention, many other bands, also inspired by the mid-'80s sound of industrial, dance, and metal, began springing up around the world. One of those bands, KMFDM, also began elevating their profile rather quickly. The origin and meaning of the German band's name has long been up for debate among fans over the years. (In 1994, at the peak of their popularity, they even held a contest for fans to submit prospective guesses of its meaning. The actual meaning is "Kein Mitleid für die Mehrheit," which, when translated, means "No Pity for the Majority.")

KMFDM's bandleader, Sascha Konietzko, has been around since their inception, but, like Jourgensen and other computer-based musicians, has worked with an extensive cast of supporting talent. Konietzko does the lion's share of the work, including writing, producing, singing, sampling, and mixing. The band debuted in 1984 with *Opium*. It took them almost ten years to attract a commercial audience, which happened with 1993's *Angst*. The band split in 1999, but reformed in 2002 for an all-new album, *Attak*.

Another German band that attracted attention from the early industrial rock underground was Die Krupps. Formed in the early '80s by the duo of Ralf Dorper and Jurgen Engler, the band best characterizes the subgenre of European industrial sounds called "Body Music." This subgenre is dense, a wall of sound with a dance beat and bleak lyrics. Although Die Krupps came together early in the industrial era, they didn't enjoy much acclaim in the States until the '90s, when they released their larger-than-life disc *One* and its follow-up, *Metal for the Masses*,

Volume 1: A Tribute to Metallica. This work witnessed the band augmenting their synthesized sound with metallic guitar. As the decade progressed, Die Krupps inched away from their original electronic roots to a more rock-metal sound.

Another band that made a big impact in America was UK titans Nitzer Ebb. Also formed in the early '80s, Nitzer Ebb was an early proponent of combining the dark, abrasive sounds of early industrial and gothic rock with the insistent beat of dance music. Consisting of Douglas McCarthy, Bon Harris, and David Gooday, the band moved to the fore of the industrial and dance movement in the late '80s, but had a hard time negotiating the treacherous and shifting waters of the '90s industrial movement. At the time, guitars had begun filtering into the sound of industrial music, turning it into the first popular heavy metal of the decade. Bands like Nitzer Ebb and Frontline Assembly had some trouble finding their place amid all the noise.

Nitzer Ebb remained quiet for the first half of the '90s, choosing to step up and release their first album of the decade in the tongue-in-cheek *Big Hit* in 1995. By this time, however, a handful of industrial bands had almost completely redefined the genre and Nitzer Ebb sank back into obscurity.

Another band from mainland Europe, Laibach, attempted to hijack the budding industrial genre from its home base in Yugoslavia. Their collective imagery, Hitlerian in a sardonic kind of way, made them seem ludicrous on the one hand (which didn't bother them), and quite intimidating on the other. To wit, an appearance on Yugoslavian television in 1983 pictured the band with shaved heads and military attire. The show provoked the government to issue a ban on the name Laibach in Ljubljana, a ban not lifted until four years later, in 1987.

That year, an American label, Wax Trax! signed Laibach to its imprint and gave them their first real exposure stateside. Their 1992 album, *Kapital*, was done in a minimalist techno-industrial style. But their 1994 album, *NATO*, recorded while their homeland was being ravaged by war, saw the band returning to a more blustery, rock-derived noise. A subsequent tour and album, *Jesus Christ Superstars*, in 1996, kept the band on the industrial map in light of the sonic changes perpetrated by the blending of industrial and metal. They've remained on the scene right up until the present day—a miraculous twenty-five years together—recording most recently in the United States in 2004.

Jim Thirlwell, a native of Melbourne, Australia, moved to London during the height of the punk era. Put off by the constraints of punk, he began experimenting with tape loops and rhythmic syncopations, a project he originally called Scraping Foetus Off the Wheel, but often changed to other variants on the Foetus concept. Thirlwell's modus operandi was clear. He constructed a relentless sonic attack all by himself, with a rather tall edifice of synthesizers. He combined the fury of punk with the tonal flexibility of electronic music. In the late '80s, operating under the alias Clint Ruin, Thirlwell teamed with Roli Mosimann, a former member of the bleak post-punk outfit the Swans. They called this collaboration Wiseblood and released an important album: *Dirtdish* in 1986. The sheer range of Thirlwell's material was evidenced by his vast imagination and his incredible facility on electronic instrumentation, which had virtually no limitation. Thirlwell utilized this freedom to avoid being pigeonholed as an industrial rock artist. While much of his material certainly qualified as such, Thirlwell was far too ambitious and wide-ranging to settle for just one genre. In the '90s, he remained active, forming Steroid Maximus for several recordings and ultimately signing onto a major label where he recorded albums simply as Foetus. He released his most recent album in 2001, the disturbing cinematic/industrial soundscape of *Flow*.

Industrial Rock versus '90s: Ministry and Company

Much of what happened in the '80s—Skinny Puppy, Laibach, KMFDM, and Nitzer Ebb—continued through the '90s, looking to build upon their already substantial audiences. But one band, Ministry, really blew the whole genre wide open. In the late '80s, industrial noise had already given way to a new school of rock, one heavily influenced not only by the computerized sound of industrial itself but by heavy metal and punk as well. Like the other punk-influenced electronic artists in industrial music, Ministry came together in the early '80s. But where many industrial bands peaked early, Ministry would go on to do their most impacting work later, in the '90s. They landed at the fulcrum of industrial, metal, and rock 'n' roll, and for that reason, they are ranked as one of the decade's most influential and critically important acts.

Helmed by Alain Jourgensen, Ministry didn't make the move to a hardcore industrial sound until 1985, with *Twitch*. Jourgensen recruited a band for his next album in an effort to approach Ministry as less of a personal computer project and more of a full-band effort. William Rieflin, Paul Barker, Chris Connelly, and Mike Scaccia aligned with Jourgensen to record the landmark set *The Land of Rape and Honey*. The recording crystallized the vision of the new industrial rock genre. Thick guitars, electronic soundscapes, throttling, computerized percussion all characterized the Ministry approach. Its sequel, *The Mind Is a Terrible Thing to Taste*, followed with similar intentions. Both recordings were hailed as groundbreaking and Ministry became the first industrial act to sell recordings in substantial figures.

Capitalizing on Ministry's success, Jourgensen and Barker in particular began to expand their ideas beyond Ministry into an infinite array of permutations. Among these side projects was Ministry's alter ego, the Revolting Cocks. Also known as "Revco," the band was essentially the same band with the addition of Belgian vocalist Luc Van Acker. Jourgensen and Barker joined the Dead Kennedys frontman Jello Biafra to form Lard. The duo created Acid Horse with Cabaret Voltaire, 1000 Homo DJs with future industrial rock kingpin Trent Reznor of Nine Inch Nails, and Pailhead with Ian Mackaye of Minor Threat and Fugazi.

Rieflin formed a partnership with Martin Atkins, formerly with the grinding rock band Killing Joke, while on tour with Ministry in 1989. They called the alliance Pigface and based the concept loosely around the idea of inviting guests in to record in a variety of different settings on each album. They recorded a dozen albums between 1990 and 2004, most on Atkins' own Invisible imprint, an essential label in the '90s industrial pantheon. Guest appearances include Jello Biafra, Steve Albini, Trent Reznor, Lydia Lunch, and former Sex Pistol/Public Image Ltd. chief Johnny Lydon.

Ministry's Paul Barker released his own material as Lead into Gold and Jourgensen worked as a producer for Skinny Puppy's divisive *Rabies* LP. This album brought a more commercial sound to Skinny Puppy, and many fans, disgruntled with the result, attributed the subsequent Skinny Puppy split to the band's effort with Jourgensen.

Big Black was another one of the initial wave of bands fusing industrial with metal and punk. Led by Steve Albini, Big Black was essentially a one-man show, at least at first. A Chicago resident and a nonconformist, Albini played guitar and bass, programmed the rhythm tracks, and sang—doing everything, basically—much like the industrial duos before him. Albini began putting out Big Black albums in the early '80s but didn't reach his apex until 1986, the year he released *Atomizer*. It would become a sourcebook for virtually all other aspiring industrial rock bands, including the trendsetting Ministry. Big Black also set trends as far as the business end of rock music was concerned. They paid for their own recordings, booked their own shows, handled their own management and publicity, and remained stubbornly independent, all at a time when the alternative revolution lured many independent bands to major labels. It is for this reason too that Big Black remains an archetype for DIY indie rockers as well as industrial rock bands.

Nine Inch Nails

One of the biggest beneficiaries of the opening blasted by Ministry and Big Black was Nine Inch Nails (NIN), a one-man show spearheaded by mercurial persona Trent Reznor. The most commercially successful and popular industrial group to date, NIN was responsible for bringing the battering style to a vast audience.

As Nine Inch Nails, Reznor began recording his own Ministry- and Skinny Puppy–styled compositions in 1988, playing all the instruments himself. At first, he simply hoped to release a 12" single on a small European label, but when he sent demo tapes to a handful of domestic companies, many of them offered him contracts. Like the other computer-powered noise hawkers, Reznor was a one-man show by and large—recruiting a touring band for the road—but essentially accomplishing his studio projects alone. There was one element of his music, though, that set Reznor apart from his colleagues and served as one of the reasons for his success: his ability to structure more melodic and traditional rock and pop songs within the harsher sonic framework of industrial music. His lyrics—about rage and frustration and alienation—also became a focal point, another deviation from industrial, which frequently placed little emphasis on singing, let alone lyrics.

Reznor's pop instincts tempered the corrosive instrumentation and made it more readily empathic and identifiable. By becoming a personality within the genre, Reznor also put a face on what had until now been a faceless style. As a result, his brooding persona, accompanied by noisy rhythmic layers and angry vocalizing, helped him become a provocateur, an anti-sex symbol for the '90s. In 1989, he released his first album, *Pretty Hate Machine*, while he was working at a Cleveland recording studio. At the time, he had a background in dance and synth-pop and that experience surfaced on the album. While it was entirely generated by synthesizer, Reznor was able to inject his pop sensibility, even ballads, into the material. That innovation was the most critical aspect of Reznor's debut and it went a long way in introducing industrial music to a wider audience.

Pretty Hate Machine received only minimal attention on its release. But as time passed it picked up steam, eventually yielding three college radio hits and selling a million copies. Reznor assembled a band to support the record's success; three years of subsequent touring, including a gritty, often violent main stage appearance on 1991's inaugural Lollapalooza and opening for Guns N' Roses in Europe, helped advance the cause. Reznor's taut, manic bleakness had hit a chord. It didn't take long for controversy to kick in. In the '80s, industrial was controversial but its profile was low. Now in the '90s, with the popularity of industrial spreading and the video age disseminating graphic pictures into living rooms everywhere, the controversies sparked public ire immediately. A video of the song "Sin" was refused by music television for its graphic sexual barbarism. (MTV later picked up on a NIN video for the more rock-oriented "Head Like a Hole.")

Reznor petitioned to free himself from his label after the company, TVT, meddled, or attempted to meddle in the follow-up to his debut. But he was contractually bound. A joint release with Interscope followed, and Interscope set Reznor up with his own label, Nothing. *Broken*, an EP full of scathing sentiment and tortuous intensity, was released during this upheaval. Despite its excessive nature, it peaked in the Top 10 on the *Billboard* album chart. A video from that disc, "Happiness in Slavery," also riled viewers with its grotesque imagery, while outtakes from "Down In It," presumed to be taken from real snuff films, were investigated by the FBI. "Wish," a song from the album, won a Grammy for Best Metal Performance. Moving forward, Reznor, still miffed at his label's interference, only wrote for side projects, including Pigface and 1000 Homo DJs, where he dabbled in similar-sounding industrial rock ideas.

Soon, writer's block also set in. It wasn't until 1994, a full five years after releasing *Pretty Hate Machine*, that he had enough material for his second full-length album, *The Downward Spiral*. To conjure the appropriate mood for recording that material, Reznor migrated to Los Angeles, specifically to the home where model Sharon Tate was murdered by Charles Manson's gang. The anticipation grew. The seething work, a pinnacle of Reznor's creative production, debuted at No. 2 on the album chart. It would, in retrospect, become one of the darkest, most unforgiving albums to achieve multiplatinum status ever recorded. The single off the album, "Closer," had highly suggestive sexual content, but Reznor was so in demand that both the song and the equally radical video managed to dominate television and radio. He had reached a new apex.

In the summer of 1994, Reznor appeared at that year's Woodstock concert. The band appeared onstage covered in mud. Soon after, a remix album, *Further Down the Spiral*, was also released and it also charted high, unusual for a remix album. Reznor invested revenues from *The Downward Spiral*, building a state-of-the-art studio in New Orleans in a building that had once been a funeral home. While pondering his next move in the wake of sudden stardom, he produced Nothing signee Marilyn Manson's second album, *Antichrist Superstar*, which made Manson a superstar as well. But ultimately, Reznor was unsure about his next move. The hesitation precipitated another case of writer's block, one that lasted another five years.

Despite the lack of consistency in generating new material, Reznor's output proved remarkably influential. Dozens of high-profile bands adopted his sound. Groups like Filter, starring former NIN guitarist Richard Patrick, Pitchshifter, Stabbing Westward, Orgy, Godhead, Static X, God Lives Underwater, Skrew, Prick, and many more all dwelled within the same industrial confines laid out by Reznor.

Nine Inch Nails finally returned in 1999 with *The Fragile*, a two-disc set that featured Reznor continuing on his own downward spiral. Strong first-week sales gave it the top slot on the album chart, but it slipped down from there quickly, largely due to a change in musical climate, and Reznor's long absence. Since then, a remix album of *The Fragile* has emerged, as has a live disc, *And All That Could Have Been*. A new album, *With Teeth*, was released in 2005.

Marilyn Manson

Florida shock-rockers Marilyn Manson, led by Brian Warner, are discussed more fully in Chapter 4 of this book. But they also played a large role in the popularization of industrial rock. As mentioned earlier, Manson was discovered by Reznor and signed to his Nothing label, after having conceived an image that was more comic-bookish than threatening. Reznor took Warner, the leader of the band, under his wing, and created the monster Warner had always dreamed of becoming. His very nature was ghoulish, his photographic image, carefully contrived, depicted the kind of rock star that frightened parents and thrilled alternative rockers. His first album in collaboration with Reznor, *Antichrist Superstar* was the kind of stunning record that shocked listeners and bemused critics.

Beyond its purposely shocking content and grotesque imagery, the Manson sound was derived from equal parts industrial and glam-rock/glam-metal of the late '80s. A super-saturated guitar, highly processed and computerized, helped give Manson their signature sound. The similarity to Reznor's own sound, striking at first, would grow more distant and disparate as the two bands progressed through the '90s. Reznor remained steadfastly devoted to his one-man studio band, while Manson handed more creative responsibility to his bandmates. Indeed, as Manson continued recording throughout the '90s, layers of industrial sound peeled away until, most recently on the album, *The Golden Age of Grotesque* (2003), he most resembled a metal/hard-rock band, with virtually none of the dressage that characterized his industrial roots.

INDUSTRIAL ROCK, PART II: THE METAL EDGE

As Reznor's image began to fade, bands of his ilk also began to earn less attention. In its place rose up a harder, more aggressive sound, derived as much from the sound of metal as from the machine-gun clang of industrial. These artists were now beginning to base their songs around distorted, metal-style guitar riffs, which helped the style cross over to metal and alternative audiences accustomed to guitar-driven music. That is, the new sound of industrial rock was crossed with the sonics of heavy metal, and filtered through the disillusion and acute alienation of alternative rockers.

Some of the most notable bands in this category, Godflesh, for example, and Fear Factory, combined the pummeling grandeur of iconic metal bands like Black Sabbath with twisted electronics. Godflesh, formed in Sabbath's hometown of Birmingham, England, in 1988, was influenced early on by experimental performers such as Can and Throbbing Gristle. Justin Broadrick, the band's leader, was a founding member and guitarist of the seminal grindcore outfit Napalm Death, an extreme metal band, with whom he released the landmark *Scum* album in 1987. After that Broadrick formed the semi-industrial outfit called Head of David, which continued his penchant for excessive noise. Finally, he teamed with a bassist, traded his guitar for a drum machine, and formed Godflesh. On their 1990 album *Streetcleaner*, Godflesh was one of the first bands to merge metal with industrial rock. They were active and, for the most part, vital, throughout the '90s, as both a touring and recording entity. Broadrick announced their dissolution in 2002.

Several worthwhile bands took their cue from Broadrick and Godflesh, most notably dour outfits like Scorn (featuring Napalm Death drummer Mick Harris), Fear Factory, Coal Chamber, and Pitchshifter. Fear Factory formed in

1990, soon after Godflesh came together. Their sound, uniquely spread over industrial, electronic, and metal styles, reflected a modern society fixated on the cold harshness of technology. Their 1995 album *Demanufacture* epitomized the band's sound. For the better part of the '90s, the band fit neatly into the alternative metal boom alongside bands like Rage Against the Machine and Korn, sharing with them a certain manic relentlessness. Vocalist Burton C. Bell left the band in 2002.

Other bands that attempted to fill the bill in the second wave of industrial metal were Gravity Kills, Coal Chamber, and Grotus. Another band, the East German act calling itself Rammstein, took the idea of heavy metal to an electronic extreme, mixing disco-dance rhythms with the surging force of guitars, computers, and other electronics. Formed in 1993, the band blended industrial noise with a theatrical element: lead singer Till Lindemann often sang onstage momentarily engulfed in flames. Their second album, *Sehnsucht*, made such an impact in their home region that it debuted at No. 1. So far, the band's American presence has been limited, but titillating enough that they remain viable as a metal act on these shores.

 INDUSTRIAL RECORD LABELS

As with any rock 'n' roll niche, industrial had its most comfortable home, at least at first, in the hands of the independent labels that knew the music better than anyone. Here are a few of the most prominent.

Mute: Along with Wax Trax! the London-based Mute family of labels, including Blast First and NovaMute, was the most important of the forward-thinking industrial imprints, giving a home to artists as seminal as Laibach, the Birthday Party, Cabaret Voltaire, Erasure, and Depeche Mode.

Wax Trax!: The label was a mainstay of industrial music in the '80s. Founders Jim Nash and Dannie Flesher consistently managed to sign and produce many of the most vital acts of the genre at one time, including the many incarnations of Ministry's Al Jourgensen, and others like the Young Gods, Psychic TV, and Foetus.

Metropolis: Home to Front Line Assembly, Front 242, Juno Reactor, Peter Murphy, and many others.

Cleopatra: Founded in 1992 by Brian Perera, Cleopatra came about as an offshoot of the Los Angeles club scene, before becoming the home of many gothic, dark wave, and industrial acts.

Invisible: Martin Atkins of Killing Joke formed this label in 1989, and it was home to Sheep on Drugs, Bile, and Pigface.

Earache: Specializing in grindcore and other hardcore metal bands, Earache began releasing music by bands with more futuristic and computerized sounds in the early '90s: Godflesh, Scorn, Pitchshifter, and Ultraviolence.

BIG-BEAT TECHNO: ELECTRONIC ROCK

Just as bands like NIN, Ministry, and Marilyn Manson bridged the worlds of electronica and heavy metal, so too did many other bands, but from a slightly different angle. The Chemical Brothers, Prodigy, Crystal Method, Orbital, Meat Beat Manifesto, Daft Punk, Lo Fidelity Allstars, Fatboy Slim, and to a lesser degree bands like Propellerheads, Leftfield, and Dub Pistols all came at rock music from electronic backgrounds and were derived from other dance movements like Rave and Acid House. But rather than playing rock music with electronic instrumentation, these acts place the emphasis on electronica and the remixing of classic rap, hip-hop, soul, and R&B tunes: they play electronic music with a rock/R&B beat. The Chemical Brothers, Crystal Method, and Prodigy specifically keep their electronica firmly based in the predictable rhythms of rock music. Other electronica acts, like Fatboy Slim and Orbital, only occasionally lapse into rock beats, as on the former's 1998 classic "Rockafeller Skank," but they do frequently dip into R&B and soul for their inspiration and their sampling.

The Chemical Brothers, also known as Tom Rowlands and Ed Simons, made their name first as party DJs in the United Kingdom. But when they ran out of records rockin' enough for their parties, they set their sites on remixing classics and writing their own tunes. Their rap-rock-dance-electronic mixture was the first of the electronica acts geared to large venues.

> They pioneered a style of music (later termed "Big Beat") remarkable for its lack of energy-loss from the dance floor to the radio. Chemical Brothers albums were less collections of songs and more hour-long journeys, chock full of deep bomb-studded beats, percussive breakdowns and effects borrowed from a host of sources. All in all, the duo proved one of the few exceptions to the rule that intelligent dance music could never be bombastic or truly satisying to the seasoned rock fan; it's hardly surprising that they were one of the few dance acts to enjoy simultaneous success in the British/American mainstream and in critical quarters. (All Music Guide)

The result was a whole new club culture and dozens of indie and techno acts dumped their old analog tools for breakbeats and computerized rock/dance sounds in the wake of the Chemical Brothers' initial success.

America's response to the Chemical Brothers was the Crystal Method. The duo of Las Vegas natives Ken Jordan and Scott Kirkland emerged from the Los Angeles Rave scene as DJs and notable personalities, a switch from the customary anonymity enjoyed by most within the underground culture. Their notoriety earned them a major-label recording contract in 1996 and their debut, *Vegas*, a powerful collection of funk, rock, house, and big beat, appeared in 1997.

Another close offshoot of industrial rock sound was Prodigy, a UK act formed in 1990. Based on a rock/punk look and a more traditional rock band approach to live performance, Prodigy, fronted by Keith Flint and arranger

Liam Howlett, proved more than any others that an electronica act could make it on the rock circuit. As a result, they played less and less in the rave underground scene and in front of more mainstream rock audiences. The fact that Howlett was capable of writing anthems in this electronic/rock style made them one of the more successful acts of the genre. "Firestarter," for example, their 1996 single, debuted at No. 1 on the British charts and fared reasonably well in America as well.

As the electronica buzz was fully underway in the mid- to late '90s, Prodigy dropped its third album, *The Fat of the Land*, in 1997. Ironically, though the band was largely responsible for the growing electronica revolution, *Fat* was their most "rock" album to date. Underground fans saw it as a sell-out, but mainstream fans fully embraced it. The LP entered both British and American charts at No. 1, selling several million copies internationally.

My Life with the Thrill Kill Kult (TKK), out of Chicago, also contributed to the commercial aspirations of the genre. Formed in 1987 by the duo of Groovie Mann and Buzz McCoy, the team originally intended to make cheesy movie soundtracks. Their first soundtrack work, for a prospective film called *My Life with the Thrill Kill Kult*, never made it to the big screen. But the two decided to take the title of the aborted film and start working on a legitimate album. Their over-the-top treatment of odd and perverse themes, including sex, Satanism, violence, and gore, became their identity and they soon built an audience eager for their humorous but substantial approach. They released recordings throughout the '90s and beyond, and even returned to the original movie soundtrack work, on Paul Verhoeven's *Showgirls* and others, that they had intended early on.

The Lords of Acid followed the same trail as TKK, perpetrating an exaggeratedly sexual sort of house/industrial blend that kept the dance floors moving and imaginations titillated. They debuted in 1991 with *Lust*, a classic, if twisted mix of dance-floor raves. Entertainment value was high, but so was shock value, as the Lords utilized eye-opening, often violent samples on which they based their songs.

MOVING FORWARD

From the period of 1992 to roughly 1998, industrial rock, industrial metal, and its many permutations held sway in the court of the '90s rock 'n' roll music. While few bands broke through in a big way, only NIN, Ministry, Prodigy, and a few others actually made a huge commercial impression; the general impact of the movement served to tweak the overall sound of rock 'n' roll in the decade. Rock bands began using computers and samples. Smashing Pumpkins, for example, on their 1998 release *Adore*, implemented aspects of electronic music in their sound. In the studio many traditional rock bands began to see the possibilities that electronic instrumentation presented.

But the turn of the century was not kind to most industrial and big-beat bands, especially those that had made their mark with the house/industrial mix popular for a short while. The leaders of the scene failed to hold the imagination of their audiences, which was especially important considering the rapid pace at which change took place in the music industry during the same time period.

12

THE BRITPOP FAMILY

Throughout the history of rock 'n' roll, the emergence of genres and subgenres can nearly always be traced to the adage, "for every action there is a reaction." Punk rock came about, for example, as a response to the self-indulgent and self-important hard rock of the '70s. In the '90s, grunge, rock for the common man, exploded in the face of the more audacious, excessively stylized heavy metal of the late '80s. These actions and reactions can be clearly traced because so many styles crystallized so quickly. And reactions to those styles cropped up within just a few years.

Britpop, the style of United Kingdom–originated guitar rock that commandeered the charts in the mid-'90s, also came of age as a reaction to a prevailing trend. In the late '80s in England, electronic dance music had become all the rage. Weekend "raves" and underground dance clubs dominated the social music scene with its computer-generated grooves and drug-oriented culture. Rock audiences reacted to this with a hunger for guitar, and so guitar bands came of age quickly in light of that dance music.

Another element that inspired—both positively and negatively—the growth of Britpop was the grunge movement. The Seattle rock sound had made a huge impact on the London scene in the early '90s; some would even say the buzz about Seattle actually began in London when Sonic Youth, a New York band, brought Seattle's Mudhoney on a UK tour with them in 1989. The response was overwhelming and it helped ignite the excitement for the grunge storm quickly amassing over America.

But as grunge began saturating the airwaves, a reaction was taking place among British rock musicians. Rather than jump on the grunge bandwagon, many began fleeing from it, choosing their own course. Grunge was a decidedly

American phenomenon, and in rock 'n' roll terms the British were as accustomed to leading (the Beatles and British Invasion styles) as they were to following (blues rock, for example). So when the British scene sensed it was falling too hard for American grunge, they pulled back and chose their own path to guitar music. Britpop was a result.

Britpop is the common term used for a variety of popular British bands from the mid- to late '90s. It was a distinctively British form of rock music, much as "mod" bands like the Who, the Kinks, and the Small Faces—as well as glam bands like T. Rex and David Bowie, and mod punks the Jam—had been overtly British in lyrics, style, mannerisms, and dress.

> Its bands prized . . . the sense that they were creating the soundtrack to the lives of a new generation of British youth. And it was very definitely British youth they were aiming at; Britpop celebrated and commented on *their* lives, *their* culture, and *their* musical heritage, with little regard for whether that specificity would make them less accessible to American audiences. (All Music Guide)

INFLUENTIAL BANDS IN BRITPOP

The Smiths

Many Britpop bands were inspired by the Smiths, a groundbreaking pop-rock band from Manchester. They were the definitive English band of the '80s indie rock scene. Their guitar-oriented approach, at the hands of lead player Johnny Marr, rose up in the face of the proper, synth-based New Wave dance acts so popular in England earlier in the '80s, like Depeche Mode, Ultravox, and Spandau Ballet. The Smiths' impressive presence established the foundation for much of the guitar rock that followed in the '90s.

Two bands that capitalized on the Smiths' popularity also became hugely influential on the Britpop scene. Stone Roses, also from Manchester, served as a bridge spanning the guitar pop of the Smiths with the heavier, more electric Britpop bands. In May of 1989, they released their self-titled debut album, a recording that exhibited not only a predilection for the '60s guitar sound of the Kinks, but also a contemporary dance sensibility. The disc received rave reviews and almost immediately a throng of similar-sounding bands rose up in their wake. By the end of the summer of that very same year, Stone Roses, led by singer Ian Brown and guitarist John Squire, were fingered as the leaders of a wave of bands that coupled vintage rock 'n' roll with acid-house culture.

Happy Mondays

Another band that helped push the Britpop movement forward was the Happy Mondays. Also from Manchester, the band differed from the Stone

Roses in that they derived less of their sound from the '60s and more from the contemporary dance culture. They soared, briefly, rising quickly to the top of the scene, and becoming the most recognizable of the early Britpop bands, thanks in part to their maniacal frontman Shaun Ryder.

But the Happy Mondays flamed out as quickly as they zoomed to prominence. Despite the rave scene's rather pacific mood—fans of the scene, though drug-consuming, were nonviolent, even placid—Ryder and the Happy Mondays were not. They drank, they fought, they were controversial, irascible, and overly sexual. Their music conveyed all of this on albums like *Pills n' Thrills and Bellyaches*, but in a disjointed way. The Happy Mondays were also one of the first to incorporate hip-hop elements into their rock music. But all of these innovations were dwarfed by the band's self-destructive behavior. By 1992, they had disappeared into the background.

Stone Roses

While the Happy Mondays were busy partying, the Stone Roses were embroiled in a controversy of their own: a bitter dispute with their label, Silvertone. The group wanted to leave its ranks, but Silvertone took out a court injunction against them, preventing them from releasing any new material. For the next two years, the band fought that decision, all the while preparing the follow-up to their monumentally successful debut. When the band was released from their contract in the spring of 1991, they signed a multimillion-dollar deal with Geffen Records.

Unfortunately, the record they said they'd been working on never materialized—some say it never even existed, given the band's penchant for loafing—and the band took an additional three years, over five years total, to put a second album together. The hiatus proved disastrous. Exacerbating things, the album, titled *Second Coming*, was only lukewarmly received. The first single didn't make much of an impact on radio, and when the band tried to pull it together and tour, a rare occurrence, the operation kept unraveling. Drummer Alan John "Reni" Wren left, guitarist Squire broke his collarbone biking before their headlining appearance at the Glastonbury Festival, the band's first UK gig in over five years. Respect deteriorated. Morale faltered. The band dissolved. Squire left the band in 1996 to form the Seahorses, a more active outfit. Brown initially intended to keep the group together upon discovery of a new guitarist, but he instead decided to shed all the baggage and embark on a solo career in 1998. He is still recording albums.

As a postscript to this story, it's interesting to note that in many polls taken by the English music press during the '90s, the Stone Roses are rated more highly even than the Beatles in terms of overall popularity in the United Kingdom. So it wouldn't be a stretch to opine that their descent into irrelevance was perhaps the most spectacular nosedive of a rock band in the history of the modern era.

THE MADCHESTER SCENE

"Madchester" refers to a period during the late '80s and early '90s when the city of Manchester was the focus for a lot of the new musical talent hitting the UK independent music scene.

During this period, bands like the Inspiral Carpets, Stone Roses, the Charlatans UK, and the Happy Mondays commanded the attention of the rock scene. Electronic outfits like 808 State and the Chemical Brothers, tipped toward the dance end of the rock spectrum, complemented this sound too.

Manchester was no stranger to a big rock 'n' roll reputation. The city had earlier seen the birth of such iconic punk outfits as the Buzzcocks, Magazine, and Joy Division (later New Order) in the '70s and '80s, as well as the Chameleons U.K. and the band that started all the Britpop talk in the first place, the Smiths. The tenor of "Madchester" music included a commingling of indie rock, psychedelic sound, and dance music. Dance DJs and producers like Paul Oakenfold and Stephen Hague had a tremendous impact on the Manchester scene, while bands like the Happy Mondays and the Charlatans had a huge impact on electronic outfits like the Chemical Brothers.

The Manchester scene also had reach outside of the city, particularly with bands like Primal Scream (from Glasgow) and the Las from Liverpool, both of which are often associated with "the Madchester sound." Interestingly enough, the city proved to be a portal for not only a great musical revolution, but an intense drug culture as well. Because of the rock scene's close relationship with the underground dance scene (notoriously drug-focused), the rock scene became drug-centric as well. And while the altered states helped give birth to some terrific music, they also destroyed the careers of some promising bands, including the Happy Mondays and Primal Scream.

Charlatans UK

Ironically, just as the Stone Roses had begun their descent into oblivion, the Britpop movement began to take shape. The Charlatans, still another band from Manchester—who, incidentally, tacked a "UK" on their name to to avoid confusion and legal entanglement with an American band of the same name—took advantage of the opening first. Together since 1989, the band has built an impressive career for themselves that has continued through the millennium with keyboard-based grooves and lasting melodies. One of the reasons why they were able to endure was their ability to make subtle shifts in sound. Their reputation as "survivors" ripened, especially following the death of their keyboardist Rob Collins in 1996. Collins had been critical to the band's sound. Their subsequent disc, *Tellin' Stories*, debuted at No. 1 on the British charts.

In America, the Charlatans UK managed to earn the same respect they enjoyed from their countrymen. Although they failed to maintain the same presence in the States and their commercial radio impact barely registered, their records impressed fans enough to keep them on lists of critically acclaimed albums throughout the decade and beyond. Since the turn of the century, the band has released three albums, including a live album, a b-sides collection, and a new studio album, *Up At the Lake*, issued in 2004.

SHOEGAZERS

Shoegazer is a genre of late '80s and early '90s British indie rock, named specifically after the bands' motionless performance styles. Specifically, many so-called shoegazer bands were self-conscious performers who, by definition, refrained from initiating eye contact with audiences. But the fact is, the sound of shoegazer rock was more about atmospherics than about a reluctant performance style. The bands didn't call attention to themselves because they preferred to let their music do the talking. Many original shoegazer bands justified that sonic focus, some did not.

Of all the shoegazer bands to emerge in both the United Kingdom and the United States, My Bloody Valentine (MBV) stood out. They established the blueprint for the style with their debut LP *Isn't Anything* in 1988, and followed it with the momentous *Loveless* in 1991. If the band's debut created the shoegazer scene, *Loveless* epitomized and legitimized it. Controlled by withdrawn guru Kevin Shields, MBV redefined, frankly, what it meant to be a pop band, injecting their gauzy melodies with sheafs of white noise and distortion, while still retaining a sense of melody. Along with Sonic Youth and Jesus and Mary Chain, MBV became one of the most important genre-altering presences in '80s and '90s pop.

Unfortunately, the party didn't last long. Shields, a reticent perfectionist, didn't feel compelled to follow-up *Loveless*, even though—and perhaps because— the indie rock scene was near-breathless with anticipation. Shields virtually retired from sight, electing to take production jobs rather than tackle the challenge of another album. The band broke the financial back of its label, Creation, before getting dropped. In turn, MBV signed with Island Records for a hefty advance. Shields built an elaborate home studio with the money. Then he recorded, reportedly, two albums, both of which he subsequently scrapped. They recorded a few one-off songs for compilations and tributes, but a lack of touring and consistent recording tore the band apart. Talk of a new MBV album continued until 1996, after which it became something of an industry joke, as if to say, "Don't hold your breath." Still, like the Stone Roses, MBV made an incredible impact with a modest recording history. Their innovations in sound, both live and in the studio, gave forward-thinking musicians a new high-water mark.

Other bands that served to lay the foundation for shoegazer rock included indie bands like the elegant Lush, led by Miki Berenyi and Emma Anderson. Lush took the guitar feedback of My Bloody Valentine and added Girl Group-vocal harmonies. The Cocteau Twins were also tremendously important to the '90s British pop scene. They got their start in the '80s as an avant-garde act— with otherworldly singer Elizabeth Fraser at the microphone. But during the '90s, after they signed with a major U.S. label (Capitol), the band rounded out into a super-sophisticated, almost pop-oriented force with whimsical albums like *Heaven or Las Vegas* (1990) and *Four Calendar Cafe* (1993).

Bands that followed through the shoegazer door opened by My Bloody Valentine were, most notably, Ride, Chapterhouse, and Slowdive. But the list also includes the heavy Swervedriver, the enigmatic Cranes, Springhouse, and

Pale Saints. All of these bands at one time or another made significant impact on the American scene, whether on college radio or on an early version of alternative radio, which was beginning its introduction in several major metropolitan markets like Boston, Chicago, and Seattle.

The shoegazers came to the United States about three years after dominating the charts in their homeland. But there was a problem. As bands, many had an indefinable inability to capture the imagination of large American audiences, most of which were looking to grunge for their decibels. But while shoegazer bands were compelling to enthusiastic indie rock fans, they were not empathic personalities. They didn't distinguish themselves in interviews, and they didn't make the kind of news that would show up in the tabloids. Thus, many of the bands failed to hold attention stateside. Soon, the movement retreated back to the United Kingdom where they had their own war for attention to wage with the glistening personalities of the new Britpoppers.

SOLIDIFYING THE BRITPOP REVOLUTION

London Suede

One band that helped solidify the arrival of Britpop revolution after the Stone Roses disappeared was Suede. With the lyrical depth of the Smiths, and healthy daubs of English sounds like Marc Bolan (T. Rex) and David Bowie, Suede—also known as "London Suede" in America, for legal reasons—trumpeted the arrival of the Britpop revolution. So heightened was the anticipation for their debut, the unrestrained English press heralded them as "The Best New Band in Britain."

Their debut, *Suede*, released in 1993, became a smash with its commingling of glam-rock and intelligent introspection. Frontman Brett Anderson was a first-rate showman, utilizing humor, ribaldry, and passion in his writing and his foppish style. Guitarist Bernard Butler, the band's chief musical talent and principal melodist, stood alongside his gallant frontman with quiet majesty. The balance was perfect. Anderson's girlfriend, Justine Frischmann, joined the band as second guitarist early on, only to leave in 1992 to form her own act, the punk-derived Britpop act Elastica.

Suede entered the charts in the United Kingdom at No. 1 and earned the band a prestigious Mercury Prize for Best Album that same year. In an attempt to capitalize on their momentum, they took their show to America, but their progress was halted when Butler's father died and he returned home. To that point, the tour had been faltering. The band's performance didn't hold together, and their opening act, the Cranberries, a Dublin act with MTV support already in place, began upstaging them.

For their sophomore effort in 1994, *Dog Man Star*, Suede ventured ever closer to glam-rock, embracing the illustrious past of British rock passionately.

But the critical balance between Anderson and Butler grew tenuous during the making of the album; the tension escalated and their differences magnified as the band grew in stature. Butler left the band soon after to set out on a solo career, and Anderson began picking up the pieces of Suede, not easy after losing such an integral member. Eventually, Anderson discovered young guitarist Richard Oakes and the band released *Coming Up* with its new lineup. The record returned the band to the top of the British charts.

Blur

While Suede was reintroducing glam-rock to young audiences, another band, Blur, set out to capture the same English audience. The band debuted in 1991 with *Leisure*, a bland but commercially successful album that led to the moderately more interesting *Modern Life Is Rubbish*. The second disc featured the band moving in a decidedly less pop and more "British" direction. The move was finalized in *Parklife*, a Kinks-inspired rock opera of sorts that featured Blur as that most English of English pop-rock bands. The project crowned them, at least temporarily, co-chairs of their homeland's Britpop department.

Released in 1994, *Parklife* would render Blur the second widely recognized entry in the newly opened Britpop category. It resulted in a string of singles in the United Kingdom, but like its two previous albums, failed to make much of an impression in America. Frontman Damon Albarn and guitarist Graham Coxon, the principals of the band, were reluctant personalities and too English, apparently, for American audiences. In fact, that was also the problem with Suede. Although they created the kind of music designed to appeal at least in part to American guitar-hungry rock fans, they were pegged as "too British." Both bands paid little attention, as many others did, to courting the American audience. Both chose to veil their material with British references to London high life and times, often choosing site-specific settings and referring to local color, both urban and rural, whenever possible, much like the Kinks did in their '60s heyday. In the case of Suede's Anderson, the dress was gentlemanly, similar to another proper Englishman, Roxy Music's Bryan Ferry. Ironically, Suede was so English, they were slapped with the tag "London" to distinguish themselves from an admittedly irrelevant American lounge singer. The name in the States, "London Suede," was more emphatically English than ever.

This snubbing of American listenership prevented both Blur and Suede from breaking through significantly. Although there was a groundswell of Britpop recognition among American rock fans, radio didn't pick up on it with much enthusiasm. Grunge was well underway and post-grunge pop bands like Collective Soul and the Goo Goo Dolls were just beginning to take off. The jam scene, then embryonic, was also starting to weave its own spell on listeners. Alternative rock had taken root and the festival scene was blossoming. Britpop was just another entrant in the sweepstakes of '90s rock music. Until Oasis arrived.

Oasis

Led by brothers Noel and Liam Gallagher, Oasis was the first band to legitimize the Britpop movement in the eyes of the American rock fan. Perhaps that legitimacy came at the hands of its music, which, intensely Beatle-influenced, managed to linger longer than that of so many other Britpop bands eager to make an impression. Then again, perhaps that legitimacy came in the form of their combative personalities. Stories drifted to these shores of how the brothers often fought (reminiscent of how Ray and Dave Davies, brothers in the Kinks, often behaved), how they trashed hotel rooms, how they lived the life of rock stars without guilt or hesitation.

Formed in Manchester by Liam Gallagher (vocals), Paul "Bonehead" Arthurs (guitar), Paul McGuigan (bass), and Tony McCaroll (drums), Oasis wasn't fully together until they invited Liam's brother Noel into the fold. Then a guitar technician for another popular Manchester band, the Inspiral Carpets, Noel consented to join the group if he was given full control and complete songwriting responsibility. He was, and Oasis became an official entity. One of their first few gigs involved filling a last-minute slot that had opened up at a Glasgow venue. The band piled in the van, with no time to assemble their fans for the evening, convinced the gig would be a washout. But Alan McGee, head of the cutting-edge Creation label, happened to be there early enough to catch the opening act (he was a Glasgow native). He had heard about Oasis and their belligerent reputation, and was reluctant to even consider them. But after he witnessed the show, he signed them on the spot.

Oasis shot to stardom quickly. Two smash singles, "Supersonic" and "Shakermaker," built anticipation for their debut album, *Definitely Maybe*, which came out in August 1994 and became the fastest-selling debut album in British pop history.

Oasis journeyed to America in 1995, after weathering a difficult fall tour in the states in late 1994, and released the single "Live Forever," which did well on music television and radio, pushing *Definitely Maybe* to gold status in the United States and helping the band sell out their subsequent American tour.

THE SECOND WAVE OF BRITPOP

The band's success spawned a second wave of Britpop bands, including Supergrass, Mansun, Cast, Embrace, Kula Shaker, Gene, Marion, and the Boo Radleys, all of which made some strides, and built modest audiences, in America. In England, they were widely praised. Gene, for example, was named Best New Band in 1995 by the tabloid press. Kula Shaker, led by Crispin Mills, debuted at No. 1 with its first album, which went on to become the fastest-selling debut since Oasis' own. Many of these bands parlayed their immediate rise into long-term success, like Supergrass, who are still together, released their greatest hits package, *Supergrass Is 10: The Best of 94-04* in late 2004, and a new album, *Road to Rouen*, in late 2005. Stereophonics and Travis, both melodic pop-rock bands in the mold of Oasis, are also still together, and busy building an American audience.

A handful of other bands attracted a fair share of attention during this time, without a real affiliation to Britpop. Pulp, James, and the Manic Street Preachers all had very different histories. Pulp and the Manics had careers long before Britpop came together. And James, an early Manchester act, had nearly captured the same audience as the Smiths in the late '80s. During the summer of 1995, Oasis recorded their follow-up (What's the Story) Morning Glory? Released in the fall of that year, the record became the second-biggest album in British pop history, thanks in part to the popularity of the disc's hit single "Wonderwall." The recording did well in America, selling 5 million copies. Oasis had become the biggest band in the world, leaving every other Britpop band in the dust. Their third album, Be Here Now, topped the charts upon its release and nearly did the same in the States. But tensions within the band rose, as they typically did while on tour, and the members separated for a time to collect themselves. The fact that Be Here Now was reviewed unfavorably, the first time the band had been hit with critical disapprobation, didn't help.

Arthurs left unceremoniously in 1999 of his own accord as the band was recording its fourth album. The Gallaghers were unmoved by the estrangement, and their callousness met with fan disapproval. The album, Standing on the Shoulders of Giants, emerged in 2000, but was also received with a less-than-enthusiastic response. The tours still grew, and the band's worldwide reputation as premier rockers remained intact. Heathen Chemistry (2002) found the band's sales eroding further, as the Gallagher brothers ended up on more tabloid pages than rock 'n' roll stages. Oasis began to collapse under the weight of celebrity expectations. The leading light of the Britpop movement began to fade as a result. Don't Believe the Truth, in 2005, recaptured some of Oasis' American audience.

One band stepped up in Oasis' place in the late '90s, but fell well short of taking the throne. Ocean Colour Scene, a musicianly R&B/pop/rock act out of the industrial city of Birmingham, actually formed in the late '80s but didn't attract much attention until ten years later, when their 1996 album, Moseley Shoals, their second release, rocketed to the top of the charts. Their third album, Marchin' Already, bumped Oasis' Be Here Now off the top slot on the charts. Their American impact, despite glowing reviews and the championing of the band by Oasis and others, has been negligible.

THE DOWNFALL OF BRITPOP

Blur versus Oasis

One of the other defining moments in the downfall of Britpop actually had to do with a band rising, rather than descending. Blur was a band that had been so popular at home there was actually a music tabloid war addressing who was best: Blur or Oasis. (This feud recalled the old Beatles versus Stones debate in the mid-'60s.) But Blur began to sidle away from its emphatic British-isms in favor of a more introspective, indie rock sound, ala Sonic Youth, Pavement, and the like. After recording the very British *The Great Escape*—an album that debuted at No. 1 in the United Kingdom—the band felt they had exhausted that approach; a change was in order. They were losing the toe-to-toe battle with Oasis, whose American popularity was much coveted, and they were eager for some kind of reinvention. It was either that or break up. Blur almost opted for the latter in 1996. Instead, they chose to take the year off.

The band's ultimate shift to a more indie rock/grungy sound, the first strains of which are found on Blur's 1997 album, served as a reintroduction to the band and proved a commercially successful risk. While British fans weren't keen on the change, U.S. rock fans approved of the arty Blur sound, as did radio. "Song 2," the single off the new *Blur* disc, became the band's biggest hit in the United States and launched their career in a big way on this side of the Atlantic. But America's gain was Britpop's loss. The band's transmigration cast another blow to the already weakening subgenre.

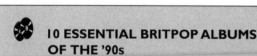

10 ESSENTIAL BRITPOP ALBUMS OF THE '90s

Oasis, *Definitely Maybe*

Suede, *Dog Man Star*

Blur, *Parklife*

Gene, *Olympian*

The Boo Radleys, *Wake Up!*

Ocean Colour Scene, *Moseley Shoals*

Pulp, *Different Class*

Cast, *All Change*

Supergrass, *I Should Coco*

Reef, *Glow*

Content with its own lateral move, Blur issued the equally impressive *13* in 1999. The album, which addressed the changes experienced by the band as well as singer Damon Albarn's star-crossed relationship with Elastica leader Justine Frischmann, saw the band experiment in ways it had only hinted at in the past. Perhaps the success of Radiohead (see below) had unveiled possibilities for Blur. Or perhaps it was headed that way in its own cosmic alignment. For the moment, Blur had sealed its transition and had begun to enjoy a more firmly rooted audience because of it.

But their momentum screeched to a halt when guitarist Coxon, after seven albums and twelve years, departed the band to kick some bad habits and embark on a solo career. He has since cleaned up and released a half-dozen or so albums in a flurry of productivity. Damon Albarn, for his part, also remained active after the Blur split, releasing a solo album, forming a cartoon-oriented dance/electronic music act called Gorillaz, and immersing himself in the music of Africa. He released an album, *Mali Music*, in 2002, did some film score work, and guested on several albums, including Fatboy Slim's *Palookaville* (2004) and classic composer Michael Nyman's *Ravenous*.

BRITISH POP BEYOND BRITPOP

Even after the movement's star began to fade, several individual bands kept going strong internationally, and the less-youth-oriented British trad-rock movement kept its classicism alive.

Radiohead

Originating in Oxford, England, Radiohead rose up during the early years of Britpop, but shared more in common with the soaring rock sounds of U2 and Nirvana than the cheeky British tones of Blur and Suede. Their first set, *Pablo Honey*, released in 1993, managed to hit it big from the outset, with the catchy single "Creep," a song that became something of an anthem in the States and an unexpected hit. The single prompted immediate touring in America. Ironically, Britain did not respond to the band until the single was reissued in their homeland some months later.

The band's sound, characterized by Thom York's angsty lyrics and a textured three-guitar approach, attracted a loyal base of fans. On their follow-up, *The Bends*, the band continued their ascent into soaring, deeply felt hard rock. The record was unanimously well received, but sold slowly, mainly because radio didn't respond to the band's single, "Just." A second single, "Fake Plastic Trees," fared better. But competition in the States at the hands of grunge and Britpop prevented the band from taking off. That would soon change. Britpop and grunge sailed off into the sunset. In 1996, the band disappeared to record their third album, a collection that would ultimately change their course, musical and otherwise, for the rest of their career. Radiohead is discussed in further detail in Chapter 4.

Coldplay

A band that has made as much impact in the United States as in their native United Kingdom, Coldplay came together rather casually within the scholarly confines of the University College in London. Although all four of its members had been musically inclined, they were never intent on making a go of a career in music until 1999, when some of the tossed-off recordings they were making caught the attention of Parlophone, a major British label and a home, of course, to the Beatles. Their style, simple, acoustic-based pop with sublime melodic flair, earned them large amounts of praise quickly. Their debut album, *Parachutes*, came out in the States in late 2000 and captured a prestigious UK nomination for the Mercury Prize. By the end of the year, the first single, "Yellow," became a massive hit on both sides of the Atlantic.

The debut album from Coldplay marked a clear change, a hard left turn, in direction for modern UK rock music. The days of the straight-rocking Britpop of bands like Oasis had come to a close and most of the musical world shifted its sites to Radiohead. Still, Radiohead was unpredictable, and had been inactive following *OK Computer*. A band was needed to fill the void; Glasgow's Travis, led by singer Fran Healey, stepped up for a while. But the United States didn't fully respond. Reef, a band out of Glastonbury, rose up out of the pack momentarily with a Stonesy flavor, even making a slight impact in the States. But it was Coldplay that entered the fray, in the late '90s, and took control of the British music scene with their 2000 debut.

Parachutes propelled Coldplay directly into the limelight. Radiohead comparisons surfaced. They both shared a certain subtlety and an aversion to rock clichés. But Coldplay distinguished themselves with a simplistic approach to making moving, introspective rock. Soon, the demands on the band began in good measure, and the labor that accompanies popularity took its toll. Singer Chris Martin, in particular, reacted adversely to the strain of performing every night, as a singer and as a celebrity. They did few photo shoots and interviews, and actually ended up canceling a good number of dates on their inaugural U.S. tour. They also canceled a slate of dates on the band's European tour.

By the fall of 2001, Coldplay returned to the studio for a second album, defying expectations of their quick demise. Their sophomore collection, called *A Rush of Blood to the Head*, was released in August 2002 to some skepticism, but accolades as well. The band supported the album for a time, before going on hiatus. During that time, Martin married Hollywood actress Gwyneth Paltrow and started a family, all the while being challenged to defend his privacy vis-à-vis the paparazzi. A June 2005 album, *X&Y*, along with an important single, "Speed of Sound," cemented Coldplay's stature as rock's newest superstars.

The Verve

Formed in the northern English city of Wigan in 1989, the Verve existed far from the center of the Britpop maelstrom happening in Manchester and London. Their debut in 1993, *A Storm in Heaven*, out amid the ballyhooed project by the Stone Roses, succeeded in distancing the band from the growing Britpop movement and avoiding any confusion about their being a contender in that genre. While the band did share some affinity for the Beatles, a Britpop staple, they also incorporated elements of psychedelia, krautrock, classical, and jam-rock. Fronted by the gangly singer Richard Ashcroft and guitarist Nick McCabe, the Verve lived on the edge. They had a famous appetite for hallucinogens and a penchant for violence. Their second recording, *A Northern Soul*, proved to be their undoing. Done in 1995, the sessions were recorded under the influence of the narcotic Ecstasy. The result was intense and critically acclaimed, but sales were poor and tensions grew. Ashcroft handled the failure by leaving just three months after the record's release.

His estrangement didn't last long. He reformed the band for their 1997 release, *Urban Hymns*, an impressive recording that yielded the band's first commercial hit, "Unfinished Symphony," a single built around a looped sample of a symphonic recording of the Rolling Stones' "The Last Time." The disc launched Verve into an elite group of British bands successful in America. But even at their peak, the curse of their ill-fated past remained. A court awarded 100 percent of the song's publishing rights to ABKCO Music, which controls the Stones' catalog, tempering the band's success considerably, both financially and creatively. The second single from the album, the haunting "The Drugs Don't Work," became the Verve's first UK No. 1 hit, and "Lucky Man" and "Sonnet" followed. Guitarist McCabe left the group while on a 1998 U.S. tour, and the band officially split in the spring of 1999. Since then, both McCabe and Ashcroft have focused on solo careers.

WHO'S NEXT?

By the year 2000, the initial wave had subsided: Oasis had all but collapsed under the weight of fame, Blur had rejected pop for a more introspective sound, and Radiohead had eschewed nearly all rock convention and gone its own separate way. Coldplay took a good deal of 2004 off, and plans to release their third album in mid-2005.

So what next for British rock in America? A few bands have recently planted seed over the last two years. All have exhibited promise, though it's too early to tell which of those seeds will take root and which will wither.

Travis has the most established roots of all the existing British rock bands. Along with Cast, Reef, Kula Shaker, Ocean Colour Scene, and Embrace, Travis was one of the most prominent of the British trad-rock bands on the scene in the mid- to late '90s and beyond. Their down-to-earth traditional rock followed Oasis' lead in the latter part of the '90s and to overwhelmingly positive notices. The Glasgow act has received an avalanche of positive reviews over the years for the albums, including *Good Feeling* (1997), *The Man Who* (1999), and *12 Memories* (2003).

Placebo, formed in 1995 and signed by the next year, exhibited great promise as a band, but insisted on existing well outside the confines of Britpop. Fronted by androgynous personality Brian Molko, the band emphasized their sexual ambiguity as a way to distinguish themselves. Molko, a mercurial performer, seemed to specialize in leading their listeners into unpredictable directions musically and in interviews, where he often embraced an androgynous sexual orientation.

In 1997, Placebo got a big break from David Bowie, a friend of the band who, obviously, readily identified with Molko's androgyny, having perfected the art himself decades before. Bowie invited Placebo to perform at his fiftieth birthday party at New York's Madison Square Garden. In 1998, the band signed a major-label deal in the United States and released *Without You I'm Nothing*. *Black Market Music* came out in 2000, and *Sleeping with Ghosts* emerged in 2003.

The new pride of Manchester now must be Doves, a band centered around the twin-brother act of Andy and Jez Williams. Officially formed in 1998 from the remnants of a feel-good dance band called Sub Sub, the band debuted in April of 2000, after a series of anticipation-building hit singles. That record, *Lost Souls*, would become one of the most acclaimed discs of the year and it launched the moody trio into an elite cadre of quality bands, both at home and abroad. It was nominated for a Mercury Prize and prompted the British press to proclaim the band "the new Radiohead." In 2002, Doves' second album, *The Last Broadcast*, went straight to No. 1 upon its release in the United Kingdom.

American audiences responded with respect and enthusiasm, helping the band to sell out its second and third tours in the United States. But in classic British fashion (Coldplay, Radiohead), the band has held back following its early success, cautious not to create overexposure and anxious to build anticipation. So far, the strategy has worked.

Another relatively introspective indie rock act in the lineage of Travis and Coldplay calls itself Starsailor. Hailing from the same town as Verve (Wigan in the north of England), the quartet was heralded in February 2001 as "Britain's best new band." Created by music students James Walsh (vocals/guitar), James Stelfox (bass), and Ben Byrne (drums), the band's sound went through several guitar-heavy incarnations before the arrival of keyboardist Barry Westhead cemented their sound. Influenced by Van Morrison, Neil Young, and Tim Buckley (whose 1970 album gave the band their name), Starsailor played their first London show at the Heavenly Social in April 2000. They released their first single, "Fever," in late winter of the next year. The single was a smash, and led to a sold-out headlining tour of the United Kingdom that spring. After the tour, and after a double bill in the States with the Doves, they made their debut album, *Love Is Here*, which came out domestically in January 2002.

Franz Ferdinand came a-roaring in 2004, receiving three Grammy nominations, including one for Best Performance for their tune "Take Me Out." Their appearance on the list came as something of a surprise, even though their self-titled debut had received vibrant reviews and their live shows became highly anticipated events.

13

THE METAL SCENE

Heavy metal, or "metal" for short, had a rough go of it during the first half of the '90s. Grunge had, almost famously, buried the limping corpse of hair metal with a barrage of downtuned riffs and its downplayed sense of style. Hair metal (and its kissing cousin "shred") were the last vestiges of commercially viable metal at the time, the last in a long line of illustrious genres and subgenres. Most burrowed further underground when they heard the grunge stampede coming. They were simply down, however, not out.

Metal's history began way back in the late '60s with acts like Cream, Vanilla Fudge, and Iron Butterfly. But because those acts stemmed from the psychedelic and blues movements, most credit the popularity of metal proper to Black Sabbath, a working-class group of occult-obsessed hippies from Birmingham, England. Sabbath honed in on a devastating sound of downtuned bleakness, reflecting the dull, industrial region of their upbringing, with evil, some say satanic, overtones. The "evil" interpretations helped by pouring fuel on an already raging fire. When Sabbath came to America for the first time in 1972, they were picketed and boycotted. It was the perfect marketing ploy.

About the same time, Led Zeppelin had ventured over to the States, oddly enough, from the same area of England. More blues-derived than Sabbath, but cut from the same deafening cloth, Zeppelin turned audiences on with their crazed adoration of decibels and power chords. Both Sabbath and Zeppelin served to form the basis of most of the heavy metal that followed during the next three decades.

Fast-forward to the '90s and the advent of grunge, or the Seattle sound. All eyes were once again focused on the seminal sounds of Sabbath. Most of the premier grunge bands, including Soundgarden, Alice in Chains, the Melvins, and Mudhoney traced their roots directly back to Sabbath's industrial England. Fans of the music and the musicians themselves overlooked the metal of the more recent past. Metallica and Megadeth had dominated the '80s, along with the slick and sexist hair metal of the mid- to late '80s. Iron Maiden, Judas Priest, and Def Leppard mined the more commercially viable side of thrash and classic metal. Shred, pivoting on the indulgent contributions of mind-bogglingly skilled guitar players like Yngwie Malmsteen and Joe Satriani, also had its time and place in the spotlight.

But grunge looked beyond these significant moments in metal in deriving its sound from Sabbath. It suited the musicians of the grunge movement perfectly, with its bleak outlook, unkempt appearance, and passionate approach. Ozzie Osbourne and Tony Iommi, Black Sabbath's singer and guitarist, were the ultimate role models for many of grunge's integral performers. The problem was, grunge squashed everything that came before it. It doused hair metal and bad pop, even indie rock, with a sobering bucket of cold water. When grunge came to life, much metal died, at least momentarily.

Another blow to metal occurred when Metallica, one of its mainstays, began to change its own musical course. Seeing the writing on the wall, and its message—which seemed to say, "Death to Metal!"—Metallica took the "if you can't beat 'em, join 'em" approach. On its 1991 self-titled release and two subsequent recordings—*Load* and *Reload*—Metallica lightened up, drained the power from its normally corrosive thrash. In addition, they turned their precision power chords into a sloppier approximation of grunge. Alternative music was swallowing everything in its path; it was bigger and stronger than anything heavy metal could throw at it, so Metallica bowed down and affiliated themselves with it. The band headlined the alternative festival Lollapalooza. They appeared on the cover of *Rolling Stone* uncharacteristically, with greased-back hair and eyeliner. The band's fans were distraught, devastated at the betrayal. And while the Metallica records may have unearthed a new audience, they drove their faithful legions away in large numbers. Metal had lost its leader; the torch that lit the way was extinguished.

As grunge rose up and asserted itself, and Metallica joined the club, rap music began stealing fans of metal as well. The same suburban kids that listened to Mötley Crüe, Poison, and Skid Row turned to rappers for their randy entertainment. Gangsta rap, an especially strident form of hip-hop, was a loud and obnoxious form of entertainment based on money, girls, partying—the same topics favored by the hair metal bands. Metal's audience, already imperiled, took another big hit.

To be fair, a few metal acts remained active and successful. Ozzy Osbourne, formerly of Black Sabbath, made one of the metal scene's most remarkable comebacks in the '90s, jumpstarting the phenomenally successful Ozzfest touring road show, which he often headlined. And Pantera, one of the decade's most successful bands, stayed the course perhaps more than any other metal band during the same period.

The fact is, it would take more than a few bullets to bring this sonic monster to its knees. Often referred to as "The Beast That Never Dies," metal is a multi-headed Medusa of music with many strains, a multiplicity of bands within each, and dedicated followings to keep each strain viable. Simply because metal disappeared from the popular music charts, it didn't mean metal was dead. The genre thrived in Europe and South America, making greater commercial strides outside the United States during this time than inside. Also, metal spent some time gestating in the American underground, gathering its forces on independent labels and touring the country in smaller, more niche-oriented clubs. Metal itself began fragmenting into more focused subgenres and niches as well: power metal, symphonic metal, black metal, dark wave, and others. This scaled-back and multipronged version of metal (vis-à-vis the extremely successful commercial metal of the '80s) helped keep the genre's pulse strong.

In time, several of these subgenres would rise to the surface of American popular music and assert themselves as powerful presences. In the interim, metal began gaining strength in the musical substrata. Festivals began popping up like Milwaukee's long-running MetalFest, which began in 1986, and New Jersey's own version, called the New Jersey Metal and Hardcore Fest. Both festivals came from the enterprising entrepreneur/promoter Jack Koshick. So while MTV dropped its "Headbanger's Ball" program, a video rundown of metal acts, through much of the '90s, momentum continued to build for metal in less visible areas. And because those areas were low profile, they were scrutinized less by the mainstream press. This under-the-radar status allowed metal and its related forces to grow more and more extreme with each passing year. This unchecked growth resulted in metal becoming a much more wild-eyed beast than in the past, less and less commercially viable, and more the bastion of extreme and disaffected fans.

The Internet also began playing a greater role for metal fans. Just as commercial music magazines neglected or ignored metal, scores of underground fanzines and Web sites began picking up the slack, feeding what was becoming a serious appetite for metal in the music marketplace. These Web sites and newsgroups helped metal establish a sense of community among its legions. No longer were fans alienated by their extreme musical tastes. They were now connected in cyberspace by a common bond.

CATEGORIES

Drawing a molecular-structure diagram of metal in the '90s would be an imposing task. Not many bands remain in or fit cleanly into a single container. Because so many of metal's niches during the '90s are so narrowly defined, a band can, and often does straddle two, three, or even six different subgenres on a single album. Still, it helps when attempting to describe a particular sound or style. The following are the eight major underground metal styles that developed a strong identity and loyal following during the '90s. There were more offshoots, and offshoots of offshoots, but for this purpose only a few need further explanation.

Death Metal

Of the many underground styles that came of age during this time, death metal was the most pervasive. Influenced by the rising status of thrash bands like Celtic Frost and Slayer, death metal is a downtuned, bass-heavy product with double-kick drums and singing that sounds like what you might hear emanating from Hell itself. Singers, almost to the person, attempt to outdo each other with profoundly deep, throaty vocals. Bands in this ilk also adopted names conjuring up bloody or grotesque imagery. Death itself splintered into several genres, including grindcore and doom.

ESSENTIAL ALBUMS:

> Deicide, *Deicide*
>
> Death, *Human*
>
> Entombed, *Clandestine*
>
> Morbid Angel, *Covenant*

Power Metal

In contrast to death metal, power metal is more symphonic and reaching. Derived mainly from classic metal of the '80s like Judas Priest, Helloween, and Iron Maiden, power metal focuses on epic themes based on virtuosic singing and playing. Some bands in this column also veer toward progressive metal, with elongated jamming and circuitous arrangements.

ESSENTIAL ALBUMS:

> Blind Guardian, *Nightfall in Middle-Earth*
>
> Iced Earth, *Iced Earth*
>
> Hammerfall, *Glory to the Brave*
>
> Stratovarius, *Dreamspace*

Progressive Metal

Progressive metal, or prog metal, blends elements of jazz, classical, and ambient/acoustic musics with nontraditional song structures in creating an elaborate product that emphasizes more cerebral than emotional qualities. Often the music is more technical than conventional metal styles, played by musicians interested more in sophisticated musicianship than visceral dynamics. Prog metal is an extension of progressive rock (prog rock), made popular in the early '70s by bands like Genesis, Rush, and Yes. In the late '80s and '90s, a variety of traditional progressive bands rose up again, led by Marillion and Porcupine Tree. Progressive metal combines the power of traditional metal with classical aspirations and arrangements. Some prog metal can emphasize power and aggressiveness, while others can veer closer to progressive rock, with acoustic elements blended in for diversity and dynamic effect.

ESSENTIAL ALBUMS:

King's X, *Gretchen Goes to Nebraska*

Fates Warning, *Chasing Time*

Dream Theater, *Images and Words*

Queensryche, *Operation: Mindcrime*

Black Metal

In the '80s, black metal was originally coined as a foil to "white metal," which was a term used to describe heavy metal with overtly religious or Christian lyrics. In contrast, purveyors of black metal believed in Satan, and sang about their convictions. Today, black metal is more used to describe the type of metal that originally came from Scandinavia in the early '90s. These musicians did in fact also worship Satan, or demons of some sort, and rebelled against the church and its Christian teachings in Scandinavia. They believed in their Viking heritage, their pagan upbringing. Some even burned Christian churches in protest. Today, that violence has dissipated and so has the original message.

Sonically, black metal combines death-metal deepness with eerie, almost psychedelic keyboard patterns and screeching vocals. Most black-metal bands smear white paint on their faces for horrific effect and some even make sacrificial animal offerings onstage.

ESSENTIAL ALBUMS:

Emperor, *Anthems to the Welkin at Dusk*

Mayhem, *De Mysteriis Dom Sathanas*

Dimmu Borgir, *Enthrone Darkness Triumphant*

Burzum, *Filosofem*

Hardcore Metal

A strand of metal combining punk with thrash rose up naturally in the '90s. The resurgence of Slayer and Pantera, two icons of thrash, coupled with the popularity of old-school punk made this hybrid a natural by-product of current musical trends.

ESSENTIAL ALBUMS:

> Hatebreed, *Satisfaction Is the Death of Desire*
>
> Killswitch Engage, *Alive or Just Breathing*
>
> Soulfly, *Soulfly*
>
> Napalm Death, *Fear Emptiness Despair*

Stoner Rock, Stoner Metal, Doom Metal

If grunge pilfered its sound from '70s metal like Black Sabbath and punk like MC5, stoner rock merely took the Sabbath part of the equation, stripping its sound down to the barest Sabbath-related elements: downtuned guitars and aggressive, though not affected, singing, all played through the haze of marijuana smoke. Add a tinge of psychedelia, and you've got a popular, but rather short-lived metal subculture. Many bands of the ilk popped up on the heels of genre originators Kyuss, including Electric Wizard, Nebula, Fu Manchu, and Masters of Reality, a band named after a Sabbath album.

ESSENTIAL ALBUMS:

> Kyuss, *Blues for the Red Sun*
>
> Sleep, *Sleep's Holy Mountain*
>
> Queens of the Stone Age, *Queens of the Stone Age*
>
> Monster Magnet, *Dopes to Infinity*

Industrial Metal

In many ways, industrial metal (discussed at greater length in Chapter 11) houses a multiplicity of genres on its own. In addition to the more commercial contributions of bands like Ministry and Nine Inch Nails, industrial metal also exists in a more extreme and underground form. Some bands, like Rammstein, take dance bands and overlay metal-sounding guitar parts. Others, like Godflesh and Fear Factory, use electronics and other syncopated techniques to create a maelstrom of precision noise.

ESSENTIAL ALBUMS:

> Godflesh, *Streetcleaner*
>
> Fear Factory, *Manufacture*
>
> Nine Inch Nails, *The Downward Spiral*
>
> Rammstein, *Sehnsucht*

Rap Metal, Nü Metal, Aggro

The most popular of all metal hybrids is also the most controversial among metal-ites. Rap metal and its kissing cousin nü metal exploded in the aftermath of grunge. Led by several remarkable personalities and a high-decibel, high-energy, yet somehow reasonably melodic sound, it blitzed the charts in the mid-'90s, making superstars of many of its acts.

The problem was, many metal fans didn't feel like this type of music deserved to be called "metal" at all. Recording techniques, radio programming, and the public taste changed in favor of louder guitars, heavier songs, more aggressive and provocative personalities. The rock world had been building toward this from the early '90s with bands like Nirvana, Helmet, and Ministry each putting forth heavier, more guitar-dominated tunes, the likes of which had never been favored before on commercial radio. Nine Inch Nails overwhelmed radio with its barrage of compressed noise, manic vocals, and electronic power. The demand for this type of music escalated as the '90s progressed and bands rose up quite willingly to meet that demand.

ORIGINS OF THE RAP AND METAL MERGER

In the late '80s, a New York City thrash band, Anthrax, combined a heavy guitar riff with rapping. It would be the first of many rap and metal mergers, and the first volley in a revolution of high-decibel, cross-cultural hybridization. Anthrax followed that song up with another in 1991, "Bring the Noise," a potent blast of metal with rap vocals that turned even more heads than the first. The song was a remake of the Public Enemy (PE) tune of the same name. PE had, just a few years earlier, stunned the rap world with the gangsta-esque *It Takes a Nation of Millions*, released in 1988. Anthrax, widely respected in the metal community, introduced, with its rendition of the tune, a commercially viable hybrid heretofore unrealized.

The Anthrax experiment opened a door to opportunity for many aspiring metal musicians, many of which had previously been disillusioned at the genre's prospect for the immediate future. Grunge had assumed control, and alternative music was fast creating converts of rock and metal fans. Real metal was losing its market share and needed a quick fix. Rap metal was its savior. But was rap metal, also called nü metal, an acceptable substitute for metal itself? Many consider the genre too diluted to be considered authentic metal. Its approach, a mix of grunge, rap, and thrash, certainly owed more to the alternative music and hip-hop than to metal. The most notable nü-metal guitar players, including Rage Against the Machine's Tom Morello, Limp Bizkit's Wes Borland, Deftones' Stephen Carpenter, and Korn's James "Munky" Schaffer and Brian "Head" Welch, relied less on the archetypal riffing and soloing of true metal and more on weaving sloppy but occasionally elaborate guitar lines in and out of turntable scratching and rapping front men.

Rage Against the Machine

Of the first wave of rap metal bands, Rage Against the Machine was, arguably, the first to make a national impact. Led by frontman Zack de la Rocha and guitarist Tom Morello, Rage debuted with a cassette-only, self-released project in 1992. The songs, pivoting on de la Rocha's zealous rapping and Morello's innovative metal riffing, were intensely political, designed to light the fire under what they perceived as a blasé public.

The approach worked. While they were criticized for compromising their anti-corporate values and signing with Sony, they also got their message out to a vast audience, which would have been unavailable to them had they stayed true to their DIY approach. In 1992, they released their official national debut, also self-titled, and began their mission of ranting against political regimes, cultural imperialism, and oppression. Their convergence of styles—namely rap, punk, and thrash metal—was effective both in conveying its polemics and waking up metal audiences. Their existence was turbulent both onstage and off. There were threats of disbanding, inner conflicts, and the like, but the band managed to stay together to record *Evil Empire* in 1996. By this time the band had built a massive, rabid fan base, and the record, long awaited, debuted at the top of the *Billboard* album chart.

The band's next album, *The Battle of Los Angeles*, also debuted at No. 1 and reaffirmed their intoxicating mix of musical and political effectiveness. But de la Rocha, interested in going his own way as a hip-hop artist, announced plans for a solo project in 2000. Producer Rick Rubin, the man responsible for many successful recordings in the '90s (the Offspring, Slayer, Johnny Cash), assembled the band one final time for *Renegades*, a recording of cover songs issued in December 2000. The band's label finally released a long-overdue live recording, titled *Live at the Grand Olympic Auditorium*, at the end of 2003.

After de la Rocha left, the remaining members of Rage hired former Soundgarden frontman Chris Cornell and became Audioslave. With experience and good pedigree the band was an instant success, debuting in November 2002 with a self-titled effort and following that with a set in late 2005.

Limp Bizkit, Deftones, and Korn

Along with Rage, Limp Bizkit, Deftones, and Korn were perhaps the most notable and notorious of the new wave of metal bands making strides in the '90s. This wave, often referred to as "nü metal," dominated the commercial metal scene of the '90s and, along with rap metal, has become commercial metal's legacy in the new millennium.

Korn was perhaps the one band that jumpstarted the nü-metal trend. The Bakersfield, California, band, led by singer Jonathan Davis, emerged with their debut album in 1994, featuring a distinctive, aggressive noise combining the manic guitars of grunge and metal with the stream-of-consciousness vocalizing of

Davis. In fact, it was Davis' vocals that provided Korn with a personality bordering on insanity. The abused product of a broken home, Davis often sang of the dark side, of going crazy, of a being an angst-ridden paranoid in a world gone wrong. The extreme dysfunction connected with a wide swath of similarly disaffected youth, and Korn, based on this agitated approach, became an instant draw.

After releasing their debut, they toured constantly with a variety of popular bands, including Marilyn Manson, Megadeth, and Ozzy Osbourne. All the touring paid off when the album went gold. Their second album, *Life Is Peachy*, picked up where the band left off, debuting at No. 3 on the album chart in 1996. The band was invited to headline Lollapalooza the next year, but had to bail out when guitarist Munky Shaffer contracted a serious illness. Still, it didn't slow them down long. They released their most successful album to date in 1998: *Follow the Leader* was both critically acclaimed and best-selling. It led to the genesis of an annual tour, coined cheekily "The Family Values Tour," which invited similarly controversial artists like Ice Cube, Limp Bizkit, and the arson-friendly Rammstein, among others over the years. The band released *Issues* in 1999 and followed that with *Untouchables* in 2002 and *Take a Look in the Mirror* the next year. In early 2005, guitarist Brian Welch left the band to devote his life to religion and religious rock music. But it was Korn's brazen approach to the metal idiom and their haywire performances that opened the door for a stampede of likeminded acts.

Deftones began their career a bit earlier, but didn't make waves until Korn had created opportunity. As high school students early on, they were traditional metal and thrash. But after hearing outfits like Faith No More and Rage Against the Machine in the early '90s, they began making adjustments to their sound, growing more experimental in the process. They debuted in 1995 with *Adrenaline*, an apt title for the project, which oozed energy and brooding dynamics. A few high-profile tours with Ozzy Osbourne and Korn later, to name a couple, ended up pushing them near the fore of the nü-metal stampede. They secured their position with credible discs and tours, maintaining integrity and making good decisions. Albums like *Around the Fur* (1997) and *White Pony* (2000) solidified their reputation.

Limp Bizkit, led by singer/rapper Fred Durst, guitarist Wes Borland, and turntablist DJ Lethal, fused metal, punk, and hip-hop in an energetic brew designed to attract audiences of all three. For the most part, they succeeded, becoming one of the most successful rock acts of the '90s and making their frontman Durst a powerful music industry insider. Durst, formerly a tattoo artist in Jacksonville, Florida, befriended Korn bassist Reginald "Fieldy" Arvizu, after Korn played the city. The relationship became the foundation of the band. Durst impressed the band, and later producer Ross Robinson with a demo, prepared in 1995, which led to a contract with Flip/Interscope. Their debut album impressed unaware rock fans with its feral chemistry and the disc cinched them a slot on the Family Values tour in 1998. The follow-up to their debut, *Significant Other*, featuring their hit, "Nookie," made them superstars.

Durst would go on to assert himself as a celebrity, dating starlets and showing up on red carpets with characteristically casual panache. His backwards baseball cap served as a signature fashion statement. Controversy followed the band almost from the beginning. In 1999, Durst was heavily criticized for inciting a near-riot at the Woodstock '99 show. His inflammatory "Break Stuff" became a self-fulfilling prophecy. The violence became so intense at the show that organizers were forced to pull the plug midway through their set.

In 2000, Durst became an outspoken advocate for Napster and its free online file-sharing concept—this at a time when many musicians were speaking out against it. He also fought frequently with his bandmates. Guitarist Borland left the band in 2001, admitting musical boredom, among other things, as the reason for his departure. Unfortunately, the move didn't satisfy either side. Borland couldn't get a solo project in flight and his former band, now with guitarist Mike Smith in the fold, couldn't maintain any momentum either. Smith's work on 2003's disappointing *Results May Vary*, was sketchy. Borland rejoined the band in the summer of 2004. A new album with Borland, *The Unquestionable Truth, Pt. 1*, served to regain the band's impact.

LOUD ROCK

Several bands in the mid- and late '90s ambushed metal and loud rock in the wake of nü metal's successes. Many argue, some vehemently, that these bands shouldn't be considered metal at all, even though, had this music been around in the '70s or even the '80s, there would have been nothing else to call it. Today, this group of bands has a more generic catch-all phrase binding them together: Loud rock.

Like nü metal and rap metal, this strain took much of its sound from grunge and other alternative ideas—thrash metal, punk rock, funk, and progressive rock—in creating a palatable hybrid of styles and approaches. System of a Down, for example, took the outspoken politics of Rage Against the Machine and, rather than rap over metal chords, they sang (albeit idiosyncratically) over unpredictable metallic-based arrangements bordering on progressive metal. Highly regarded discs like *Toxicity* and *Mezmerize* have vaulted system to the fore of loud rock after just three studio albums.

Puddle of Mudd, led by singer guitarist Wes Scantlin, first came off as a Nirvana knock-off on the band's debut, *Come Clean*. His intensely personal lyrics and garbled vocals closely adhered to the work of Kurt Cobain. But he has since moved beyond those comparisons into less explored territory.

Godsmack took the Boston metal scene by storm, debuting in 1997 with their self-titled release. Singer-songwriter Sully Erna and guitarist Tony Rombola front the band, which has had impressive success with albums like *Awake*, which earned them Grammy recognition for Best Rock Instrumental Performance in 2000, and *Faceless*, which arrived in 2003.

Staind, a veteran band from western Massachusetts led by Aaron Lewis, crashed the loud-rock scene in 1998 with their debut *Dysfunction*. A band signed by Limp Bizkit's Fred Durst, Staind followed up their successful debut with the career-making *Break the Cycle*, a disc that spent more than a few weeks at No. 1. Since then, they have established themselves as an important loud-rock act.

Sevendust, from Atlanta, has not yet reached the heights of many other of the most successful loud acts, but they've built a dedicated following throughout the '90s with a steadfast touring schedule and solid, if not hit, recordings. On acclaimed discs like *Home* and *Seasons*, the band distinguished themselves by layering the soulful vocals of Lajon Witherspoon over a bottom-heavy guitar attack.

Disturbed, a band with roots on the South Side of Chicago, came together when guitarist Dan Donegan teamed with singer/rebel Dave Draiman. The outfit debuted in 2001 with *The Sickness*, a hugely popular set that earned the band a multiplatinum record and a slot on Ozzfest's main stage the following summer. *Believe*, their follow-up, emerged in 2002, and a new album in 2005.

Guitarist Jerry Horton and singer Coby Dick of Papa Roach turned a criminal existence in northern California into gold when they decided to form a band with Tobin Esperance and Dave Buckner. In 1996, three years after uniting, they debuted with *Old Friends from Young Years*. But it wasn't until the follow-up, recorded for the Dreamworks label, that the band received any attention. *Infest*, powered by the hugely successful single "Last Resort," ended up selling over 3 million copies following its 2000 release. *Lovehatetragedy* came in 2003, with lukewarm reception. *Getting Away with Murder* was made in 2004, and began to recapture the band's fan base.

ALTERNATIVE METAL

Incubus, P.O.D., Linkin Park

A handful of bands cut their loud rock with elements of Latin, hip-hop, funk, progressive, and DJ elements. These bands were aggressive enough to be called, in some circles, metal acts, but diverse enough to be shunned by true metal heads. Alternative metal (alt-metal) seemed to be the catch-phrase for this bunch of acts. And depending on how one views metal, any number of the bands already mentioned could qualify as alt-metal as well. At this point, the mix-and-match nature of rock 'n' roll labeling throughout the '90s isn't sufficiently past for any sort of definitive categorization.

Of all the alt-metal bands to enjoy success in the '90s, Primus is by most counts the most original. Based on the bass playing of Les Claypool (rather than the *de rigeur* sound of power chords on the guitar), Primus concocted a willfully strange brew of odd tempos and quirky song subjects ("Winona the Beaver," "Jerry Was a Race Car Driver"), of unorthodox performances, and

Frank Zappa–esque surprises. Claypool is an eccentric talent with a vision of his art that encompasses as much the visual end as the sonic side. Supported by gifted guitarist Larry "Ler" Lalonde and drummer Brian "Brain" Mantia, Claypool has been able to present the most unusual mainstream entertainment in rock music. In fact, it's so unusual, the band, which is arguably less metal than "jam band," has been able to cross over and appeal to many different types of audiences. Primus headlined Lollapalooza in 1993.

Incubus formed early in the '90s as high school classmates, but it wasn't until 1997 that they released their first recordings. Their second recording, *Make Yourself*, delivered in 1999, didn't make its impact until 2001, when the third single from the album, "Drive," hit it big on radio. Constant touring kept the band's profile high, while a subsequent album, *Morning View*, debuted on the charts at No. 2, in late 2001. *A Crow Left of the Murder* (2004), helmed by R.E.M. producer Scott Litt, proved the band was interested in a permanent expansion beyond their nü-metal origins.

Southern California's P.O.D. tinted their own loud rock with a variety of diverse elements, including Latin rock and hip-hop. But the thing that separated P.O.D. (stands for "Payable on Death") was their unflinching stance as a Christian act, born-again rockers. Their outward spirituality didn't deter legions of fans from flocking to their 2001 breakthrough disc, *Satellite*. The recording yielded a number of hit singles, including "Set It Off" and "Alive"; the latter has since become the band's anthem.

The young Linkin Park gang succeeded in recording one of the best-selling rock recordings of the '90s with their *Hybrid Theory* which sold 8 million copies. The "Hybrid Theory" in question is the one mixing hip-hop and thrash metal, something Linkin Park does with smooth efficiency. Singles "Crawling" and "One Step Closer" were massive radio hits and video favorites, while well-planned joint tours with Family Values and the Project: Revolution led the band to play 324 shows in 2001. Linkin Park received three Grammy nominations for Best Rock Album and Best New Artist, and received the hardware for Best Hard Rock Performance for "Crawling." The band spent the remainder of 2002 in the studio, working on a follow-up. In 2003, they released *Meteora*, which spawned another hit, "Somewhere I Belong." But the recording didn't reach the heights of its predecessor.

THE RETURN OF METAL

Sabbath, Maiden, Priest, Megadeth, Metallica, Van Halen

Following the blitzkrieg of nü-metal, alt-metal, and loud-rock bands in the '90s, and conjoined with the ongoing success of Ozzfest (see Chapter 7), the climate for metal warmed substantially. This receptivity was accorded not only to new bands and newly coined niches of metal, but also to veteran bands who saw an opportunity to recapitalize.

Ozzy Osbourne, who had been the driving force behind Ozzfest, and who had often headlined that festival as a solo act, consented to a reunion of his legendary outfit, Black Sabbath. They released a live album in 1998, which went platinum in the United States and proceeded to tour throughout 1999. In 2001, Sabbath announced it would reunite again to headline the sixth year of Ozzfest and entertained the idea of producing a new studio album, the original lineup's first since 1978. That never materialized, but the group did win a Best Metal Performance Grammy for "Iron Man," a song originally written in the early '70s and reunited for several successful tours.

Sabbath wasn't the only major metal outfit to return in the '90s. Metallica, who never technically went away, surged back to the front of the movement with a new album and a few other surprising revelations. During the '80s, Metallica had changed the rules for all heavy-metal bands. They were the undisputed leaders of the genre, and commanded respect from huge numbers of both fans and critics, unusual for a thrash-metal band. In the '90s, however, the band saw their large foundation begin to erode.

In 1996, they released *Load*, the long-awaited follow-up to the well-received *Metallica*, issued in 1991. But the album stunned and disappointed fans for the way it presented the band as moving toward an alt-metal sound. Rather than sticking to their original mission, as they had since forming in the early '80s, through many a trend, Metallica was seen as bowing to the pressure of staying relevant. Even image-wise, the band made concessions: they cut their hair and had their picture taken by popular photographer Anton Corbijn for the cover of *Rolling Stone*. They consented to headline the sixth Lollapalooza, an alternative music festival. Although *Load* was a hit when it came out, entering the charts at No. 1 and selling 3 million copies in the first two months, the band's legion complained vociferously about the shift in image and sound. But there were no concessions made. Metallica issued *Reload*, a collection of new and leftover material from the *Load* sessions. That too sold briskly, but also permanently alienated their fans. *Garage Inc.*, a double-disc collection of b-sides, rarities, and newly recorded covers, followed in 1998. In 1999, Metallica maintained their unconventional string of releases with *S&M*, a concert collaboration with the San Francisco Symphony Orchestra. Despite being rather strange bedfellows, the disc debuted at No. 2, reemphasizing their popularity.

In 2000, the band again made headlines in an unorthodox way, this time spearheading a legal assault on Napster, a file-sharing community that allowed users to download music files from other members' computers free of charge. Metallica disapproved of the file-sharing and accused Napster and its users of pirating already copyrighted material. The outcry eventually ousted over 300,000 members of that file-sharing community. This controversial procedure, seen in some circles as Metallica acting out against its own fans, sparked a widespread debate over the availability and cost of digital music. In July 2001, Metallica dropped their lawsuit against Napster, perhaps sensing that their stance harmed the band's plebeian image. The debates—and lawsuits—still rage today.

In April 2001, the band, minus departed bassist Jason Newsted, entered the recording studio to begin work on a new album, with rhythm guitarist James Hetfield lined up to handle bass duties alongside original drummer Lars Ulrich and lead guitarist Kirk Hammett. In 2003, Metallica released *St. Anger*, a disc full of bold tunes that featured the band staying away from its metal roots, but compensating for that with aggressive and thrashy playing. The disc debuted bassist Robert Trujillo. Metallica remained in the spotlight of controversy once again, when a feature-length film, *Metallica: Some Kind of Monster*, debuted at the Sundance Film Festival in 2004. Directed by Joe Berlinger and Bruce Sinofsky, the movie presented a warts-and-all view of the band during the two-year period surrounding the recording of *St. Anger*, including the band's retention of a $40,000-a-month psychotherapist who helped them resolve intraband tension.

Megadeth

Another metal band that rose up against incredible odds happens to have roots in Metallica. Dave Mustaine, founder and leader of Megadeth, was also an original founder of Metallica. Bounced out of that band early on, Mustaine went on to form his career-making outfit in 1983, distinguishing himself from his former band by streamlining his thrashy approach and making it more instrumentally aggressive. Megadeth went on to become one of the best-loved and most loyally followed metal bands of the '80s with a series of successful albums, culminating in 1992's *Countdown to Extinction*, which debuted at No. 2 on the *Billboard* album chart. In fact, all of Megadeth's '90s albums rose to at least a Top 10 chart position.

Countdown to Extinction ultimately went double-platinum and became the band's biggest hit, confirming that they had retained their audience in the wake of grunge. Megadeth was now one of the most popular metal bands in the world, supplanting Metallica, who had been on hiatus since releasing the important *Metallica* disc in 1991. Taking advantage, Megadeth moved into the mainstream with *Youthanasia*, a 1994 set that entered the charts at No. 4 and earned platinum status. The next year, Mustaine issued a disc of rarities called *Hidden Treasures*, featuring some of the soundtrack tunes that had helped expand the group's MTV audience in the early '90s. *Cryptic Writings* in 1997 earned Megadeth much love from album-rock radio, something that never happened in the '80s.

But substance abuse and personnel problems dogged the band and Mustaine had trouble managing the operation. In 2002, while drying out at a facility for substance abusers, Mustaine incurred a freak arm injury, losing all nerve sensitivity in his picking hand. He was diagnosed with radial neuropathy and told he'd never play again. At that point, he officially disbanded Megadeth and announced to his following that his playing days were over. Of course, with Megadeth, nothing goes as planned, and so it was with Mustaine's injury, which cleared up at the end of 2003 after extensive rehabilitation. In 2004, Mustaine returned with a vengeance, producing a new album, *The System Has Failed*, and embarking on an extensive national and international tour.

Iron Maiden/Judas Priest

Two of metal's most popular bands worldwide, Judas Priest and Iron Maiden, rekindled their popularity in the '90s with new albums and world tours. Both bands emerged from Britain in the late '70s and went on to conquer the world throughout the '80s as flamekeepers of the so-called New Wave of British heavy metal.

Iron Maiden dominated the '80s with a sort of galloping virtuosity, led by a strong two-guitar battery and vocalist Bruce Dickinson, who joined the band in 1982. They'd go on to release such power-metal classics as *Number of the Beast* (1982) and *Seventh Son of a Seventh Son* (1988). Maiden foundered for much of the '90s, releasing a few live albums, witnessing the departure of Dickinson, and missing the mark on a couple of new studio releases (which found the band attempting to change with the times) with replacement Blaze Bayley. In 1999, Dickinson rejoined the band, nearly a decade after leaving, and the band seemed to undergo a rejuvenating period. In 2002, after a couple of world tours, the band, recast in prime form, released the well-received *Fear of the Dark*. In 2004, Maiden continued their improbable run in the new millennium with *The Dance of Death*. They celebrated their twenty-fifth anniversary together in 2005.

Like Maiden, Judas Priest spent much of the '80s at the forefront of heavy metal. Albums like *Stained Class* (1978) and *British Steel* (1980) helped the band establish the very sound and foundation of the genre. While they steamrolled through the '80s based on their early reputation and an ever-growing fan base, the band attempted to stay impervious to trends, remaining steadfast and faithful to their original sound. This worked until the '90s, when tastes changed so dramatically that many of the more veteran bands, unable to identify and roll with those changes, decided to call it quits. Like Maiden, Priest searched their way through the '90s. Singer and image-leader Rob Halford left early in the decade, replaced by Tim "Ripper" Owens, a singer from a Judas Priest tribute band. Halford went on to create a gaggle of projects: his own band called Fight, another project, called Two, in conjunction with Nine Inch Nails leader Trent Reznor's label, and Halford, a self-monikered band. None of these were particularly successful, and in 2003, Judas Priest reunited, first collaborating on liner notes and song selection for the career-encompassing box set *Metalogy*, then for a global tour in 2004.

Van Halen

Thanks in large part to their brilliant lead guitarist Eddie Van Halen, Van Halen became one of the heavy-metal genre's defining bands. As the prototype for much of the guitar players who followed, Eddie Van Halen created the template for heavy-metal guitarists, raising the bar with his eye-popping skills. Additionally, singer David Lee Roth's vocal approach, with an inimitable tongue-in-cheek flair, became a role model for the vocalists (who took his act seriously) of hair metal in the late '80s.

Formed in the late '70s, the band's success permeated the subsequent decade. Albums like *1984* (1984) and *5150* (1996) hit high-water marks for heavy-metal innovation, and sold accordingly.

But when the '90s rolled around, and heavy metal begrudgingly took a backseat to the far less pompous rock of grunge, Van Halen stalled. They had experienced some trouble with vocalists—Sammy Hagar replaced David Lee Roth, and was in turn replaced briefly by Gary Cherone in the mid-'90s. Their sales flagged in the mid-'90s as well, reflecting the current trend of alternative music dominating the decade. To aggravate the situation, Eddie Van Halen had to undergo treatment for alcoholism in the '90s and cancer in 2000, making it impossible to develop any sense of continuity as a band, even though the interest and demand remained high.

When Cherone was dismissed as vocalist in 1999, rumors had it that the band was about to rehire original singer Roth, helping to heighten the anticipation of a reunion. Ultimately, that never happened. But in 2004, to coincide with a greatest hits collection, the band, fronted by Hagar and starring a healthy Eddie Van Halen, toured the country.

METAL MOVING FORWARD

Discussion of metal in the '90s invariably addresses the death of the genre at the hands of alternative rock (alt-rock). And, in fact, grunge and similar styles did grant a murderous end to most commercial metal, hair metal (Poison, Mötley Crüe, Warrant, etc.). That style of music had run its course and the new alt-rock of the '90s was too exciting to ignore.

But metal did come back in the '90s, and in a much bigger and stronger form. Like a plant pruned back in timely fashion that grows back fuller and with greater health, metal itself returned with gusto. Both in the underground and commercially speaking, heavy metal returned as if in defiance to prove that it was indeed a multiheaded beast incapable of being felled.

In the underground, metal gathered strength and accumulated fans increasingly discontented with alternative rock. Commercial metal, in the form of alt-metal and nü metal, siphoned off fans of alt-rock as well. While those styles were derided by fans, they did heighten the presence (and the decibels) of metal on a much wider scale. It also forced the independent metal found in the burgeoning metal underground to distinguish itself with extremist noise and refreshing, ever more innovative, sounds.

14

MUSIC TECHNOLOGY

The music industry, since the latter part of the '90s, has been coping with significant change. Major record labels have seen their sales drop sharply in the past several years, and have blamed the falling revenue in large part on a new phenomenon among music consumers: free music downloads available via the Internet. Courtesy of several Web sites such as Napster, Morpheus, and Gnutella, avid and casual music fans alike can find the music they want with a few simple clicks. This transaction, called file-sharing, involves searching for a song or songs within a large network of participating computers, finding that song, and copying it. What's more, the transaction is free. Since the practice began in the mid-'90s, labels have felt strongly that this has played a monumental role in the economic slide plaguing the industry.

Others cite additional factors for the lag in sales, such as lower household spending during the late-'90s recession, and increased competition from other entertainment forms like DVDs and video games, the sales of which have risen precipitously over the same time period.

Record company business has also been affected by copying. One telltale sign of digital copying—that is, reproducing music on blank CDs—is a steep drop in an album's sales in its second week out. Second-week sales of a hit album typically fall 25 percent or less; now 40 percent is the norm. For example, Alanis Morissette's 1999 release, *Alanis Unplugged*, fell just 17 percent in Week-Two sales, but her 2003 release, *Under Rug Swept*, fell 44 percent. Brandy's 1998 album, *Never Say Never*, fell a mere 4 percent in its second week, but her new release, *Full Moon*, dropped a whopping 44 percent. On the same hand, sales of blank CDs, that is, CDs used for transfering pre-recorded music, have skyrocketed.

"There's no doubt about it," says Thomas Dolby Robertson, in an editorial for the Recording Industry Association of America (RIAA) Web site, "these are risky times. New technologies can punch a hole in your bank balance and your business model, and music companies that don't adapt will sink without a trace" (RIAA).

Not all studies done on the effects of downloading find that the practice adversely affects record sales. One 2003 study of the effects of file-sharing on music sales found that online music trading appears to have had little to do with the recent slide in CD sales. For the study, researchers at Harvard University and the University of North Carolina tracked music downloads over seventeen weeks in 2002, matching data on file transfers with actual market performance of the songs and albums being downloaded. Even high levels of file-sharing seemed to translate into an effect on album sales that was "statistically indistinguishable from zero," they wrote. "We find that file sharing has only had a limited effect on record sales," the study stated. "While downloads occur on a vast scale, most users are likely individuals who would not have bought the album even in the absence of file sharing" (Oberholzer 2004, 24–25).

INDUSTRY DOWNTURN

Whether or not file-sharing has had an impact on sales, the music industry has indeed been slumping. Music sales overall are continuing a distinct downward trend begun in the late '90s. For the first six months of 2002, CD sales dropped 7 percent. Total U.S. music sales during that time declined 10.1 percent. Since 2000, total record sales have dropped nearly 25 percent. The Recording Industry Association of America points to illegal Internet downloading and CD piracy as contributing factors.

As a result of this sales downturn, the recording industry underwent radical consolidation during this time. Most significantly, there was an unprecedented merging of companies. Currently, there are only four major recording labels: the Universal Music Group, Warner Music Group, Sony BMG Music Entertainment, and the EMI Group. This is a stunning reduction, down from twice that earlier in the decade. These four groups of labels now control 75 percent of the market share and over 90 percent of recorded product. Such control maximizes the exposure of big stars while minimizing the ability to expose audiences to lesser-known talent. The budget for talent development has shrunk considerably over the past three years.

As a result of these shrinking budgets, scores of artists have been dropped from their labels in an attempt to streamline the financials and enhance chances for the retained artists to break through. Conversely, and perhaps at odds with the aforementioned industry goals, thousands of major-label staffers were laid off as well.

A QUICK BUCK

During the '90s, critics identified a disturbing trend in artist development, even before sales went south. The alternative music boom of the decade proved that just about any band could break through to the mainstream given the right song, with little positioning and marketing. Nirvana, for example, rose to the top of the charts almost completely under the radar, only to become the biggest rock band in the country for several years. Seeing this happen, industry executives and A&R reps were constantly on the lookout for the "Next Big Thing," the next Nirvana. A copycat industry even before the alternative boom, record companies were looking under rocks for whatever they deemed unusual or alternative. First they were intent on finding the next Nirvana or Pearl Jam sound-alikes; then their search widened to include bands in whatever trend happened to break through on its own: electronic, boy band, Britpop, punk rock, and anything else.

The downside of all this was that record labels had little margin for error. Their bottom lines were such that if a band didn't make an impact immediately, with an album's first single, or if they didn't in some way make an impression on the press or the public, the label would reposition its resources to the next artist. Tour support for that act was cut back and the promotional budget slashed, leaving said band to do most of the work for itself. On the other hand, if a band showed promise in some way or if radio latched onto a song, a company would shift its full effort in that direction. Artist development, that is, the practice of nurturing and cultivating the music and presentation of a band over time—became moribund.

This business practice, charged critics, was troubling in many ways. The major labels were scurrying around the country signing young, independent bands at an alarming rate. But when these bands—many of them eccentric alternative acts that labels felt were only marginally worth the risk of signing—failed to capture the imagination of a sizable audience, they were dropped from the label. Often, that action resulted in promising bands breaking up, discouraged and humiliated, without reaching their potential. This precipitated a drop in quality bands on the scene industry-wide. It also left independent labels, home to those bands prior to their signing with a major, in difficult straits, without their marquee bands to rely on for financial survival.

Eventually, following the record industry bust of the late '90s and beyond, the indie labels would get a modicum of revenge on the majors. Still, because of this dubious practice of signing and dropping bands, the complexion of the music industry changed. More than ever, these labels were seen as villainous. Throughout the '70s and most of the '80s, labels would spend a great deal of time and energy developing talent, helping bands focus on attaining quality output. In the '90s though, that all changed as labels took the short cut in signing bands, stamping them with an image, and tossing them out into the marketplace to see what would happen. Would a band sink or swim? If a band sank, as often was the case given the small promotional budgets of the labels, the record company no longer threw them a life preserver. The practice did immense damage to the perception and reputation of the industry.

TEEN-POP PREVAILS

Another questionable move the recording industry made in the '90s was its decision to focus on the teen and pre-teen market for its business. While rock has always been the biggest market for its product, the pop audience also contributed mightily to the music industry's bottom line, especially in the mid-'90s when boy bands and teen-pop idols briefly overtook radio and music television. Yet there was an irony here that was overlooked. While the record companies honed in on the teen demographic, many within that demo were engaging in frequent downloading, not purchasing, of their music. Rather than buying the CDs at the store, they were either copying and distributed music to friends, or downloading the radio single through Web sites like Napster.

Oblivious of the trend, record companies were set on marketing to this group because, they perceived, they had the most disposable income. This was, in retrospect, seen as a grave error. As the teen market eroded, so did industry revenues. Now, music executives were faced with a dilemma. In order to enforce the prohibition of downloading, which is an illegal practice, they could do one of two things. Either pursue, threaten, even sue the demographic guilty of pirating music—that very same demographic they were so eager to capture a few years before. (In a sense, this meant alienating their most desirable consumer market.) Or, they could leave the file-sharing community alone and pursue alternate technological means on their end, such as creating a musical format impervious to copying. They ended up doing both. "Though it would appear that record companies are still making their money and that artists are still getting rich," states an essay on the RIAA Web site, in justifying its legal pursuit of downloaders,

> these impressions are mere fallacies. Each sale by a pirate represents a lost legitimate sale, thereby depriving not only the record company of profits, but also the artist, producer, songwriter, publisher, retailer, and the list goes on. . . . Each year, *the industry loses about $4.2 billion to piracy worldwide.* We estimate we lose millions of dollars a day to all forms of piracy. (RIAA)

In March 2004, in the latest in a series of similar actions, the recording industry sued 532 people, including scores of individuals using computer networks at 21 universities, claiming they were illegally sharing digital music files over the Internet. The defendants, which the trade group claims offered "substantial amounts" of music files, face potential civil penalties or settlements that could cost them thousands of dollars. Settlements in similar previous cases have averaged $3,000 each.

CHANGING OF THE GUARD?

Since 2001, the recording industry has been able to identify a change in consumer trends and an opportunity to bounce back from the woes inflicted by downloading. Now, instead of holding on to the teen market, they've refocused efforts to reach out to their baby-boomer parents. The shift has been successful. Today, the biggest percentage of music sale dollars comes not from teens but from their parents. And baby boomers' diverse musical tastes contribute to the recent splintering of the market. No longer is rock the predominant genre. Music sales are now as likely to come from the folk/bluegrass/gospel set *O Brother Where Art Thou?* as from U2. Since 1990, the older segment of the population has steadily increased its share of the music market. In 2001, those forty and older made up 34 percent of music buyers, according to the RIAA 2001 Consumer Profile. "Those from 40 to 60 form the largest single group of people purchasing music," says Jeannie Novak, president & CEO of Indiespace, which pioneered the online distribution model for independent music products in 1994. "Through the '90s, they took a larger share of the market than the younger group." This means, at the turn of the century and through the present, the baby-boomer generation is essentially keeping the record industry in business. "If things in music keep going the way they are, boomers may be the only music market left."

Artist Norah Jones might be the best example of this. The Texas-raised, Brooklyn-based Jones released her debut on February 26, 2002, on Blue Note Records. That album, a folky, jazzy, mellow, very adult-oriented pop set of tunes called *Come Away with Me* sold an incredible 18 million copies virtually out of the blue. Jones' piano-based style, languid and comfortable, appealed to older listeners. The demand for that kind of music, made visible by *Come Away with Me*, was palpable. Jones' remarkable year culminated at the 45th Grammy Awards on February 23, 2003, when she took home an unprecedented eight awards out of eight nominations, including major categories Album of Year, Record of the Year ("Don't Know Why"), and Best New Artist. Jones' follow-up, *Feels Like Home*, sold a record-setting 1 million copies its first week in early 2004, but hasn't since become the selling tsunami of its predecessor.

Another recording that took the industry by surprise—and revealed a dramatic shift in the record-buyer demographic—was the soundtrack to the feature film *O Brother Where Art Thou?* This unlikely disc featured an array of gospel, bluegrass, and roots music, and jumped to the top of the *Billboard* album chart a year after its 2001 release, over acts like U2 and Bob Dylan. It became the first soundtrack to win the album of the year prize since 1994 on its way to scooping up four Grammys and selling over 6 million copies.

The record industry, now awakened to the potential of selling records to an older demographic, began to rethink its marketing strategies in the new millennium. In 2003, the industry regained some sense of balance—still focusing on the youth market with a preponderance of pop and rock, but also now considering the boomer generation, and their continuing interest in buying music. Although 2003 sales still decreased for the fourth consecutive year, U.S. album sales came on strong in the second half of the year, remained strong in the first half of 2004, and ended the year with a brief growth spurt. But midway through 2005, sales were again lagging, down 7 percent from a year ago.

THE RISE AND FALL OF NAPSTER

It was simply the most revolutionary music technology to emerge in the feverish months of the Internet investment boom. The peer-to-peer MP3 file transfer system developed by a 17-year-old named Shawn Fanning powered a company that at its peak claimed 70 million users and ranked as the fastest-growing company in history.

Essentially, Fanning designed a computer program that transformed the Internet into an unlimited library of free music. It also turned long-standing notions of property rights, copyrights, and demand-and-supply pricing completely around. Napster challenged the protocol of the world's music business. It defied the enduring business model of the industry, insisting that music was over-priced and could be distributed free electronically without consequences. But there were.

> What was most striking about the battle over Napster was the assumption that what was at issue was rock music. (Napster was not seen as a threat to classical or country music.) Significantly, the first widely successful use of MP3 technology, Napster, involved a global network of home "tapers" and drew on the rock ideology of DIY, community, and anti-commerce. Whatever Napster's fate, it ensured that rock music would be central to 21st-century ways of doing things. Rock, in short, not only reflects (and reflects on) social and cultural change; it is also a social force in its own right. (*Encyclopaedia Britannica.com*)

The music industry declared war on Napster and other peer-to-peer systems. The battle engaged the biggest entertainment and technology companies in the world. Artists, the one group caught in the middle, came down on both sides of the argument. The most notable against the service was Metallica, who spoke vehemently on behalf of artist rights. Limp Bizkit's Fred Durst sided with Napster and downloaders. His opinion, shared by many, held that downloading simply fostered consumer excitement to make purchases. Still, amid much hullabaloo, Napster received a court injunction to shutter its services.

Other file-sharing transfer systems have arisen in its wake, including Gnutella, Morpheus, KaZaa, and Aimster. These services now boast worldwide user bases larger than Napster's, and are proving harder to shut down. But it was Fanning's own peer-to-peer network that started it all.

NAPSTER, THEN AND NOW

January 1999

Shawn Fanning, 19, creates Napster, enabling online music enthusiasts to open their hard drives to other people and swap MP3 files. In May, Napster Inc. is founded.

December 7, 1999

The record industry charges Napster with violating federal and state laws through copyright infringement.

May 8, 2000

U.S. District Judge Marilyn Hall Patel orders Napster to stand trial for copyright infringement.

June 13, 2000

The Recording Industry Association of America (RIAA) seeks a preliminary injunction against Napster, raising the possibility that the service will end.

July 26, 2000

Patel orders Napster to halt the trading of copyrighted material. A few days later, an appellate court allows Napster to remain in operation while it prepares to hear an expedited appeal.

October 31, 2000

German media conglomerate Bertelsmann forms an alliance with Napster to develop a subscription service.

March 6, 2001

Napster wins a small reprieve in court and remains in business as long as it is filtering out copyrighted material from its networks.

August 8, 2001

Napster Chief Executive Konrad Hilbers outlines the company's planned subscription service.

September 24, 2001

Napster agrees to pay $26 million to settle its ongoing legal disputes with music publishers and songwriters.

NAPSTER, THEN AND NOW *(continued)*

March 8, 2002

Napster cuts 10 percent of its staff as the company returns to court to fight copyright battles. A subscription service is put on hold as the court case drags on.

May 17, 2002

Bertelsmann Music Group (BMG) agrees to buy Napster for $8 million and retains CEO Hilbers and Fanning.

June 3, 2002

Napster files for Chapter 11 bankruptcy protection.

September 3, 2002

A federal judge blocks the sale of Napster to Bertelsmann.

October 29, 2003

Purchased by technology company Roxio, Napster is reborn as Napster 2.0, a legal online music service.

ALTERING THE LANDSCAPE: THE RISE OF LEGAL MP3 DOWNLOADS AND PLAYERS

The fear within the music business, the anxiety that keeps it hot on the trail of illegal downloaders, is that sales will continue to fall. Consumers now buy more blank CDs than recorded CDs. And executives watch nervously as millions of Internet users trade slower Internet connections for faster broadband access, such as cable modems. These high-speed lines make it fast and simple to download music.

Still, it is starting to get tougher and tougher for RIAA statisticians to align CD sales numbers with allegations that piracy is killing the music business. Peer-to-peer network traffic is still going strong, even after thousands of RIAA lawsuits against alleged pirates. Now the public learns that CD music shipments in the first half of 2004 have risen 10 percent over the same period a year ago. The RIAA still wants to make a case that piracy is hurting sales, but their own statistics show that changes in music listening habits, Internet single sales, and other economic factors are playing a great part in the music sales upturn. As with any set of statistics, cases can be made for many different points of view and can lead to diverging statements like these:

Better technology and an improvement in quality are also pushing more people to legitimate sources. Many consumers always wanted to do the right thing, but just couldn't. And now that's changing.
—Michael Gartenberg, vice president and research director
at Jupiter Research in Washington, DC.

Piracy, both online and on the street, continues to hit the music community hard, and thousands have lost their jobs because of it.
—Mitch Bainwol, chairman and CEO of the RIAA.

Certainly, the advent of online music download services has exposed music listeners to a wider variety of music than the mega-stars radio constantly promotes. This statistic could be used as proof that the music listening public has moved away from the big hits and is opening its ears to an array of music. One can argue that because of this, the overall music industry is now in more robust financial shape. One could further argue that the increase in sales of non–top 100 albums could be directly attributed to exposure to the larger pool of artists available on music download sites, in which you can sample an act before making a purchase.

iTunes and Legal Downloading Sites

In the wake of all the turbulence surrounding the illegal file-transfer sites, a number of legal download companies have risen to compete for the business. Apple's iTunes was launched in April 2003, offering songs for 99 cents. In its first year of service, users acquired 70 million songs and it anticipated selling twice that in the next year. The company says it averages 2.7 million songs a month. Its inventory amounts to over 700,000. Napster, by contrast, the leading site among iTunes competitors, is selling, at the time of this publication, just over 1.2 million songs a month. In the summer of 2005 Apple was celebrating the sale of 500 million songs.

Other legal sites such as Rhapsody, Pressplay, and Musicnet sell considerably fewer tunes and have smaller libraries. But because the download market is still relatively untapped, with only Apple fully capitalizing on the idea, companies will stick it out to see this technology through. Surely, the idea of selling songs rather than albums is one that the more profitable, album-oriented music business will be slow to embrace.

DVD Growth

Global music sales fell by only 1.3 percent during the first half of 2004, suggesting the market is showing some signs of recovery. But much of that recovery concerned the growth of DVD music videos. While music sales have been in decline for the past four years, DVDs, whose sales have increased by over

20 percent this year, have helped bring up the entertainment dollar's bottom line significantly. Music videos have, more and more, become a factor in major music releases. Many successful recording artists are jumping on board the music industry's latest trend and adding a DVD to their CD release. Live concerts, music videos, behind-the-scenes footage, and tour documentaries have all added value to major CD releases in an effort to enhance the overall package and make it more attractive for purchase. Elsewhere, labels might embed an exclusive video in a CD-ROM format to entice buyers. Bands that have opted for this enhanced package include Linkin Park, the Red Hot Chili Peppers, and Simple Plan, among many others. This is also a powerful tool to dissuade would-be downloaders, and encourage fans of a band to choose this value-added package over a stripped-down version of the same disc.

SATELLITE RADIO

Another reason for optimism within the music industry over the past few years has been the advent and subsequent growth of satellite radio. Satellite radio, which became widely available in 2001, involves the broadcast of 100 channels of digital audio programming via satellites directly to 3-band AM/FM and satellite-compatible radios. The service is subscription-based and offered by two companies, Sirius Satellite Radio and XM Satellite Radio. They both offer high-quality, uninterrupted digital audio signals throughout the continental United States. Both serve up a vast menu of music stations, all of which are dedicated to airing a single genre, from blues and reggae to punk and metal. These car radios, which also receive traditional signals, are manufactured by the leading names in consumer electronics and available at retail stores nationwide or as an option with the purchase of a new car.

Satellite radio will primarily widen the options for music fans tired of listening to thirty minutes of commercials every hour, and to songs they don't like. Subscribers can now tune in to hear not only music they know they will like, but they will be exposed to music within the genres they like that they have not heard. This will undoubtedly stimulate sales, especially among baby-boomer commuters, who spend much of their time every day in their automobiles, can afford the subscription price, and have a little extra income to spend on pre-recorded music.

THE FUTURE OF TECHNOLOGY AND ROCK MUSIC

The availability of music through new technology like satellite radio and Internet downloading will contribute to the broadening of genres. The Web enables people to sample music prior to buying, as well as to research musicians and bands. Satellite radio has the same effect. Earlier generations didn't have this simple access to new music.

Over the coming years, downloading will continue, but it will become more of a precursor to buying as older downloaders utilize the technology to research music before purchasing. An Ipsos-Reid survey from June 2002 revealed that 14 percent of those aged 35 to 54 had downloaded music or MP3 files from an online file-sharing service. The same study showed that nearly one-third of downloaders said their preferred genre of music had changed since they began downloading. This suggests that online music activities can influence offline listening and purchasing.

While brick-and-mortar stores continue to experience shortfalls in profits, the likes of which most small "Mom & Pop" stores cannot endure, Web stores are thriving. These e-merchants are more likely to stock music made years ago and back catalog items; many of these titles are not available in stores.

In the coming years, labels will finally come to an agreement on a standard download contract that supports burning and a greater range of devices. (As of 2004, there is no standard contract with artists involving the royalties for downloaded songs.) As a result, legal downloading will begin to take off as the availability of content becomes more consistent. By 2007, one estimate states, a new business model for the music industry will generate as much as $2 billion worldwide, or 17 percent of music business revenues. As a result of the growth potential, artists will embrace the Internet and sign downloading rights over to their labels.

Still, these emerging technologies guarantee not only that new commercial opportunities are most certain to arise, but that the music industry will be faced with finding more and more ways to legislate those technologies. In 2005 and beyond, that means not only a cornucopia of red tape, but endless fascination and anticipation among consumers of today's music.

A-TO-Z OF ROCK, 1991–2005

Bold-faced terms refer to other entries in this A-to-Z chapter.

Adult Alternative Pop/Rock. A strain of commercial pop-rock geared to a slightly older audience, and with an alternative twist. Bands of the ilk include the **Spin Doctors**, **Blues Traveler**, Gin Blossoms, and Vertical Horizon, and more recently, Train and Five for Fighting.

Albini, Steve. See **Big Black**

Alice in Chains. Seattle-based metal-grunge band led by Layne Staley and Jerry Cantrell that released several acclaimed and chart-topping albums, including *Dirt* and *Jar of Flies*, the only EP to debut on *Billboard*'s top spot. Staley died of a drug overdose in 2002. Members also included Mike Starr and Sean Kinney.

Alternative Country (Alt.Country). A style of music blending country, roots rock, and punk. The earliest purveyors include **Uncle Tupelo**, the **Jayhawks**, the Silos, and Jason and the Scorchers. *No Depression*, the name of an Uncle Tupelo recording from 1990, is now a magazine of the same name covering the genre.

Amos, Tori (born Myra Ellen Amos, 1963–). Evocative, piano-playing singer-songwriter with a poetic vision. Her confessional writing style, especially on recordings like *Under the Pink* (1994) and *Little Earthquakes* (1991), has gained her legions of empathic fans and has made her one of the '90s' most consistent sellers.

Babes in Toyland. Minneapolis indie-grunge trio of the late '80s and early '90s, led by Kat Bjelland, that was influential, especially on their major-label debut *Fontanelle* (1992), part of the **Riot Grrrl** movement that would begin soon after. Members also included Lori Barbero, Michelle Leon, and Maureen Herman.

Bad Religion. California punk rockers that served as the backbone for the resurgence of punk in the '90s. Beginning in 1982 and through 1993, the band released records on their own Epitaph label, run by guitarist Brett Gurewitz. That label would go on to become one of the country's most successful independent imprints, releasing albums by the **Offspring**, Tom Waits, and Merle Haggard. Members include Greg Graffin, Greg Hetson, Brian Baker, and Bobby Schayer, who replaced drummer Peter Finestone.

Barenaked Ladies. Toronto outfit whose first album, *Yeloow Tape*, was released in 1991 merges pop/rock/rap/jazz/folk and any other style with comedy in becoming a successful draw on the concert circuit. Came perilously close to being considered a novelty act, but grew more serious on later recordings like *Maroon* (2000) and the aptly titled *Everything to Everyone* (2003). Members include Ed Robertson, Steven Page, Jim Creeggan, Andy Creeggan, and Tyler Stewart.

The Beastie Boys. Punk trio turned demonstrative hip-hop/rock/punk mélange on albums like *Licensed to Ill* and *Paul's Boutique*. Adam Yauch, Mike Diamond, and Adam Horovitz established their own eclectic label, Grand Royale, before slowing down the pace of recording and touring in the late '90s.

Beat Happening. Seminal Northwest indie rock trio of the '80s and '90s known for their primitive, charming sound. Their rise as a band—the lineup of which included Calvin Johnson, Heather Lewis, and Bret Lunsford—coincided with the founding of their label, K, which was critical in bringing attention to the **indie rock** and **Riot Grrrl** movements of the '90s.

Beck (born Beck Hansen, 1970–). Eclectic, colorful singer-songwriter capable of playing within a startling variety of genres, from **indie rock** and punk to blues, funk, and folk. Best known for his debut single "Loser" in 1994, but also for his 1997 recording *Odelay*. He has since become a reliable critic's favorite.

Big-Beat Techno. Acts like the **Chemical Brothers** and Crystal Method whose electronic recordings closely approximate rock music and rock-music tempos.

Big Black. Chicago act led by guitarist and music scholar Steve Albini and flanked by Santiago Durango and David Riley. Big Black's noise helped usher in the age of industrial rock, also practiced by **Ministry** and **Nine Inch Nails**. Albini would go on to produce important recordings by the **Pixies** and **Bush**.

Bikini Kill. Seminal **Riot Grrrl** punk group from Olympia, Washington, led by Kathleen Hanna, that did more to further the political and social causes—and empower the women—of the Riot Grrrls than any other. Other members included Tobi Vail, Kathi Wilcox, and Bill Karren. The group disbanded in 1998, with Hanna going on to form another, less confrontational act, Le Tigre.

Bjork (born Björk Guðmundsdóttir, 1965–). Unusual and progressive singer-songwriter originally from Reykjavík, Iceland, Bjork made a name for herself with an adventurous pop-rock outfit called the Sugarcubes. She left that band in 1992 to become a solo performer and actor, and has since made a number of popular recordings, including *Post* (1995) and *Homogenic* (1997).

Black Metal. A form of metal music originating in Scandinavia that sounds somewhat similar to death metal but puts forth an anti-Christian stance. Many bands of the black-metal movement, particularly from Scandinavia, were on a mission to return their countries to their Viking or pagan roots. Some bands went so far as to burn churches, sixty of which were burned in Norway alone.

Black Sabbath. The single most influential heavy-metal band on the school of grunge acts to emerge in the late '80s and early '90s. Sabbath's distorted, heavy sound, apparent on seminal albums like *Paranoid* (1992), shows up in virtually all of grunge's most popular bands, including **Nirvana**, **Soundgarden**, and **Alice in Chains**. Founding members include Tony Iommi, Bill Ward, Geezer Butler and **Ozzy Osbourne**.

blink-182. Rowdy punk rock trio featuring Mark Hoppus, Tom Delonge, and Scott Raynor, and a taste for scatological humor. In 1998, Raynor left the band and was replaced by drummer Travis Barker. The new lineup appeared on *Enema of the State*, which hit record store shelves in 1999. A live album, *The Mark, Tom and Travis Show*, was released in 2000, followed by *Take Off Your Pants and Jacket* in 2001.

Blues Traveler. New Jersey band that built its reputation on touring relentlessly and selling albums along the way. Fronted by singer-harpist John Popper and including Chan Kinchla, Bobby Sheehan, and Brendan Hill, Blues Traveler also established an annual tour called **H.O.R.D.E.** (Horizons of Rock Developing Everywhere), to run every summer from 1992 through 1998.

Blur. Premier **Britpop** act of the '90s led by singer Damon Albarn and guitarist Graham Coxon. Their rise, simultaneous to **Oasis'** own rise in Britain, was limited to their homeland until they released the smash single "Song 2" in America in 1997. Band members also include bassist Alex James and drummer Dave Rowntree.

Bonnaroo. The current top of the festival heap right now, the Bonnaroo festival draws nearly 100,000 people for its four-day run every summer. Located on a 700-acre farm in Manchester, Tennessee, the event's first three installments have all sold out, with acts as diverse and well-known as Neil Young, Bob Dylan, the **Grateful Dead**, and **Dave Matthews**.

Britpop. A self-explanatory term describing a trend that originated in the late '80s in Britain with bands like the **Smiths** and the **Stone Roses**, then surged in popularity at the hands of bands like **Oasis, Blur,** and **London Suede.**

Buckley, Jeff (1966–1997). Massively acclaimed songwriter-guitarist and son of respected folk singer Tim Buckley. Jeff made a name for himself with his wide-octave vocal range and his passionate performing. Buckley only managed to release one official album, *Grace* (1994), before dying in a freak swimming accident in the Mississippi River in 1997. His reputation has grown significantly since his death.

Bush. A London band that made its fortune selling records in America, Bush was initially criticizing for debuting with a sound suggesting **Nirvana** following Kurt Cobain's death. But their bow, *Sixteen Stone* (1994) and follow-up recordings like *Razorblade Suitcase* (1996), which received better but mixed reviews, were vastly popular and sold well. The lineup features frontman Gavin Rossdale, guitarist Nigel Pulsford, bassist Dave Parsons, and drummer Robin Goodridge.

CCM (Contemporary Christian Music). The evolving state of Christian-oriented music includes such diverse and contemporary styles as rock, jazz, blues, dance, metal, rap, alternative, New Age, grunge, punk, thrash, death, gothic, and industrial. Yet regardless of form, the essence is a fondness for Christian themes and an appreciation of religion. The subgenres saw a tremendous explosion of popularity in the '90s.

Cassidy, Eva (1963–1996). Talented singer-songwriter and interpreter who became popular after her death in 1996 at the age of 33. She earned local fame in and around Washington, DC, but was never able to capitalize on her reputation until after her death. *Songbird*, a collection of songs culled from her first three recordings, has since gone on to sell over a million copies.

Charlatans UK. One of Manchester, England's most popular bands, Charlatans UK made its name as a groove and dance-oriented act with a penchant for deep melodies. Experienced modest success in the States. Band members include Tim Burgess, Martin Blunt, Jon Brookes, Mark Collins, and Rob Collins. Tony Rogers replaced Rob Collins after his tragic death from an automobile accident in 1996.

Chemical Brothers. Marquee electronic and big-beat recording duo consisting of programmers Tom Rowland and Ed Simons. They have, since their formation in 1994, become one of the cornerstones of "electronica" based on hit records like *Dig Your Own Hole* (1997) and *Exit Planet Dust* (1995).

Chicago Post-Rock. A school of progressive, jazz-inflected **indie rock** with unpredictable arrangements and accomplished musicianship. Significant bands in the movement include Tortoise, Sea and Cake, Trans Am, LaBradford, Karate, and Louisville's Slint. An intentional backlash to the hard-rock sounds of grunge.

Childish, Billy (1958–). Unsung torchbearer for the garage-rock movement past and present. Beginning in the early '80s, Billy Childish recorded over 100 LPs with half a dozen different bands, including the Thee Headcoats, the Del Monas, and under his own name. He's also finished 2,000 paintings, written two novels, and thirty-plus volumes of poetry.

Coldplay. London pop outfit with a flair for simple, infectious, and passionate melodies, enjoyed crossover success with their debut album *Parachutes* in 2000 and again in 2002 with *A Rush of Blood to the Head*. Chris Martin, Jon Buckland, Will Champion, and Guy Berryman comprise the band.

Collective Soul. A rock group from outside Atlanta led by songwriter/guitarist Ed Roland. The band almost didn't exist, when Roland became so discouraged by his lack of success that he gave up writing music altogether. But a breakthrough song, "Shine," became an instant sensation in 1994 and sent the band on its career path. Ross Childress, Ed's brother Dean Roland, Will Turpin, and Shane Evans round out the band.

Corporate Rock. In the '70s, when this term originated, successful rock bands became, literally, corporations, employing dozens and earning money in several ways—onstage, on recordings, and through merchandise. That definition changed in the '90s. Beginning in 1990, many popular alternative bands bit on the big-money contracts waved at them by the major labels. Many even became the subject of bidding wars. As a result of their substantial investment in these big-money contracts, many underground and marginally commercial bands became willing corporate partners with the labels.

Counting Crows. Adam Duritz–led outfit based in Los Angeles with a jangly, Van Morrison-esque sound. Their debut album, *August and Everything After* (1993), popularized the band, helped by the epic pop-rock of "Mrs. Jones." Their approach hinted at a return to the downhome classic sound of rock in the face of grunge. But it ultimately took a backseat. Dave Bryson and Dan Vickrey played guitar, Charlie Gillingham, Dave Immergluck, Ben Mize, and Matt Malley comprise the band's early lineups.

***Cracked Rear View* (Atlantic, 1994).** Hootie and the Blowfish breakthrough album became one of the best-selling recordings of the '90s, selling over 13 million copies. The band was heavily criticized in the media for producing easy listening pop music, but mainstream audiences responded.

The Cranberries. Formed in 1990 in Limerick, Ireland, the Cranberries were one of the early '90s' most successful pop-rock bands in America, led by former church choir singer Dolores O'Riordan. *Everybody Else Is Doing It, So Why Can't We?* (1993) is regarded as their best and breakthrough disc. O'Riordan was flanked by Noel and Mike Hogan, and Feargal Lawler.

Creed. Immensely successful and commercially popular Florida-based rock band whose '90s oeuvre featured multimillion-selling albums like *My Own*

Prison (1997) and *Human Clay* (1999). Their music, loud and metallic with anthemic choruses, put a mainstream spin on the sound of **Seattle** grunge. Scott Stapp and Mark Tremonti served as Creed's principal songwriters, while Brian Marshall and Scott Phillips assumed bass and drum duties.

Crow, Sheryl (1962–). One of the '90s most successful singer-songwriters, Crow made her debut in 1993 after countless sessions in which she performed as a backing singer. *Tuesday Night Music Club*, named after her songwriting group, featured several hits and pushed Crow into the mainstream as a credible artist. More hit records would follow, including the self-produced *Sheryl Crow* (1996).

Deftones. Sacramento-based metal act with the fury of punk and a subtle hip-hop influence. Singer Chino Moreno and guitarist Stephen Carpenter form the core of the band, which also includes bassist Chi Cheng and drummer Abe Cunningham. Albums have been consistently creative, including *White Pony* (2000).

Difranco, Ani (1970–). Defiantly independent upstate New York native who runs her own record label, has developed a unique style on acoustic guitar, and has developed a fanatical following among the acoustic and folk audiences. Album highlights include *Little Plastic Castles* (1998) and *Not a Pretty Girl* (1995).

Dinosaur Jr. Influential grunge act out of rural Massachusetts formed by guitarist and songwriter J. Mascis. The band's early LPs like *Bug* (1988) and *Green Mind* (1991) would serve as the guitar foundation of much of the grunge music to follow, especially that of **Soundgarden** and **Pearl Jam**. Lou Barlow would splinter off to create **Sebadoh** in 1988. Mike Johnson and someone known only as Murph served as Mascis' rhythm section after Barlow left.

The Dixie Chicks. Country roots trio consisting of Natalie Maines, Emily Irwin, and Martie Seidel, the Dixie Chicks formed in Dallas in the late '80s. They set themselves apart from their country counterparts with their skilled musicianship and classic cowgirl approach to the idiom. Their albums sold in vast numbers throughout the '90s and beyond, despite the fact that their liberal leanings ran counter to their conservative fan base.

The Donnas. The Donnas, an all-girl act, began in 1993 as teenage delinquents in the Bay Area, inspired by punk and hard-rock bands like the Ramones, KISS, and AC/DC. They grew in popularity in 2001 when they released a heavily promoted major-label debut, *The Donnas Turn 21*. The band assumed cutesy nicknames like Donna A., Donna R., etc., but their given names are Brett Anderson, Allison Robertson, Maya Ford, and Torry Castellano.

Doves. Critically acclaimed Manchester, U.K., pop trio that gained in popularity in the wake of **Radiohead**'s abstract pop and **Coldplay**'s critical successes. Twin brothers Jez and Andy Williams formed the group with Jimi Goodwin.

Drag City. Prominent indie rock label based in Chicago. Released recordings by influential bands like **Pavement**, Royal Trux, Gastr del Sol, and **Palace**.

Drive By Truckers. A country/roots rock outfit with roots in Alabama and Athens, Georgia. Led by Patterson Hood and boyhood friend Mike Cooley, the band has enjoyed widespread acclaim for albums like *The Dirty South* (2004) and *Decoration Day* (2003).

Earle, Steve (1955–). One of the more intriguing personalities to emerge from Nashville in the late '80s, Earle flourished in the '90s, first as a rocker and then in areas of roots rock, country, bluegrass, and folk. In 2002, he released an album, *Jerusalem*, which garnered much controversy in the light of Earle's criticism of what he considered false patriotism in post-9/11 America. Known as an artist who insists on playing by his own rules, Earle has emerged from a checkered past to become one of the country-roots scene's most acclaimed artists.

Elephant 6. One of the more intriguing musical developments in '90s **indie rock** was the birth of something called Elephant 6, a musical commune located in Athens, Georgia. Premier bands within the Elephant 6 community include Apples in Stereo, Neutral Milk Hotel, Olivia Tremor Control, Beulah, the Music Tapes, Elf Power, the Sunshine Fix, Marbles, the Minders, and Chocolate USA.

Emo. Short for "Emotional," Emo is a form of punk or rock music that is sung and played with great emotion. Generally credited to originator Ian Mackaye of Minor Threat/**Fugazi** in the '80s, the style has since produced a good number of well-known bands in the '90s and later, including the Used, Dashboard, Confessional, and Finch.

Exile in Guyville. Seminal recording by **Liz Phair** released in 1993, which went on to win the *Village Voice* poll for album of the year. Intended as a song-by-song remake of the Rolling Stones album *Exile on Main Street*, the disc seizes the stereotypical man's approach to rock and subverts it to great effect.

Farrell, Perry (1959–). Important creative mastermind in the '90s, first responsible for his critical output as a bandleader for **Jane's Addiction**, and then for putting together the annual traveling, alternative rock tour package called **Lollapalooza**. Also formed **Porno for Pyros** following the dissolution of Jane's Addiction in 1992.

Fatboy Slim (1963–). Also known as Norman Cook (1963–), Fatboy Slim has been one of the more important house electronic artists of the day, working within a variety of electronic styles, from rave and techno to hip-hop. Significant recordings include the influential "Rockafella Skank." His remixes of other artists, including Cornershop's "Brimful of Asha," have reached the top of the English charts.

Fear Factory. One of the first bands in the '90s to incorporate technology into their extreme form of metal, Fear Factor's disc *Demanufacture* proved that you didn't have to be an industrial band to utilize digital elements. Dino Cazares, Burton C. Bell, and Raymond Herrera were key members.

File-Sharing. A form of transfer that takes place between home computers and usually involves music files called MP3s. **Napster**, Gnutella, Morpheus, KaZaa, and Aimster are among the most popular file-sharing transfer systems.

Flaming Lips. Oklahoma band together since the mid-'80s whose wild blend of psychedelic hard rock and wiggy pop has attracted its share of fans since forming. They released some of their most acclaimed work in the '90s, including *The Soft Bulletin* (1999) and *Yoshimi Battles the Pink Robots* (2002). Wayne Coyne, Michael Ivins, and Stephen Drozd comprise the band's creative core.

The Fluid. Grunge band from Denver, Colorado, often in the shadow of other more well-known grunge acts on the same label (**Sub Pop**) like **Nirvana** and **Mudhoney**, despite releasing a couple of landmark genre recordings, like *Clear Black Paper* (1988) and *Roadmouth* (1990). The Fluid lineup included frontman John Robinson, guitarist James Clower, drummer Garrett Shavlik, bassist Matt Bischoff, and guitarist Richard Kulwicki.

The Foo Fighters. Dave Grohl, drummer of **Nirvana**, formed the Foo Fighters in the wake of Nirvana's demise and saw immediate success with albums like *The Colour and the Shape* (1997) and *There Is Nothing Left to Lose* (1999). Grohl had always written songs, but his work was not welcome in the context of Nirvana. Frequent lineup changes have marked the group's existence.

Franz Ferdinand. Named for the Archduke that was assassinated to spark World War I, Glasgow's **indie rock** quartet came together in 2001 and has since become one of the rock scene's trendiest bands. The band features bassist Bob Hardy, guitarist Nick McCarthy, drummer Paul Thomson and singer-guitarist Alex Kapranos.

Fugazi. Seminal indie punk outfit from Washington, DC, led by singer Ian MacKaye, a former founding member of hardcore punk act Minor Threat. Fugazi made many important records in the '90s and toured relentlessly, giving birth to the **Emo** art form. They were also socially and politically active, kept their ticket and CD prices down, and essentially proved that art can triumph over commerce. Guy Picciotto, Joe Lally, and Brendan Canty round out the Fugazi lineup.

Garage Rock. Originally coined in the '60s, the school of garage rock in the '90s and later resembled the raw, primal sound of the original wave as well as its organic trappings. New purveyors of the style include the **Hives**, the **White Stripes**, and the **Strokes**, all of which are characterized by a tough urban feel and little studio polish.

Generation X-ers. A generation of kids born between 1961 and 1981 characterized by their desire to hop off the merry-go-round of status, money, and social climbing that often frames the modern American ethos. This generation is in harsh contrast to the baby boomers, whose births range between 1945 and 1964.

The Gits. A Seattle band formed in 1986 and featuring singer-songwriter Mia Zapata. Zapata, however, was murdered in 1993, after issuing just one record and beginning a second. The homicide was a seismic event in the history of Seattle rock music, and helped give rise to a powerful independent women's movement in rock music.

Godflesh. Justin Broadrick, fresh off a seminal outing with industrial music icons Napalm Death, formed Godflesh in 1988 in Birmingham, England. They made an important debut with *Streetcleaner* in 1989, a recording that melded downtuned guitars with relentless drum loops. It has become an **industrial-metal** milestone.

Godsmack. Heavy-metal band out of Boston featuring singer-guitarist-songwriter Sully Erna and guitarist Tony Rombola. Their early recordings, including *Godsmack* and *Awake*, established the band's downtuned, visceral sound, and singles like "Voodoo" and "Keep Away" proved the band could succeed on a commercial level as well. Godsmack also includes drummer Tommy Stewart and bass player Robbie Merrill.

Goo Goo Dolls. A fun-loving punk band turned tuneful pop-rockers, this Buffalo trio featuring Johnny Rzeznik, Robby Takac, and drummer George Tutuska (replaced by Mike Malinin in 1995) started out in 1986. But it wasn't until they released *A Boy Named Goo*, which yielded the hit single "Name," that they began their commercial ascent up the charts. More hits would follow, but by 2000, popularity began to fade.

Gov't Mule. Jam-oriented band renowned for their musicianship and exploratory live sets and their willingness to delve into blues and jazz as well as rock. Formed in 1995 as a side project while guitarist Warren Haynes and bassist Allen Woody played together with the reunited Allman Brothers. Matt Abts controls the drums for GM.

The Grateful Dead. Important progenitors of the '90s jam band movement, which is still a vital creative concept. The Dead disbanded after the death of their spiritual leader Jerry Garcia in 1995, but their raison d'être was continued by experimental and jam-oriented bands like **Phish**, **.moe**, and **Blues Traveler**. Garcia was accompanied by a long list of players, including original members Phil Lesh, Bob Weir, and Mickey Hart.

Green Day. Punk trio out of Berkeley, California, central to the rise of punk rock in the '90s. Consisting of Billie Joe Armstrong, Mike Dirnt, and Tres Cool, the band issued their breakthrough *Dookie* in 1994 and went from an unassuming but talented bunch of scruffy kids to superstars playing arena-sized venues. Their 2005 album *American Idiot* found the band reaching yet another high-water mark for the punk genre.

Green River. Significant early grunge act in Seattle that predated the official emergence of the genre. It was important in that it featured in its lineup members of **Mudhoney** and **Pearl Jam**, both of whom would go on to make a pronounced impact on the rock scene during the '90s grunge era. Members included Jeff Ament and Stone Gossard from Pearl Jam, Mark Arm and Steve Turner from Mudhoney, and Bruce Fairweather from Love Battery.

Guided by Voices. An **indie rock** band headed by former elementary school teacher Robert Pollard and his songwriting partner Tobin Sprout. Recorded frequently, churning songs out by the dozen, once, that is, Pollard decided to abandon his teaching career in the mid-'90s and dedicate himself to music. At one point, around 1995, GBV stood as one of the most celebrated underground/indie rock bands in the country.

Guns N' Roses. Formed in Los Angeles in 1985, Guns N' Roses rose quickly to prominence in the rock world with albums like *Appetite for Destruction*. They were well on their way to becoming the next Led Zeppelin when feuds and interpersonal troubles began to consume the band and their chemistry was destroyed. They began an extended hiatus in the early '90s and haven't regrouped since. Axl Rose, the band's temperamental lead singer, has threatened to release a new album since the early '90s, but has burned through millions of dollars and scores of musical support in a futile effort. Their label, Geffen, ultimately lost patience in the process and dropped the band from its roster in 2004. Founding members include Rose (born William Bailey), Slash (born Saul Hudson), drummer Steven Adler (later replaced by Matt Sorum), second guitarist Izzy Stradlin (born Jeff Isabelle), and bassist Duff McKagan.

H.O.R.D.E. The Horizons of Rock Developing Everywhere tour, or H.O.R.D.E. Festival, began in 1992 as a showcase for bands that excelled playing live but who also wanted to avoid playing the summertime club circuit. Conceived by **Blues Traveler** frontman John Popper and colleague David Frey, the festival, which rallied annually during summers through 1998, also served to assemble like-minded **jam bands** that appealed to an audience big enough to sell out amphitheaters.

Happy Mondays. Ill-fated **Britpop** group out of Manchester that started out promisingly with a dance-oriented pop sound. Band frontman Shaun Ryder, responsible for turning out what was essentially considered the soundtrack for Britain's "Ecstasy Culture," succumbed to drugs himself and was in and out of rehab frequently during the '90s. The band eventually broke up in 1993; Ryder went on to form Black Grape. The group also included Paul Ryder, Paul Davis, Gary Whelan, Mark Day, and Bez Berisford.

Hardcore Metal. A strand of metal combining punk with thrash rose up naturally in the '90s. The resurgence of Slayer and Pantera, two icons of thrash, coupled with the popularity of old-school punk, made this hybrid a natural by-product of current musical trends.

Harper, Ben (1969–). California native with a folk music upbringing who has gone on to embrace genres as diverse as blues, soul, and gospel. Famed for playing his lap steel guitar called a Wiessenborn, Harper tours relentlessly and records sporadically. He collaborated with the Blind Boys of Alabama gospel group in 2004 on *There Will Be a Light*.

Harris, Emmylou (1947–). One of the leading lights of Nashville, Emmylou Harris became the Grand Dame of the alt.country movement in the '90s with an impressive canon of roots rock projects. *Wrecking Ball*, her 1995 album produced by Daniel Lanois, helped Harris reinvent herself as an alt-country chanteuse and an eager collaborator, which she did with Linda Ronstadt, Dolly Parton, and scores of others throughout the '90s and beyond.

Harvey, P. J. (1969–). UK artist Polly Jean Harvey paved the way for much of the honest and expressive work heard from other women songwriters like **Liz Phair**, Alanis Morissette, and the **Riot Grrrls**. Her debut album *Dry*, in 1992, made substantial impact on the alternative rock scene as did later work like 1995's *To Bring You My Love*.

Hatebreed. One of the foremost purveyors of '90s hardcore metal, the Connecticut band formed in 1993 with charismatic singer Jamey Jasta and toured aggressively with anyone and everyone in metal before debuting on record in 1997 with *Satisfaction Is the Death of Desire*. Hatebreed consists of frontman Jamie Jasta, guitarists Boulder Richards and Sean Martin, bassist Chris Beattie, and drummer Rigg Ross.

Helmet. New York City proto-metal band made a big impact in the independent underground scene before going on to make an even bigger splash on the national scene during the grunge era. Their heavily syncopated sound and deep, primal riffs would be one of the inspirations for the nü-metal movement of the late '90s. The founding lineup of Helmet consisted of frontman-guitarist Page Hamilton, bassist Henry Bogdan, drummer John Stanier, and second guitarist Peter Mengede.

The Hives. Outrageous garage-rock act from Sweden, the Hives have served as the leading light of the young new wave of garage bands. Characterized by a raw, early rock sound, the Hives, always dressed in some combination of black and white, have proved to be capable leaders of that movement, on the road, and on recordings like *Tyrannosaurus Hives* (2004).

Hole. One of the most controversial rock bands of the '90s, led by the flamboyant **Courtney Love**. Hole was formed in Los Angeles in 1989, but soon became associated with the grunge movement in Seattle. Love eventually married leading grunge rep Kurt Cobain and the two were together until his death in 1994. Hole recorded some of their best work during that difficult time, including the powerful and prophetic *Live Through This* (1994), released just four days after Cobain's death. Two months after Cobain died, the group lost bassist Kristen Pfaff to a drug overdose. Hole held together following these traumas, for better or worse. Love became a celebrity, even made a few feature film appearances, including a leading role in *The People vs. Larry Flint* in 1996. Other albums followed, including *Celebrity Skin* (1998). But a string of run-ins with the law, as well as a legal battle with the remaining members of **Nirvana**, have both kept her on the police blotter and out of her more suitable role as leading rock lady of the '90s. The band also included Hole's significant songwriter collaborator Eric Erlandson, drummer Patty Schemel, and bassist Melissa Auf Der Maur.

Hoobastank. The post-grunge/alt-metal quartet was formed in a suburb of Los Angeles back in 1994. Their sound, informed by the heavy melodicism of **Nirvana** and the progressive rock of Tool, leavened their approach with pop elements. The result was a radio-friendly rock/metal sound that found a willing audience. Their debut album, *Hoobastank*, went gold, and the band's more mature follow-up, *The Reason*, with the hit title song became a huge hit. Frontman Doug Robb, guitarist-songwriter Dan Estrin, bassist Markku Lappalainen, and drummer Chris Hesse make up the Hoobastank lineup.

Hootie and the Blowfish. Darius Rucker led this band, which formed at the University of South Carolina. Their chief form of rock consisted of Rucker's passionate singing and edge-less but feelgood melodies. The chemistry didn't earn them rave reviews, but it sold more albums than just about any other act throughout the '90s. Their debut, *Cracked Rear View* (1995), racked up 14 million in sales. Oddly, they had trouble following that debut with anything of substance, and their career as pioneers of a southern folk sound stalled in the late '90s. Rucker is joined by guitarist Mark Bryan, bassist Dean Felber, and drummer Jim Sonefeld.

Huggy Bear. Just as **Bikini Kill** was spearheading the **Riot Grrrl** movement in the States, Huggy Bear was doing the same in the United Kingdom. They debuted in 1991, recorded sporadically, then disbanded just three years later. A multigender unit comprised of vocalist Chris, vocalist/bassist Niki, guitarists Jo and Jon, and drummer Karen. In addition to their refusal to reveal their full names, they also turned down requests for interviews and photographs.

***Human Clay* (Wind-Up, 1999).** Creed's second album, and the follow-up to the massively successful *My Own Prison*, solidified the Florida band's place among the biggest rock acts in the world. Their anthemic songs took grunge and polished it into singalong rock hits, many of which made it onto *Human Clay*, an album that entered the *Billboard* album chart at No. 1 and stayed in the upper reaches for months.

Hüsker Dü. See Mould, Bob/Hüsker Dü/Sugar

***Hybrid Theory* (Warner Brothers, 2000).** Linkin Park's "hybrid theory" is that of the merger of rap and rock, which, in itself, was not terribly new when the Los Angeles band got its hands on it. Still, audiences responded in a big way to the sound of Brad Delson's heavy guitar and Chester Bennington and Mike Shinoda's rapping/singing. *Hybrid Theory*, Linkin Park's debut, went on to sell in the millions, and jumpstarted the band's near-term career.

Incubus. Like its alt-metal colleagues **Hoobastank**, Incubus combines the power of progressive rock and metal with pop melodies in creating a commercially viable heavy-music experience. The Incubus trip began in Calabasas, California, in the early '90s, as grunge was beginning to take hold. The band members, including singer Brandon Boyd and songwriter guitarist Mike Einziger formed Incubus in tenth grade. Their breakthrough recording, *Make Yourself* (1999), eventually went double platinum, and the band began to draw larger numbers on the concert circuit. Einziger and Boyd are supported by bass player Dirk Lance (born Alex Katunich), drummer José Pasillas, and DJ Lyfe (born Gavin Koppel).

Indie Rock. An extension of the so-called "college" or "underground" rock of the '80s—which originally included bands like the **Replacements, R.E.M.,** and **U2**—and a forbear of the alternative rock explosion of the '90s. Indie rock literally addressed the thousands of bands who recorded their music for independent labels; that is, labels not owned by large corporations. In the wake of the alt-rock boom, however, indie rock became more specific, defined more by its sound than its anti-corporate stance. That sound was, and still is, characterized by spare production values; primitive, stylized playing; and the freedom to explore a greater range of emotions lyrically and artistically, largely because it is bound by fewer commercial constraints.

Indigo Girls. Amy Ray and Emily Saliers emerged during the late '80s as a two-women-with-guitars folk act, following on the heels of success by women like Suzanne Vega and Tracy Chapman. But they quickly became heroes to a new generation of acoustic music fans. Saliers and Ray complement each other skillfully, with different styles and diverging approaches to the acoustic idiom. Their albums, lyrical and intelligent, reflect that range and have sold consistently well, not only to their rabid core following, but to the mainstream audience as well.

Industrial Rock/Industrial Metal. Stemming from the late '70s and early '80s computer music orthodoxy of bands like Throbbing Gristle and Kraftwerk, the industrial musics of the '90s have come a long way. The music, still powered by a bank of synthesizers, resembles rock and metal, with large numbers of overdubbed guitars and an aggressive approach to song composition that almost reflects hardcore punk. **Ministry** and **Nine Inch Nails** are widely regarded as touchstones of the genre, and their influence was widely felt throughout the '90s and later in bands like Garbage and My Chemical Romance.

iTunes. Apple Computer's revolutionary Music Store went online in 2003—specializing in selling individual songs for .99 cents—and has been the market leader ever since, moving millions of songs every month. The iTunes solution came as a response to the illegal downloading and **file-sharing** that occurred, and continue to occur only now to a lesser degree.

***Jagged Little Pill* (Maverick, 1995).** Alanis Morissette recorded this album for Madonna's Maverick label and it went on to become one of the top-selling albums in all of the '90s, bolstered by singles like "You Oughta Know" and "Ironic."

Jam Band. The jam band methodology came about most memorably in the music of the **Grateful Dead**. That band would often launch into unpredictable flights of fancy, or improvisatory jams, during a song, the destination of which was never actually known by the audience or by the band itself. Following the demise of the Dead, hundreds of other groups aspired to the jam band throne, including **Widespread Panic**, **Gov't Mule**, **.moe**, and **Phish**, but no act has quite taken over the Dead's reign.

Jane's Addiction. Perry Farrell's integral alternative band, Jane's Addiction formed in Los Angeles in the mid-'80s and made their major-label recording bow in 1988 with *Nothing's Shocking*. The band broke into the mainstream with *Ritual de lo Habitual* in 1990 and went gold. From there, Farrell took advantage of the young alternative rock revolution and conceived **Lollapalooza**, the first alternative rock festival of the '90s. The first installment of Lollapalooza went on the road in 1991 and it would continue for most of the decade. Jane's Addiction recorded sporadically after this point, and had some lineup changes, ultimately leading to their breakup in 1993. But they reunited first in 1997 and a couple of times thereafter, mainly to tour. They released the well-received *Strays* in 2003. Jane's seminal lineup included drummer Stephen Perkins, guitarist Dave Navarro, bass player Eric Avery, and singer-frontman Farrell.

Jars of Clay. The folky jangle and textured guitar pop of Illinois' Jars of Clay took mainstream rock by surprise, not only because they were largely unknown, but because they were all devout Christians who took their name from a bible verse. No matter, they penetrated deep into the mainstream rock charts with their breakthrough album *Jars of Clay* in 1995. Although there was a slight backlash to their subtle preaching—both on the secular side and on the Christian side (many of their fans thought they had become too secular), they debuted at No. 8 with their second album, *Much Afraid*, in 1997. Their success set the stage for other Christian rock acts like dc Talk and Sixpence None the Richer, both of whom became commercially viable pop acts. They released their fifth studio album, *Who We Are Instead*, in 2003. The band is led by Dan Haseltine, with keyboardist Charlie Lowell, guitarists Steve Mason and Matt Odmark, and drummer Scott Savage.

The Jayhawks. Alternative country took a giant step when this Minneapolis outfit released its creative defining moment *Hollywood Town Hall* back in 1992. The band, helmed by Gary Louris and Mark Olson, made downhome music with sublime harmonies, and in so doing, helped to establish the idea that **Uncle Tupelo** wasn't the only one able to bring country-styled music to the mainstream. Olson eventually left the band to record as a solo artist and with the Original Harmony Ridge Creek Dippers, as well as with his life partner Victoria Williams. The Jayhawks, meanwhile, went on to record epic roots pop recordings like *Tomorrow the Green Grass* (1995) and *Smile* (2000). Beside Olson and Louris, key contributors to the Jayhawks include bassist Marc Perlman, keyboardist Karen Grotberg, drummer Tim O'Regan, and guitarist Kraig Johnson.

Jet. When Jet stormed the rock world with its debut recording, the aptly titled *Get Born*, in 2003, few expected the sweeping impact this Australian quartet would have. Cameron Muncey, brothers Chris and Nic Cester, and Mark Wilson stormed into America virtually unannounced but left with millions of fans, and the kind of radio domination only seasoned rock bands such as Aerosmith could expect. Singles like "Look What You've Done," "Cold Hard Bitch," and the milestone garage-rock hit "Are You Gonna Be My Girl" featured the band retaining a super-raw guitar sound, but somehow managing to cross over to mainstream pop audiences in 2004. Their success was as unlikely as any rock band in the new millennium.

Jewel (1974–). Throughout the mid- to late '90s, Jewel, born Jewel Kilcher, commanded magazines and radio airwaves with her light acoustic pop songs. Her debut, *Pieces of You*, released in 1994, would end up selling an astonishing 7 million copies. Not bad for a young songwriter from Alaska who spent part of her life growing up in a van. Jewel eventually matured, both as a songwriter and as a personality. In 2003, she took a left turn and recorded *0304*, a dance-pop album that ran counter to her heretofore organic image. Still, the record sold well.

Jimmy Eat World. Formed in Mesa, Arizona in 1994, Jimmy Eat World consists of childhood pals that would go on to much bigger things as the decade progressed. They signed with a major label in 1995 and released their debut, *Static Prevails*, the next year. Some lineup changes and a few tweaks to their sound followed over the next few years. Eventually, they changed labels to record their breakthrough, *Bleed American*, later retitled *Jimmy Eat World* (it was released just before the World Trade Center bombing). The record sold strongly for a year, and the band supported it with two years of constant touring. They released *Futures* in 2004. Band members include Jim Adkins up front, drummer Zach Lind, Tom Linton on guitar, and Rick Burch on bass.

Jones, Norah, *Come Away with Me* (Blue Note, 2002). This was the single album that managed to change the way recording companies looked at their marketing plans. Norah Jones (1979–), the daughter of renowned sitarist Ravi Shankar, was a waifish, half-folk, half-jazz chanteuse who sang quirky, laid-back arrangements to spare accompaniment. Released on the legendary jazz imprint Blue Note, the record went on to sell 18 million copies worldwide and earn the singer eight Grammy awards. Throughout the '90s and later, record companies set their sites almost exclusively on a young buying demographic, and they released "young" and pop music accordingly. But that demographic had turned to illegal downloading for their music and had curtailed their spending on legally issued CDs. When Norah Jones emerged, and in so doing proved that more adult-oriented pop music could sell in big numbers, record labels began to shift their marketing focus and their release schedule to an older audience—one that didn't care to download their music.

KMFDM. Industrial rock icons, who got their start in the early '80s in Paris. Officially conceived by Sascha Konietzko (the name stands for "Kein Mitleid für die Mehrheit" or "No Pity for the Majority"), the band's first performance—at a gallery opening—consisted of guitar feedback, five basses, and four coal miners banging on the museum's foundation. Since then, they've sampled audio collages and run it over their often heavy-sounding industrial backdrops. They did much of their best work in the '90s on discs like *Virus* (1993) and *XTORT* (1996). Principals include Sascha Konietzko and En Esch.

Korn. Important **nü-metal** act who exerted their influence on heavy-metal music when they debuted in 1994. At its best, their haunting, ear-splitting sound embodies the very nature of alternative metal and is a creative study in aggressive music. The band toured relentlessly throughout the mid-'90s, and issued *Life Is Peachy* in 1996. Virulent singer Jonathan Davis seethed his way through the recording in helping to define himself as one of the most compelling and troubled voices in all of rock, and the manic guitars and rhythm surrounding him only enhanced the final product. By the mid-'00s, the band's sound had grown slim of ideas. Davis is supported by guitarists James Shaffer and Brian Welch, bassist Reginald Arvizu, and drummer David Silveria.

L7. Formed in Los Angeles in 1985 and comprised of an all-girl lineup, L7 served as a critical inspiration for the **Riot Grrrl** movement. They proved that women could match the testosterone-fueled rock 'n' roll of the grunge bands (they even signed briefly with the grunge imprint **Sub Pop**), and they could be just as outrageous as well. Created as a sort of post-punk version of bands like the Runaways (late '70s) and Fannie (early '70s), L7—Suzi Gardner, Donita Sparks, Jennifer Finch, and Dee Plakas—made a commercial impact with their 1992 effort, *Bricks Are Heavy*, but had trouble maintaining a high level of popularity. They split in 2000, after releasing *Slap Happy*.

Lilith Fair. The brainchild of **Sarah McLachlan**, Lilith Fair was conceived as a vibrant meeting place for fans of women in music, an outlet that gave a host of emerging female singer-songwriters room to showcase their talents. At the time, women were being embraced as never before by radio stations, record labels, and the broader pop industry, and Lilith Fair gave them a platform. The Fair began with a small handful of dates in 1996 and ran through the summer of 1998. Founder McLachlan was the toast of fans and media alike for assembling artist bills. In spite of the festival's success, it still was met with criticism. Ardent feminists didn't think McLachlan's Fair was feminist enough while some in the mainstream media thought it was too exclusive. Finding herself at the center of controversy, she hesitated. Pregnant, she decided to discontinue the festival to raise her baby in 1999.

Limp Bizkit. A poster child for the **nü-metal** movement in the mid- to late '90s, Limp Bizkit came together in Florida, when Fred Durst, then a tattoo artist, inked one for a member of **Korn** after they played a show in Jacksonville. From there Durst and company busted out of the Sunshine State in a big way. Their debut, *Three Dollar Bill, Y'All* (1997) started the Bizkit trip, which also included stops at Woodstock, where their exhortation of the crowd to "Break Stuff" that night (after their single of the same name) jumpstarted a full-on riot. Throughout their spotty career, the band served as a wedge between the metal of the commercial alt-metal world and the underground metal scene, which despised the band's purpose. Still, the band sold records in large numbers, especially *Chocolate Starfish and the Hot Dog Flavored Water* (2000). Frontman Durst is flanked by Wes Borland on guitar, Sam Rivers on bass, drummer John Otto, and DJ Lethal.

Linkin Park. Rap metal made a big commercial impact on alternative music in the '90s, particularly following the demise of grunge. **Korn** and **Limp Bizkit** began rapping over their metal riffs, giving way to a tsunami of imitators, all young white bands eager to merge their fondness for hip-hop with the prevailing rock vibe. Linkin Park, united in Los Angeles in the late '90s, may not have been the first rap metal group to emerge within that trend, but they were certainly one of the most successful, selling millions of copies of their debut, *Hybrid Theory* (2000), its title a reference to their rap/metal combination, and their follow-up, *Meteora*, in 2003. The assembled lineup includes frontmen Chester Bennington and Mike Shinoda, guitarist Brad Delson, drummer Rob Bourdon, DJ Joseph Hahn, and bassist Dave Farrell.

Live. Small-town kids from York, Pennsylvania, Live quickly made a name for themselves with their passionate live performances and brawny hard rock, which was heavily influenced by **U2** and **R.E.M**. Led by singer Ed Kowalczyk, and rounded out by guitarist Chad Taylor, bass player Patrick Dahlheimer, and drummer Chad Gracey, Live debuted on record with the cerebral *Mental Jewelry* in 1991. But they saw their stock soon rise toward superstardom with the commercially successful *Throwing Copper* (1994), their career high point thanks to impressive rock singles like "Selling the Drama," "I Alone," and "Lightning Crashes." Live never recaptured that glory, though their catalog throughout the '90s always challenged their listeners and enjoyed reasonably good sales.

Lo-fi. Lo-fi recordings have been produced in rock 'n' roll ever since the '60s, but the term became a genre in the late '80s and throughout the '90s when it was coined to describe a type of artist who recorded material at home on cheap four-track recording equipment. Prominent lo-fi discs include early recordings by Beck, **Guided by Voices**, **Liz Phair**, and **Sebadoh**, as well as select work by Lamb Chop, Smog, and East River Pipe.

Lollapalooza. **Jane's Addiction** frontman Perry Farrell came up with the idea to put together a touring roster of prominent alternative rock bands in the early '90s—the precise time the alt-rock movement had begun to explode. Initially, Farrell envisioned Lollapalooza to be a farewell tour for his band, along with a few special guests. But it blossomed into a genuinely alternative festival where a single audience could enjoy electronica, punk, rock, rap, and metal all in the same day.

The first Lollapalooza tour happened in the summer of 1991, and it continued through 1998. Headliners included the **Red Hot Chili Peppers**, **Alice in Chains**, **Smashing Pumpkins**, and **Metallica**. Lollapalooza didn't just feature musical acts, however. Performers like the Jim Rose Circus, a modern-day freak show, or the chanting Shaolin Monks defied the limitations of traditional rock shows. There was a tent for display of art pieces, virtual reality games, piercing booths, poetry readings, and political/environmental activism. After 1991, the festival incorporated a second stage (and, in 1996, a third stage) for up-and-coming bands or local acts. By 1997, the idea was faltering, and by 1998, the search for a willing headline act turned up nothing, and the tour was scrapped. A 2003 reunion-type tour was in the works, and had even begun to sell tickets, but they were moving so slowly, tour producers and Farrell had to scrap that tour as well.

London Suede. London Suede helped solidify the arrival of the **Britpop** revolution after the **Stone Roses**, the movement's standard-bearer, disappeared in a tangle of legal problems. London Suede—known simply as Suede in the United Kingdom—possessed the lyrical depth of the **Smiths**, and healthy daubs of very English sounds like Marc Bolan (T. Rex) and David Bowie. So heightened was the anticipation for their debut, the English press heralded them as "The Best New Band in Britain." Their debut, *Suede* (1993), trumpeted their arrival, but *Dog Man Star* (1994) solidified their place as top-notch glam-rockers. The band featured key members singer Brett Anderson, guitarist Bernard Butler (replaced in 1994 by Richard Oakes), and bassist Matt Osman.

Louisville Scene. Full of fertile indie, **lo-fi**, and post-rock talent, Louisville, Kentucky, proved to be an unlikely breeding ground for independent bands in the late '80s and early '90s. Squirrel Bait would emerge first from the city in the mid-'80s as an important post-punk band. That trailblazing led to other bands finding their way out of Louisville and into the collections of avid **indie rock** fans: Slint, Gastr del Sol, King Kong, Bitch Magnet, and **Palace**, to name a few.

Love, Courtney (1964–). See **Hole**

Luna. When Dead Wareham split from the influential Boston **lo-fi** rock act Galaxie 500 in 1991, he brought his inimitable, wistful sadness with him to a band called Luna. Throughout the '90s up until the 2003 release *L'Avventura*, Wareham and Luna put out consistently riveting **indie rock** and pop, with a tendency toward self-pity. They experienced little in the way of commercial notoriety, but their recordings made substantial impact on the urban underground and **indie rock** scenes. The band's seminal lineup included Justin Harwood (ex-Chills) and Stanley Demeski (ex-Feelies). In 2004, Luna released *Rendezvous* and announced their break-up.

Luscious Jackson. This New York City group began with friends Jill Cunniff and Gabrielle Glaser, who then recruited Kate Schellenbach and Vivian Trimble to round out the lineup. Their funky, all-female take on the dance-pop idiom opened doors for them; they secured opening slots with **R.E.M.** and **Live** as well as a second stage slot on **Lollapalooza**. Their early material, especially *In Search of Manny* (1992) and *Natural Ingredient* (1994), were important records in the alternative rock movement.

Lynne, Shelby (1968–). First a dolled up country singer, then a big-band chanteuse, and finally an **alt.country** roots rock and folk singer, Shelby Lynne has been searching for an artistic identity throughout much of the '90s. With her arrival at a soulful acoustic roots and pop sound on albums *I Am Shelby Lynne* (2001) and *Suit Yourself* (2005), Lynne has at last found an audience.

The Madchester Scene. Burgeoning rock scene of late '80s through the mid-'90s, Manchester, England, nicknamed "Madchester" for its rock 'n' roll fervor and high-energy dance scene, gave birth to many of England's biggest acts. The phenomenon began with the **Smiths** in the '80s, one of England's most beloved acts. The **Stone Roses** followed, as did the **Happy Mondays**, Inspiral Carpets, the **Charlatans UK**, and electronic acts like 808 State and the **Chemical Brothers**.

Mann, Aimee (1960–). Aimee Mann made a name for herself originally as a singer for the '80s Boston pop act "'Til Tuesday," who had a hit with the song "Voices Carry" in 1985. After 'Til Tuesday broke up in 1989, Mann, the bassist and singer for the band, went solo, releasing a string of acclaimed work, beginning in 1993 with *Whatever*. But her solo career was plagued by bad luck, legal entanglements, and her own scornful attitude toward the corporate side of the recording industry. Mann's career got a kick-start in early 2000, however, when she released her soundtrack for the critically acclaimed film *Magnolia*; the song "Save Me" was later nominated for an Academy Award. She released *Lost in Space* in 2004, an album that received the requisite critical praise, but only modest commercial reception; the same occurred for 2005's *The Forgotten Arm*.

Manson, Marilyn. Dismissed by critics and denounced by fundamentalist groups for his anti-religious/blasphemous comments and stage shows, Marilyn Manson, born Brian Warner (1969–), was one of the most controversial figures of the '90s. Against great odds, and passionate enemies, the band, also named Marilyn Manson, with its thundering blend of hard rock, punk, and '80s metal climbed the charts, slotting Manson behind Alice Cooper and KISS as the latest in a long line of shock rockers. Manson was discovered by **Nine Inch Nails'** Trent Reznor, who signed him to his Nothing label. The band, populated by musicians who renamed themselves after beauty icons/serial killers ("Marilyn Manson," "Madonna Wayne Gacy"), made their recording debut in 1994 with *Portrait of an American Family*, a scathing and heavy-rock effort that would set Manson on the fast track to superstardom. High-profile tours would follow, including a set at **Ozzfest** in 2004, serving to keep the flamboyant personality in the public eye. The band released a greatest-hits collection, *Lest Ye Forget*, also in 2004.

Maroon 5. The Los Angeles band spent the latter part of the '90s recording as Kara's Flowers. But they broke off that contract and renamed themselves Maroon 5 in 1999. They went about tweaking their sound and eventually signed a new deal with indie label Octone. That led to an album, *Songs About Jane*, and years of touring. All the work and perseverance paid off, as their singles "Harder to Breathe" and "This Love" hit radio. Ironically, Maroon 5, a band since the mid-'90s in one form or another, earned a Grammy award for Best New Artist in 2004. Adam Levine, Jesse Carmichael, Mickey Madden, and Ryan Dusick were the band's original members, with James Valentine joining in 1999.

Matchbox 20. Matchbox 20 is Florida songwriter Rob Thomas's pop-rock vehicle. Brian Yale, Paul Doucette, Adam Gaynor, and Kyle Cook are the other members of the band, who proved themselves more than a one-hit wonder when their 1996 album, *Yourself Or Someone Like You*, yielded a handful of singles and charted highly well into 1998. By 2000, the recording had sold 10 million copies. At first the band was just another post-grunge rock band dotting the commercial landscape. But Thomas was a confident songwriter whose songs seem to consistently strike chords with radio. Another notch in Thomas' belt was his collaboration with Carlos Santana on the hit single "Smooth." The song earned the duo three Grammy awards in 2000, including Song of the Year. Thomas shared songwriting duties on the band's 2002 follow-up *More Than You Think You Are*.

The Dave Matthews Band. One of the breakthrough superstar acts of the '90s, the Dave Matthews Band was started in Charlottesville, Virginia, by the band's namesake (1967–), a former bartender originally hailing from South Africa. Other members are Stefan Lessard, Leroi Moore, Boyd Tinsley, and Carter Breauford. Early on, the band established a strong word-of-mouth reputation by playing anywhere and everywhere, especially on the college circuit. Their blend of world-beat, **jam band**, pop, and jazz sounds proved unique. One independent release, *Remember Two Things*, kicked the band's canon off stylishly, leading to a major-label deal. *Under the Table and Dreaming*, their major-label debut, came through in 1995 and proceeded to sell in large numbers, ultimately moving over 4 million units in the States alone. Touring remained the band's hallmark; the more the band toured, the more fans they converted, and soon they were selling out stadiums with alarming regularity. *Crash* followed in 1996, as well as a few side projects and live albums, none of which disappointed fans. A 2005 album, *Stand Up*, is his fifth studio recording in ten years.

Mayer, John (1977–). Blues rock guitar whiz kid turned adult/alternative songwriter, John Mayer is looking to mold himself into an enduring artist ala **Bruce Springsteen**. His musical roots run deep, in blues, rock, and jazz; but he also has a flair for writing commercial melodies like "Your Body Is a Wonderland," a lite-FM staple from 2002. *Room for Squares*, originally released independently in 2000, was picked up and released by Sony, to good result. It would go on to sell in multiplatinum numbers, and turn Mayer into a superstar on the brink. Touring followed, as did *Heavier Things*, his second album, in 2004. That recording won the artist a Grammy award and continued his reputation as a smooth, nonconfrontational writer with the ability to jazz up simple tunes with nifty guitar textures and a stylish singing voice.

McLachlan, Sarah (1968–). Since debuting in 1988, Sarah McLachlan has grown in both stature and ability, proving herself to be an accomplished songwriter and pianist, an able spokesperson and personality, and a woman in full command of her artistry. Through the years, McLachlan has developed a reputation as a major player in the music business. The Halifax, Nova Scotia, native has sold enough records to be taken seriously as a superstar, and also has credibility on the business end of the industry with her organizational work on **Lilith Fair**, a women's music festival she established. But it's her music, and her expressive voice that will remain, on albums like *Solace* (1991) and *Fumbling Towards Ecstasy* (1993). *Afterglow*, her 2003 recording, came after a short hiatus in which McLachlan raised her first child.

Megadeth. Dave Mustaine (1961–), the leader of Megadeth, which currently includes Glenn Drover, James MacDonough, and Shawn Drover, got his start as one of the founding members of **Metallica** in the early '80s. He was unceremoniously ousted from that band for his dangerous behavior, but not before co-writing some of the band's early classics. Megadeth came of age in the late '80s and kept going strong through the '90s on albums like *Rust in Peace* (1990) and *Countdown to Extinction* (1992). The band's hard-rocking recordings sold consistently through this period, despite his inability to find a stable lineup. In 2002, Mustaine sustained a serious injury to his arm, which prompted him to declare his days as a guitarist were finished. Sad news indeed for his legion of fans. Somehow, he experienced a miraculous, near-religious recovery, and in 2004 he released his comeback recording, *The System Has Failed.*

The Melvins. The Melvins were one of the Pacific Northwest's first bands to become enamored with the downtuned, sludgy sound of '70s metal heroes **Black Sabbath**. Members over the years have included Dale Crover, Joe Preston, Matt Lukin, Kevin Rutmanis, Mark Dutrom, Buzz Osborne, Lori "lorax" Black. It is often believed that the Melvins were the first real grunge band; corroborated by the fact that **Nirvana**, the quintessential grunge act, was profoundly influenced by the Melvins' approach. Nirvana's Kurt Cobain, in turn, would secure the Melvins a major-label contract after years of toiling in indie obscurity. Still, the band's sound was uncompromising, some would say even uninviting: walls of feedback, gibberish lyrics, and confrontational stage shows that almost literally challenged fan to endure the noise. Creatively speaking, the band reached an early high point with *Houdini* in 1993. Ironically, while most of the grunge bands they influenced and led to temporary prosperity have since vanished, the Melvins remain, defiantly individual, still releasing music.

Merchant, Natalie (1963–). The former lead singer of the successful New Jersey pop-rock band 10,000 Maniacs, Natalie Merchant ventured out on her own in 1995, one year after leaving the band. Her solo career managed to keep Merchant in the public eye—she had gained many fans while in the Maniacs—and they remained with her throughout. *Tigerlily*, her first solo album, demonstrated that she could cut it on her own, as did *Ophelia* in 1998. Merchant also began distributing her own recordings through her Web site rather than hassling with a record company. This risky ploy succeeded and she has since become a business model for her efforts. In addition, Merchant has used her celebrity status to leverage her in campaigns against domestic violence, homelessness, and for animal rights.

Mercury Rev. Psychedelic and unpredictable **indie rock** band that enjoyed a few major recordings in the '90s, beginning with the epic *Yerself Is Steam* in 1991, and *Boces* in 1993. But intraband squabbles, and a sporadic touring and recording schedule prevented the band from truly being able to take advantage of any sort of commercial momentum. After a long hiatus, they reconvened for a 2005 release. Original members included David Baker, Jonathan Donahue, Grasshopper (born Sean Mackowiak), Suzanne Thorpe, Dave Fridmann, and Jimy Chambers.

Metallica. Legendary thrash band out of San Francisco, Metallica made a name for themselves in the '80s with their blend of punk fury and metallic power, later called "Thrash metal." They would go on to become the most influential metal band of a generation, and their firepower rubbed off on virtually every metal band that formed in their wake. In the '90s, Metallica was the leader of the metal movement, and could do no wrong. But the band suffered through some rocky times. In 1991, they released *Metallica*, which sold 7 million copies in the United States, but featured the band moving slightly away from their gold standard of songwriting. In 1996, the band moved further away from their core audience by issuing the "alternative"-sounding *Load*. A headlining slot on the **Lollapalooza** alt-rock festival seemed ill-advised for both the band and the festival, but still they powered through. They recorded a sequel album for *Load*, called *Reload*, laid down tracks for a covers album, and issued a collection of symphonic versions of their songs. In 2000, they distanced themselves from their audience by going after illegal downloaders, a move that painted them in an elitist light. The band's bassist, Jason Newsted, left in 2001. And the band began to come apart further after that. A film of the band teetering on the brink of disintegration, *Some Kind of Monster*, saw national release in 2003. A controversial 2003 album, *St. Anger*, received mixed reviews. James Hetfield, Lars Ulrich, and Kirk Hammett, and the late Cliff Burton (replaced by Newsted) were the original members of the band.

The Mighty Mighty Bosstones. As the original Third Wave ska/punk/ metal band, the Bosstones, from Boston, influenced many bands, like **No Doubt** and **Sublime**, who'd go on to see greater success. But the Bosstones, who formed in 1985, became one of the hardest-working and most entertaining of the Third Wave ska. They recorded consistently throughout the '90s on both indie and major labels. Original members included Tim Bridewell, Dicky Barrett, Nate Albert, Joe Gittleman, Josh Dalsimer, Tim "Johnny Vegas" Burton, and Ben Carr.

Ministry. Al Jourgensen and Paul Barker formed Ministry in Chicago in 1981, but began making their mark as a powerful industrial in 1987 with *Land of Rape and Honey*, an unrelenting work combining the crush of synthesizers with the buzz of big guitars. The door now open, Ministry slammed through it with a variety of highly regarded **industrial metal** recordings, including their bilious *A Mind Is a Terrible Thing to Taste* and *Dark Side of the Spoon*. Jourgensen battled personal demons of his own throughout his career, leading to a sporadic touring and recording schedule. But they did solidify their place among the '90s' most significant style milestones, exerting their influence on acts like **Marilyn Manson**, **Nine Inch Nails**, and Garbage, themselves influential acts as well.

.moe. Many refer to .moe, a **jam band** from Utica, New York, as the heir apparent of **Phish**'s legacy. The group was founded by Rob Derhak, Chuck Garvey, and Ray Schwartz in 1990. Phish, who wore the **Grateful Dead**'s jam mantle for a few years before breaking up in 2004, in turn has seemingly passed it on to .moe. And while .moe doesn't indulge as deeply in the improvisational side as either Phish or the Dead, they do write consistently more engaging songs and are just as willing to spend massive amounts of time on the road. Their late-'90s release *Tin Cans and Car Tires* found them placing increasing importance on traditional song structures and their appearances at major jam festivals like Bonnaroo have also elevated their profile.

Mother Love Bone/*Temple of the Dog*. An early bright light in the Seattle area, Mother Love Bone wasn't exactly grunge, but they did bring attention to the area in the late '80s and early '90s with their classic hard-rock and slightly glam sound. Singer Andrew Wood, the band's leading man, was a dazzling performer and headed, most agreed, for greatness. But he wasn't the only one in the band headed for history. Jeff Ament and Stone Gossard would later join **Pearl Jam**. Unfortunately, Wood died of a heroin overdose in 1990, before fulfilling his potential. Their debut, *Apple*, emerged later that same year.

To celebrate Wood's life, and to cement him as an important cog in the development of the "Seattle Sound," his fellow musicians rallied to record *Temple of the Dog*. Gossard and Ament joined up with **Soundgarden** members Matt Cameron and Chris Cornell to record a pair of songs that Cornell had written for the late singer. But the session grew more ambitious and soon the group had written an album's worth of songs. *Temple of the Dog* (named after a phrase from one of Wood's lyrics) was issued in 1991, and would go on to enjoy surprisingly substantial success, as would Pearl Jam and Soundgarden soon thereafter.

Mould, Bob/Hüsker Dü/Sugar. In the '80s, Bob Mould was a member of post-punk icons **Hüsker Dü**, one of the most influential underground bands of the decade. They were one of the first indie bands to sign with a major label and the first to blaze the trail from the underground to commercial success. Mould abandoned Hüsker Dü and went solo in 1988, and began releasing highly anticipated and impassioned albums like *Workbook* and *Black Sheets of Rain*. In 1992, the restless Mould formed Sugar, a power trio, looking for a fresh means of expression. After a few Sugar records, he put that band on hiatus and returned to record as a solo act. Mould would never go on to capitalize on his potential and would never claim the success commensurate with his stature as a songwriter, despite having several opportunities to do so. In 1998, Mould began dabbling in electronica, a turn that dismayed fans. In 2005 he returned to guitar rock with *Body of Song*.

Mudhoney. One of the grunge movement's most dedicated and enduring purveyors, Seattle's Mudhoney grew their reputation with outrageous, distorted singles, and relentless live performances. Mark Arm and Steve Turner, along with bassist Matt Lukin and drummer Dan Peters, soldiered through the ups and downs of grunge in the '90s, releasing some landmark recordings (*Mudhoney* in 1989, *My Brother the Cow*, 1995). Their work virtually defined the grunge sound, courtesy of Turner's messy guitar sound and Arm's belligerent vocals. Ironically, they had to go to London, on a tour with **Sonic Youth**, to be discovered in the United States. Upon their arrival, and after playing a few gigs, the reviews were so positive, critics in the United States felt they had to take a second look at a band they had already looked beyond. After recording throughout the decade, the band closed its first phase with an anthology, *March to Fuzz*. At that point, many had anticipated the band's dissolution. But Mudhoney remained viable with *Since We've Become Translucent* (2002).

My Bloody Valentine. The British quartet led by Kevin Shields that would preliminarily become the poster child for the so-called **shoegazer** movement, and then go on to be considered one of the '90s most influential guitar bands. Unfortunately, the band, for reasons still unknown today, was never able to fully take advantage of their reputation. Bandleader Shields, a notorious recluse, seemed reluctant to produce a follow-up to the era-defining *Isn't Anything* (1988) and their magnum opus of 1991, *Loveless*. Their creative repercussions— a sound that shimmered with dense and quirky guitar washes and ethereal, open-ended explorations—went on to influence other shoegazer bands like Ride, Chapterhouse, and the Pale Saints. The band entered the studio in 1992 and again in 1993 to record a new album, but nothing came of it. Rumors began to circulate that an album would emerge any time. But it never did. Shields built a home studio with the band's sizable signing advance, but My Bloody Valentine did little recording of any official material. Shields took up much of his professional time producing projects for other bands.

Napster. Watershed moment in the controversial **file sharing** concept of the mid- to late '90s. The company, owned by Shawn Fanning, established a system whereby members of the Napster community could pull songs off each others' computers without paying the artist or copyright holder of that song any licensing or royalty fees. The record industry was up in arms, as was the artist community, who, albeit briefly, saw their livelihoods going up in smoke, as more and more file-sharers envisioned a world full of free music. Napster would spawn several imitators before going out of business. They would re-emerge in 2004 with a more legitimate pay plan, Napster To Go.

Nickelback. Vancouver band directed by songwriter Chad Kroeger, Nickelback began as a cover band near Calgary, before moving to Vancouver. In 1998, the group invested their own money to record *The State*, their debut, in 2000. The record, released independently, was quickly picked up by Canadian radio and soon the band became stars in their homeland. That popularity also awaited them in the United States, where the band's clean, hard-rock sound found an even larger audience. Nickelback's follow-up, *Silver Side Up*, sold in even larger numbers, and made the band international stars. Their hit single off that record, "How You Remind Me," was only the second time a song by a Canadian band that topped both the Canadian and American charts at the same time. It did so in 2002.

Nine Inch Nails. This **industrial metal** act blazed a trail in the '90s with its delirious and maniacal computer/guitar-based maelstrom. Trent Reznor (1965–), the man solely responsible for the band's artistic direction, was reclusive and moody. He wrote haunting songs of despair and tragedy on momentous sets like *The Downward Spiral*. Unlike most industrial artists, Reznor was unafraid to put a face on the genre; he humanized it, and attracted throngs of fans eager to empathize with his frustration.

Nirvana. The single most important band of the '90s, Nirvana accomplished nothing less than changing the course of rock music throughout the decade. Despite being an unpretentious couple of roughneck kids out of small-town Washington state, Kurt Cobain, Chris Novoselic, and original drummer Chad Channing, later replaced by Dave Grohl, would become unsuspecting poster children for the grunge movement, and later, alternative rock as a whole. They proved that heavy music could indeed appeal to a wider audience, sending A&R reps scurrying to sign the next big, off-the-beaten-path act. Nirvana's success also opened the door for dozens of other types of alternative music, from **indie rock** to **industrial rock**, from **nü metal** to electronica.

Nirvana released their first full-length album, *Bleach*, in 1988. It was recorded, famously, for less than $700 in Seattle. The set served to put Nirvana on a singular hard-rock map, but it didn't succeed commercially. Their Zeppelin/**Black Sabbath** '70s influences combined with punk rock and post-punk of bands like the **Pixies** came fully formed on their follow-up, *Nevermind*, in 1991. Out of nowhere, the record struck a huge chord with a radio and record-buying public that was desperate for a new sound. That sound came in the form of the band's hit single "(Smells Like) Teen Spirit," a rollicking rock song (now with Dave Grohl on drums) that captured the imagination of the nation. The record topped the charts, knocking Michael Jackson out of the No. 1 spot in early 1992, and its fate as one of the most important and influential rock outings of the decade was sealed.

Unfortunately, that fate meant greater attention and a brighter spotlight for bandleader Kurt Cobain. He didn't fare well in that spotlight, even though he married the flamboyant **Courtney Love**. The band released *In Utero*, an abrasive album designed to help the band shed some of its pop-leaning audience. Cobain disliked the accountability a high profile brought him, and he turned to drugs to escape. He committed suicide in April 1994.

Nitzer Ebb. Before industrial music added guitars and became the heavy metal of the 1990s thanks to **Ministry**, Nitzer Ebb, formed by Douglas McCarthy,

Bon Harris, and David Gooday, in Chelmsford, Essex, England, produced hard-hitting electronic music informed by the abrasive edge of early industrial music. But as metal began to infiltrate electronic music in the '90s, Nitzer Ebb held its ground with assaulting dance music.

No Doubt/Gwen Stefani. One of the more commercial successful acts of the '90s, No Doubt debuted in the '90s with an unusual fusion of pop music and ska. Led by charismatic lead singer Gwen Stefani, the Southern California band hit it big with their 1995 album *Tragic Kingdom*, which contained a seemingly endless string of hits such as "Just a Girl" and "Spiderwebs." The success continued with *The Return of Saturn*, which finally saw the light of day five years later, in 2000. *Rock Steady* followed that with ska revival and New Wave sounds, a tribute to their roots. From their humble roots of 1987, No Doubt had over the course of the '90s and through the present, become one of the best-selling and most important acts on the pop-rock scene. Gwen Stefani broke temporarily from the band to record an album, *Love. Angel. Music. Baby*, introduce a fashion line, and dabble in artist management with Japan's Harajuku Girls.

NOFX. Formed as a post-punk punk band in 1983 in Berkeley, NOFX never signed a contract with a major label, choosing instead to remain independent. The band remained true to its roots, and remains so today. Under the creative guidance of bandleader Fat Mike Burkett, the band was dragged under the spotlight by virtue of its association with other punk bands like **Bad Religion** and the **Offspring**. Their political roots and crass humor set them apart from their colleagues, however. They recorded many of their best albums for the Epitaph label, run by Bad Religion's Brett Gurewitz.

Nü Metal. Nü metal was the most controversial form of metal to arise in the '90s, for it polarized fans. Hardcore metal fans didn't consider the maniacal, punky, hard-rock guitar of the metal bands to be true metal. Its appeal to mainstream rock fans affirmed that belief. Still, more fans than ever flocked to the sound of bands like **Limp Bizkit, Korn**, the **Deftones**, and **Staind**. Groups labeled nü metal have, since its announced demise in the new millennium, tried to shake the nü-metal branding, somewhat successfully.

Oasis. After the **Stone Roses** jumpstarted **Britpop**, Oasis took over and elevated the subgenre to a new level. The band, featuring brothers Noel and Liam Gallagher on guitar and voice, combined the muscular guitars of the time with an overt Beatles melodicism and a Stonesy thuggishness in creating some of the decade's most memorable rock music. Oasis debuted in 1994 with *Definitely Maybe* and followed that with *(What's the Story) Morning Glory?*, both of which yielded a number of singles and sold well, especially in their native Britain, where there was a sort of Beatlemania about the band. The *Morning Glory* album has since become the second-biggest-selling album in British history, thanks to its single "Wonderwall." The United States welcomed Oasis into its Top 10 as well. *Be Here Now* in 1997 topped the UK charts again, and made a similar impact on the States. But in-fighting, personal injuries, and plain arrogance eventually began to undo the band. They released recordings fairly consistently, but it was obvious they had lost their focus and desire. A 2005 album, *Don't Believe the Truth*, succeeded in recapturing some of the band's focus and excitement.

O'Connor, Sinead (1966–). Dublin-born singer Sinead O'Connor burst on the scene in 1987 with a remarkable debut, *The Lion and the Cobra*. She would go on to become one of the era's most influential and controversial talents. She railed against stereotypes, demanded to be taken seriously, and refused to play by the restrictive rules laid out for women artists. Her second album, *I Do Not Want What I Haven't Got*, released in 1990, boosted O'Connor from a rising talent to a superstar.

Eventually, her outspoken nature worked against her. She refused to perform one night after "The Star Spangled Banner" was played at her show, and, perhaps in the most damaging publicity stunt of the decade, she tore up a picture of the pope on *Saturday Night Live* in 1992. She would never go on to reclaim her stardom after that, though she still commands respect as an artist, and for bringing popular music one of the most vibrant singing voices of a generation.

The Offspring. One of the bands that elevated melodic punk rock to a commercial level in the mid-'90s. Its members included Dexter Holland, Kevin "Noodles" Wasserman, Greg Kriesel, and Ron Welty. The Offspring sold millions of records based on their combination of so-called "skatepunk" and heavy-metal guitar riffs. The band's prophetically titled 1994 album, *Smash*, released five years after their debut in 1989, turned the group into megastars. It would go on to become the biggest-selling independently released rock album of the decade. The band did some soul-searching after that, torn between remaining true to their indie roots or moving on to a bigger corporation that could better handle their demands. They chose the latter, and suffered a backlash from fans because of it. But in 1997 they issued the highly anticipated follow-up, *Ixnay on the Hombre*. It fell short of expectations. For their next album, the band made headlines when they decided to offer their album, *Conspiracy of One*, free on the Internet. Their label, however, disagreed and they abandoned the plan. They released *Splinter* in 2003 and a greatest hits collection in 2005.

OK Computer, Radiohead. Few of Radiohead's fans were prepared for the stunning creative achievement of *OK Computer*, the band's 1997 milestone. The band's first two albums, *Pablo Honey* and *The Bends*, employed hard-rock guitar heroics to good effect, but *OK Computer* abandons that style in favor of a more abstract, more textured approach. They stripped away the more obvious aspects of rock, yet still managed to make the record listen and feel like a rock recording. Reviews were ecstatic and the disc, while too abstract to sell in huge numbers, became one of the most lauded rock albums of the decade.

Olympia, Washington. Olympia was an unlikely place to be designated as the **indie rock** hotbed of the '90s. But, based on efforts of a musically active population and the support of Evergreen State University, Olympia became a mecca for indie rock and **Riot Grrrl** bands throughout the '90s. **Lo-fi** indie rockers **Beat Happening** jumpstarted the scene back in the early '80s, and bands like **Sleater-Kinney** and **Bikini Kill** came in and preserved the small town's musical integrity. Today, hundreds of bands continue to hail from Olympia.

Osbourne, Sharon and Ozzy. One of the oddest success stories of the '90s pertains to Ozzy and Sharon Osbourne. The former was the original frontman for Black Sabbath and later a prominent hard rock solo artist. He married Sharon, his manager, in 1982, and she went on to handle his many business affairs, largely because the doddering Ozzy couldn't fathom handling them himself. Sharon was named by *Entertainment Weekly* as one of the most powerful women in show business. In 2002, MTV network introduced the family in a reality show. The series succeeded overwhelmingly—largely due to the family's frank dialogue and the chaos that seemingly characterizes their real-life existence.

The Other Ones. Formed after Jerry Garcia passed away in 1995, the Other Ones consisted of guitarist Bob Weir, bassist Phil Lesh, drummer Mckey Hart, and keyboardist singer Bruce Hornsby. They headlined the Further Fest in 1998 and released an album *The Strange Remain* in 1999.

Ozzfest. Ozzfest originated in the mid-'90s and began officially in 1996. **Ozzy Osbourne**, the former lead singer of **Black Sabbath**, assembled this metal concert bill in order to compete with the alt-rock roadshow, **Lollapalooza**. With the help of his manager/wife **Sharon**, Ozzfest became a true force on the summer concert scene. The metal barrage came at the perfect time during the '90s. Popular music had emerged from grunge and the **Lilith Fair** sound with a vengeance. Bands like **Limp Bizkit**, **Korn**, **Rage Against the Machine**, and the **Deftones** were overthrowing the gentler rock acts already on the radio with an edgy, aggressive noise of their own, and Ozzfest was there to take advantage.

Palace. The enigmatic country-blues franchise that goes by a variety of names—Palace, Palace Brothers, Palace Songs, and Palace Music—is the creation of the mysterious Will Oldham. Like many indie and **lo-fi** artists, Oldham possesses an eccentricity that keeps him well away from the glare of the spotlight. But that eccentricity also serves as a fascinating focal point for many **indie rock** fans. But because Oldham has prefered to remain in the shadows— he refuses interviews and chooses not to list his musical collaborators in his record notes—it's difficult to trace Oldham's evolution as an artist. Rather, all his fans have are his recordings, and perhaps a few performances.

Parsons, Gram/The Flying Burrito Brothers. Coined the father of country rock, Parsons made it acceptable for rock bands to play country and vice versa. His influence is far-reaching, from the Byrds (of which he was a member) and the Stones to **Uncle Tupelo** and Ryan Adams. Parsons died in a motorcycle accident in 1973, at the age of 26.

Pavement. Formed in Stockton, California, in 1989 by principal members Stephen Malkmus and Scott Kannberg, Pavement initially originated as a studio entity exclusively. But the band, encouraged by their material, recruited a full band, including basist Mark Ibold and percussionist Bob Nastanovich, for their 1992 debut, *Slanted and Enchanted*. The recording, widely acclaimed by critics as one of the best "alternative" albums of that year, and certainly the first high-profile indie rock album in the wake of the alternative explosion, helped Pavement establish themselves, reluctantly, as a high-profile act. They went on to record throughout the '90s, and even sold good numbers of records. But the band's two principal members, Scott Kannberg and Stephen Malkmus, began solo projects around 2000 and the band broke up.

Pearl Jam. After Andrew Wood died of a heroin overdose, his bandmates Stone Gossard and Jeff Ament of **Mother Love Bone** started over, forming their own band with guitarist Mike McCready and drummer Jack Irons. Irons recruited San Diego surfer Eddie Vedder and Pearl Jam was formed. The year was 1990. It didn't take long for their star to rise. Pearl Jam's debut, *Ten*, hit the charts in 1991. It was a heady blend of arena rock and post-punk rawness. The chemistry pushed the recording into the upper reaches of *Billboard*'s album charts. When **Nirvana** hit in 1991, Pearl Jam rode grunge's coattails, becoming the second major band to breakthrough from Seattle, on its way to becoming superstars of the '90s.

Many more albums followed, including *Vs.* (1993), which bowed at No. 1 and sold a million copies in its first week of release. The band expanded its canon throughout the '90s, and kept a low profile in the media. They toured consistently, backing up Neil Young during one stint in 1995. In 2001, the band toured worldwide. In order to circumvent bootleggers, their subsequent European and American tours were recorded in full and released in an unprecedented series of double-CD sets, each of the 72 volumes featuring a complete concert.

Phair, Liz (1967–). Chicago lo-fi queen Liz Phair began her career auspiciously in 1993, with the controversial *Exile in Guyville*, a purported female's response to the Stones' *Exile on Main Street*. Phair's work was unanimously acclaimed. Although it sold over 200,000 copies over two years, Phair wasn't able to break into the mainstream, even after her follow-up recordings brought out a more polishing sound. Problems with stagefright, and raising a family took time away from her career. But she resurfaced in 2003 with the eponymous *Liz Phair*. The record marked a change of style for the singer, toward a more pop sound and away from her indie roots.

Phish. The most successful of all the so-called **"jam bands,"** Phish formed while at the University of Vermont, the brainchild of Trey Anastasio, Mike Gordon, and Jon Fishman. Through the '90s, they crafted their eclectic sound, which embraced rock, jazz, country, bluegrass, pop, avant-garde, and folk, with equal gusto. Like the **Grateful Dead** before them—the band many insist set the template for Phish and the entire jam-band contingent—they built their reputation on constant touring. They consistently inserted surprises in their set for their so-called "Phans," many of whom would follow the band around ala the Dead's "Deadheads." Phish also had a loose onstage image, which offered plenty of humor to go along with their improvisational performances. They also made huge spectacles of their shows, spending hundreds of thousands of dollars on concert props and setup so their weekend shows in far-flung areas would be genuine destinations.

The band's recorded history is inconsistent. Their releases never sold particularly well. But their fan base was active, attending shows and trading tapes, similar again to the fan base the Dead enjoyed. Phish ultimately went on hiatus in 2000, with each of its members going on to record solo albums. They bowed to pressure and reunited in 2002, only to dissolve permanently in mid-2004.

Pixies. Boston's Pixies, which includes Kim Deal, Joey Santiago, Black Francis, and David Lovering, made most of their impact in the late '80s with albums like *Surfer Rosa*, one of the most important albums of the alternative era. They broke up in 1991 after releasing *Trompe Le Monde*. Reunite in 2004–2005 for an international tour.

P.O.D. The name means "Payable on Death," which may at first connote violence. But P.O.D., from Southern California, was above all a Christian band. Formed in 1994, they debuted on a major label in 1999 with *The Fundamental Elements of Southtown*. The album showcased the ability to write chorus-friendly hard rock and metal, with rapping on the side. *Satellite* followed, and better defined the band's mix of hip-hop, punk, and reggae. The band's single, "Alive," saturated the airwaves with spiritual chaos and a memorable chorus. Curiel left the band in 2003, replaced by guitarist Jason Truby.

Porno for Pyros. See **Jane's Addiction**

Primus. Quirky, near cartoon-ish group led by bass player Les Claypool, Primus formed in 1986 with guitarist Larry Lalonde and drummer Tim Alexander. Their sound, centered on Claypool's quirky singing and virtuosic bass playing, had a bizarre element suggesting Frank Zappa that served to separate Claypool from his alt-rock peers. In 1991, the band released *Sailing the Seas of*

Cheese and in 1993 they issued *Pork Soda*, which penetrated the Top 10. A year-long tour followed, which also included a headlining slot on the 1993 **Lollapalooza** tour. Claypool went on to form his own label (Prawnsong), record under a few different monikers (Sausage, Oysterhead, Colonel Claypool's Bucket of Bernie Brains), and pretty much go wherever his muse took him.

Prodigy. Prodigy was the one band that, for a time, represented the great hope of electronica to cross into the mainstream. When they broke out in 1996 with their third album, *Fat of the Land*, they were on the brink of worldwide popularity. Their electronic output, peppered by rock and metal guitar samples, helped their live show approximate the original atmosphere of the British rave scene while leaning toward arena-rock showmanship and punk theatrics. *Fat* debuted at No. 1 on both the UK and U.S. charts. But the electronica wave subsided and Prodigy, perhaps miscalculating their importance, waited three years before issuing another recording. Members include Keith Flint, Liam Howlett, Maxim, and Leeroy Thornhill.

Puddle of Mudd. Alt-metal outfit led by Wes Scantlin, a down-on-his-luck songwriter who wrote material that reflected his **Nirvana** infatuation as well as his Pink Floyd appreciation. *Come Clean* appeared in 2001, and a more ambitious follow-up, *Life on Display*, came out in 2003. Both fared well commercially.

Queercore: Team Dresch/Pansy Division/Tribe 8/The Butchies. Queercore is a subgenre of punk originally spawned out of the politically explosive environment of the Reagan years. It gained momentum by latching onto the **Riot Grrrls** before becoming its own entity after that movement dissolved. Queercore was most visibly exemplified by Team Dresch, Pansy Division, God Is My Co-Pilot, and Tribe 8 on labels like Mr. Lady, Candy Ass, Chainsaw, Kill Rock Stars, Agitprop!, and Heartcore. Queercore also intersected with an alternative folk movement that embraced more commercial acts like the **Indigo Girls**.

Radiohead. The acclaimed Oxford, England, band, comprising members Thom York, Collin Greenwood, Jonny Greenwood, Ed O'Brien, and Phil Selway, had two promising albums, *Pablo Honey* and *The Bends*, before issuing their genre-defining **OK Computer** in the summer of 1997. The band's sound until then, hard rock with power chords and fairly conventional songwriting, somehow morphed into something vastly different. With its three-guitar lineup and singer Thom Yorke's expressive vocals, the band twisted rock convention into something extraordinary. It was a crowning achievement and one of the most acclaimed recordings of the '90s. Radiohead would continue in the same vein thereafter, recording quickly and sporadically in an attempt to capture the spontaneous beauty of great musicianship and revelatory ideas. *Kid A*, the sequel to *OK Computer*, debuted in the United States at No. 1. *Amnesiac*, created from remnants, also fared well upon release.

Rage Against the Machine/Audioslave. Harvard grad Tom Morello formed this band in Los Angeles with Zack de la Rocka, Brad Wilk, and Tom Commerford. Initially, they fused hip-hop beats, politically informed rap vocals, and metal guitar in creating the foundation for the **nü metal** that would follow. Their first few recordings, including their 1992 eponymous debut, set the standard for their incendiary formula, and started a decade-long quest for converts. Albums in 1995 and 1999 followed, both of which topped the charts. But de la Rocka left the band in 2000, effectively ending the original RATM combo. Morello and the rest of the band recruited **Soundgarden** singer Chris Cornell and the quartet moved forward as Audioslave.

Rancid. As one of the main pillars of the '90s punk movement, Rancid drew on ska and the classic sound of the Clash for their inspiration. Begun by Berkeley, California, friends Tim Armstrong and Matt Freeman, they added Brett Reed to form their original group. Lars Frederiksen later joined them. Their 1995 album, *And Out Come the Wolves* (a veiled reference to the way major labels were signing **indie rock** and punk bands), sold over a million copies and made them an MTV staple. But enthusiasm tapered from there, on both ends. The band, left-leaning politically and defiantly independent, pulled away from the mass-market attention they were getting, and subsequently lost a great deal of commercial interest. But that decision enabled them to retain a devoted core audience as the new wave of revivalist punk-pop began to slip off the fickle, mainstream' musical radar in the late '90s.

The Red Hot Chili Peppers. Los Angeles–based superstars of pop-rock and funk, the Red Hot Chili Peppers (whose original members were friends, Anthony Kiedis, Michael Balzary [Flea], and Hillel Slovak), formed in 1983 and proceeded, over the course of twenty years, to break down barriers between genres. Their albums, including the epic *Blood Sugar Sex Magik* (1991) and *Californication* (1999), would help to define the music of the '90s and their work spawned many imitators. The Peppers' story, however, was not without its cautionary chapters. They suffered through death and intense drug addiction, only to emerge stronger and more effective as a band.

R.E.M. Michael Stipe, Peter Buck, Bill Berry, and Mike Mills dominated the '80s with their jangly rock music, a style that came to be known as "college rock." But by the time the '90s rolled around, the band left its indie roots and began selling large numbers of records for the Warner Brothers label. Their 1991 disc *Out of Time* and their 1992 opus *Automatic for the People* are high water marks for the band creatively and commercially, as well as for rock music in the '90s, even coming at a time when harder-edged alternative rock preoccupied music audiences. As the decade progressed, R.E.M. continued to release albums, all of which seemed to elevate its superstar status. Drummer Bill Berry left the band in 1997. *Around the Sun*, the band's most recent album, was released in 2004. 2005 has seen a complete revamping and remastering of the band's 1990's titles.

The Replacements/Paul Westerberg. When Westerberg disbanded his much-loved **indie rock** garage punk outfit the Replacements in 1991, he proceeded to head out on a solo career that would sustain him, if not commercially, at least creatively, throughout the '90s and beyond. Highlights of that solo career include *14 Songs* in 1993, *Eventually* in 1997, and a few **lo-fi** projects, including an acclaimed project called Grandpaboy. Another indie moment, 2003's *Folker*, focused on Westerberg's introspective side.

Reverend Horton Heat. The Reverend, aka Jim Heath, specializes in psychobilly, a combination of revved up rockabilly and punk rock. More than any other artist, he and his trio remained true to the psychobilly cause, updating it for today's audiences. They debuted in 1991 with *Smoke 'Em If You Got 'Em* and would go on to record well-received sets throughout the decade, releasing a record every two years through 2004's *Revival*.

Riot Grrrls. A movement with blurred beginnings, the Riot Grrrls came of age in the Pacific Northwest partly as a response to the grunge movement of the early '90s, and partly as a politically active, frustrated contingent seeking an equal voice not only in art, but in politics and society. **Sleater-Kinney**, **Bikini Kill**, Bratmobile, and **Huggy Bear** were among the first Riot Grrrl bands. The movement began in the early '90s and ran out of steam around 1997. The spirit of the Riot Grrrls remains, but the rigid subgenre has disappeared.

Sadcore/Slowcore. A style of **indie rock** music characterized by slow, quiet tempos and plaintive singing. Bands include Calliope, Low, Codeine, and many others. This subgenre also arose in direct response to the high-decibel approach of early '90s grunge.

Screaming Trees. One of the more highly regarded early grunge purveyors, led by singer Mark Lanegan, with Van Conner, Gary Lee Conner, and Mark Pickerel who together provided a creative, psychedelic guitar attack. They signed with a major label in 1989 and released much of their best material, including *Uncle Anesthesia* in 1991.

Scuzz Rock. Intentionally crude anti-musicianship usually stemming from in-the-know urban hipsters purposely uninterested in any sort of commercial success. Many of these bands emerged from New York, some from Chicago. The list of prominent players within this category includes: Pussy Galore, the **Jon Spencer Blues Explosion**, Honeymoon Killers, Royal Trux, Boss Hog, and many others.

Seattle, Washington. The original alt-music mecca of the late '80s and early '90s and the home of grunge, the sound that incited the alt-rock revolution of the '90s.

Sebadoh. Like **Pavement**, Sebadoh, formed by **Dinosaur Jr.**'s Lou Barlow, is something of a template for indie rockers. His sound included everything from noise rock to jangle, from punk rock to folk music. Barlow left his old band to enjoy the songwriting freedom of his own band. As soon as he left, the material came gushing forth. Sebadoh, at first a home-recording project, blossomed into a fruitful collaboration with Eric Gaffney and Jason Lowenstein. The Sebadoh project spun off into Folk Implosion, which enjoyed an inadvertent hit with the song "Natural One" in 1995. The Sebadoh set that followed the hit, *Harmacy*, became the band's first-ever charting album. Another Folk Implosion album came out in 2002 and Lou Barlow released a solo album in 2005, *Emoh*.

Shoegazers. A category of **indie rock**, populated mainly by UK bands that play a low-energy kind of rock music with loud, buzzing guitars. The shoegazing refers to these bands' shy and undemonstrative performance style. Important shoegazer bands include **My Bloody Valentine**, Pale Saints, Swervedriver, Chapterhouse, and the Cranes.

Sleater-Kinney. The powerful **Olympia, Washington**–based punk trio formed in the wake of a couple of **Riot Grrrl** bands, and has since gone on to become one of the region's most notable bands.

Corin Tucker, Carrie Brownstein, and Janet Weiss gained recognition for the fierce and visceral punk-inspired performances and recordings—*Call the Doctor* and *Dig Me Out*, particularly—that managed to capture the same intensity.

Smash Mouth. Commercial pop rock from San Jose, California, that flecked its musical approach with dashes of surf and punk. The good-natured group formed in 1994, including Steve Harwell, Kevin Coleman, Greg Camp, and Paul De Lisle, and enjoyed hits out of the gate, with the Zombies-inspired "Walkin' on the Sun." The band's records sold well, especially the breakthrough effort, 1999's *Astro Lounge*. The band's cut "All Star" also helped make them a household name through its use in the animated feature *Shrek*.

Smashing Pumpkins. One of the most important alt-rock bands of the '90s, Smashing Pumpkins traversed the decade with a series of creative releases, including the genre-defining *Mellon Collie and the Infinite Sadness* in 1995. Bandleader Billy Corgan (1967–) began the Pumpkins in Chicago in 1988, as a kind of grunge/hard-rock band with subtle psychedelic tendencies. As they progressed, however, Corgan became a nuanced hard-rock songwriter who understood good dynamics and the importance of passion in performance. Backed by guitarist James Iha, bassist D'Arcy Wretzky, and drummer Jimmy Chamberlin, the band took alternative rock as far as it could go before crumbling at the hands of in-fighting and egotism. They headlined **Lollapalooza** in 1994. The group split up in late 2000. Corgan emerged in 2005 with a solo album, also expressing his desire to reform the Pumpkins.

Smith, Elliott (1969–2003). The Portland, Oregon, folk-punk singer-songwriter rose from indie obscurity (Heat Miser) to mainstream success in 1997 on the strength of his "Miss Misery," which earned him an Academy

Award–nomination for its appearance in the popular film *Good Will Hunting.* Reluctant in the spotlight, Smith would go on to record a couple of more widely acclaimed recordings, including *XO* (1998) and *Figure 8* (2000). But despite his considerable talent, he was a morose, tragic figure, often difficult to read. He was found dead in 2003, an apparent suicide.

The Smiths. Influential outfit to England's **Britpop** movement; many say the Smiths were the first Britpop band. Certainly, they influenced the **Stone Roses**, a band that is most often credited with being the spark that set the movement in motion. Still, they made their impact in the '80s, disbanding in 1987. Morrissey, the band's fey lead singer, lingered throughout the '90s as a solo artist. Other members included co-founder Johnny Marr and Andy Rourke and Mike Joyce.

Son Volt. When the vital alt.country act **Uncle Tupelo** broke up, its two leaders, longtime friends Jay Farrar and Jeff Tweedy, went their separate ways. Tweedy formed **Wilco**, while Farrar established Son Volt. Both recorded actively. Tweedy (see **Wilco**) became a critical favorite, while Farrar struggled to retain his commercial viability. Albums like *Straightaways* (1997) and *Trace* (1995) showed promise, but Farrar never hit his stride with Son Volt. He embarked on a solo career, only to return with a new Son Volt disc in 2005.

Sonic Youth. Few underground bands can claim to be as influential throughout the '90s as New York City's Sonic Youth. Beginning in the early '80s, the band started out experimenting with song structures and chordal variations, never settling on a conventional approach to rock, even while many of their colleagues in the post-punk underground were. They brought a sort of free-form intensity to their music, and a performance-art aesthetic that was totally unique. When they adhered subtlely to the standards of rock convention, as on 1988's *Daydream Nation*, the results were masterful. Throughout the '90s, they veered closer and closer to orthodox song structures on albums like *Dirty* (1992) and *Goo* (1990). Members include founders Thurston Moore, Lee Ranaldo, and Kim Gordon, along with later members Steve Shelley and Jim O'Rourke.

Soul Asylum. Throughout the '80s, this Minneapolis-based rock band of Dan Murphy, Karl Mueller, Dave Pirner, Grant Young, and later Sterling Campbell who replaced Young, plied a tough brand of post-punk heavy rock. By the time the '90s rolled around, the band, tired of their approach, began altering it slightly to include more acoustic and rootsier-type sounds. The change of vibe proved a boon for the band, and they began selling records in greater numbers. *Grave Dancers Union* in 1992 and *Let Your Dim Light Shine* proved that Soul Asylum could write good melodic radio hits, even after spending over a decade avoiding them.

Soundgarden. Along with **Nirvana** and **Pearl Jam**, Soundgarden was one of the biggest bands to emerge from grunge-era **Seattle**. Originally comprising Kim Thayil, Chris Cornell, Hiro Yamamoto, Bruce Pavitt, and Scott Sundquist, later replaced by Matt Cameron, their Zeppelin-esque aesthetic was first heard on 1987's *Screaming Life* EP, but best heard on 1991's *Badmotorfinger* and 1994's *Superunknown*. They disbanded in 1997, and their lead singer Cornell joined **Rage Against the Machine**, changing the name of that band to **Audioslave**.

Spencer, Jon/Pussy Galore/Blues Explosion. Spencer spent his early years crafting the dubiously musical "scuzz-rock" of Pussy Galore in the late '80s, a controversial New York City outfit infamous for its primitive "anti-rock" stance. He later went on to form the Blues Explosion with Judah Bauer and Russell Simmins, a band that would take the anti-rock stance and turn it into something more blues and viable.

The Spin Doctors. *Pocketfull of Kryptonite* was the Spin Doctors' debut, and it came out in 1991 with a bang. The New York City pseudo-hippie **jam band**, with Chris Barron, Anthony Krizan, Mark White, Aaron Comess, and Eric Schenkman, wrote catchy songs like "Two Princes" and "Little Miss Can't Be Wrong." The album went on to sell millions, but the band had trouble following that success and was dropped from its label in 1996.

Springsteen, Bruce. Springsteen made headlines in 1989 when he gave his long-standing friends in the E Street Band notice that he'd no longer require their services. In March of 1992, he released two albums, *Human Touch* and *Lucky Town*, both of which fared well. Springsteen continued to tour until July 1993. In the fall, he wrote and recorded "Streets of Philadelphia" for the soundtrack to the film *Philadelphia*, which concerned a lawyer dying of AIDS. The song became a Top 10 hit in 1994, winning the Academy Award for Best Song and cleaning up at the Grammys the following year. *The Ghost of Tom Joad* was his next milestone, released in 1995. Seven years later, he issued *The Rising*, in July 2002, a paean to the World Trade Center disaster. He reunited the E Street Band for a subsequent tour. Another acoustic release without the band, *Devils & Dust*, emerged in 2005.

Staind. Springfield, Massachusetts, was an unlikely breeding place for a multiplatinum alternative metal band, but that's just where Aaron Lewis, Mike Mushok, and company of Staind hail from. Their 2001 disc, *Break the Cycle*, their third official release, was a leading seller for that year and it topped the charts thanks to their uncharacteristically quiet single "It's Been A While." *Chapter V*, the band's fifth album, came out in the summer of 2005.

Stone Roses. As the band that broke open the idea of **Britpop, Stone Roses**, with original members John Squire, Ian Brown, Reni (Alan John Wren), Andy Cousins, and Pete Garner, carried quite a responsibility on their shoulders. Unfortunately, it wasn't the kind of burden the band was built to handle. Their debut, *Stone Roses*, released in 1989, was the beginning of the

British movement to increase the presence of guitars in their pop. In 1991, the band would get tangled in a bitter lawsuit with their label. The turmoil curtailed the band's touring and recording activities for years. By the time they reemerged in 1994 with *Second Coming*, the anticipation for new music had subsided. Other misadventures ensued and the band called it quits in 1996, one of the greatest busts in all of British pop.

Stoner Rock/Stoner Metal. A distinctly '90s offshoot, Stoner metal bands brought the low, psychedelic jams of the '70s metal acts like Blue Cheer and Sabbath into the '90s. Essentially, it was this psyche-metal combined with **Sub Pop**–esque grunge that came together as Stoner Metal. Monster Magnet, Kyuss, and Electric Wizard are among the bigger names that have refined and focused the genre.

Stone Temple Pilots/Talk Show. Eric Kretz, Scott Weiland, and Dean and Robert DeLeo joined to form Stone Temple Pilots in 1992. Their flamboyant style and rock star charisma gave them a leg up on the competition and their debut, *Core*, made them instant stars. Their sound adhered to the alt-rock conventions of the time. Soon, though, confidence grew and the band began to alter their sound and try variations on the formula. Their experimenting paid off on discs like *No. 4* and *Purple*. Scott Weiland, however, the band's lead singer, melodist, and lyricist battled drug addiction during the course of their career, disappearing at critical times during recording sessions and tours. Ultimately, the frustration built and the band called it quits. The year was 2003. Weiland made it through rehab and joined **Velvet Revolver** with members of **Guns N' Roses**. The remaining STP members tinkered with an ill-fated side project themselves, called Talk Show.

The Strokes. Critical band in the garage-rock/urban-rock revival of the new millennium. The Strokes, including Julian Casablancas, Nick Valensi and Albert Hammond Jr., Nikolai Fraiture, and Fabrizio Moretti, have thus far released two albums: *Is This It* came out in 2000 and *Room on Fire* arrived in the fall of 2003. They've been received with critical acclaim and popular reception.

Sublime. Brad Nowell (1968–1996) spearheaded the Long Beach–based good-time ska, punk, reggae act who rose quickly to fame during the punk resurgence of the mid-'90s. The band released just two albums during its seven years together before Nowell died of a drug overdose in 1996. A third recording, *Sublime*, was released just months after his death.

Sub Pop Records. The single most important recording company of the grunge era, Seattle imprint Sub Pop virtually ignited the alternative revolution by signing bands central to the movement: **Nirvana**, **Soundgarden**, Tad, **Mudhoney**, and the Fluid. Started by Bruce Pavitt and Jonathan Poneman, the label began as a folksy underground indie label and grew into something much bigger, especially after Nirvana, a Sub Pop band, had struck it big.

Superchunk. Highly regarded **indie rock** band led by Mac McCaughan was the toast of Chapel Hill, a true independent act with little interest in stardom. They followed their own rules, and believed heartily in the DIY ethic. The autonomy gave them unlimited freedom to record and release whatever product they wished. This included Superchunk albums and singles as well as a side project, Portastatic, which served as the buzzing Superchunk's quieter alter ego.

Tad. Idaho butcher turned guitar grinder, Tad Doyle and five band members helped to put the punctuation mark on the grunge movement with this band's slow, guttural delivery and steamrolling tempos. While his albums never sold as well as many of his grunge compatriots, he did manage to embrace the grunge sound better and more consistently than most, especially on albums like *God's Balls* (1989) and *8-Way Santa* (1991).

Tenacious D. Acoustic-rock comedy duo Tenacious D features Jack Black and Kyle Gass. They got their start debuting a skit on *Saturday Night Live*. That led to a brief program on HBO, which led to their zany video image. The exposure began their rise to cult stardom. Strangely enough, they also proved to be quite capable musically. Black wrote songs about juvenile subject matter while Gass lent the material musical credibility. They released the single, "Tribute," billed sarcastically as "the greatest rock song ever written." Their first full-length recording, *Tenacious D*, hit stores in 2001.

3 Doors Down. The Mississippi post-grunge rock band of Brad Arnold, Matt Roberts, Todd Harrell, and Chris Henderson opened their recording careers with a hot hit single, "Kryptonite," which turned the heads of local radio stations, and then, in turn opened doors for them nationally and internationally. The band would sign with Universal in 1999, and they opened with *The Better Life* the next year. The record went on to sell 6 million copies. So far, the band's two follow-ups, including 2005's *Seventeen Days*, have yet to equal that level.

Throwing Muses/Kristin Hersh/Tanya Donelly/Breeders/Belly. The Throwing Muses made a name for themselves in the '80s as a college band and independent underground rockers fronted by cousins Kristin Hersh and Tanya Donelly. They earned audiences on both sides of the Atlantic thanks to a record deal that stressed presence in both London and the States. They never sold records in large numbers, but their angular, quirky sound did command respect from music lovers and their albums rarely disappointed. In 1992, Donelly left the band to first play with the Breeders, an all-girl alt-rock supergroup with Kim Deal (**Pixies**), Kelley Deal, and Josephine Wiggs (Perfect Disaster). Following that short-lived stint, Donelly moved on to form Belly. She experienced some radio success with Belly, but their rise was brief and ended in discord. Hersh carried the Muses' cause forward and released records under the Throwing Muses moniker as well as under her own name. She still records as Throwing Muses. Her last record, 2003's self-titled effort, featured Donelly as a guest backing singer.

***Tuesday Night Music Club* (A&M, 1993).** The name of **Sheryl Crow**'s breakthrough album as well as the name of the writing clique with which she received critical inspiration for the album.

U2. Having made great gains in the '80s, the Irish band U2, with Bono (Paul Hewson, 1960–), the Edge (David Evans), Adam Clayton, and Larry Mullen Jr., began experimenting in the '90s. Albums like 1993's *Zooropa* and 1997's *Pop* were highly stylized outings that took the band far from its solid rock roots and into uncharted territory. In 1995, they collaborated with Brian Eno on *Original Soundtracks, Vol. 1*, and released the album under the name the Passengers. The effort was greeted with reservation by critics and fans. Still, few could fault the Dublin quartet for experimenting and their albums still sold well, but they became regarded as rather indulgent, bloated caricatures of their former selves. They began to change all that with their return to roots outing in 2000, *All That You Can't Leave Behind* and 2004's *How to Dismantle an Atomic Bomb*.

Uncle Tupelo. Formed in Belleville, Illinois, in 1987, Uncle Tupelo would go on to become a pivotal band in the development of alternative country. Many even credit the genre directly to UT. Led by Jeff Tweedy, Jay Farrar, and a talented group of musicians, the band prided itself on commingling seemingly disparate concepts—punk and country—into one rather exciting hybrid. Many feel the Byrds with **Gram Parsons** accomplished this in the late '60s, but at the time it didn't trigger the kind of groundswell and influence as many bands as when Uncle Tupelo debuted. The band released three independent records before signing with a major, all of which featured their folksy blend of roots music combined with the snappy fury of alternative rock. *Anodyne*, their major bow, was heard by more people, and influenced more bands, than anything the band had done before it. It has come to be known as a cornerstone of the alt.country genre. Farrar and Tweedy split acrimoniously following a tour in support of *Anodyne*. Tweedy left to form **Wilco** with other members of Uncle Tupelo, while Farrar assembled a band of his own: **Son Volt**.

Urge Overkill. Cheeky Chicago rock featuring Nash Kato, Eddie "King" Roeser, and Jack Watt, later adding Blackie Onassis, bordered on grunge that turned heads in the '90s not only because of their suave sense of style, but because the band, a trio, always challenged rock conventions. They released a few independent albums in the '80s, but went on to sign with Geffen Records following the alt-rock revolution. The records they made thereafter, such as *Exit the Dragon* (1995) and *Saturation* (1993), were slicker and sold better. But ultimately, the band lost their purpose and broke up in 1997.

Velvet Revolver. Formed from the pieces of two broken bands—**Guns N' Roses** and **Stone Temple Pilots**—Velvet Revolver has combined the power and promise of those two bands in just a short time together. First assembled in 2002 as the Project, the band—guitarist Slash, bassist Duff McKagan, and drummer Matt Sorum, three-fifths of Guns N' Roses—came together to re-test the waters after years apart. The chemistry still existed, and so the band only needed to find a frontman. Enter Scott Weiland, the bad-boy that broke up Stone Temple Pilots due to his personal demons. The band was willing to take a chance on the talented singer, and soon they had pulled together enough material for an album. They released *Contraband* in 2004 and, powered by the lead single "Slither," became one of the year's rock success stories.

The Verve. The Verve started out in the early '90s as a hard-rocking post-grunge band from the rural north of England. For much of the decade, until their breakthrough in 1997, they paid their dues, enduring a major breakup, multiple lawsuits (one at the hands of the Rolling Stones) and an appetite for narcotic destruction. Their 1997 album, *Urban Hymns*, would be their key to success, as well as their undoing. Guitarist Nick McCabe eventually parted ways with unpredictable frontman Richard Ashcroft, and the band, having just experienced their first No. 1 song (ironically titled "The Drugs Don't Work") in their homeland, couldn't enjoy the fruits of their labor.

The Vines. The Vines were perhaps the luckiest and the unlikeliest of all the bands to break through the New Garage door. The Australian trio rose to prominence in 2002 after only a handful of gigs, and an incredible wave of hype generated by a few demo recordings. Led by Craig Nicholls (vocals, guitar), and joined by Patrick Matthews (bass, vocals) and David Olliffe (drums, later replaced by Hamish Rosser), the band's debut album, *Highly Evolved*, released in July 2002, charted at No. 11 in the United States and No. 5 in Australia. Touring followed and the band developed a reputation for short, unpredictable, even violent performances. Their follow-up, *Winning Days*, shows a band growing exponentially, and coming into their own as a studio entity.

The Wallflowers. Son of Bob Dylan, Jakob Dylan fronts the Wallflowers, a melodic pop-rock band with a flair for straight-ahead, Tom Petty and the Heartbreakers–styled rock 'n' roll. Their self-titled EP sold poorly in its year of release, 1992, and the band was dropped from their first label. But they resigned and issued their second recording, *Bringing Down the Horse*, in 1997. It became a Top 10 hit and the band asserted themselves commercially. The gutsy *Breach* followed in 2000, *Red Letter Days* in 2002.

Warped Tour. With two stages and upwards of twenty bands, the Vans Warped Tour is the longest-running of the summer festival concepts. As a less pretentious and less pricey alternative to tours like **Ozzfest** and **Lollapalooza**, the Warped Tour, which celebrated its tenth year in the summer of 2004, has shown some real staying power. The festival combines punk-based musicians with extreme sports—BMX, skateboarding, rock climbing, and motocross stunts. Similar to Lollapalooza, the Warped Tour also features a village of sorts, with shops and activist tents where concertgoers can learn about nonprofit organizations and political causes. The tour's low ticket prices guarantee a diverse and sizable audience, and its interest in punk rock—long a bastion of the underground underdogs—fosters a warm, communal spirit.

Weezer. Drawing on the inspiration of power-pop bands like Cheap Trick and post-punk rockers like the **Pixies**, the members of Weezer, led by temperamental singer-songwriter-guitarist Rivers Cuomo, have become unusual stars. Their music, infused with a quirky sense of humor and an endearing awkwardness, is crystallized in hit singles like "Undone (The Sweater Song)," "Buddy Holly," and "Say It Ain't So," all big modern rock hits in 1994 and 1995. Weezer also made innovative videos, which helped promote their nerdy but somehow hip image. A sharp turn in the climate of late-'90s rock pushed Weezer off the radar. But the band would return in 2001 with what has come to be known as "The Green Album." More hit singles followed, as did albums, *Maladroit* in 2002 and *Make Believe* in 2005.

Welch, Gillian (1968–). Born in Manhattan and bred in Los Angeles, Gillian Welch somehow managed to sing as if she grew up in Appalachia in the early twentieth century. Her appearance on the folk scene was nothing less than stunning. Her ability to evoke vivid scenes from rural mountain life earned her plenty of recognition early on, and her partnership with multi-instrumentalist David Rawlings helped bolster her authenticity. Welch and Rawlings released a handful of stellar recordings, including *Revival* in 1996 and *Soul Journey* in 2003.

Whiskeytown/Ryan Adams. A mercurial and destined-to-fail independent alt.country band, Whiskeytown managed to build up a substantial fan base before imploding in 1999 after five years together. With the irascible Ryan Adams (1974–) at the helm, Whiskeytown was anything but predictable. Adams was a belligerent but brilliant presence, able to sing Minor Threat punk as well as Hank Williams country. The band stayed together long enough to record three proper albums, including 1999's *Pneumonia*, a highly sought-after album that never saw proper release. When Whiskeytown disbanded in 1999, Adams immediately began working on solo material, releasing *Heartbreaker* the next year. Adams has since become something of an icon, a pop singer who has smoothed out the abrasive aspects of his music and his personality. His fans have benefited, especially on albums like *Gold* (2003), the near-crooner disc, *Love Is Hell* in 2004, and *Cold Roses* the next year.

The White Stripes. In 1997, Jack and Meg White, a Detroit couple alternately assumed to be husband and ex-wife or brother and sister, came together as a bass-less duet, with Meg (b. Megan Martha White) on drums and Jack (b. John Anthony Gillis) on guitar and vocals. One of a new breed of back-to-basics rock acts to emerge from the city, Jack and Meg were obsessed with returning the music of the Motor City, and rock 'n' roll in general, back to its roots. They proceeded to do so on brilliant and well-received outings like *White*

Blood Cells (2001) and the follow-up, *Elephant*, in 2003. *Elephant* was issued to nearly unanimous critical acclaim and charted as high as No. 6 on the *Billboard* albums chart. It has sold nearly 2 million copies. *Get Behind Me Satan* was released in the summer of 2005. The White Stripes' presence reenergized the flagging U.S. rock scene.

Widespread Panic. One of the many neo-hippie **jam bands** that took its rightful place as a possible heir to the **Grateful Dead** touring mantle. Widespread established a grassroots following on the strength of constant touring and their loose brand of Southern rock, which shows elements of jazz as well as blues. The group has origins dating back to the early '80s, but it wasn't until they were given a slot on the 1992 and 1993 **H.O.R.D.E.** tours that their reputation began taking on a national pallor. Throughout the '90s, their records sold in increasingly greater numbers, and the band's summer tours became true events on the receptive jam-band circuit. Founding member and lead guitarist Michael Houser died in 2002, but despite the tragedy, the band soldiered on. It was Houser's wish. Since then Widespread gigs have been consistent sell-outs and their albums have done reasonably well.

Wilco. Jeff Tweedy's vehicle following the dissolution of **Uncle Tupelo**, Wilco has become one of the most acclaimed bands of the '90s and early twenty-first century. Each successive album has enjoyed broader and broader acclaim, from their more or less predictable rootsy debut, *AM*, in 1995, through efforts like 1996's sprawling *Being There*, 1999's *Summerteeth*, and 2001's *Yankee Foxtrot Hotel*. Throughout his career, Tweedy has consistently challenged expectations, and over time morphed into a satisfying, occasionally sublime, even brilliant songwriter, veering from folk tenderness to Brian Wilson quirky to Neil Young drone without much trouble. Ironically, they were dropped in 2001, in a widely publicized estrangement, by their label, Warner Brothers. Nonesuch Records picked up the album and the official release came out in early 2002 to widespread critical acclaim. Meanwhile, an independent film documenting the drama surrounding the album entitled *I Am Trying to Break Your Heart* followed in the fall of 2002. Their most recent album, *A Ghost Is Born*, has also been hailed.

Williams, Lucinda (1953–). Lucinda Williams, during the late '90s, took a stagnant, often nonexistent career and shifted it into high gear. A recording artist since the late '70s, Williams went through droughts of productivity, whether due to writer's block, label complications, or her legendary perfectionist attitude in the studio. There have been spans of six and eight years between albums. But beginning in 1997 with her recording *Car Wheels on a Gravel Road*, the rootsy, country-folk singer has made up for lost time, writing and recording frequently and releasing albums every few years. Like **Wilco**, she is a perennial presence in critics' polls during the years she's released records, and her uncompromising quality has kept her standards high. For *Car Wheels*, she won a

Grammy for Best Contemporary Folk Album. *Essence*, in 2001, won her another Grammy, this time for Best Female Rock Vocal, an unusual award for Williams, whose voice was always an acquired taste. She released *World Without Tears* in 2003, and *Live at the Fillmore* in 2005.

Yeah Yeah Yeahs. Hinging on the manic vocal histrionics of frontperson Karen O, the trio made a name based on their unusual chemistry. They consist of only two instrumentalists—guitarist Nicolas Zinner and drummer Brian Chase—supporting O's vocals, making for a lean presentation that allows each element to stand out. Their latest album, *Fever to Tell*, released on the major label Interscope, was typically acclaimed, but failed to make commercial impact. Still, the band's unusual sound, and Karen O's unorthodox performing style, has helped the band amass a dedicated following.

Yo La Tengo. New Jersey **indie rock** band with a long-standing legacy, cruised into the '90s with enough laurels for a good long rest. But instead, the band—Ira Kaplan, James McNew, and Georgia Hubley—made compelling alterations in their sound to keep what has always been a strikingly fresh sound fresh enough to remain vital. '90s outings like 1993's *Painful* and 1997's *I Can Hear the Heart Beating As One*. In 2005, the forward-thinking band reluctantly released their first career retrospective, *Prisoners of Love: A Smattering of Scintillating Senescent Songs*. Prolific and moody, the band has been able to transcend their myriad influences and become an indie rock icon and a much-loved presence on the alternative scene.

 **APPENDICES**

List of Top-Selling Albums, 1991–2005

These albums are those with sales in the millions. Their peak chart positions are given.

1. *Cracked Rear View Mirror*, Hootie and the Blowfish, 1994, 14 million, peak chart position, #1, June 1994.
2. *Hybrid Theory*, Linkin Park, 2000, 14 million, peak chart position, #1, 2001.
3. *Jagged Little Pill*, Alanis Morrisette, 1995, 13 million, peak chart position, #1, 1995, 2001.
4. *Ten*, Pearl Jam, 1991, 12 million, peak chart position, #2, August 1992.
5. *Yourself or Someone Like You*, Matchbox 20, 1996, 12 million, peak chart position, #5, 1997.
6. *Human Clay*, Creed, 1999, 11 million, peak chart position, #1, 1999.
7. *Devil Without a Cause*, Kid Rock, 1998, 11 million, peak chart position, #5, 1999.
8. *Dookie*, Green Day, 1994, 10 million, peak chart position, #2, 1994.
9. *Greatest Hits*, Tom Petty & the Heartbreakers, 1993, 10 million, peak chart position, #5, February 1994.
10. *Nevermind*, Nirvana, 1991, 10 million, peak chart position, #1, 1992.
11. *1*, The Beatles, 2000, 9 million, peak chart position, #1, 2000.
12. *Mellon Collie and the Infinite Sadness*, Smashing Pumpkins, 1995, 8 million, peak chart position, #1, 1996.
13. *Core*, Stone Temple Pilots, 1992, 8 million, peak chart position, #3, 1993.
14. *Achtung Baby*, U2, 1991, 8 million, peak chart position, #1, 1991.
15. *Throwing Copper*, Live, 1993, 8 million, peak chart position, #1, May 1994.
16. *August and Everything After*, Counting Crows, 1993, 7 million, peak chart position, #4, March 1994.

17. *Hell Freezes Over*, Eagles, 1994, 7 million, peak chart position, #1, 1994.
18. *Get a Grip*, Aerosmith, 1993, 7 million, peak chart position, #1, 1993.
19. *Vs.*, Pearl Jam, 1993, 7 million, peak chart position, #1, 1993.
20. *Significant Other*, Limp Bizkit, 1999, 7 million, peak chart position, #1, July 1999.
21. *Crash*, The Dave Matthews Band, 1996, 7 million, peak chart position, #2, August 1996.
22. *Blood Sugar Sex Magik*, The Red Hot Chili Peppers, 1991, 7 million, peak chart position, #3, 1992.
23. *Purple*, Stone Temple Pilots, 1994, 6 million, peak chart position, #1, June 1994.
24. *Under the Table and Dreaming*, The Dave Matthews Band, 1994, 6 million, peak chart position, #2, 1995.
25. *Chocolate Starfish and the Hot Dog Flavored Water*, Limp Bizkit, 2000, 6 million, peak chart position, #1, 2000.

List of Most Significant Rock Albums, 1991–2005

Pearl Jam
Ten
August 1991

Nirvana
Nevermind
September 1991

The Red Hot Chili Peppers
Blood Sugar Sex Magik
September 1991

My Bloody Valentine
Loveless
November 1991

Pantera
Vulgar Display of Power
February 1992

Pavement
Slanted and Enchanted
May 1992

The Jayhawks
Hollywood Town Hall
September 1992

Rage Against the Machine
Rage Against the Machine
November 1992

Liz Phair
Exile in Guyville
June 1993

Smashing Pumpkins
Siamese Dream
July 1993

Nine Inch Nails
The Downward Spiral
March 1994

Soundgarden
Superunknown
March 1994

Hole
Live Through This
April 1994

The Beastie Boys
Ill Communication
May 1994

Jeff Buckley
Grace
August 1994

Oasis
Definitely Maybe
August 1994

Sleater-Kinney
Call the Doctor
March 1996

Beck
Odelay
June 1996

Wilco
Being There
October 1996

Radiohead
OK Computer
July 1997

Lucinda Williams
Car Wheels on a Gravel Road
June 1998

Flaming Lips
The Soft Bulletin
June 1999

The White Stripes
The White Stripes
June 1999

Coldplay
Parachutes
July 2001

The Strokes
Is This It
September 2001

REFERENCE GUIDE

PRINT

Christgau, Robert. *Christgau's Consumer Guide: Albums of the '90s*. New York: St. Martin's Griffin, 2000.

Cobain, Kurt. *Kurt Cobain: Journals*. New York: Riverhead Books, 2002.

Crampton, Luke, and Dafydd Rees. *Rock & Roll: Year by Year*. New York: DK Publishing, 2003.

DeRogatis, Jim. *Milk It!: Collected Musings on the Alternative Music Explosion of the '90s*. New York: DaCapo Press, 2003.

Erlewine, Michael, Vladimir Bogdanov, Chris Woodstra, Stephen Thomas Erlewine, and Richie Unterberger (eds.). *All Music Guide to Rock*. San Francisco: Miller Freeman, 1997.

Frey, Darcy. "Lucinda Williams Is In Pain." *New York Times*, September 14, 1997.

Gaar, Gillian. *She's a Rebel: The History of Women in Rock & Roll*. 2nd ed. New York: Seal Press, 2002.

Graff, Gary, and Daniel Durchholz (eds.). *MusicHound Rock: The Essential Album Guide*. Detroit: Visible Ink, 1999.

Gulla, Bob. "Hometown Hero." *Guitar*, 1996.

Hype! Surviving The Northwest Rock Explosion, The Motion Picture Soundtrack. Sub Pop. B0000035ID. Compact disc liner notes. October 1, 1996.

McDonnell, Evelyn, and Ann Powers (eds.). *Rock She Wrote: Women Write About Rock, Pop & Rap*. New York: Cooper Square, 1999.

Oberholzer, Felix, and Koleman Strumpf. "The Effect of File Sharing on Record Sales." Available at: http://www.unc.edu/~cigar/papers/FileSharing_March2004.pdf.

Reynolds, Simon. *Generation Ecstasy*. New York: Routledge, 1999.

Robb, John. *The Nineties: What the F**k Was That All About?* London: Ebury Press, 1999.

Robbins, Ira (ed.). *The Trouser Press Guide to '90s Rock*. New York: Fireside, 1997.

Samuels, Dave. "Rock Is Dead." *Harper's*, November 1999.

Strong, Martin C. *The Great Rock Discography*. London: Times Books, 1998.

Thigpen, David. "Irish Passion." *The New York Times*, March 28, 1994.

True, Everett. "True Stories." *Melody Maker*, January 1992.

True, Everett. *Live Through This: American Rock Music in the '90s*. London: Virgin, 2001.

Woodworth, Marc (ed.). *Solo: Women Singer-Songwriters in Their Own Words*. New York: Delta, 1998.

WEBSITES

About.com. http://altmusic.about.com.

    All-encompassing Web site with multiple facets, including this one about alternative rock. Also handy for punk, industrial, and heavy metal.

All Music Guide. http://www.allmusic.com.

    Created by the *All Music Guide* (AMG) Staff. Provides up-to-date biographical and discographical information on the musicians and music of the day.

Billboard. http://www.billboard.com/bb/index.jsp.

    Industry and entertainment news from a respected source.

British Broadcasting Company (BBC). http://news.bbc.co.uk/2/hi/entertainment.

    Editorials and news items on artists and issues in the music industry from a British viewpoint.

C/NET News. http://news.com

    Breaking news in technology.

Creem Magazine Archives. 2004. http://www.creemmagazine.com.

    Web site for rock music magazine originally founded in Detroit in 1969. Provides reviews, articles, links, and cross-generational perspective on rock 'n' roll.

The Dave Matthews Band. http://www.davematthewsband.com.

    Official Web site of the Dave Matthews Band.

Detroit Free Press. http://www.freep.com/index/entertainment.htm.

    The entertainment section of the Detroit daily.

Elephant 6 Recording Company. http://www.elephant6.com.

    A Web site devoted to the bands and recordings of the Elephant 6 indie rock collective.

Encyclopedia Britannica. http://www.encyclopediabritannica.com.

    Official Web site of the reference organization.

Geek News. http://www.geek.com/news/geeknews.

    A variety of news on subjects of technology, including music industry issues like peer-to-peer and MP3.

Inside Connection. http://www.insidecx.com.

    Music industry news service.

Jam Bands. http://www.jambands.com.
    Exploration of the bands on the current jam scene.

Lilith Fair. http://www.lilithfair.com.
    Official site of the women's music festival.

Little Steven's Underground Garage. http://www.littlestevensundergroundgarage.com.
    A discussion of the garage-rock scenes past and present.

Molinaro, John. 1998. http://xroads.virginia.edu/~MA98/molinaro/alt.country/jm-thesis.html.
    A thesis presented to the Graduate Faculty of the University of Virginia on
    the origins and directions of the alternative country genre.

MTV. http://www.mtv.com.
    Music television Web site with background and news items on popular musi-
    cians.

Nationmaster. http://www.nationmaster.com/encyclopedia/List-of-Britpop-musicians.
    Thorough annotation of the musicians of the Britpop era.

No Depression. http://www.nodepression.net/archive/nd01/index.html.
    Archive of interviews, reviews, and essays from the predominant authority on
    alternative country.

Pitchfork Media. http://www.pitchforkmedia.com.
    Reviews and interviews with indie rock musicians.

Punk Bands. http://www.punkbands.com.
    A tribute to the bands, labels, and organizations that make up the punk genre.

Recording Industry Association of America (RIAA). http://www.riaa.com.
    Official site of the recording industry, with statistics, essays, and editorials on
    the business of music.

Riot Grrrl. http://riotgrrrl.com.
    Master site for the Riot Grrrl movement.

Scaruffi, Piero. 2002. History of Rock Music 1990–1999. http://www.scaruffi.com/
    history/cpt50.html.
    European perspective on the history of modern rock.

Sweden. http://www.sweden.se.
    The official national tourism Web site also includes articles and essays about
    the Swedish rock/pop music scene.

trakMARX. http://www.trakmarx.com.

Trouser Press. http://www.trouserpress.com.
    Touted as "the bible of alternative rock since 1983."

Unterberger, Richie. http://www.richieunterberger.com.
    Noted rock historian and former editor of *Option* magazine touts his own
    books and others as well as interesting rock 'n' roll links.

VH1. http://www.vh1.com.
>   Music television Web site with background and news items on popular musicians.

Warped Tour. http://www.warpedtour.com.
>   Official site of the popular punk rock tour.

Whitburn, Joel. http://www.recordresearch.com.
>   Oft-consulted chart data Web site.

Wikipedia, the Free Encyclopedia. http://en.wikipedia.org/wiki/Rock_and_roll.
>   Offers a wealth of information, definitions, and perspectives on the origins, movers, and important events of the rock 'n' roll era.

Yahoo! http://dir.yahoo.com/Entertainment/Music/Genres/Rock_and_Pop/Punk_and_Hardcore.
>   Reference guide and point of origin for information on alternative styles of music.

FILMS

While the music of the '90s was not defined by many feature films, there were several that played an integral role in helping to solidify the alternative music ethos of the period.

The Decline of Western Civilization. Spheeris Films, 1981.
Stop Making Sense. Arnold Amusement Group/Cinecom Pictures/Talking Heads, 1984.
Sid & Nancy. Channel 4/Goldwyn Films/Killer Films/Newmarket Films/Single Cell Pictures/Zenith, 1986.
The Decline of Western Civilization 2: The Metal Years. IRS/New Line Cinema, 1988.
Singles. Warner Brothers, 1992.
Kurt and Courtney. Strength, Ltd., 1998.
Velvet Goldmine. Channel 4/Goldwyn Films/Killer Films/Newmarket Films/Single Cell Pictures/Zenith, 1998.
Almost Famous. Vinyl Films, 2000.
High Fidelity. Dogstar Films/New Crime Productions/Touchstone Pictures/Working Title Films, 2000.
Hedwig and the Angry Inch. Killer Films/New Line Cinema, 2001.
I Am Trying to Break Your Heart. Experience Music Project/Fusion Films/Plexifilm, 2002.
End of the Century: The Story of the Ramones. Magnolia Pictures, 2003.
Dig! Interloper, 2004.
Mayor of the Sunset Strip. First Look, Samuel Goldwin Films, 2004.
Metallica: Some Kind of Monster. IFC Films, 2004.

RECORDINGS

Anthologies consist of various artists; all recordings refer to compact disc (CD) format.

Sub Pop 200. Sub Pop, 1988.
Where the Pyramid Meets the Eye—Tribute to Roky Erickson. Warner Brothers, 1990.
Gabba Gabba Hey: A Tribute to the Ramones. Triple X, 1991.
Never Mind the Main Stream: The Best of MTV's 120 Minutes, Vol. 2. Rhino, 1991.
Tom's Album. A&M, 1991.
Virus 100: Dead Kennedy Covers. Alternative Tentacles, 1992.
Born to Choose. Rykodisc, 1993.
No Alternative. Arista, 1993.
Sweet Relief: A Benefit for Victoria Williams. Columbia, 1993.
Teriyaki Asthma, Vols. 1–5. C/Z, 1993.
The Crow: Original Motion Picture Soundtrack. Atlantic, 1994.
The Grunge Years: A Sub Pop Compilation. Sub Pop, 1994.
If I Were a Carpenter. Polygram, 1994.
Punk-O-Rama, Vols. 1–8. Epitaph, 1994–2003.
Star Power. Pravda, 1994.
Every Band Has a Shonen Knife Who Loves Them. Positive, 1995.
Saturday Morning Cartoons' Greatest Hits. MCA, 1995.
Victory: The Early Singles. Victory, 1995.
Working Class Hero: A Tribute to John Lennon. Hollywood, 1995.
You Sleigh Me: Alternative Christmas Hits. Atlantic, 1995.
California Ska-Quake, Vol. 2: The Aftershock. Moon, 1996.
M.O.M., Vol. 1: Music for Our Mother Ocean. Interscope, 1996.
Sweet Relief II. Columbia, 1996.
Twisted Willie: A Tribute To Willie Nelson. Justice, 1996.
MTV Buzz Bin, Vols. 1–3. Mammoth, 1997.
Some Songs: From the Kill Rock Stars Singles. Kill Rock Stars, 1997.
For the Masses: An Album of Depeche Mode Songs. Polygram, 1998.
Everything Is Nice Matador Records. Matador, 1999.
Industrial Strength Machine Music: Framework of Industrial Rock 1978–1995. Rhino, 1999.
KCRW: Morning Becomes Eclectic. Mammoth, 1999.
Oh, Merge: Merge Records 10 Year Anniversary Compilation. Merge, 1999.
Another Prick in the Wall: A Tribute to Ministry, Vol. 2. Invisible, 2000.
Emo Diaries, Vol. 5: I Guess This Is Goodbye. Deep Elm, 2000.
Family Values Tour 1999. Interscope, 2000.
KCRW: Sounds Eclectic. Mammoth, 2001.
Warped Tour: 2001 Compilation. Side One Dummy, 2001.

EVENTS

All Tomorrow's Parties
Camber Sands, England
Los Angeles, CA
http://www.atpfestival.com/

> The ATP Festival is held at two locations, the first and original on England's south coast and the second in Los Angeles, California. The idea here is to invite a curator—a musician, artist, or writer—to choose a selection of performers that reflect his or her musical aesthetic.

Apple & Eve Newport Folk Festival
Newport, RI
http://www.newportfolk.com

> Annual multi-day summer music festival founded by George Wein in 1959; one of the premier American music festivals presenting legendary popular music artists and many new roots and pop artists of the day.

Coachella Valley and Arts Festival
Indio, CA
http://www.coachella.com

> Large, multiperformer music and art festival begun in 2003 and held in April or May of each year in a large field in Indio, California, near Palm Springs. 2005 festival includes Weezer, Coldplay, Wilco, Nine Inch Nails, the Chemical Brothers, and dozens more.

The Glastonbury Festival of Contemporary Performing Arts
Glastonbury, England
http://www.glastonburyfestivals.co.uk/

> Long-standing British festival, and one of the most popular music festivals in the world, specializing in big-name alternative pop and rock acts, with smaller stages featuring music, theater, circus, and cabaret.

International Pop Overthrow
http://www.internationalpopoverthrow.com/

> IPO is a new, young pop music festival held for the past seven years in Los Angeles, and more recently in Chicago, New York, Boston, Philadelphia, Baltimore, Nashville, San Francisco, and Liverpool, England.

Metalfest
Milwaukee, WI
http://www.metalfest.com

> Long-running festival and the premier metal gathering in North America, celebrating the rise of heavy metal.

New England Metal and Hardcore Fest
Worcester, MA
http://www.metalandhardcorefestival.com

> Now in its seventh year, the New England Metal and Hardcore Festival has been lauded as one of the best heavy-music festivals in the United States.

New Orleans Jazz & Heritage Festival
Fair Grounds Race Course
New Orleans, LA
http://www.nojazzfest.com
> Annual ten-day spring cultural festival; features cooks, craftspeople, and internationally renowned musicians; music encompasses every genre, including some of the biggest alternative rock acts.

Ozzfest
Nationwide
http://www.ozzfest.com/
> Another summertime metal festival, only this one features bands that have more commercial aspirations. Organized and run by the Osbournes, Sharon and Ozzie, formerly of Black Sabbath.

The Reading Festival
Reading, England
http://www.readingfestival.com
> Held in late August, the young Reading Festival features the top names in loud rock and heavy metal as well as many up-and-coming indie bands.

INDEX

About the Author

BOB GULLA has been a professional writer and editor for over fifteen years. His work has been published in *Rolling Stone*, *People* magazine, and the *Boston Globe*, among other publications. Bob also served a five-year stint as Executive Editor of *Guitar One* magazine, taking the niche-based publication from startup to an international title with a worldwide circulation of 150,000. This is his first book.